This study provides the first systematic account of John Henry Newman's treatment of heresy and heretics in the early Church, and thus sheds light on an area hitherto unexplored in books about Newman. It shows how Newman's 'rediscovery' of ancient patristic writers and heretics was part of a strategy to revive 'Catholicism' within the Anglican Church, and also how his reading of the Church Fathers relates to the controversies and personalities of early nineteenth-century England during the period of The Oxford Movement. The author demonstrates how Newman's eventual conversion to Roman Catholicism in 1845 may be understood as a change in his perception of heresy, his preoccupation with which – up until his conversion – bordered on the obsessive.

NEWMAN AND HERESY

Portrait of John Henry Newman by Sir William Ross.
Reproduced by permission of the Fathers of the Birmingham Oratory.

NEWMAN AND HERESY

The Anglican Years

STEPHEN THOMAS

Senior Lecturer
Department of Theology
La Sainte Union College of Higher Education
Southampton

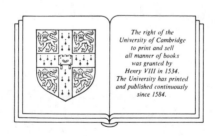

The right of the
University of Cambridge
to print and sell
all manner of books
was granted by
Henry VIII in 1534.
The University has printed
and published continuously
since 1584.

CAMBRIDGE UNIVERSITY PRESS

Cambridge
New York   Port Chester
Melbourne   Sydney

Published by the Press Syndicate of the University of Cambridge
The Pitt Building, Trumpington Street, Cambridge CB2 1RP
40 West 20th Street, New York NY 10011, USA
10 Stamford Road, Oakleigh, Melbourne 3166, Australia

First published 1991

Printed in Great Britain at the University Press, Cambridge

British Library cataloguing in publication data

Thomas, Stephen, *1951–*
Newman and Heresy: the Anglican Years.
1. England Catholic Church. Newman, John Henry, 1801
1. Title
282.092

Library of Congress cataloguing in publication data

Thomas, Stephen (Stephen Colquitt), 1951–
Newman and Heresy: the Anglican Years/Stephen Thomas.
p. cm.
Includes bibliographical references and index.
ISBN 0-521-39208-x
1. Newman, John Henry, 1801–1890 – Views on heresy and heretics.
2. Heresies, Christian – Study and teaching – England – History – 19th
century. 3. Oxford movement – England. 4. Church of England –
Doctrines – History – 19th century. 5. Anglican Communion – England –
Doctrines – History – 19th century 1. Title.
BT1317.T46 1991
273'.092 – dc20   90-20359
CIP

ISBN 0 521 39208 x hardback

For Pippa
My old flame, my wife.
hic demum collectis omnibus una defuit

Contents

Acknowledgments

I owe an infinite debt of gratitude to my scholarly mentor and friend, Dr Sheridan Gilley, of Durham University for his kind erudition, warm humanity and generous encouragement during the period of the writing of this book.

I remember also with great pleasure discussions with Dr Richard Roberts, of Durham University, now Professor of Divinity at St Andrews University whose combativeness never failed to sharpen my thinking and encouraged me to push my conclusions further.

During my time of research at the Birmingham Oratory Archive, I received, from the Librarian, Gerard Tracey, unstinting help and advice in finding my way around the riches of Newman's manuscript legacy, for which I remain most grateful.

Thanks are owed also to Stephen Sykes, then Van Mildert Professor at Durham University, without whose help in initiating my research this book would have remained only an idea.

Finally, and most of all, my thanks to Pippa, not only for typing the manuscript, but also for appreciating and understanding my work – for she, perhaps, understands it best of all.

A short glossary of heresies

APOLLINARIANISM: the denial that Christ had a human mind or intelligence; Apollinarians saw the human mind in Christ as replaced by the Divine Mind.

ARIANISM: the denial of the full divinity of Christ; more precisely, the refusal to accept that the Divine Word or Logos is one in substance or essence with God the Father.

DOCETISM: the view that the bodily life of Christ only seemed to take place: the crucifixion was an illusion, Christ remaining always totally a divine being, incapable of really suffering.

DONATISM: the followers, in the fifth-century African Church, of Donatus. They formed a schismatical sect, claiming to be the True Church, which was strict about matters such as sin and martyrdom. They were *doctrinally* orthodox.

ERASTIANISM: the identification of Church with State, so that the Church becomes merely an expression of the State's needs.

EUTYCHIANISM: the view that Christ had one divine person and nature and that the human in Christ was completely swallowed up in the divine.

GNOSTICISM: a term for a variety of second-century mystical, intellectual and myth-making Christians, who made salvation depend on the reception of secret, spiritual knowledge or illumination. Gnostics tended to see matter as bad and the non-material as good. Salvation was salvation from matter and from the body.

LATITUDINARIANISM: the view, originating in the late seventeenth century, that, since there is so much uncertainty about dogma, 'latitude', or freedom of opinion, should be granted to all in matters of religious truth.

LIBERALISM: a term whose application to theology Newman virtually invented, but which even he found difficult adequately to define. It is similar in meaning to Latitudinarianism (q.v.), and is often used to refer to those who seem to be reducing dogmas to the status of human opinions.

MANICHEANISM: a religion based on the teaching of a third-century Persian sage, Manes, which held that the world had been created by Satan, and that salvation was from matter and the body. It practised extreme self-denial.

MONOPHYSITISM: the theology of Egyptian Christianity after the fifth century, teaching that, after the union of divine and human in Christ, there was one divine nature only. The Mono-physites saw the Council of Chalcedon's two-nature theology as an heretical, Nestorian (q.v.) denial of the teaching of St Cyril of Alexandria.

NESTORIANISM: the view that in Christ there are two per-sons, both a human person and the Person of the Divine Word. It is unlikely that anyone ever held such a view explicitly, and Nestorius, the originator of the controversy, certainly did not. Nestorianism was based on an over-sharp distinction between the divine and the human in Christ, at the expense of the unity of his person.

PELAGIANISM: the view, attributed to Pelagius, that a human being can earn salvation by his own good actions, without the grace of God. Pelagius probably actually only argued that human actions have an important part to play in salvation. His opponent, St Augustine, stressed – some would say over-stressed – the importance of grace.

SABELLIANISM: the denial of three distinct persons as part of the very nature of God; Sabellians preferred to talk of the one God making himself known under three aspects, or faces.

SEMI-ARIANISM: a term to describe those who, for a variety of differing reasons, refused to describe Christ as one in substance or essence with God, but preferred the term 'similar in essence'.

SOCINIANISM: a term, originally referring to the Italian theologian Fausto Sozzino, used to describe certain seventeenth-century deniers of the Doctrine of the Trinity. Socinians believed God was one, not three, and are the ancestors of modern Unitarians. They also denied that Christ's death was a sacrifice to atone for human sin.

Introduction

Orthodoxy is my doxy: heterodoxy is another man's doxy
(Bishop William Warburton)

Two Jews, three opinions
(Rabbinic joke)

Christians have always disagreed about fundamentals, a cause of much perplexity – if God's truth be one. No Church Father would have been happy to proclaim, with one contemporary theologian, that Christianity's very essence may be best defined as a chronic set of disagreements.[1] The Fathers were made of sterner stuff: they spoke of orthodoxy, right belief and worship, and of heresy, the sin of preferring one's own opinion to what Christ had revealed and the Church taught. The vehemence of this view conceals a difficulty: in practice it is often hard to distinguish heretic from orthodox. An orthodoxy eventually emerged concerning the natures of Christ and the Trinity, held by Byzantium and the medieval West, but leaving behind major rifts in the East, in Egypt and Palestine. Later, Protestant and Catholic argued about other things. When Michael Servetus, a sixteenth-century denier of the Trinity, escaped burning by Catholics only to be burnt by Calvin, he found out the hard way that there were some things all the big churches still agreed about. This consensus went up in smoke with Servetus. In the protest about his treatment, the modern idea of toleration was born.[2]

By 1800, toleration was fashionable in England, and dogmatism had itself almost become a heresy. The Unitarians, or Socinians, were an articulate and well-educated minority, the heirs of earlier anti-trinitarian movements, who argued for a rational monotheism, untrammelled by dogma. Along with other, more orthodox, Dissenters they were demanding their place in the sun. Not all

Anglicans felt they could long be denied it. Since the Revolution of
1688, an influential school of Hanoverian theologians had argued
that, whenever doctrinal disagreement arose, latitude should be
given to the other man. Bishop William Warburton's often-quoted
witticism only takes latitudinarianism a little further, into comedy.
The Church Fathers and Councils were much sniped-at by latitudinarian cleric and atheist alike. The Fathers were presented as
repulsively narrow-minded and hopelessly confused – nowhere
more amusingly than in the atheistic Edward Gibbon's *Decline and
Fall of the Roman Empire*.

Some were not amused. A school of eighteenth-century divinity,
deriving especially from the Non-Jurors, made a spirited defence
of early Church dogma. The young John Henry Newman was not
amused. He joined with his friends John Keble, Hurrell Froude
and Edward Bouverie Pusey on the side of ancient credal orthodoxy. They were emphatically against latitude and compre-
hensiveness.

Newman differed in one important respect both from his friends
and from the dry seventeenth- and eighteenth-century divines he
often over-praised. He was a writer of genius, a brilliant storyteller,
a biting polemicist. He was a provocative, alarming and romanti-
cally compelling personality. He started a reactionary revolution,
challenging the idea of toleration just as it was beginning to
dominate. Does toleration mean, Newman asked, that one belief is
as good as another? Newman always used the word 'latitudinarian'
derogatively. He introduced another term, its synonym, still acridly
resonant in ecclesiastical circles today – liberalism. To call a man
'liberal' was, for Newman, the worst thing that one could say of
anyone.[3]

Newman's interest in the Early Church has as much to do with
the controversies of the early nineteenth century than the impartial
investigation of scholarship. This is why the story of Newman's
treatment of heresy cannot be straightforwardly told: his writings
have a makeshift and improvised quality. A more systematic
theologian than Newman might have restricted himself to specific
treatises, which could then be interpreted and compared, and a
theory of their relation constructed. Not so with Newman. There
is the problem of how to relate a thematic investigation of heresy
to historical background and biography. His treatment of heresy
cannot easily be presented in terms of a chronological progress in

his understanding: several ways of treating heresy co-exist; a treatment of heresy characteristic of one temporal point abruptly re-emerges later; some attitudes to heresy are there all the time. Heresy appears to be rather a function within a shifting set of strategies than the object of sustained reflection. It is, perhaps, for this reason that no account of Newman's treatment of heresy has hitherto appeared, despite its obvious importance in his writings.

The *terminus a quo* for Newman's treatment of heresy is the period of his early manhood: the troubled times from Waterloo to the Reform Bill, which illustrate the political and social roots of his first treatment of the Arian heresy (1832). Newman's *Arians of the Fourth Century* is a scholarly examination of the first great heresy to split the Church; it was the view that Jesus was something less than divine. The bitter debates culminated in the Church's first Ecumenical Council, at Nicea (AD 325), where the divinity of Christ was defined. But Newman's narrative is also an oblique satire upon liberalism in his own age. The dual currency of the word 'Arianism' is significant here: as well as meaning the fourth-century heresy, it was also a term used, along with 'Socinianism', to describe contemporary Unitarians. Newman's point was that too much toleration would eventually result in a virtually unitarian Church of England. His treatment of Arianism is, then, *rhetorical*: he is trying to persuade his contemporaries of present dangers by a skilful comparison with Christian Antiquity. This rhetorical exploitation of history characterises all his discussions of heresy. Paradoxically, it was the *heretics* that Newman described as rhetoricians, as arguers too clever by half. The fact that Newman is himself a rhetorician is not so obvious, because his rhetoric is a matter of a strategy underlying his narratives, rather than logical surface brilliance. Part I examines the origins of this strategy in the early 1830s and shows how Newman continued this method of narrating Antiquity throughout the decade.

Overlapping this, was a more theological and philosophical approach to liberalism, characteristic of the mid-1830s. Its immediate occasion was a squabble about whether Dissenters should be allowed to study at Oxford, then a purely Anglican preserve. This coincided with Newman's study of two heresies; first, Sabellianism, which argued that the persons of the Trinity were only names for the activities of a single God, rather than eternal distinctions, and, secondly, Apollinarianism, which denied that Christ had a human intellect. It is difficult to see where academic activity ends and polemic begins. Part II describes how Newman found correspondences between these heresies and modern theology.

In the 1840s, Newman's interest turned to the fifth-century Christological heresies; Monophysitism, the view that Christ had only one nature, and that a divine, and Nestorianism, a heresy, which, if it ever existed, was supposed to teach that Christ was actually two persons, a divine and a human. At roughly the same time Newman re-examined Arianism, concentrating on the moderate party of so-called 'Semi-Arians'. This was the period when Newman's confidence in his own, Anglo-Catholic, 'Via Media' position was cracking: he was on the path to Rome. Part III shows the importance of the idea of heresy in the long process leading to Newman's conversion in 1845, and the reformulation of his whole picture of orthodoxy in the *Essay on the Development of Christian Doctrine*.

The *terminus ad quem* for this book is the end of Anglicanism for Newman. As a Tractarian, he tried to strengthen an Anglicanism which was losing political power and influence by proposing it as the inheritor of patristic orthodoxy – as the Catholic Church in England. He presented Anglican orthodoxy as a bulwark against the crypto-infidelity of Dissent. But like all such apologists before him – like his seventeenth-century forebears – he had to hold a steady course to avoid drifting Romewards. By 1845, he saw his Anglican position as hopelessly compromised. Thereafter, Newman proposed the stark alternative of Roman Catholicism as the Church of the Fathers, the only bulwark against the infidelity towards which all other forms of Christianity, 'Via Media' Anglicanism included, either openly or secretly tended. Although this story ends at 1845, two works from the Roman Catholic period will be considered, as they bear upon the collapse of the 'Via Media': both *Difficulties of Anglicans* (1850) and the *Apologia* (1864) are sources, albeit problematic ones, for the period 1839–45.

In his Roman Catholic period (1845–90), Newman's interest in heresy waned. In the years following his conversion, he compared Anglicanism with Monophysitism – but this is really a sequel to his Anglican period, as he turns his guns upon his former self in a final dismissive act of repudiation. The writings on heresy published during his Roman Catholic period are re-workings of what he had written as an Anglican. His obsessive heresy-hunting belongs almost entirely to the embattled and contested background of his attempt to maintain the Catholicity of the Church of England. Once 'safe'[4] in the Roman fold, the impulse to find heresy *everywhere* waned.

Although 'safe', he was by no means comfortable with the neo-ultramontanism fashionable throughout his life in the Roman Church. The mind-set of ultramontanism was hostile to criticisms made even on patristic grounds. Newman found himself to be a liberal within Roman Catholicism; actually delated to Rome for heresy without his knowledge in 1859,[5] he was regarded by Mgr Talbot as 'the most dangerous man in England'.[6] Suspected, marginalised, cut off from the forum provided by his beloved Oxford, his attitude towards heretics, or those suspected of covert heresy, softened. In *The Trials of Theodoret*, Newman cannot repress his sympathy for the maligned and misrepresented Theodoret of Cyrrhus, who was accused of Nestorianism, nor can he stifle the suspicion that Cyril, the great Alexandrian upholder of orthodoxy, was, nevertheless, a bit of a scoundrel.[7] Concerning assent to doctrines in the Roman Church, Newman consistently pursued the line allowing the greatest freedom of conscience.[8] On the matter of the promulgation of dogma, such as Papal Infallibility, he took the view that it was inopportune to define.[9] Always professing the most humble obedience to authority, he was often nevertheless regarded by his superiors much as he had himself regarded the latitudinarian Hampden: as a man of dangerous tendencies. Newman's ambiguous position as a Roman Catholic, then, is so different from his Anglican situation as to be quite a distinct area from the one being pursued in this book.

Newman the Roman Catholic became a very different person from the intense young clergyman of Tractarian times. But he did not *want* to be different: he liked to see himself as the same as he had always been. Accordingly, he usually attempted to adjust his earlier texts to something resembling his later position. He was an inveterate tinkerer. Sometimes, when an earlier position is hopelessly irreconcilable with Romanism, he disagrees with his earlier self in footnotes.[10] But, more often, he will make a minor adjustment, edit out, smooth over or conflate, usually without acknowledgment. As a result, the text of the (Longmans) *Collected Edition* is not necessarily a reliable guide to what he actually wrote when he was an Anglican. First editions, original articles or manuscripts have therefore been consulted and have been cited when they differ from the Collected Edition. The object of this study is Newman's Anglican period – the very tract of time which later he strove so seductively to re-tell. All efforts have been made to resist the seduction.

PART ONE

Defence: Arianism and the Church–State Crisis

Well, old boy, you've made the ancients modern.
('Le Douanier' Rousseau to Constantin Brancusi)

CHAPTER ONE

Heresy and orthodoxy in the 'Evangelical' period

When Newman was only fifteen, Walter Mayers, the schoolmaster responsible for converting him to a form of Calvinistic Evangelicalism, gave him a number of standard Evangelical books to nourish his sanctification.[1] Two of these were to have such an important effect upon him that, although written nearly half a century later, the account in the *Apologia Pro Vita Sua* still conveys a sense of idealistic youthful enthusiasm. One was *The Force of Truth* by Thomas Scott of Aston Sandford, 'to whom (humanly speaking) I almost owe my soul'.[2] The other was Joseph Milner's *History of the Church of Christ*: he was 'nothing short of enamoured'[3] of the long patristic extracts he found there.

In the *Apologia*, Newman identifies Scott as having taught him orthodox Trinitarianism, 'that fundamental truth of religion'.[4] Moreover, Scott's own journey towards orthodoxy was made in the milieu of the ascendancy of heresy – Unitarianism or Socinianism: 'He followed truth wherever it led him, beginning with Unitarianism, and ending with a zealous faith in the Holy Trinity.'[5]

Scott's own autobiographical section in *The Force of Truth* records more about the nature of heresy, and particularly about its human psychology, than Newman's own compressed account, so that it is possible to elaborate upon what is only sketched in the *Apologia*. Scott relates how, when in a state vacillating between regeneration and apostasy, he was influenced by an instrument of the devil – a Socinian commentary on the Scriptures. This soothed his conscience, so that despite his sinfulness, he considered himself 'a very worthy being'.[6] This commentary reduced revelation to the human understanding, enabling infidelity and pride to be concealed beneath a mask of reason.[7] Scott declares that he had been 'a Socinian, or very little better',[8] having concealed my real sentiments under the mask of general expressions.[9]

9

Scott was influenced by the moderate 'Arianism' or adoptionism of Samuel Clarke's *Scripture Doctrine of the Trinity* and the related controversy became a 'favourite part' of his 'study'.[10] He shows how the rationalist principle, once it has begun to work, is not content with moderation: those who are first 'Arians' and believe that Christ was, in some sense, divine, but only by adoption will, Scott argues, eventually fall into Socianism, the more radical heresy, which holds that Christ was no more than a mere man: 'This is the natural progress of unhumbled reason: from *Arianism* to *Socinianism*; from *Socinianism* to *Deism*; and thence to *Atheism*.'[11] This is the 'down-hill road' which many learned and philosophical men have trod 'almost, if not quite, to the bottom'.[12] It is, then, possible to conclude that Newman encountered at a very early age a haunting vision of the potential tragedy faced by every person – the slide into infidelity via heresy.

Scott does think it possible, however, 'to return by the retrograde path, first to *Arianism* and then to the received doctrine of the Trinity'.[13] In the description of such a journey towards the orthodox faith, Newman would have found some of his first references to the doctrines of the early Church. It was, for instance, reading the Prayer Book article about the Athanasian Creed, which first made Scott, while still a crypto-Socinian, consider the Trinitarian orthodoxy of the Church to which he belonged:

When the psalm was named, I opened the prayer book to turn to it: but (accidentally shall I say, or *providentially?*) I opened upon the articles of religion; and the eighth, respecting the authority and warrant of the *Athanasian* creed, immediately engaged my attention. My disbelief of the doctrine of the Trinity of *coequal persons in the unity* of the Godhead, and my pretensions to candour, had both combined to excite my hatred for this creed. No sooner did I read the words . . . than my mind was greatly impressed and affected.[14]

Moreover, in his correspondence with 'Mr N.', an orthodox Calvinist, Scott was daunted by the demonstration that his own position had 'in all former ages of the Church . . . been branded heretical'.[15]

Only a year or so after Newman had acquired his copy of *The Force of Truth*, his early undergraduate diaries show the influence of Scott's Trinitarianism. One of his earliest private reflections, in the form of 'sermonets', was composed on the subject of the Athanasian

Creed, which had played such a central part in Scott's autobiography.[16] By 1819, in his *Hints on the Athanasian Creed*, Newman was asserting its importance by associating it with what was at that time for him the authority of the Reformers. In the same diary entry, he stressed the necessity of dogmatic belief, dismissing as absurd that, in relation to the Divinity of Christ, 'it matters not whether men believe him such or not'.[17] The entry immediately following points out that Jesus condemned as 'crimes' equally faults of conduct and errors of belief.[18] By 1821, Newman seems to have begun to adopt his later characteristic distinction between the *economy*, or provisionality, of the human language of revelation and the real, but mysterious, distinctions within the life of the Trinity which human language is trying to express:

The second person of the Blessed Trinity is called the Son of the Father, the Only-begotten, not in a literal sense, but as the nearest analogy in human language to convey the idea of an incomprehensible relation between the Father and the Son.[19]

Two months later, he recorded a dream in which the exhortation of a 'mysterious visitant' reinforced this distinction between the difficulties of the human language of revelation and the transcendent realities to which they point:

Among other things it [the 'visitant'] says that it was absolutely impossible for the reason of man to understand the mystery (I think) of the Holy Trinity and in vain to argue about it; but that every thing in another world was so *very, very* plain that there was not the slightest difficulty about it.[20]

It would, however, be misleading to suggest that the statement in the *Apologia* about Scott's Trinitarian influence be taken at its face value, and that Newman had, between 1816 and 1821, evolved a clearly articulated Trinitarian theology which he regarded as the fundamental Christian dogma. On the contrary, the undergraduate Newman was more likely to regard belief in Christ's atoning death for human sin as the 'keystone of Christianity';[21] the shift in emphasis from Atonement to Trinity has not yet taken place, still less the later characteristic polemic against Evangelicalism, whereby it is suggested that preaching which centres attention on Christ's sacrifice for humanity endangers the objectivity of revelation to be found principally in the Trinity. Once, it is true, in 1821, Newman says he is against the preaching of the Calvinistic doctrines of election and perseverance in order to convert the unregenerate.[22] In this he anticipates the Tractarian doctrine of 'Reserve'[23] which often made the same point about the doctrine of the Atonement. It is, however, generally true of the period 1816–21 that Newman saw the Trinity as less important than the Atonement: for example, he defends the *divinity* of Christ as essential to a real sacrifice for the sins of the world.[24]

During this early period, Newman, like Scott, regards the main threat to Christian orthodoxy as Socinianism, seeing it as a form of rationalism by which revelation is rejected if it transgresses the bounds of human understanding:

I should like to know what the Socinians understand by *faith*. As I understand the Bible it is *a (perhaps the)* most difficult Christian grace, viz. the believing of something which is beyond our powers of reason and contradictory to the imaginations of our sinful nature . . . They walk by sight.[25]

Here, heresy is intellectual independence of revelation, a characterisation he later develops in his attack upon theological liberalism.

However, the later antithesis between Trinitarianism as the fundamental of Christianity, and Socinianism as, either overtly or in some concealed form, its denial – an antithesis which the later perspective of the *Apologia* presupposes – is not yet evident. Rather, Socinianism is only indirectly a threat to the Trinity: what it really challenges is the Atonement, and the reality of human sin, for which sacrifice must be made. It is from this perspective that Newman attacks the Socinian denial, or modification, of the Divinity of Christ:

It is most strange that so philosophical a sect as the Socinians should believe Christ to be a mere man, yet to be 'far exalted above all principality and power etc *not only* of this world, *but also* etc' and to have 'all things put under his feet'. For, according to their Creed, sin is a venial, trivial matter, nor is this world extraordinarily circumstanced. How then is it to be believed that the Almighty should have distinguished this little globe?[26]

Newman cannot see the need for a Christ at all without the urgent need for Atonement. If, however, Atonement *is* necessary, then the full divinity of Christ must be upheld:

Except on the orthodox scheme, how is the *need* of a Mediator explained? If He made no atonement, what need of a creature praying his Creator to be merciful (to man)? What an empty, unmeaning formality, to make a being who would be without authority, influence & etc requisite to induce God to pardon sinners.[27]

God does not pardon 'without any atonement' because 'the law is immutable like its Divine Author'.[28] There can be no true honouring of God's law without the Atonement, as the 'Socinian scheme' claims, for to omit the Atonement is to admit adjustment in the divine standard – and therefore in God's very holiness.[29]

Although Scott's influence may be discerned between 1816 and 1821 to be promoting both an awareness of heresy and a sense of Trinitarian orthodoxy, it is not true to say that in these years Newman necessarily saw the importance of the Fathers and heretics in the history of the early Church. There is little evidence that the early impression made by the long extracts in Joseph Milner, to which Newman so eloquently testified, had any influence upon his thinking while he was an undergraduate, although – as will be seen later – Milner's *History* did have a marked effect upon his writing of *The Arians of the Fourth Century*. Significantly, for all his preoccupation with Socinians, the obvious comparison between them and fourth-century Arians is completely absent, nor is there any attempt to discern a similar 'rationalism' in the heretics of the early Church.

The series of events which was to transform Newman from an Evangelical to an upholder of patristic orthodoxy were under way as he was writing the last of his diary notes about the 'Socinian scheme': in late 1820, there had been the *fiasco* of his performance in the Schools,[30] and soon to come was the news of his father's insolvency in late 1821.[31] Then followed his election to the Oriel fellowship,[32] bringing him into contact with the 'Noetics', powerful personalities, obsessed with logical analysis, who were to cause him first to modify, then to abandon, his Evangelicalism. Particularly important were Edward Hawkins, who between 1824 and 1825 brought to Newman's attention the role of Tradition in 'unauthoritatively' interpreting Scripture – 'the *quasi*-Catholic doctrine of Tradition, as a main element in ascertaining and teaching the truths of Christianity'[33] – and Richard Whately, who first sowed the idea of the independence of Church from State, and the wrongness of 'that *double usurpation*, the interference of the Church in temporals, of the State in spirituals'.[34] There was also the experience of his first pastoral work, in the often harrowing conditions of St Clement's, Oxford, that convinced him 'that the religion which he had received from John Newton and Thomas Scott would not work in a parish'.[35] Calvinism was a 'system' which did not answer to human experience, and was 'unreal'.[36]

Towards the end of the six years, 1822–28, of his transition from Evangelical to 'Apostolical', under the influence of the 'Noetics', Newman became aware of a dangerous drift into 'the Liberalism of the day': a critical attitude to the creeds and disparagement of the Fathers. Whately accused him of 'Arianising'. Such, at any rate, is the testimony of the *Apologia*.[37] Here, however, his very phraseology betrays a later perspective: 'I was just then very strong for that ante-Nicene view of the trinitarian doctrine, which some writers, both Catholic and non-Catholic, have accused of wearing a sort of Arian exterior.'[38] He attributes to himself the disparagement of pre-Nicene orthodoxy, arising from a view of the early Fathers which he himself later attacked in both 'liberals' and Roman Catholics.

The *Autobiographical Memoir*, compiled a decade after the *Apologia*, also averts to his transition from Evangelicalism. Here, he describes his early faith as having been half-Trinitarian and Incarnational, and half-Evangelical. The 'four doctrines' which he held as 'certain truths' were 'the Holy Trinity . . . the Incarnation . . . Predestination . . . and the Lutheran apprehension of Christ'.[39] The first three, he argues, being true Catholic doctrine and hence matters of indefectible certitude, remained with him, but the last, not being Catholic doctrine, could not be held with certitude – and so just faded away. It hardly needs to be pointed out that Newman is schematising his early life in terms of the 1870 *Grammar of Assent*.[40]

The *Autobiographical Memoir* also touches upon the 'liberal' phase of Newman's transitional period, but in a manner somewhat different from that of the *Apologia*: 'A cold Arminian doctrine, the first stage of Liberalism, was the characteristic aspect, both of the high and dry Anglicans of that day and of the Oriel divines.'[41] This is a unique passage in Newman: the potential slide into liberalism is presented *not* – as so often later – via Evangelicalism, Protestantism, popular or otherwise, or biblicism,[42] but via the upholders of creed, liturgy, establishment, Arminianism and orthodoxy – the 'Z's',[43] who are lumped together with Noetics such as Whately and Hawkins. By contrast, the Evangelicalism from which Newman is departing is praised for its holiness and spirituality, and criticised, not for a heretical, or liberal, tendency, but for impracticality![44] From the cold intellectualism of Arminianism, Newman declares he was 'saved' by 'imaginative devotion' to the Fathers of the Church, gained from Joseph Milner's *History* during schooldays. As if to reinforce the impression of the patristic basis of even his early days, he details occasions of patristic study undertaken in 1823, 1825–6 and 1828, *before* the systematic reading of the Fathers, begun in 1828.[45]

These two accounts, taken together, raise some difficulties and contradictions with regard to Newman's brief 'liberal' phase. He was 'Arianising' and disparaging the pre-Nicene Fathers, who were at the same time the objects of his devoted study! Moreover, the source of his liberalism is by no means clear: one might expect it to be derived from 'Noetics' such as Whately – yet the latter was Newman's orthodox accuser, while the High Church orthodox seem to share the blame for his liberalism.

Some clarification is provided by reference to Newman's writings *at the time* of his 'Arianising', which reveal a complex picture of his understanding of heresy and orthodoxy somewhat different again from the foregoing accounts. In his *Journal* in early 1828, he wrote as part of his retrospective account of the previous year:

At Easter I had to preach the usual sermon in the College chapel and got into some little controversy about it. The Provost Copleston liking it, recommended it to Whately (part of it was on the Divinity of Christ), who accused it of Arianism. Hawkins thought it dangerous, and Blanco White thought it systematized more than Scripture does. So it must have been faulty more or less.[46]

The offending sermon was *On the Mediatorial Kingdom of Christ* (No. 160), preached on 15 April 1827, which Newman did not choose to include in any of the volumes of his published sermons.[47] The criticisms to which it was subjected in the form of marginal annotations made upon the manuscript by Whately, Hawkins and Blanco White are extant, and provide a clear picture of the varying kinds of censure to which Newman was being subjected.

These criticisms centred upon the second 'point' of the sermon, 'the economy of the Mediatorial Kingdom of Christ – from a review of which, it follows . . . that the Son of God, as Mediator, is *inferior to the Father*'.[48] Whately was the most definite of the three to say that Newman had 'Arianised'; Hawkins is, for example, altogether more cautious. Newman argued that, 'whatever the original glory and power of the Son of God', he is not denying His pre-existent eternity. Nevertheless, when we consider Him as the Mediator and restorer of fallen humanity, it is 'more agreeable' to this redemptive scheme to see Him as 'in a subordinate character, in the form of a servant', and to represent Him as 'inferior to the Father'. Whately drew the strictly logical conclusion: 'This leaves no alternative between supposing Christ to be the Mediator in his human capacity alone (the *man* Jesus) and downright *Arianism* or at least the most objectionable part of it.'[48] Against the central idea of the sermon – that there was a mediatorial Kingdom of Christ, to be distinguished from the Kingdom of God the Father, Whately inveighed: 'How then on your view, can He, the head of this kingdom, be Himself God, if He is to resign it in order that God may be all in all?'[48]

Whately is not suggesting that Newman was deliberately Arianising, but, rather, commenting upon a tendency in Newman's use of language when describing Christ's salvific 'incomprehensible condescension' and self-abasement: '*the impression which it leaves on the feelings* of those who dwell on it (however cautiously stated) will inevitably be either Tritheism, or such a conscious danger of it as will turn men's thoughts from the whole subject'.[48] A note Newman himself added to the annotated sermon implies that, although 'quite aware' of the 'difficulty' to which his approach was leading, 'the scanty limits of a sermon prevented my entering into it'.

If Newman was deemed Arian, it is possible to see Whately as verging upon the Sabellian, in seeming to reduce the three persons of the Trinity to mere names. Commenting upon one of Newman's quotations from I Corinthians, 'To us there is but one God, the Father, of whom are all things and we in Him – and one Lord Jesus Christ, by whom are all things and we by Him'.[48] Whately demanded rhetorically, 'Is not this (as well as numberless other texts) against the notion of any divine character in the Son distinct from the Father who is the One God?'[48] Whately's view sprang from extreme scepticism about the capacity of human language to express, or of the mind to comprehend, the Trinitarian distinctions: since no good 'practical result' could accrue, he declares it better 'to waive the discussion' and to 'dwell on the *practical* doctrine of the Trinity, viz: the relations of God to us'. From this distinctively

Whatelian position, Hawkins somewhat demurred: 'Doubtless there are hosts of texts on the great doctrine of the Unity – but there is some mysterious distinction too.'[48]

Newman's main accuser, then, tended to deny Trinitarian distinctions upon practical grounds and to hold the Trinity should be seen as the expression of certain 'relations' between God and us. This encounter between Newman and Whately was a fateful one, for it provided the germ of an idea which Newman was to expand very considerably eight years later, when, at the height of the Hampden controversy, he used the concept of Sabellianism to describe theological liberalism.[49] A comment written against the *Journal* entry of this time is clearly a gloss written from this later perspective: he mentions the seventeenth-century defender of the Nicene Creed, Bishop George Bull,[50] whom he had not read by 1827. It is still, of course, possible that he accurately records the distinctive line taken by the protagonists in discussions on the sermon at the time: 'It [the sermon] took without knowing it Bull's doctrine of the "subordinatio filii". Whately, Hawkins and Blanco White were all then verging towards Sabellianism themselves.'[51] Another later reminiscence of the incident virtually repeats this view:

It [the sermon] took the view of the doctrine of the Holy Trinity, which I afterwards (i.e. in 1831, 1832) found to be the ante-nicene [*sic*] view, especially on the point of the 'subordination of the Son'. Bull (whom at that time I had not read) brings it out in one of his chapters.[52]

Newman's *Memorandum*, written a little less than a month after the sermon itself, and therefore very close to the discussions about it, presents a very different picture from these accounts coloured by a later perspective, although, indeed, it shares one characteristic with his later remarks – an exquisite amalgam of remorse and self-abasement with self-justification and special pleading. Newman admits, in this *Memorandum*, that, although there is 'nothing wrong' with it, the 'partial view . . . one view out of several' might, in the case of the Trinity, be 'very inexpedient' and he admits that he ought to have added, 'some strong sentences explicitly stating that the foregoing statement was only *one* view of the Scripture doctrine, one side and aspect of the great structure of the economy of the redemption'.[53] On the other hand, 'I do not see at present that I am wrong.'[54] He justifies his peculiar position in the sermon as having been adopted to account for the 'difficulty' presented by the idea of divine *Sonship*, one solution being 'to understand "the Son" always of our Lord's human nature'.[55] Surprisingly – in view of later developments in Newman's life – his view of the Trinity as a result of the discussion is almost identical with that of Whately, and indicates an influence of the latter upon him, or at least substantial agreement, which later accounts of the incident altogether suppress:

I as cordially dislike all discussions concerning the nature of God, and speculations about the *mode* of His Existence as Three and One, as the most strong opposer of Bishops Pearson and Beveridge. I do not even like the words Trinity, Person, Procession, etc etc – indeed any systematic exposition of the doctrine but what is *relative to us and practical*.[56]

The *Memorandum* culminates in Newman's first reflection upon the nature of early Church heresy, in its relation to orthodoxy:

The Church has at times been accused of Arianism – Arianism (in the main) is true – so is Sabellianism – (in its first outline) Unitarianism – but not the *whole* Truth – yet for *particular purposes*, according to particular occasions, it may be useful to represent the Catholic doctrine in this or that form.[57]

Newman explains the process whereby he slipped into an appearance of heresy by reference to the calling of the preacher, his being 'all things to all men', in order to bring them to Christ. The preacher may, Newman argues, for a 'particular' occasion, present a partial view of Christian doctrine. How, then, does the orthodox preacher differ from the heretic, who *also* articulates a partial view, true enough as far as it goes? Newman's approach to this problem anticipates his future bearings with regard to heresy: the orthodox is, in the best and most humane sense, a rhetorician – he is adapting the material of the Christian Tradition, in order to persuade his audience either to conversion or repentance, a *metanoia*; yet the 'form' is to be distinguished from 'the Catholic doctrine', to which the particular rhetorical forms are obedient and implicitly refer.[58] Thus the Church on certain occasions – and Newman on this one – may be vindicated from heresy, and the heretical appearance of the preacher explained, because the latter was merely concerned 'to account for a difficulty'.[59]

Newman's grasp of the importance of Trinitarian orthodoxy tightened during the months following the criticisms to which his sermon was subjected. By June 1828,[60] for example, he was referring to the Doctrine of the Trinity with a wholehearted assent, very different from the 1827 *Memorandum*'s reservations about 'persons' and 'processions'. In fact, the sermon on the *Mediatorial Kingdom* has been described as 'the watershed between the mainly evangelical style at St Clement's, and the patristically inspired sermons at St Mary's'.[61] However, by 1828, events were beginning which were to effect a profound modification in Newman's view of heresy and orthodoxy.

In conclusion, Newman absorbed the 'moderate' and Trinitarian Calvinism of Thomas Scott, but his own picture of his early years overestimates the presence of what were later positions. His own brush with heresy, his 'Arianising' and the 'Sabellianism' of those who were at that time his friends, colleagues and accusers, was to gain importance in the light of future events: the break with Whately, the tragic fall, in Newman's view, of Blanco White into Unitarianism. One might add the fact that one of Newman's nearest approaches to heresy on his own part had arisen from a peculiarly Evangelical emphasis: the presentation of the doctrine of the nature of Christ in terms of its redemptive *effect*, by the preaching of the Atonement. The mature Newman was consistently hard upon this wherever he met it, censuring it as a dangerous form of anthropocentric subjectivism. Perhaps the reason is because he had once found it in himself.

CHAPTER TWO

'The Arians of the Fourth Century' and its Background 1828–1832

(A) FROM EVANGELICAL TO HIGH CHURCHMAN

By 1828, Newman was in a state of transition[1] between Evangelicalism and a new party he was to create for himself, variously termed Tractarianism, Anglo-Catholicism, and, least appropriately, Puseyism. His strictures during this period upon Evangelical excesses *resemble* later Tractarian language, but are in fact no more than would have been acceptable to moderate evangelicals within the Church of England, such as the Clapham sect, who were also appalled by the pentecostal excesses of such as Edward Irving.[2] Neither does Newman's defence of the Established Church in the late 1820s necessarily mean that he can no longer, in some sense, be called an evangelical himself, for the Clapham Sect also revered the visible, sacramental authority of the Church of England.[3] Indeed, a number of Tractarians, later converts to Rome, came from evangelical backgrounds – Henry and Robert Wilberforce and Henry Manning. Newman's first contributions towards ecclesiastical politics, therefore, at least *began* from a moderate evangelical position.

In early nineteenth-century England, legislation against heterodoxy, Dissent and Roman Catholicism was slowly being relaxed. In 1812, the Conventicle and Five-Mile Acts had been repealed,[4] and, in the same year, a Bill was passed without debate, publicly supported by the Primate, removing criminal penalties against those who denied the Doctrine of the Trinity.[5] In 1828, upon the Repeal of the Test and Corporation Acts, what had for some years been practically admitted by annual acts of indemnity was finally and officially recognised, that those outside the Church of England could hold public office without being compelled first to subscribe to the Church of England's articles.[6] This had passed off without

20

widespread controversy. Such measures are an indication of the Church of England's sense of security, rather than of any impending threat.[7] However, alarm began to spread with the Bill to emancipate Roman Catholics in 1829, a measure which was mainly an attempt to placate a potentially rebellious Ireland.[8] By 1832, the Reform Bill[9] had widened the franchise in such a way as to give power to those hostile to the Church, and the newly constituted House of Commons could no longer be seen as the lay synod of the Church of England, of one mind with the clergy, in the promotion of a national faith. Suddenly, the great cry was reform of the Church of England – its wealth, its sees, its liturgy, creeds and anathemas. The bishops, who had opposed the widening of the franchise in the Lords, were never more unpopular. Parliamentary committees, not necessarily friendly to the Church or even composed of its members, were being set up. It was widely believed that the days of the established Church were numbered.[10] A political party arose, influenced by Utilitarians such as Jeremy Bentham and James Mill, whose 'vital principle'[11] was the destruction of the Establishment.

Newman was first fired to defence of the Establishment over Catholic Emancipation in 1829. In taking a definite political stance over this issue, and campaigning vigorously against the re-election of Robert Peel, High Churchman and chosen representative of the Oxford Tories, who had, in 1829, executed a complete *volte face*,[12] he was not obviously aligning himself with any particular ecclesiastical party: churchmen, and for that matter, opinion in the country generally, were divided. There was much nostalgia for George III,[13] who had always opposed Emancipation for fear of violating his Coronation Oath. Surprisingly, some later seen as 'liberals' were *against* – for example, the Provost of Oriel, Edward Copleston. The Evangelicals, usually unanimous on Church–State issues, were divided – William Wilberforce was *for*, and suffered opprobrium from his own party on this account; Daniel Wilson changed his mind from *against* to *for*. Similarly, the High Church party failed to present a united front – Daubeney was strongly *against*, but Alexander Knox was *for*.[14] Newman and Pusey campaigned on opposite sides. Blanco White and Newman both switched abruptly from previously held positions.[15]

It is therefore important to understand Newman's precise reasons for his venture into politics, and in order to appreciate his triumphant feelings at the return of the mediocre reactionary, Sir Robert Inglis,[16] and the discomfiture of Peel. Newman saw such reforms as proposed by Parliament, not as goods in themselves, but as part of a progressive strategy to erode the authority of the Church of England. Writing to his sister, Jemima, in March 1829, Newman explained the motivation behind his by now successful campaign: 'I am in principal [sic] Anti-Catholic – i.e. I think there is a grand attack on the church in progress from the Utilitarians and Schismatics – and the first step in a long chain of events is *accidentally* the granting of these claims.[17] Here, Newman identifies a process of secularisation as concealed beneath apparently benign reforms. The potential slide into national infidelity is equated with an attack upon the visible Church's social dominance. Significantly, the rationalist and infidel prong of this attack ('the Utilitarians') is not distinguished from Dissenters ('Schismatics') – they are both alike threats to the visible mediation of grace through ecclesial structures.

Newman elaborates this idea in a letter to his mother, written just over a week later than the letter to Jemima. Here, he expresses at length what might be described as a theory of secularisation, in order to make clear the principles upon which he is defending the established Church. He argues that the context of the 'novel era' to which the crisis of the times is the inaugural sign is 'an advance towards universal education'.[18] Whereas in the past, people depended upon others – particularly the clergy – for their opinions, 'now each man attempts to judge for himself'.[19] Although 'liberty of thought' and 'free inquiry' are not, in principle, enemies of Christianity,[20] they are so at the present, because they are directed towards dissolving the very structure by which it had been mediated, a structure functioning by subordination and deference. Newman therefore places Christianity and independence of mind in direct antithesis one to another:

Christianity is of faith, modesty, lowliness, subordination; but the spirit at work against it is one of latitudinarianism, indifferentism, republicanism, and schism, a spirit which tends to overthrow doctrine, as if the fruit of bigotry, and discipline as if the instrument of priestcraft.[21]

This is the first occurrence in Newman of 'latitudinarian', a word to be revived in the Tractarian period as an equivalent of heresy:[22] it is the view that opinions on religious subjects are a matter of indifference, that one truth is as good as another. The question of orthodoxy ('doctrine'), and the latitudinarian challenge to it, is presented both in an ecclesial framework ('schism') and in a political one ('republicanism'). Newman is anticipating with dread the disestablishment of the Church, a 'revolution' which will leave 'the upper classes' religionless, and the clergy dependent on their congregations for 'voluntary contributions'. He also fears the withdrawal of parliamentary protection for the Church of England's doctrine.[23]

Newman's list of the upholders of 'liberty of thought' and enemies of Christianity reveals his profound social and political conservatism at this time: they are the uneducated or partially educated in towns ('deistical or worse'), Utilitarians ('political economists, useful knowledge people') schismatics ('in and out of the Church'), Calvinistic Baptists, 'the high circles in London', and 'political indifferentists', men so far gone they might become Roman Catholics or Socinians as circumstances dictate. Again, Dissent – the schismatics – is identified with infidelity. Calvinism is firmly repudiated – and even Thomas Scott's moderate Calvinism dismissed as inconsistent with itself and therefore likely to produce men unreliable in a crisis.[24] The suggestion that Roman Catholicism is also in some way tending to infidelity is explained in another letter of the same time, to his sister, Harriet:

though I am used to think the country has not so much to dread from Romanistic opinions, (the danger seeming to be on the side of infidelity), yet there is a general impression which Blanco White's book confirms, that infidelity and Romanism are compatible, or rather connected, with each other.[25]

Blanco White, himself a lapsed Roman Catholic priest, had endeared himself to the Establishment by his writings revealing the scepticism and indifferentism of continental Romanism – and Newman here accepts Blanco's line quite uncritically. The enemies of Christianity are, in fact, *anything at all* which is *not* the established Church.

The last two paragraphs of Newman's letter to his mother take on an altogether more sophisticated air, as he expounds a 'theory' of secularisation: 'Listen to my theory.'[26] This 'theory' arises from the idea to which he had first adverted, the link between the Church–State crisis and the spread of education: 'the talent of the day is against the Church',[27] which depends on – he admits it – 'prejudice and bigotry'.[28] Upon this unpromising foundation, he builds a defence of the established Church, explaining how it is capable of mediating Christianity not only to the educated, but also to the ignorant. It is one of his earliest suggestions of the connections between, on the one hand, doctrinal truth with moral soundness, and, on the other, error with moral shallowness.

Newman begins by applying to the social sphere an argument from individual conscience:

As each individual has certain instincts of right and wrong, antecedently to reasoning, on which he acts and rightly so, which perverse reasoning may supplant, which then can hardly be regained, but, if regained, will be regained from a different source, from reasoning, not from nature, so, I think, has the world of men collectively.[29]

Newman's later distinction between 'moral sense' and 'sense of obligation'[30] is not yet in place: rather, he argues that individuals have an *a priori* instinct about the rightness or wrongness of specific actions. If, however, a certain kind of perverse intellectualism tampers with this, the instinct will be lost, the spontaneous communing with 'nature' broken, so that a moral code will then have to be reconstructed – laboriously, it is implied – by means of reason, if, indeed, the individual is capable of this. Newman applies this idea to revelation. He is not suggesting that – as with moral truths – doctrine is in some way innate; the point of comparison is rather the *tacitness* of both morality and doctrine. In the case of revelation, truths have been unquestioningly handed down, as an implicit part of the history of a society – he does not *call* this 'Tradition':

These [revealed truths] are transmitted as the 'wisdom of our ancestors', through men, many of whom cannot enter into them, or receive them themselves, still on, on, from age to age, not the less truths, because many of the generations, through which they are transmitted, are unable to prove them, but hold them either from pious and honest feeling (it may be) or from bigotry or from prejudice.[31]

These truths are only in principle or in theory rationally provable. In practice, it is 'for great men alone', such as Richard Hooker in the seventeenth century or Joseph Butler in the eighteenth, 'to prove great ideas or grasp them'. The authority of such theologians derives from their *moral* profundity. But in the field of argument what requires moral depth for its apprehension will not normally win the day: 'as moral evil triumphs over good on a small field of action, so in the argument of an hour, or the compass of a volume'.[32] This explains how the dissenting Whig Lord Brougham or John Wesley gain the advantage over Hooker or Butler in people's minds – Newman's premises commit him to the conclusion that dissenting theology is inferior to Anglican, even in the case of such a great man as Wesley. Newman sees the established Church as mediating to the English people truths which, because of the proneness of the large part of humanity to shallowness, can only be received tacitly:

Moral truth is gained by patient study, by calm reflection, silently as the dew falls, unless miraculously given, and, when gained it is transmitted by faith and by 'prejudice'. Keble's book is full of such truths; which any Cambridge man might refute with the greatest ease.[33]

The final reference to John Keble points to the probable ultimate source of Newman's connection between the capacity to receive revealed truth with full assent, and moral character or *ethos*.[34] Although he had already, simply and briefly in his 1819 *Journal*, made this connection,[35] Keble's characteristic exaltation of *ethos*[36] over intellect would have reinforced it, providing a powerful means of explaining the presence of heterodoxy. Moreover, we may see in Newman's advocacy here of the transmission of the 'wisdom of our ancestors', Keble's socially conservative reverence for the daily round of rural peasant life, steeped in the liturgies and traditions of the Church of England.[37]

Keble's ardent disciple, and, until his early death, Newman's closest friend, Hurrell Froude, who was largely responsible for bringing Newman and Keble together, had in July 1827, written *On the Connexion between a Right Faith and Right Practice; on the Ethos of Heresy*. In four closely argued pages, Froude achieves a level of systematic speculation upon the nature of heresy, which Newman had yet not attained. Froude's argument is directed against the idea that two distinct principles of causality, that is, right faith and right practice, operate in relation to salvation. Rather, the two must be connected, since it is possible to be as *responsible* for one's beliefs as for one's actions. Froude advances his argument in three stages. First, he asserts that opinion and character are 'homogeneous': opinions generate a 'temper' of mind, a 'temper', conversely, generates specific opinions. Now, when condemning an *opinion* as 'vicious', we are really condemning 'the same temper which developes [*sic*] itself indifferently either in opinions or actions'.[38] Secondly, working from the premiss that 'variety' of opinions cannot be accounted for by variety in the 'reasoning faculty', he concludes that such variation must be derived from difference of character (*ethos*).[39] Thirdly, the partisan spirit in which disagreements are conducted shows that the 'affections' are 'engaged' – it is not simply a question of reasoning; similarly, unity between those holding the same opinion is a sharing of *ethos*: 'we cannot suppose that opinion, *quatenus* opinion, has any power to attach or segregate'.[40] Moreover, some 'affections' have 'an *essential tendency* to produce particular opinions'.[41] There is, then, an *ethos* of heresy.

The common atmosphere between Froude and Newman is clear: both identify intellectual with moral soundness, and it is likely that Froude influenced Newman in this instance – at least in conversation,[42] if he had not by this time read the passage in Froude's *Occasional Thoughts*. However, Froude's last two paragraphs reveal a more definite relation to Newman's 'theory' expounded in the letter to his mother. Froude connects the idea of *ethos* with the *tacit* dimension of faith:

The very notion of right and wrong implies that it is wrong not to respect *it*, previous to all *rational* conviction concerning its nature. As revelation is useless without reason to prove its truth, so reason is worth nothing without instinct to enforce its suggestions.[43]

Here, Froude is discussing the rightness or wrongness of opinions – and his points apply to 'matters of faith' as well as 'questions of morality'. As evidence for the instinctual, tacit pre-apprehension of truth, Froude points to the common social requirement of responsibility for actions demanded in the case even of those who are at the pre-rational or infantile stage of existence; such a requirement

at a period of our lives when we are incapable of appreciating any other evidence than the authoritative declarations of those who take care of us, proves that the absence of implicit faith, which alone can (then) protect us from any vice, must in itself be vicious.[44]

Newman's 'theory' takes over this idea of the tacit moral instinct of infants, but applies it to the corporate life of faith in its entirety, where most people, with the exception of the 'great', are children who must accept what is handed down with unselfconscious obedience. Here, Newman considerably modifies Froude's line: the latter is concerned with the individual, and *specifically* with heresy, the former with the social mediation of Christianity and the nature of the challenges to such mediation. Newman has not yet seen the advantages of relating this to *heresy*.

(B) THE REACTIONARY PREACHER, 1829–1831

It is the sermons between the defeat of Peel in February 1829, and the composition of *Arians* in June 1831, which show most clearly his evolving response to heresy and orthodoxy, in the context of an embattled Establishment. First, he is by now clear that the Church of England upholds a distinct body of doctrine handed down from the Early Church. His systematic study of the Fathers, begun in 1828, was proceeding chronologically. By mid-1828, he had begun the second-century 'Apostolic Fathers',[45] who could hardly have been more relevant to his preaching programme in the late 1820s: St Clement of Rome and, especially, St Ignatius of Antioch,[46] never tire of stressing the apostolic authority of the bishop, the deposit of doctrine he guards and teaches, and the need for visible Church unity in the face of schism and heretical novelty.[47] Secondly, Newman characterises the opponents of the Church according to a particular *ethos* or character, so that his ecclesial and doctrinal conservatism is supported by a rhetoric employing subtle psychological analysis, often verging upon satire.

The call to obey the objective teaching of a visible Church body is clearly announced in *Religious Faith Rational*, preached on 24 May 1829.[48] Here, Newman reacts strongly against the extreme 'Evangelical' pattern of faith, against, that is, the idea of faith as a psychological process whereby a person appropriates the work of Christ: 'When faith is said to be a religious principle, it is (I repeat) the things believed, not the act of believing them, which is peculiar to religion.'[49] The deposit of teaching may, in fact, be contrary to human experience, requiring the faith of Abraham, who was led 'to believe God's word, even when opposed to his own experience'.[50] But how, if the obedience of faith is contrary to experience, do we know that we *are* obeying God? How did Abraham *know* that he was obeying the voice of a *divine* command? The implications of these questions, which Newman faces squarely

enough, may be translated, in the light of the historical background
of the late 1820s, as, 'How can it be shown that dissent from the
established body, and heterodox challenging of creeds and articles,
are acts of disobedience to God?' Newman refuses to answer this
discursively: to do so would be to disrupt the rhetorical structure
of the sermon, which functions by *assertion*, and to introduce an
agenda whereby the givenness of revelation, and the authority of
the Established Church as its mediator, might be called into
question. Instead, he sustains the rhetorical thrust of the sermon
by an appeal to *ethos*, drawing upon the tacit grounds of obedience
in innate conscience; it is a bold – and vulnerable – attempt to call
forth in his audience a sense of common, instinctual pre-apprehension: 'We obey God primarily because we actually feel His presence
in our consciences bidding us obey Him.'[51] Therefore he exhorts,
in the face of troublesome questions, 'For ourselves, let us but obey
God's voice in our hearts.'[52] But those who *pursue* such questions –
Dissenters, sceptics, infidels or heretics – have an entirely different
ethos:

They set up some image of freedom in their minds, a freedom from the
shackles of dependence, which they think their natural right, and which
they aim to gain for themselves; a liberty, much like that which Satan
aspired after, when he rebelled against God.[53]

Intellectual autonomy puts the doubters outside the reach of
Newman's rhetoric, for they have separated themselves from the
tacit and instinctual: 'Their conscience is as their reason is; and it
is placed within them by Almighty God in order to balance the
influence of sight and reason; and yet they will not attend to it.'[54]
Somewhat crudely he states the 'plain reason' for which they have
cut themselves off: 'they love sin – they love to be their own
masters and therefore they will not attend to that secret whisper of
their hearts, which tells them they are *not* their own masters and
that sin is hateful and ruinous.'[55] Newman, then, roots deference
to authority in the 'secret whisper' of conscience, in order to
legitimate the established religion against the subversive stirrings
of critical doubt.

   In a sermon of the following month, *The Christian Mysteries*,[56] in
which he treats of the Doctrine of the Trinity, Newman follows
substantially the same line: in the matter of revealed truths,
'religious light is intellectual darkness'.[57] Reception of religious

truth entails being 'told something',[58] rather than thinking something out: it is a matter of *ethos* – hence, Jesus 'spoke in parables,
that they might see and hear, yet not understand, – a righteous
detection of insincerity; whereas the same difficulties and obscurities, which offended religious men, would but lead the humble and
meek to seek for more light'.[59] It is conscience which sustains the
believer when doubts pain him, but it is only the one who cuts
himself off from conscience who gives way.

The strategy underlying Newman's rhetoric is made explicit in
a sermon entitled *Submission to Church Authority*,[60] preached towards
the end of 1829: the precepts of the Book of Proverbs – to hold
what has been *given*, 'turning neither to the left nor to the right'[61] –
are applied to the contemporary situation of the beleaguered
Church of England:

> the present time, when religious unity and peace are so lamentably
> disregarded, and novel doctrines and new measures alone are popular,
> they naturally remind us of the duty of obedience to the Church, and of
> the sin of departing from it, or what our Litany prays against under the
> name of 'heresy and schism'.[62]

Behind the outline of the embattled Establishment, Newman
discerns the maimed form of the ancient Church. He describes
with much pathos how the once united 'vast Catholic body' has
been smashed into fragments, 'just as some huge barrier cliff which
once boldly fronted the sea is at length cleft, parted, overthrown
by the waves'.[63] Buffeted by the assaults of a new paganism, amidst
'rebuke and blasphemy', stand the adherents of the Church of
England, 'clinging to our own portion of the Ancient Rock which
the waters are roaring round and would fain overthrow'.[64] The link
between the ancient Christianity out of which the creeds emerged,
and the present, is still just in place, but strained to breaking point.

Newman's discussion of heresy in this sermon starts from an
examination of the New Testament texts in the epistles about
'parties' (in Greek *haireseis*) in the earliest Christian communities:
his first two texts, from I Corinthians and Titus, refer to what the
Authorised Version translates as 'heresies' and 'heretic',[65] but it is
possible that he has in mind the New Testament, as opposed to
the early Church, sense of heretics, for the third text he quotes –
from Romans[66] – refers to those who cause 'divisions and offences'.
Influenced by the crisis of his own times, he brings heresy close to

schism. The threat of 'party spirit' emerges clearly in his definition: heresies are 'private persuasions, self-formed bodies', and a heretic is 'one who adopts some opinion of his own in religious matters, and gets about him followers'.[67]

Newman holds out only one hope for those who would avert complete 'overthrow' of the Church – *obedience*.[68] The Church cannot complacently rest in the claim of infallibility, (a shaft at Rome here!), and, since teaching error *is*, therefore, possible, the whole body of the faithful must, by deference and obedience, contribute to the holding together of that polity, the 'visible Church', which transmits revelation:

a system of laws, a bond of subordination connecting all in one, is the (next) best mode of securing the stability of sacred Truth. The whole body of Christians thus become the *trustees* of it, to use the language of the world, and, in fact, have thus age after age transmitted it down to ourselves.[69]

Deliberate Dissent, the physical separation from the Church of England, is as sinful as the intellectual separation from conscience of the rationalist sceptic: 'There is not a dissenter living, but, inasmuch and so far as he dissents, is in a sin.'[70] Separation is an 'evil' in itself. On the other hand, obedience is a good in itself: Hammond, the Laudian divine, Newman tells us, recommended 'uniform obedience' in which there was no choice at all as 'the happiest state of life'.[71]

Newman was not only addressing the tradesman and shop-keepers of Oxford while Vicar of St Mary's – he was also from time to time continuing his examination of the nature of faith in the *University Sermons*, addressed to the academic community. The second of these, preached in April 1830, examines more rigorously and philosophically than his 'parochial' sermons the relation between conscience and faith. Nevertheless, the line taken, as he applies himself to the problem of theological error, has a close relation to the approach we have already seen emerging in 1829. The existence of errors is explained by reference to a separation between, on the one hand, the abstracting power of the intellect and, on the other, an instinctive orientation, the unspecific, innate sense of obligation, which, when progressively lived out in the performance of moral acts, develops into a specific sense of duty, described as an unerring form of ethical knowledge, 'moral revelation'.[72] Newman's starting point, then, is the particular individual trying to live out concretely his or her instinct in acts, an undertaking which necessarily involves the *social*.

The discussion, later in the sermon, of the relation between the natural and revealed returns to the theme of the destructiveness of the separative intellect, in order to explain the rise of eighteenth-century rationalist movements such as Deism and Unitarianism, which Newman calls 'Arianism'. Revealed religion is, Newman explains, *concrete*: its method of communication is by the impact made upon particular individuals, that is, by 'personation'.[73] The Incarnation, the very basis of Christian revelation, is particular; consequently, the Church is 'teaching religious truths historically, not by investigation.'[74] Natural religion, on the other hand, concerns itself with 'principle'; its abstraction tends towards a form of idolatry: 'in whatever degree we approximate towards a mere standard of excellence, we do not really advance towards it, but bring it to us; the excellence we venerate becomes part of ourselves – we become a God to ourselves.'[75] Abstraction drives the individual into a tragic solipsistic state, narrow and lonely, cut off from the springs of religious life.

The philosophy of religious knowledge expounded in the second *University Sermon* was constantly being translated into the rhetoric of his parochial sermons, where characterisation, or, rather, an appeal to a psychological typification drawing upon common wisdom and experience, does the work of argument and analysis. Newman's task of popular exposition is, of course, made easier by the compatibility of *ethos* with character-presentation. One of his most remarkable attempts at such characterisation of heresy is his sermon, *The Self-Wise Enquirer*,[76] preached six months after the second *University Sermon*. It is a miniature biography, in which the 'self-wise' main character proceeds on an infidel's progress, terminating in the formal profession of heresy. It describes the life of one 'in whom intellectual power is fearfully unfolded amid the neglect of moral truth'.[77] The slide into what eventually becomes heresy begins with a 'contest between our instinctive sense of right and wrong and our weak and conceited reason'.[78] The rationalistic element wins, and, now trusting in his own powers, our character begins to despise the *given* revelation; he is impatient of it, fearing that it will 'interfere with his own imaginary discoveries.'[79] This moral and religious collapse takes place 'when childhood and boyhood are past and the time comes for our entrance into life'.[80] In childhood, the innate moral sense had been unquestioningly obeyed (there is, perhaps, an echo of Hurrell Froude here), but the pressure of adult life engenders a desire to be 'independent', 'original' and 'manly'. There follows 'a light unmeaning use of sceptical arguments and assertions',[81] which is really 'the beginning of apostasy'.[82] The gift of reasoning, when 'clear, brilliant or powerful' is dangerous because it causes 'men of superior under-standing . . . to *value* themselves upon it and look down upon others'.[83] Such people cast down 'moral excellence' from its 'proper eminence' and set up reason in its stead.[84] Then a terrible delusion takes place: having cut themselves off from the moral, they begin to believe that when all are intellectuals, all will be moral: 'they labour to convince themselves, that as men grow in knowledge they will grow in virtue.'[85] Needless to say, such a delusive conviction screens its adherent from the necessity of practical virtue. The collapse of faith is now complete, nor is profligacy far behind. Our character settles down into heresy in old age, having spent his prime in 'the pursuit of wealth, or in some other excitement of the world'.[86] The effort to repent according to orthodox Christian demands is now too much, arduous and humiliating as it would be; he now needs religion, but one with an accommodating creed, for he is unwilling to struggle against vicious habits, now entrenched. Heresy fits the bill: 'Thus it happens that, men who have led profligate lives in their youth . . . not unfrequently settle down into *heresies* in their latter years.'[87]

But what of those who, unlike the frivolous self-wise enquirer, have genuine doubts about orthodox dogmas. The title of a sermon of November 1830, indicates Newman's responses – *Obedience the Remedy for Religious Perplexity*.[88] Here he holds ruthlessly to the idea of *ethos*: 'Revelation was not given to us to satisfy doubts, but to make us better men.'[89] Therefore, to those who are perplexed and 'who wish for light but cannot find it', he will give one answer only – 'Obey!' The doubter must bear his doubt 'manfully', all the while striving 'meekly' at a practical acquiescence in 'God's will'; the more this is done, the sooner the 'unsettled state' will vanish and 'order arise out of confusion'.[90] Deference to the established, the abnegation of critical thought, intellectual passivity, the daily round of virtue – these are the qualities guaranteeing an inner spiritual order which mirrors the divinely ordained policy of the established Church. Heresy, on the other hand, is an impatient solution to the problem of doubt; heretics are those who will not 'wait upon the Lord', they 'seek some new path which promises to be shorter and easier than the lowly and circuitous way of obedience . . . they expect to gain speedy peace and holiness by means of new teachers and by a new doctrine.'[91]

Although the sermons between 1829 and 1831 are a defence of a beleaguered, established, visible Church against intellectual heterodoxy and 'schismatic' Dissent, this is not to say that Newman was *unequivocally* upholding the 'powers that be'. His sermons attack respectability, wealth, comfort and intellectual independence, the very qualities of the bourgeoisie.[92] In the third of the *University Sermons*, he makes a clear distinction between a secularist morality which absorbs Christian ethics, accommodating it to a refined, attractive and expedient moral system, and the stern morality of the Gospel which is offensive to the world and demands heroic sanctity. Although it is true to say that Christian morality has beneficial social effects, a utilitarian concept in which it is viewed *only* in such terms, is a 'shallow philosophy'.[93] Newman is, in his own Romantic way, a revolutionary, challenging the cherished assumptions of an increasingly bourgeois culture: 'May God arise and shake terribly the earth (though it be an awful prayer), rather than the double-minded should lie hid among us, and souls be lost by present ease.'[94] Newman depreciates the qualities which support the restless, tampering, bustling spirit of bourgeois Christianity: 'Eloquence and wit, shrewdness and dexterity, these plead a cause well and propagate it quickly.'[95] What he is so rhetorically assailing is itself a form of rhetoric. But he sees its force as ephemeral, because it manipulates its audience with cleverness, rather than appealing to the universal stock of wisdom, innate to humanity: 'It has no root in the hearts of men and lives not out a generation. It is the consolation of the despised truth that its works endure.'[96]

Newman, then, appeals to the past – orthodoxy has, as it were, been vindicated by time, as it has accumulatively found an answer deep within human hearts. His Romantic conservatism, supported by a philosophy and psychology of conscience, deployed in order to defend from reform the Anglican Church, gives an original turn to the ancient maxim that heresy is *novelty* and that novelty is always wrong.

(C) THE COMPOSITION OF 'ARIANS OF THE FOURTH CENTURY,
1831–1832'

(i) *The Occasion*

In March, 1831, when Newman's preaching was in full flow, Hugh
James Rose presented him with an opportunity to write a full-
length work – what eventually became *The Arians of the Fourth
Century*. Rose's conception of the kind of work Newman should
write for the *Theological Library* could not be more different from
the book – ultimately 'plucked'[97] – which came from Newman's
pen: 'I hope to see your work the standard work on Articles for
students of Divinity.'[98] In such a dogmatic text-book, the history
of the Councils was to be *background* to an exposition and defence
of the articles of the Christian religion, taking in the meaning of
doctrinal terminology and its relation to Scripture proof. It was to
be a judicious and scholarly tome of High Church divinity.

Newman's work was certainly learned and dogmatic, but it was
also more than Rose bargained for: structurally a highly original
combination of systematic exposition, vivid narrative and brilliant
character-sketch, all co-ordinated, by means of ancient–modern
analogies of varying point and subtlety, into a rhetorical thrust
against his ecclesiastical and political opponents. His correspondence and diaries show him conscientiously doing his homework,
intensively exploiting the patristic reading which had been in
progress since 1828, and studying the standard textbooks of the
day.[99] However, a tension soon emerges between the systematic–catechetical, and the narrative–historical method of presentation. In a letter to Rose in late August 1831, Newman argues that
the best method of proceeding would be to write a *connected history*
of the Councils, rather than taking each Council in isolation and
supplying a doctrinal commentary upon it. The *acta* of Councils,
he argues, only give *conclusions*, without the process leading to
them: the Nicene Confession cannot be properly understood by an
article-by-article exposition: it can only be grasped by reference to
the historical rise of Arianism. However, such a determination
raises its own problems: how to avoid lengthy digressions and
intrusive footnotes in the discussion of doctrine, which will disrupt
the flow of the historical narrative. Newman's proposed solution to

the dilemma is to consider the structure of the work from the point of view of an imagined reader:

I propose, then, to clear my text of arguments as much as may be and state my conclusions – and to enter so far into the subject matter of debate, as to explain it generally, connect the history, introduce the subjects and excite curiosity – then to add a series of notes or discussions under various heads . . . In this way I think the book may be somewhat more attractive (if that is an object) – and beginners will be less clogged with difficulties and delays.[100]

Newman considers the disposition of his material with regard to the audience: he wants to tell a good story, to be readable, to enable his audience, who will not be learned but beginners, to 'enter into' his subject. His self-declared method is not then 'historical', in the sense of the impartial sifting of evidence; rather, he incorporates the historian's interest in causality and origins into a story in which argument and narrative are carefully woven to make the greatest popular appeal.

Newman was aware of the originality of his attempt. In a letter to Samuel Rickards, of 30 October 1831, he declares: 'I am engaged in a history of the Principal Councils as illustrative of the doctrines of the Articles . . . I am led to fancy I may be able to throw some light upon the subject.'[101] He distances himself from two main approaches: first, the huge folios of the 'standard Divines' of the past, and secondly, historians of the present. Of the former – 'Bull, Waterland, Petavius, Baronius and the rest' – he severely qualifies his admiration; they are 'magnificent fellows but then they are Antiquarians or Doctrinists, not Ecclesiastical Historians'.[102] Newman's popularist aim in the presentation of his subject accounts for his reservations about following them in their massive accumulation of citation. It is, however, surprising to find him so dismissive of Bishop George Bull, who was, by his own testimony, to exert such an important influence upon him during the Tractarian period.[103] Whatever his feelings, he drew upon these earlier writers freely when he was composing Arians. As for the historians, he can only say of these, 'I have a very low opinion – Mosheim, Gibbon, Middleton, Milner etc – Cave and Tillemont are highly respectable but biographers.'[104] In their very different ways, the historians, rather than the 'biographers' here challenged credal and patristic orthodoxy, in such a way as to make them unsympathetic. His dismissiveness is, nevertheless, again rather surprising: Edward Gibbon and Joseph Milner both exerted, as we shall see, a profound influence upon his method of presentation in *Arians*. At this point, however, Newman saw himself treading a lone path.

(ii) *'Arians of the Fourth Century' as a church–political tract: 'liberalism' and 'tests'*

What, then, *was* the purpose of his narrative? Foremost in his mind was the desire to make a polemical contribution to the Church–State crisis of 1829–32. He wanted to defend the tests which by law upheld the unique status of the Church of England, and which demanded public assent to a mixture of early Church dogmas and specifically Anglican doctrines, in return for power and privilege. Until the legislative movements of the 1820s, it was by *tests* that Dissenters and Roman Catholics had been excluded from full participation in the public life of the nation, and, in Newman's own university, were still by *tests* excluded from admission. It was the value and justice of *tests*[105] that 'latitudinarianism' was challenging. In a letter, written three weeks before the exhausting process of composition had run to its end, Newman equates such tests with the dogmas of the Early Church Councils 'The one point which I strive to show is the importance of the *Homoousion* and similar tests.'[106] Here, Newman presents the definition of Christ's divinity at the Council of Nicea (AD 325) as a 'test' in the early nineteenth-century English sense. At this stage there is no firm evidence that Newman held to the distinction, much-used in the Tractarian period, between articles of faith, the universally binding articles of the ancient creeds, and articles of religion, such as the *39 Articles*, a matter only of Church order and a product of a national church's history. Replying to Rose's original request in 1831, he shows *some* awareness that the *39 Articles* – 'our own' – are not identical with the articles of the ancient creeds: 'I had considered a work on the Articles might be useful on the following plan. First, a defence of the articles – then, the history of our own.'[107] However, the nature of the difference remains undefined, while, on the other hand, it is clear that defence of ancient and of Anglican articles belong to the same strategy, in that both uphold the ancient Christianity mediated by the Church of England.

That school of opinion which wanted to relax tests Newman called 'liberalism'. From 1830 onwards, Newman had used the term to describe those who aimed to deprive the Church of England of its 'forms' and to alter its 'system of government'; those who would broaden the national Church so as to embrace any who were, in some sense, Bible Protestants.[108] Newman therefore understood the term in a markedly party way: liberalism was the ecclesiastical form of that challenge to Toryism which triumphed with the Reform Act of 1832.

One of Newman's boldest polemical strokes was to suggest that such liberalism was a mark of the heresies of the early Church. Of the Arian prelate Acacius, he declares, 'He had lately succeeded in establishing the principle of liberalism at Constantinople, where a condemnation had been passed on the use of words not found in Scripture.'[109] With the mischievous dropping of the word 'liberalism' into the heavily patristic context – he provides the conditions by which his reader, with, as it were, newspaper and *British Magazine* at elbow, might pursue the parallel in detail. The indignant Highchurchman reading Newman's book could hardly miss the application: a wily church-politician invoking vague assent to Scripture in order to weaken the authority of a test which could be used to exclude him from power and influence in the church.

This is but one of a carefully orchestrated series of innuendos implying parallels between the most unscrupulous and least religious of the Arians, and modern liberal churchmen such as Thomas Arnold of Rugby. While Newman presents Arius as an open and honest heretic, he describes the party centred around the courtly ecclesiastic Eusebius of Nicomedia as scheming, power-seeking and dishonest. Newman even calls the followers of this Eusebius 'the Court Faction'. They are presented as 'nothing better than a political party'.[110] It directs its energies towards private ends, 'a mere political faction, usurping the name of religion; and, as such, essentially anti-christian [*sic*]'.[111] Arianism was undoubtedly successful in putting forward a plausible and reasonable face to the world and adept in the ways of the Court. The analogy with Newman's view of the reforming party – that crypto-infidelity was employing parliamentary and democratic structures and the plea of reasonable reform to dismantle the Church – lurks, unspoken, just below the surface of his vivid descriptions.

In *The Arians of the Fourth Century*, for the first time, there appears, clearly enunciated, the analogy[112] between heresy and the forces of Newman's own time which he regarded as enemies of Church and Christianity. It is, indeed, the political aspect of heresy which he takes for his peroration, pointing to the present significance of the past:

And so of the present perils, with which our branch of the Church is beset, as they bear a marked resemblance to those of the fourth century, so are the lessons, which we gain from that ancient time, especially cheering and edifying to Christians of the present day. Then as now, there was the prospect and partly the presence in the Church, of an Heretical Power enthralling it, exerting a varied influence and a usurped claim in the appointment of her functionaries, and interfering with the management of her internal affairs.[113]

(iii) The 'Ethos' of heresy: liberalism and 'neology'

Newman's sermons between 1829 and 1831 were directed against those who would tinker with the established Church. This political thrust was integrated, by an appeal to *ethos*, into a critique of the spirit of the age. From the pulpit, Newman presented modern rationalism as heresy. The same is true of *The Arians of the Fourth Century*, where he identifies rationalism as the intellectual origin of Arianism. He now points to the 'Self-Wise Enquirer', not only in his own age, but also in that of the Fathers. His discussion of rationalism links the idea of 'liberalism' with a pejorative term current in the mid-1820s – 'neology'. In this, Newman is doing more than attacking a church-political party: he identifies the origin of heresy in an all-pervasive *Geist*, an arrogant intellectualism which tends towards infidelity.

Newman acquired the idea that heresy was rationalism from the Fathers' polemic against the Arians, which accounted for their success by describing them as skilful but unscrupulous logicians. The 'place of education' of Arianism was 'the schools of the Sophists'.[114] Drawing freely – and uncritically – upon examples from the historians, Socrates and Sozomen, Newman declares, 'adroitness in debate was the very life and weapon of heresy'.[115] The great Fathers of the Church are of 'one voice' in protesting against 'the dialectics of their opponents',[116] and substantiate the adage that Aristotle was the 'bishop of the Arians'. Newman, then, just like the Fathers, rhetorically assails a form of rhetoric as inauthentic Christianity. But he gives this patristic view his own characteristic slant: Arian rhetoric is inauthentic because it does not appeal to the experience of the concrete body of the Church as it is living out its faith, but separates and abstracts theological discussion from this context, compelling with the syllogism, rather than persuading by appeal to the common stock of wisdom. Of Paul of Samosata Newman declares, 'His heresy thus founded on a syllogism, spread itself by instruments of a kindred character.'[117] Heretics view Christianity, as it were, from an external perspective, that is, the laws of argument, so that the meaning of Scripture is distorted:

And from the first, it has been the error of heretics to neglect the information thus provided for them, and to attempt of themselves a work to which they are unequal, the eliciting a systematic doctrine from the scattered notices of the truth which Scripture contains.[118]

But Newman has already decided that the Arians were 'unequal' to the total rationalistic systematisation of Christianity. In fact, for him, they wanted to 'inquire into', and – a value-laden word in the 1830s – 'reform' the creeds which had been 'received'.[119] He sees them as nineteenth-century liberals, tamperers and accommodators, whose purpose is to modify the Christian tradition in the direction of infidelity, while making apparently moderate changes to its external appearance.

The authentic, orthodox response is to point to the concrete, to people and things. Hence, the advice of Sisinnus to the Patriarch of Constantinople about how to deal with Arianism: 'to drop the use of dialectics, and merely challenge his opponents to utter a general anathema against all such Ante-Nicene Fathers as had taught what they now denounced as false doctrine'.[120] When this was tried, the heretics were reduced to silence: 'they rested their cause on their dialectic skill, and not on the testimony of the early Church'.[121]

If, then, Arianism was essentially *alien* to Christianity – the application of Aristotelian rhetoric to revelation – whence did it arise? It might suggest, as we shall see, that the Church was passing through a phase when love and faith had grown cold. This has value as a debating point in the crisis which is Newman's *own* context, not least in predisposing his audience towards the idea of *revival* or renewal.

First Newman explains how Christian theologians became Aristotelian rhetoricians. The practice of dialectical disputation about Christian truth had been early introduced into the Eastern Church, in order to 'prepare the Christian teacher for the controversy with unbelievers'.[122] This resulted in an atmosphere in which heterodox texts were defended 'by way of exercise in argument'.[123] This soon became open to abuse. Christian rhetoricians repeated the 'error of the Sophists',[124] divorcing the arguability of a tenet from its truth. This was the first step in the secularisation of Christian discourse and its absorption into the curriculum of 'a liberal education'.[125] Doctrine, having been separated by rhetoric from its form of life, was soon subjected to the criteria of the natural sciences:

Then, however, as now, the minds of speculative men were impatient of ignorance and loth to confess that the laws of truth and falsehood, which their experience of the world furnished, could not at once be applied to measure and determine the facts of another.[126]

'Then . . . as now': Newman points the analogy with his own time when Christianity has been distorted by the imposition of categories derived from 'the world', from a 'liberal education', from science and from logic.

He gives a second reason: the growth of an Eclectic mystico-philosophical school incorporating elements of Platonism into Christianity, which, while in many ways different from Arianism, nevertheless contributed to an intellectual atmosphere within the Church facilitating the spread of heresy. It was begun by Ammonius Saccas, an initiate into Christianity, who, renouncing full belief 'at least secretly', opened a syncretistic philosophical school. Arianism was Aristotelian, logical and scientific, while Eclecticism was Platonic and mystical. Newman brings them together with a sour observation on the nature of ecclesiastical politics, pointing to the essentially 'party spirit' of heresy: 'in seasons of difficulty men look about on all sides for support'.[127] Eclecticism was difficult to distinguish from orthodoxy, for it used the terminology of the latter in a manner only very subtly heterodox. It became a 'seasonable refuge' for the more radical originators of Arianism – 'the Sophists of Antioch' – when they were under pressure from orthodox criticism and authority. The originators of Arianism could shelter under the comparative respectability of Eclecticism.

When full-blown Arianism arose, it could claim earlier Eclecticism as a pseudo-Christian tradition to which it belonged.[128] But there was a profounder reason bringing Eclectics and Arians together: both were *in principle* opposed to 'mystery, in the ecclesiastical sense of the word'.[129] Newman means the failure, or even refusal, to recognise that revelation transcends the human capacity fully to comprehend it.[130]

The discussion of Eclecticism provides Newman with an opportunity for contemporary polemic. He compares it with 'what would now be called *Neologism*, a heresy which, even more than others, has shown itself desirous and able to conceal itself under the garb of sound religion, and to keep the form, while it destroys the spirit, of Christianity'.[131] It closely resembles orthodoxy by its use of such terms as 'divine', 'revelation', 'inspiration', and professes respect for the religious teachings of the Scripture, seeing them as, in *some sense* from God. However, it denies a distinctively and specifically divine intervention in human history and may be identified by its opposition to miracle. Newman's notes, made in preparation for *Arians*, provide a precise definition: 'a denial of the exclusive mission and peculiar inspiration of the Prophets and Evangelists'.[132] Neology lurks in the bosom of Christianity; its real danger is its specious resemblance to orthodoxy. This implication bears on the early nineteenth-century call for the waiving of 'tests', for, with the disappearance of these would disappear, also, Newman argued, all chance of isolating this ambiguous alien, Neology.

The reference to 'Neology' draws upon a debate in which Newman had been peripherally involved, beginning in 1825 with Hugh James Rose's lectures on *The State of the Protestant Religion in Germany*.[133] Pusey's attempt to set right Rose's misconceptions, in his *Historical Enquiry* (1828),[134] provoked a controversy[135] in which Rose, perhaps forgivably misreading Pusey's turgid[136] volume, accused him of disbelieving the inspiration of the historical parts of Scripture.[137] Pusey, shocked to be accused of 'vindicating German Neology' and of being 'a disciple of the Neologians',[138] replied with a second part to his *Historical Enquiry*, in 1829, in which he clarified his position regarding Biblical Inspiration. Newman assisted Pusey with this latter task, especially with the patristic material,[139] and would therefore have been thoroughly familiar with the terms of the debate.

Although Newman helped Pusey defend his own orthodoxy

against Rose, Pusey's own early sympathy, in the first part of the
Historical Enquiry, for the Schleiermachian theology of feeling as a
not unconstructive approach to the rationalism of the eighteenth
century[140] did not impress Newman. Indeed, it is rather the
influence of Rose that is uppermost.[141] In his identification of the
intellectual milieu out of which the political attacks on the Church
sprang, Newman applied Rose's thesis about German theology to
the *English* scene. His presentation of 'rationalism' from 1829
onwards so closely resembles that of Rose, that it may be concluded
that the latter was an important influence upon him. Many of
Rose's sentences in *The State of Protestant Religion in Germany* are
indistinguishable from Newman's statements in sermons and in
Arians; for example, take Rose's:

> The advocates for the supremacy of the human understanding . . . (not
> content with judging of the evidences offered in support of the truth of
> the Christian system) . . . establish reason as the sole and sufficient
> arbiter of the truth or falsehood of the various doctrines which that
> system contains, the umpire from whose judgment there is to be no
> appeal in matters of religious controversy.[142]

Rose contended that such an approach eventually resulted in an
attenuation of the supernatural element in revelation; it 'proceeded
from the determination that whatever was not intelligible, was
incredible; that only what was of familiar and easy explanation
deserved belief, and that all which was miraculous and mysterious
in Scriptures must be rejected.'[143] Against this – like Newman –
Rose held it better to believe too much than too little, and
advocated acquiescence in the *given*. Again like Newman, Rose
thought the bulwark against rationalism to be the authority
structure of a visible, established Church, with its liturgy and
precise articles, imposed as tests. This structure the Church of
England possessed as far as Rose was concerned, but its security,
he warned, should not be taken for granted, for German rationalism was beginning to seep into the English Church. Finally, Rose's
polemic is couched in terminology which is also a familiar feature
of Newman's vocabulary throughout his life: 'the essence of
Protestantism, the right of private judgment'.[144]

By the time of the composition of *Arians*, the Anglican hegemony
to which Rose could point in 1825 was dissolving rapidly. Newman
diverted Rose's polemic against Germany towards the *English*

reforming spirit and compared it with the process by which ancient
heresy arose. Not only did he call Eclecticism 'Neology', he also
called it *liberalism*: 'Who does not recognise in this old philosophy
the chief features of that recent school of liberalism and false
illumination, political and moral, which is now Satan's instrument
in deluding the nations?'[145] Readers of the Tractarian and Roman
Catholic Newman will be familiar with this pervasive sense of
'liberalism',[146] which stretches from *Tract 73* to the *Biglietto Speech* –
it became a catch-all for everything he saw as bad in the application of intellect to religion. Its first appearance in this very broad
sense in Newman's published writings occurs when he simultaneously gives an explanation of the origins of Arianism and
makes a parallel between modern liberalism and ancient heresy.
In doing this, Newman brings Christian Antiquity suddenly to life:
Church history is no longer just a scholarly pursuit – the past is
used to unmask what Newman sees as a present threat to Christianity: scepticism and infidelity making its way in a lukewarm
Church under the cover of philosophy and learning.

(iv) *Newman's characters*

Arians of the Fourth Century could be described as Newman's first
novel. His presentation of character has a richness and complexity,
absent in the patristic sources, as he meditates upon the tragic
failure of the inner man. Particularly in his concrete presentation
of the characters involved in the Arian dispute, Newman embodies
his points about the *ethos* of heresy. Prominent is the view that
heresy springs from worldliness. Thus, the heresiarch, Paul of
Samosata, is linked with a kind of 'ceremonial Judaism', an empty
ritualism far removed from the moral zeal of the Old Testament.
His 'grossly humanitarian'[147] attitude to the Divinity of Christ does
not surprise Newman. Similarly, he sees Julian the Apostate's
infidelity as sharing the outlook of 'men of the world', who fail to
penetrate into the 'real moving principle and life of the system'
and whose perception is restricted to its 'surface'.[148] A milder case
of worldliness, that of Eusebius of Caesaria, serves as a means of
directing a mischievous shaft at latitudinarianism: 'his conduct
gave countenance to the secular maxim, that difference in creeds is
a matter of inferior moment, and that, provided we confess as far
as the very terms of Scripture, we may speculate as philosophers,

and live as the world'.[149] Newman's satiric analogy treats Eusebius as the typical, learned Regency bishop.

On the other hand, in the case of Pope Liberius, who conceded to Arianism under duress, Newman discerns a weakness provoking, not mockery, but compassionate sympathy: his was a moral and personal failure, a tragedy, born of deficiency in the heroic quality of martyrdom. A brave man, worn down by exile, he was skilfully broken by the alternation of blandishment with mortal threat, baffled by the conflicting demands upon conscience of martyrdom and peace in the Church, a victim of the complex and ambiguous state of Church parties, humiliatingly held in exile by his tormentors. Yet, even after his lapse, he constitutes, for Newman, a miserable apostasy and a warning lesson to compromisers.[150] A gentler hint against the conciliatory spirit is his characterisation of Meletius, holy and orthodox, but tender towards heretics; his partiality towards his friends dulled his sensitivity towards heresy in particular instances, clouding his vision with a 'false charitableness' and making him a pawn of Arian plots.[151]

The last two examples – Liberius and Meletius – show Newman's capacity to cope with the shades and complexities entailed by the *embodiment* of his rhetoric in characters. The acceptance of a degree of ambiguity – that not *all* sympathisers with heresy are *grossly* worldly – is consistent nevertheless with his overall argument from *ethos*. Association with heresy must involve a character deficiency somewhere, however subtle, Newman argues, – and of such his imagination is a fertile source.

Newman also shows subtlety in his treatment of *groups*. For example, in his depiction of the moderate Arian parties, he distinguishes between the followers of Eusebius of Nicomedia, whose moderation concealed indifference to truth, and the 'Semi-Arians', whose opposition to the Athanasian *Homoousion* derived from genuine scruple. In the latter case, his portrayals take on a poignant many-sidedness. The Semi-Arians were good and holy men – 'saints and martyrs' compared with the 'Eusebians'[152] – vigorous missionaries of the Gospel,[153] whom even the uncompromising Athanasius called 'brothers'.[154] In fact, 'the men were better than their creed'.[155] Why, then, did they cleave to heresy? As so often, Newman declares the cause to lie in the intellect: the Semi-Arians were drawn by subtlety of argument into the labyrinth of dialectic. They tried 'to satisfy their intellect and conscience by

refined distinctions and perverse reservations',[156] and failed to take
a 'broad and commonsense view of an important subject',[157] while
Catholics evaded such difficulties by their 'straightforward sim-
plicity'.[158] Here, Newman comes very close indeed to identifying
the *appetitus intellectivus* with deficiency of character, unreflective
obscurantism with the fullness of orthodox truth. Yet his exploitation of the pathos inherent in the picture of Semi-Arianism as a
genuine spirituality half-stifled by rationalism transforms this
antithesis into an evocation of the fraught ambivalence and latent
tragedy of the Christian bourgeois *intelligentsia*; he detects 'amid
the impiety and worldliness of the heretical party . . . elements of a
purer spirit, which gradually exerted itself and worked out from
the corrupt mass in which it was embedded'.[159]

Newman also deploys a topology of heresy: he identifies Antioch
as the source of Arianism.[160] It was in this city, noted for worldly
corruption, that the *ethos* of the heresy germinated: 'The history of
the times gives us sufficient evidence of the luxuriousness of
Antioch; and it need scarcely be said, that coldness in faith is the
sure consequence of relaxation of morals.'[161] He describes Antioch
as imbued with the spirit of a bastardised Judaism which looked to
'the promise of temporal blessings, and a more accommodating
rule of life than the gospel revealed'.[162] Such a materialism made
heresy's rise inevitable: 'When the spirit and morals of a people
are materially debased, varieties of doctrinal error spring up, as if
self-sown, and are rapidly propagated.'[163] Antiochene Christianity,
he later adds, developed a literalist scriptural hermeneutic wholly
in accord with its *ethos*.[164] His condemnation of Antioch – a view
which survived intact the revolution in perspective of the mid-
1840s[165] – is unqualified. He sees no subtle shades and complexities, as he did in the case of the Semi-Arians. This is probably
because, in his eagerness at all costs to vindicate his beloved
Alexandrian Fathers from the charge of originating Arianism, he
has deliberately shifted the blame to Antioch.[166]

(v) *Sources and analogues*

The Arians of the Fourth Century, then, proceeds by a fertile exploitation of analogy between ancient Church history and the ecclesiastical scene of the early 1830s. How did Newman come by such an
historiographical method? The most obvious answer lies in his

reading of the Fathers, particularly Origen and Clement of Alexandria, whose influence has been traced by C. F. Harrold:

man may catch glimpses of the infinite through the 'parable' of nature and history, as well as through Scripture.[167]

The Alexandrian idea of pagan history as a preparation for the Gospel provided a means whereby he could see all history as, in some sense, parabolic.[168]

However, behind patristic typology, an earlier influence may be suggested, that of 'figuration' in the Calvinist tradition of Scripture-interpretation.[169]

In addition to these general trends, Newman had a specific historiographical model in Joseph Milner's *History of the Church of Christ*.[170] Just as Newman had overestimated the *early* influence of this work upon him, equally, he understated its *later* effect, when he declared that Gibbon was the only historian of ecclesiastical affairs to command, despite his notorious infidelity, his respect and admiration.[171] The fullest account of Milner, by J. D. Walsh, follows the testimony of the *Apologia*, concluding that 'Newman himself, for all his debt to Milner, did not take him very seriously as a Church historian'.[172]

As he progressed in scholarship, Newman may indeed have come to hold a low opinion of Milner as a modern, *critical* historian. Nevertheless, the *History* shows an uncannily close resemblance, both in method and details, to *The Arians of the Fourth Century*. Milner's typically eighteenth-century view of a uniform human nature producing constantly republicated patterns of behaviour throughout the course of history provides the basis for an analogy between ancient and modern.[173] Milner's problem was how to appropriate history for his own, distinctively – and in the English context unusually – *Lutheran* doctrine of justification:[174] early Church history finds, for him, its significance, and its heroes, in those individuals who accepted Christ by faith. What Newman therefore found in Milner was an historiographer who was responding to the past, not by the attempted extinguishment of his personal perspective, but existentially, imaginatively, and polemically.

If Milner's explicit statements about the significance of heresy are taken at face value, then he could not be more different from Newman, who turned a history of Articles into a history of heresy.

Milner, on the other hand, wanted to minimise heresy in his account, in order to concentrate on showing how the saints in every age were justified by faith, so that it would be absurd to write the history of Christianity by reference to heresies: 'as absurd were it to suppose an history of the highwaymen that have infested this country to be an history of England'.[175] However, Milner's actual procedure in his *History* closely resembles that of Newman, especially in the treatment of heresy. Indeed, it will be argued that the former adopted a rhetorical strategy almost identical with that found in *The Arians of the Fourth Century*.

One of Milner's major themes is the danger of pagan philosophy importing into Christianity a destructive rationalism. His conviction about the infidel tendency of philosophy was acquired through personal experience: born of poor parents, but a prodigy of learning, he lost his early Evangelical faith by exposure to Locke and Samuel Clarke, later undergoing a prolonged conversion from which he emerged a convinced enemy of the 'prophane philosophy'[176] which had deprived him of his faith. This experience passed into his treatment especially of heresy, whose origin he explains in terms of intellectual pride and the infiltration of paganism into Christian theology. Justin Martyr, praised for his 'Evangelical' faith, is also censured for his openness to 'philosophy': 'he was the first sincere Christian who was seduced by human philosophy to adulterate the gospel, though in small degree'.[177] Milner's definition of philosophy is precise:

I mean all along that philosophy of the ancients, which was founded in pride, was chiefly speculative and metaphysical, and at bottom atheistical. No one objects to those moral maxims of the ancient philosophers, which were in many instances excellent, though defective in principle.[178]

Despite the 'moral' qualification, Milner's condemnation of philosophy goes further than Newman's, far enough to hand out severe criticism to the Alexandrians.[179]

Nevertheless, the target of both Newman's *Arians* and Milner's *History* is identical – that modern spirit of intellectual autonomy, which separates the cultivated and refined believer from revealed truth and sets him off on the road to infidelity: 'Pride and self-conceit frequently have a peculiar ascendancy over men who have acquired knowledge in private by their own industry.'[180] Like Newman, and, before him, Rose, Milner sees the abuse of reason as an attenuation of Christianity. Such rationalism is the origin of heresy; discussing Praxeas, Milner declares:

All attempts to subvert the faith of Scripture on this subject arise from the same error, namely, a desire to accommodate divine truths to our narrow reasoning faculties: let men learn to submit; and on no account strip the Almighty of His attributes of Incomprehensibility.[181]

Like Newman, Milner characterises Arius as a logician, noted for his 'pride of reasoning': 'Arius evidently split on the common rock of all heresies, a desire of explaining by our reason the modes of things which we are required to believe on Divine testimony alone.'[182] Like Newman, Milner explains the presence in Christian theology of the corrupting influence of dialectic by reference to the Eclectic philosophy of Ammonius Saccas.[183] Finally, like Newman, he articulates a parallel with modern infidelity, 'the turbulent, aspiring, political sons of Arius and Socinus in our own times'.[184]

Milner's rhetorical strategy, then, is so close to Newman's as to make it very probable that it served as a model for the analogical rhetoric of *Arians*, albeit unacknowledged and perhaps unconsciously adopted. J. D. Walsh's description of Milner's *History* – if 'Catholic' be substituted for 'evangelical' – is an exact description also of *Arians*:

The struggle of evangelical religion and rationalistic philosophy has been renewed again and again in new disguises . . . The moderns comically deluded themselves on the modernity of their views: it was not new philosophy they propagated but ancient heresy.[185]

Both Milner's and Newman's rhetoric – despite the difference of theology – derive from a similar political and social ideology. From 1828 onwards, Newman was defending 'Establishment' against liberalism and latitudinarianism. His conservatism persisted into the Tractarian period. Similarly, Milner was, notwithstanding his 'Evangelical' concept of justification, politically a Tory, opposed equally to Jacobitism and Dissent, writing against the ominous background of the French Revolution, proliferation of dissenting chapels, liberal politics and infidel philosophy. His *History* vigorously defends the authority of the *established* Church – episcopacy, infant baptism and ecclesiastical order.[186] Here, perhaps, are the seeds of an explanation for the rhetorical use of history found in both men: the threat to the present order of things, provoking a search for authority in the remote past.

Finally, the connection between *ethos* and orthodoxy exploited in so many different ways by Newman, is found in Milner. Although the latter, typically, stresses the act of faith by which the believer appropriates Christ's merits, he also upholds the *objectivity* of orthodox doctrine – the Trinity, the Divinity of Christ, the Atonement and the 'efficacious influences' of the Holy Spirit[187] against the objection that a good life is the only requirement for a Christian, by connecting true doctrine with right practice.[188]

Milner therefore finds himself committed to the schema: orthodoxy leads to virtue, heresy to vice. The Arians he depicts as dishonest, and violent persecutors, morally inferior to the pure, if irritable, Athanasius.[189] He warns of the dangers of worldly prelacy in Eusebius of Nicomedia,[190] and can point confidently to the coincidence of immorality and heresy in Paul of Samosata.[191] Although Milner from time to time acknowledges difficulties in the application of his schemes – notably Origen (holy but heterodox)[192] – his presentation of *ethos* remains on the comparatively straightforward level of whether or not a Father or heresiarch performed good works; the *History* lacks the complexity of Newman's characterisations.

CHAPTER THREE

Newman's Tractarian rhetoric, 1833–1837: the analogy continued

Newman continued the analogy between heresy and liberalism in his poetry from abroad, composed as the Church–State crisis deepened, and in his early writings of the Tractarian period. The issues provoking Keble's *Assize Sermon*, which caused in turn the celebrated meeting at Rose's Hadleigh rectory, and which stimulated the early *Tracts* had been exercising Newman in the preceding years. The issues of the crisis were epitomised in the threefold cry of (Roman Catholic) Emancipation, Repeal (of the Test Acts), and (Electoral) Reform. Connected was the proposed reduction in the number of Anglican sees in Ireland, in view of the overwhelmingly Roman Catholic allegiance of the population there, and the imminence of rebellion.[1] Newman regarded such parliamentary reform touching upon religion as an attack upon Christ's very Church, and had vigorously opposed the re-election of the pragmatic and tergiversating Tory, Robert Peel, to the University's seat. It was not so much the reforms in themselves that he opposed, as the motives he suspected behind them.[2]

In the final sentence of *The Arians of the Fourth Century*, Newman looked forward to a 'destined season', when 'our Athanasius and Basil will be given us',[3] to release the Church from its satanic oppression. It is tempting to conclude that he saw *himself* as such an Athanasius or Basil *redivivus*, as, during his Mediterranean travels, his conviction grew of destined 'work to do in England'.[4] In his poetry of this time, the controversies about Church–State relations in England are presented against the backcloth of the eternal struggle between divine truth and the powers of darkness:

> .... she, once pattern chief
> Of faith, my Country, now gross hearted grown,
> Waits but to burn the stem before her idol's throne.[5]

But now the Enemy is *within* the Church: in *Liberalism*, written at Palermo in June, 1833, he identifies this new satanic stratagem, the 'halving' of the truth, whereby the 'dread depths of grace' and zeal for sanctity are discarded by 'Statesmen or Sages', who are 'doubters at heart' of the awesome and mysterious claims of traditional Christianity,

> .... O new-compassed art
> Of the ancient Foe! – but what, if it extends
> O'er our own camp, and rules amid our friends.[6]

On the other hand, in *The Greek Fathers*, the Fathers of the Church, have come to life as 'our fathers and our guides'. The depiction of Basil glances at what Newman regarded as the political enthral-ment of the Church of England,

> . . . saintly Basil's purpose high
> To smite imperial heresy,
> And cleanse the Altar's stain.[7]

The choice of 'imperial' as a fitting epithet for 'heresy' is character-istic of Newman's attitude to England as a political power during this period: only ten days before he wrote this, he had described England as

> Tyre of the West, prosperously
> Wielding Trade's master keys.

but,

> . . . glorying in the name
> More than in Faith's pure flame![8]

England is, in succeeding stanzas, compared both with Babel and Sodom. His poems establish the tone of the earliest Tractarian phase: the exclamatory style and intense diction generate what was, no doubt, heartfelt emotion, but the poems are also *public* rhetoric, with a clearly envisaged audience. He was not just writing for his commonplace book, he was urgently sending his packets of poems to Rose for publication in the *British Magazine*. The deploy-ment of rhetoric, of which an important ingredient was the application of the ancient struggles between Fathers and either

heretics or imperial oppressors, to the English political ferment of
Repeal and Irish Sees is the originating context for his treatment
of heresy in the Tractarian period.

His earliest writings on his return to England continue the
trends found in his poetry. These were the *Letters on the Church of the
Fathers*, written in August 1833,[9] and published from October
onwards in the *British Magazine*. They took as their subject St
Ambrose and his times. Newman begins his narrative of this period
of Church history with an immediate reference to the 'changes
which the British Constitution has lately undergone',[10] and anticipates a 'material alteration' in Church–State relations. He looks
back with nostalgia to the 'former quiet and pleasant course of
King George III'.[11] Here, certainly, is social and religious conservatism. But there is also something new, as he urges his readers to
consider 'by what instruments the authority of Religion is to be
supported should the patronage and protection of the government
be withdrawn'.[12] He is already looking beyond defence of establishment, hinting at a distinction between Church and State. Indeed,
it is possible that he was exaggerating his conservatism in order to
win over the gentry and lower clergy to the more innovative and
popular idea of the supernatural foundation of the Church which
the narrative expounds:

Who at first sight does not dislike the thought of gentlemen and clergymen
depending for their maintenance and their reputation on their flocks? of
their strength as a visible power, lying not in their birth, the patronage of
the great and the endowment of the Church (as hitherto), but in the
homage of a multitude? I confess I have before now had a great
repugnance to the notion myself.[13]

It is in terms of a struggle in Antiquity between the Church of
Milan personified in St Ambrose and the Arian Empress, Justina,
that Newman proposes a parallel between his own time and the
past. The State demanded that Ambrose cede one church for Arian
use, but, 'His duty was plain: the churches were the property of
Christ; he was the representative of Christ and was therefore
bound not to cede what was committed to him in trust.'[14] A few
pages before, Newman had prepared the reader for the force of his
analogical presentation of the 'primitive church'; the story has
been chosen 'With a view of showing the power of the Church at
that time (not as if I would persuade any one to murmur at things

as they are, but merely to *prepare* Christians for what may be and to encourage them.'[15] Newman's position is complex; he opposes the 'spoliation of the Church', but has gone beyond defence of establishment to discover a principle other than national history – that is, the apostolicity of the Church of England, a principle which can be deployed as part of a radical and spontaneous appeal to the people: 'Ambrose rested his resistance on grounds the people understood at once and recognised as irrefragable . . . They rose in a body and thronged the palace gate.'[16]

Heresy, then, in the early *Letters on the Church of the Fathers* is deployed as an element in a broad strategy, which is not concerned with the theological examination of the nature of heresy, but with fashioning a narrative of the patristic age, in such a way that it forms a perspective or framework of values whereby the significance of contemporary issues may be discerned. It is the ability to perceive the polemical potential of early Church history, which lends the essays on Ambrose their mischievous vitality:

Now some reader will here interrupt the narrative, perhaps, with something of an indignant burst about connecting the cause of religion with mobs etc. To whom I would reply, that the multitude of men is always rude and intemperate, and needs restraint, – so, it is better they should be zealous about religion, as in this case, than flow and ebb again under the irrational influences of this world. A mob, indeed is always wayward and faithless; but it may be acted upon.[17]

Newman, in his final sentence, balances his radical appeal to the populace with a more soothing prospect: the suggestion, not necessarily ironic, that an orthodox mob will, in fearing the Judgment, be susceptible of social control.

The *Letters* on St Ambrose are part of a strategy which finds expression also in other writings of the early years of Tractarianism. Dating from September 1833, though not published until 1836, was *Home Thoughts from Abroad*, which introduces some additional motifs, organising them around the theme of heresy:

When Arianism triumphed in the sees of the Eastern Church, the Associated Brethren of Egypt and Syria were the witnesses prophesying in sackcloth against it. So may it be again. When the day of trial comes, we shall be driven from the established system of the Church, from livings and professorships, fellowships and stalls; we shall (so be it) muster amid dishonour, poverty and destitution, for higher purposes; we shall bear to be severed from possessions and connexions of this world.[18]

Here, Newman uses his anti-bourgeois strain: comfort, ease and compromise are associated with the 'world' to point a contrast with the asceticism of orthodoxy, in order to exalt rationalisation of sees into a matter of martyrdom, of a kind.

The early *Tracts for the Times* confirm the shape of Newman's strategy. The fifteenth *Tract*, written in late 1833, provocatively employs the idea of the popular appeal against the very figureheads of the apostolic structure of the Church of England, the bishops. Again, Newman sets up an analogy in which the contrast between heresy and orthodoxy in Antiquity is part of his strategy:

it has always been agreeable to the principles of the Church, that, if a Bishop taught and upheld what was contrary to the orthodox faith, the clergy and people were not bound to submit, but were obliged to maintain the true religion; and if excommunicated by such bishops, they were never accounted to be cut off from the Church.[19]

Luther even gets a good mention here, for his stance against the Roman Catholic bishops, in upholding 'in main the true doctrine'.[20]

On the other hand, Newman's stance was not *always* so provocative. He was capable of advocating, in the face of the groundswell of democratic ideas, a strengthening of establishment and *status quo*, for the straightforward reason that it will be an instrument for keeping the lower orders under control, a more peaceable method of shoring up the threatened social fabric than the militiaman's rifle or the cavalryman's sabre: the Church is:

confessedly a powerful instrument of state, a minister of untold good to our population, and one of the chief bulwarks of the Monarchy. No institution can be imagined so full of benefit to the poorer classes, nor of such prevailing influence on the side of loyalty and civil order. It is a standing army, insuring the obedience of the people to the Laws by weapons of persuasion.[21]

Newman wrote these words in March 1835, in his pamphlet on the *Restoration of Suffragan Bishops*. At the same time, he disclaims recommending 'any perversion of the Church to mere political purposes',[22] since the Church's office is 'doubtless far above any secular objects'. Nevertheless,

He who has 'ordained the powers that be' as well as the Church, has also ordained that the Church, when in most honourable place and most healthy action, should be able to minister such momentous service to the

Civil Magistrate, as constitutes an immediate recompense of his piety towards her.[23]

It is tempting to conclude that Newman, here straining to reconcile an apostolic concept of the Church with one verging upon the Erastian, is, for the purposes of the public debate, attempting to have his cake and eat it. However, there is a strand in the same pamphlet which suggests that the underlying theme is the process of secularisation of English society and its resistance, 'that spirit of unbelief and systematized opposition to the vital and ancient doctrines of religion, which is the perplexity of orthodox church-men now'.[24] The antithesis of 'orthodox' here is not with 'heretical' in the sense of a precisely definable malformation of Christian discourse; rather, to 'orthodox' is opposed a *Geist*, elusive but all-permeating, of 'unbelief', and 'opposition' to the givenness of revelation. Moreover, Newman presents social disorder as a proph-etic sign of the disintegration of Christian culture – or, to use Keble's phrase, 'national Apostasy'.

The backcloth against which Newman presents the political crisis in which the Church was involved may be described as eschatological rather than political. His apocalypticism, residual from the period when as a young man he scrutinised Newton on prophecy for signs of the End,[25] identified the spread of unbelief with the dissemination of democratic radicalism arising from the French Revolution:[26] the revolutionary spirit, subversive of the powers that be, and usually atheistic, was the great apostasy heralding the approaching Judgment. This apocalypticism per-sisted in the Tractarian period and emerged in *The Patristical Idea of Antichrist*. Here the idea of heresy plays an important role. Newman presents challenges to previously established authority as signs of the times:

we actually have before our eyes, as our fathers also in the generation before us, a fierce and lawless principle everywhere at work – a spirit of rebellion against God and man, which the powers of government in each country can barely keep under with their greatest efforts. Whether this which we witness *be* that spirit of Antichrist, which one day will be let loose, this ambitious spirit, the parent of all heresy, schism, sedition, revolution and war – whether this be so or not, at least we know from prophecy that the present framework of society and government, as far as it is the representative of Roman powers, is that which withholdeth, and Antichrist is that which will rise when this restraint falls.[27]

While Newman protects himself with a becoming caution – 'whether this be so or not' – he nevertheless holds up to the imagination of his contemporaries an apocalyptic vision of history in which heresy is collated with other evils. Moreover, his deployment of the Pauline idea of the power of the Roman Empire exercising a restraining force whereby the Antichrist is held back from arriving, provides a theological legitimation for the beleaguered Toryism to which he appeals. This enables a plea for the power and privileges of the Church of England, which is integral to the powers that be:

the special and singular enemy of Christ, or Antichrist, will appear . . . this will be when revolutions prevail, and the present framework of society breaks to pieces; and . . . at present the spirit which he will embody and represent is kept under by 'the powers that be', but that on their dissolution, he will rise out of their bosom and knit them together again in his own evil way, under his own rule, to the exclusion of the Church.[28]

The movement to which Newman here calls alarm has its roots in the French Revolution, which is the fulfilment of the prophecy that the time of Antichrist will be heralded by open infidelity. In the ritualised apostasy of Jacobinism, in its dogmatic atheism and worship of Liberty, 'which scared the world some forty or fifty years ago', Newman recognised the spirit of Antichrist.[29]

He relates the role of heresy to the other ills in this *nexus* of evils preceding the End. If apostasy is a sign presaging the reign of Antichrist, then apostasy is presaged by heresy. He gives two examples of this: first, Arianism preceded Julian the Apostate's attempt to re-introduce paganism to the Empire; secondly, and more dangerously, the fifth-century heretics preceded the rise of Islam.

Nestorianism and Eutychianism, apparently opposed to each other, yet acting towards a common end in one way or another denied the truth of Christ's gracious incarnation and tended to destroy the faith of Christians not less certainly, though more insidiously, than the heresy of Arius . . . Out of this heresy, or at least by means of it, the impostor Mohammed sprang, and formed his creed. Here is another special Shadow of Antichrist.[30]

Newman's prophetic perception of the past, in which it is read as a series of predictive signs, is not necessarily in conflict with an historical approach: he is, after all, arguing that as a matter of history heresy preceded apostasy by causal connection. However, the framework in which the kinship between heresy and infidelity, and the inevitable slide from one to the other, is presented is an echatological one, in which Newman's almost hysterical dramatisation of the contemporary controversy over Church and State reaches its highest pitch.

Newman's apocalyptic presentation of Arianism, Nestorianism and Eutychianism is immediately followed by a contemporary application: 'Is there no reason to fear that some such Apostasy is gradually preparing, gathering, hastening on this very day?'[31] As his analysis of the *forms* of apostasy proceeds, it becomes clearer that he means by it a secularisation of the social patterns of English life by means of a reforming political programme, which conceals its true nature under the guise of the reasonable and the humane. Newman attacks the assumptions upon which the movement to remove the established Church from 'power and place'[32] were based: that religion has nothing to do with the State, but only with a human individual's conscience; that social norms may be constructed solely on the criterion of 'utility', so that expediency rather than Truth becomes the rule; that in matters of controversy, the majority will should prevail; that the Bible has a multiplicity of meanings making a dogmatic stance unreasonable; that religion is a matter of subjective, inner experience, rather than objective rites and doctrinal formulations. The consequences of such assumptions are the proposal that oaths and other religious practices be removed from public transactions, and that religion be removed ultimately altogether from education, the first stage of which will be the amalgamation of all religious forms into one, and the second the evaluation of religion purely in terms of its moral productivity.[33] Newman, then, shows a deep-seated antipathy towards all forms of utilitarianism.

It should by now have emerged that, if Newman may, in some sense, himself be described as 'radical', or even on occasions 'subversive', this was not in a democratic direction. He rather appears to have imbibed the Romantic reactionary spirit of his beloved friend, Hurrell Froude. This mentality survived the early years of Tractarianism, with the result that 'heresy', along with its guilty associates – dissenters outside the Church and liberals within, as well as unbelievers of varying degrees of frankness – became embedded in a stream of anti-democratic vituperation extending throughout Newman's period of activity as a 'Tractarian'.

Least equivocal of all was his *British Critic* article for October 1837, *The Fall of De La Mennais*, in which he presents himself as the patriotic Tory Churchman *par excellence*, staunchly opposed to the encroachments of Roman Catholicism on one side, and of reforming Whiggery on the other,

two parties at present wish our downfall; our ill-starred foreign brethren, in order to level us to themselves, and our own masters, to rival foreign spoliations. Whigs and Papists, the high and the low, combine, the one from ambition, the other from envy.[34]

Bitter is Newman's sarcasm for those who comfort the protesters against State encroachment upon Church by declaring that at least their Patriarch is not, as with the Greeks, appointed by the Turk: 'under the feeling that we had no right to complain as yet, when our rulers were appointed, not by pagans, but only by schismatics, latitudinarians, profligates, socinians and infidels'.[35] Newman introduces with the deftly and spitefully placed advert, 'only', a revealing list of shibboleths: the heresy towards which he has already presented all contemporary liberal errors as tending, the Socinian denial of a revealed Trinity, is collocated with dissenting bodies (it is difficult to see what else 'schismatics' could mean), ecclesiastical liberals (for which 'latitudinarians' was his usual term), the morally unsound ('profligates') and the frankly unbelieving ('infidels'). While De La Mennais associates the cry for democratic liberties as 'the voice of Truth, of our best nature', Newman identifies it with sin. The rebellion of sin, from the pride of pre-lapsarian Eve to the final onslaught of Antichrist, is identical with the spirit of *political* rebellion against the *status quo*.[36] 'Hence, he is able to draw close to the democratical party of the day, in that very point in which they most resemble Antichrist.'[37] De La Mennais' philosophy has, however, an application for Newman closer to home: 'It is not wonderful that, with these principles, he cordially approves of what the Roman Church and Mr O'Connell are doing in Ireland, sympathizes in their struggle, and holds them up for the edification of the Pope and the Papal world.'[38] Newman's contemptuous description of the people in Ireland, and his detestation of the Irish nationalist leader, Daniel O'Connell, demonstrate the profound Toryism underlying his theology: Roman Catholicism, Antichrist, heresy, and the spirit of democracy are all of a piece.

CHAPTER FOUR

Conclusions: rhetoric and politics

In 1864, Newman wrote of Hugh James Rose,

The Reform agitation followed, and the Whig government came into power; and he anticipated in their distribution of Church patronage the authoritative introduction of liberal opinions into the country. He feared that by the Whig party a door would be opened in England to the most grievous of heresies, which never could be closed again.[1]

Although Newman distances himself somewhat from the 'Movement' by presenting what was Rose's view in the 1830s, rather than what was, by 1864, necessarily his own, the bringing together of the political ('Whig', 'reform', 'Church patronage'), and the doctrinal ('grievous heresies') clearly describes that dimension of Newman's *own* public writings which we have seen between 1833 and 1837. Just as he identifies heresy with Whiggery, and liberalism, so orthodoxy is identified with the old order, on the point of collapse: 'Such was the commencement of the assault of Liberalism upon the old orthodoxy of Oxford and England.'[2]

What might appear in Newman as individual, even eccentric, insights, or localised political options, may thus be regarded as the outcome of vaster forces. It is possible, for example, to identify him as a reactionary, resisting the inevitable developments of the Industrial Revolution – democracy, capitalism and the decline of religion. Against such a 'Whig'[3] interpretation of history, however, J.C.D. Clarke's recent 'revisionist'[4] account of the period 1688–1832 argues that England remained an *ancien régime* until the sudden, unexpected collapse in the early 1830s, and that, until then, England was a hegemony of nobility, gentry and clergy, undergirded by a theological ideology giving divine legitimation to the *régime*: 'it was Anglican, it was aristocratic and it was monarchical'.[5] The first characteristic was, in the 1960s and 1970s marginalised by social historiographers who themselves had no interest in theology.

Clarke's account of theology-as-ideology among England's cultural élite between the Revolution and the Reform Bill does much to dispel the idea of Newman as unusually bigoted in his hostility to Dissent and in his insistence upon tests. Rather, his responses may be seen as arising naturally out of the contemporary climate of opinion. Trinitarian orthodoxy, apostolic succession, sacraments and Biblical providential language provided a 'story' and controlling ideology, effective in inculcating submission to the powers that be.[6] Clarke's analysis explains what in Newman, Rose and Keble appear to the modern reader as protests verging on the hysterical about the suppression of Irish Sees or the relaxation of tests: their understanding of these issues would have been bound up with allegiance to the *ancien régime*, as heterodox Dissent was attempting to dismantle it, with the connivance of liberalism within the Church of England. On this thesis, Newman may be seen to be in continuity with an orthodox Anglican ideology, which had functioned broadly in both Hanoverian and Jacobite political thought, and which, moreover, was not inconsistent with his early Evangelicalism.[7] To this social order the great challenge was heresy.

This analysis of the political context of English theology is helpful in explaining why so often the young Newman's discussion of heresy cannot be separated from defence of the Established Church. He had himself gained access only, as it were, by adoption, in his election to the Oriel Fellowship, to the benefits of that world of deference, patronage and privilege to which the term *ancien régime* refers. The ferocity with which he fought a rearguard action against all the reforming measures of the time – Irish Sees, Catholic Emancipation, marriage laws, access of Dissenters to university education – is perhaps a reflection of his adopted status: he would defend to the last the establishment which made him.

On the other hand, it would be untrue to suggest that Newman's theology was deterministically controlled by the dynamics of the *ancien régime*, in the way that Clarke sometimes appears to suggest was the case with his eighteenth-century Anglican predecessors.[8] In fact, Newman's theology began at the very point when, according to Clarke, the power of the *ancien régime* was irrevocably broken – the year 1832.[9] Newman's early *Tracts* frankly recognise that the old system of 'deference' is a thing of the past: if, he asks the clergy,

State support is withdrawn from the Church, '*on what* will you rest the claim of respect and attention which you make upon your flocks?'[10] We have already seen how, in his presentation of Ambrose's struggle against Arianism, Newman presents *apostolic* Christianity as having the power to appeal over the heads of the ruling authorities to the supernatural foundation of the Church. It is not so much that he could not conceptually separate the *ancien régime* from the supernaturally founded Church. Rather, he defended Establishment because, and for as long as, he saw its structures as mediating Christianity to the English people, in a way which was – at any rate until the time of 'George the Good' – unproblematic.

When, however, in the 1830s, the State seemed to be withdrawing its support, he initiated a creative theological movement which re-invented a concept of Catholicity. Newman's treatment of Arianism reflects the transition from the pre-1832 situation, in which it was not necessarily *party*-political to defend Establishment, to the new situation, after Reform, in which an ecclesiastical *party* had to be created in the Church of England.[11] It is thus that the ambivalence of his language may be understood, as it alternates between reactionary polemic on behalf of the *ancien régime* and an ecclesiology beginning to detach itself from the establishment and to point to the supernatural origin and nature of the Church.

Newman's public response to attacks upon *ancien régime* Christianity is not a systematically argued presentation of the history of dogma attempting to justify theologically a practical choice over an issue of Church polity. It is rhetoric. His image of an apostolic Church turned upon by a persecuting State, as the re-enactment of fourth- and fifth-century struggles against heresy, proposes a startling analogy between antiquity and the nineteenth century. Thus he provokes in his contemporary reader a sense of present distance from, and alienation from, his Christian past, forcing him to come to self-consciousness about the new position of the established religion as a result of the crisis of the 1830s. This is, as it were, Newman's primary task – to raise the alarm and to convince his public that any kind of alienation *has* taken place as a result of the dismantling of the *ancien régime*. Only then will it be possible to move on to a second stage, in which the no longer self-evident relation of Church and State may be re-defined. Newman can re-examine the nature of the Church in relation to the ancient past and *reconstruct*, in a contested context, an ecclesiology and a theology, in a sophisticated bid for his countrymen's assent.

It is precisely this purpose which he privately declared at the preparatory stage of his *Letters on the Church of the Fathers*: 'I am poking into the Fathers with a hope of rummaging forth passages of history which may prepare the *imaginations* of men for a changed state of things, and also be precedents for our conduct in difficult circumstances.'[12] Elsewhere, writing again privately to one of his companions-in-arms in the struggle against liberalism, he declares the political dimension of his work on St Ambrose, 'I am hunting into the lives of the Fathers, to see if I can pick up anything against the Ministry.'[13] His language here – he is 'rummaging', 'poking', 'hunting' and 'picking up' – discloses the rhetorical purpose of his investigations into Church history. The rhetorical concern is not, however, only polemical ('against the Ministry'), or born of the desire to tell a rattling good yarn – it also arises 'to *prepare*' for a new situation.

PART TWO

Attack: Sabellianism and Apollinarianism – Liberalism Unmasked

A horde of heresies fleeing with mitres awry.
(James Joyce, Ulysses)

CHAPTER FIVE

New directions: the mid-1830s

Sabellianism was a Trinitarian heresy, flourishing in the West in the late second and early third centuries: Apollinarianism an Eastern Christological heresy of the fourth. Yet Newman discerned such close kinship between them that he found it necessary, and even inevitable, to pass from one to the other in his detailed patristic research of the mid-1830s. Moreover, he connected *both* with Arianism.

Apollinarianism, with its high Christology stressing the identity of Christ as Divine Logos, has been suggested as an appropriate designation for Newman's *own* view of the person of Christ. Yet he saw its ultimate source as a form of the very infidelity out of which Arianism had sprung. This position he maintained despite the abundant witness to Apollinaris' suffering and struggles against Arianism at the side of the great Athanasius. Sabellianism, too, may be described as the opposite tendency to Arianism in the *trinitarian* field of debate: a concern to assert the unity of God against those very distinctions within the Trinity from which Arian subordination of the Logos emerged – certainly, Arians maintained the various forms of their theology out of a professed horror of Sabellianism.[1] But, again, Newman discerns a link, and even goes so far as to suggest that Sabellianism is a *form* of Arianism! Moreover, by exploiting the fact that 'Arian' could still mean 'Unitarian' or 'Socinian', he could point to the trinitarian heresy lurking beneath the surface of liberal theology. Here, Newman massively expands what had only been hints and conjectures in *Arians*.[2] Newman strives to articulate the essence of all heresy, and to tease it out of its manifold historical forms. The method he employs bears a close resemblance to that which he eventually applied to orthodox doctrine in the 1840s, that is, the idea of *development*. Most striking is the presentation of heresy as manifesting its true nature ever more clearly as its *history* progresses, so that its essence stands truly revealed in its later developments and consequences, in a way unintended by its originator. Heresies may also, Newman argues, legitimately be drawn out *logically* to their consequences by a critique bringing to light their hidden essence.

As the Fathers found surprising correspondences between new doctrines and old impieties, so Newman himself, in his examination of trends in the theology of his time. The virtual *identification* of Socinianism with what he usually calls 'infidelity' – he means disbelief in the revealed doctrines of Christianity, something not very far from atheism[3] – had taken place at the time he was writing *Arians*. Thus, Sabellianism's development towards the Socinianism it concealed, he was saying something, in his own terms, very sinister. The influence of Athanasius – one of the primary sources for the Arian controversy – may be crucial here, for he regularly describes Arianism as a form of atheism (*asebeia* – impiety or infidelity),[4] because, in denying the Son's consubstantiality with the Father, Arians are denying the Father too, just as Caiaphas and the Jews of old, in rejecting Christ, rejected God also; Arianism is apostasy (*apostasia*), the infidelity of a revived, but debased Judaism[5] – this is the very stuff of Athanasius' vituperative style. In Newman we can see it being transformed into an analytical tool.

Newman's heresiology of the mid-1830s marks a shift in perspective. His rhetoric centred upon Arianism, delineated in Part 1, was overwhelmingly interested in social and political developments and their relation to the ethical and religious. However, Newman's use of Sabellianism and Apollinarianism inaugurates a new interest in the analysis of the 'tendencies' underlying heretical theology: he is interested in the dangerous closeness between explaining divine truths in human terms and a virtual humanism. There is, it would seem, an interaction between Newman's patristic research and his public discourse. That his Apollinarian and Sabellian heresiology is yet another *rhetorical* strategy emerges clearly when the complex background, centred upon events in Oxford between 1834 and 1836, is considered.

The complicated chronology of Newman's encounter with Sabellianism and Apollinarianism stretches the narrator's art to its limits. He lived a hectic, fraught and intense existence, as he strove, with only partial success, to reconcile the demands upon his time of scholarly research with public controversy. The story has all the untidiness and vividness of a life lived at full stretch. An attempt will be made to tell this story according to the broad sequence of his unfolding biography. But the problems of simultaneity will not be artifically smoothed out, and constant cross-referencing will be necessary adequately to convey the complexity of the background. On the other hand, in order to make possible a coherent theological exposition of Newman's treatment of heresy, this account has been divided into sections or stages, each concentrating upon a particular facet of Newman's heresiology or application of it. Conclusions about the evolution of specific aspects of Newman's thought, in relation to the background and influences upon him, have sometimes been cautious, because it is difficult to decide if he was *applying* to the contemporary polemical scene principles discovered during scholarly research, or, conversely, if the immediate background first affected his method of research.

CHAPTER SIX

Patristic research: the edition of Dionysius of Alexandria

In March, 1834,[1] Newman began his project of an edition of the fragments of Dionysius, the third-century Bishop of Alexandria, and pupil of Origen, who had a notable correspondence with his namesake the Bishop of Rome on the subject of the Trinity,[2] Dionysius had been combating, within his own diocese, a form of Sabellianism.[3] Dionysius' defence of real distinctions within the Godhead was reported, by his enemies, to Rome, in such a way as to give the impression that he regarded the persons of the Trinity as three separated substances and that the Son did not exist before He was begotten – in other words, he seemed to anticipate a form of Arianism.[4] Such an impression would have been exaggerated when Greek terms were translated into Latin.[5] Dionysius of Rome therefore courteously protested against what appeared to be heresy in the teaching of his brother bishop.[6] In a celebrated passage from his *Refutation and Apology*, preserved in St Athanasius' defence of him against the imputation of Arianism, Dionysius clarified to the Roman Pope's satisfaction, his view of the Trinitarian distinctions: just as the sun and its radiance are one yet distinct, and co-existent with each other, so the Son and Spirit are distinct from the eternally existent Father, yet ever one with Him.[7]

Newman's interest in Dionysius arose out of dissatisfaction with the quality of research in *Arians*. As an old man, he declared, dramatically, that it was not even a 'little' book, that it was rushed and that it 'hit no mark at all'.[8] This appears an accurate reminiscence of what was more mutedly expressed in the 1830s: in August 1834, he wrote to John William Bowden explaining his decision to undertake the precise discipline demanded by patristic textual editing:

If you say, why edit books at all? I answer I have great fears of being superficial – nothing is a greater temptation in writing such a book as the

Arians, [than] to take facts and Fathers at *second hand* – and I wish to withdraw myself as much as possible from it.[9]

Newman is responding here to an enquiry about his *Arians*, and has declared that 'an opportunity of correcting my Arians is of course very uncertain and of distant date'.[10]

There is another reason for Newman's broadening of his patristic research. He had originally considered *Arians* as only a first volume – treating of the history of the Doctrine of the Trinity[11] – to be followed by a *second* volume on the Incarnation, dealing with the heresies 'falling under' this latter category.[12] Moreover, when Rose remarked of *Arians* that he had got, instead of a history of *Councils* a history of *heresy*, Newman declared that 'The succeeding volumes, if they are to form one with the volumes we have seen, will be a History of Heresies.'[13] The puzzles and complexities of the way Dionysius acted as a bridge passage between the historically unrelated heresies of Sabellianism and Apollinarianism will be considered in due course. One thing, however, is clear: *Arians* was the somewhat unsatisfactory and unpredictable outcome of an overarching concern with the history of doctrine perceived as the history of heresy.

It is therefore not surprising that Newman grasped the chance to edit, for the Oxford University Press, the fragments of Dionysius, Bishop of Alexandria.[14] He began in March 1834, and worked hard at it until the end of August 1835.[15] He took the work very seriously, collating manuscripts in the Bodleian[16] and, in July 1834, asking Benjamin Harrison, who was in Paris, to consult for him some manuscripts unobtainable in England.[17] In the same month, he told his sister, Harriet, that he was 'getting on fairly'.[18] By August, he felt that he had 'nearly broken the neck of it',[19] but was still working hard at it by November.[20] It dragged on. By the Long Vacation of the following year, he exclaimed, 'Dionysius whom oh that I could despatch this vacation.'[21] Still in August, he is 'hard at Dionysius',[22] but it only 'gets on slowly'.[23] Then at the end of the month, he declares 'Dionysius is nearly done',[24] but has to qualify his optimism, 'i.e. as far as it can till I read more'.[25] Beginning in hope and proceeding in enthusiasm, the final draft eluded him, and the project fizzled out.

Nevertheless, he kept his notes[26] – they are some of his neatest – with a Latin commentary upon the textual variants running alongside the Greek text. These provide precise information about his acquaintance with Dionysius' attack on Sabellianism. Newman edited, from Eusebius' *Ecclesiastical History*, the Second Letter on Baptism to Xystus,[27] Bishop of Rome, in which Dionysius touched on Sabellianism.[28] In a note here, Newman alludes to 'contra Sabellium scriptas' (writings against Sabellius).[29] He worked on the existing fragments of Dionysius' *Refutation and Defence*, especially that occurring in Athanasius. However, completely lacking is any recorded definition of Sabellianism, or any disquisition upon the nature and origins of that heresy. Similarly, there are no reflections upon the general nature of heresy. These notes are, perhaps, Newman's only attempt at pure scholarship. They bore fruit, as we shall see, elsewhere.

Carefully folded and bound with a pink ribbon, the sheets reside in the Oratory Archive. On the first paper of the pile appears a retrospective comment, written by a very old man, perhaps wistfully leafing through the papers of his youth, 'This inchoation of (in 1834) of [*sic*] an edition of S. Dionysius Alex, came to nothing. July 83', and then, in frail pencil, 'It was put an end to by the commencement of the Movement.'[30] This is not an entirely accurate remark – the 'Movement' was under way even before he had started the edition – but it nevertheless points to the reason for its incompletion: the distraction of public controversy was at its height, and Newman stood poised to lay bare the infidelity concealed by liberalism.

CHAPTER SEVEN

The Hampden Controversy

Newman's preoccupation with Renn Dickson Hampden began on 20 August 1834, with the publication of the latter's *Observations on Religious Dissent*, and continued until February 1836, cutting across his patristic research, and forming the background for his major work during this period, *Tract 73, On the Introduction of Rationalist Principles into Revealed Religion* (September, 1835).

The controversy may be seen as perhaps Newman's last really serious defence of the *ancien régime* – the preservation by religious tests of Oxford University as the exclusive preserve of the Church of England. Thus, he lamented to Hugh James Rose, upon the publication of Hampden's *Observations*, that it had destroyed Oxford's 'glory', by breaking down the previously unanimous position of the University that subscription to the *39 Articles* should not be waived to allow Dissenters to matriculate.[1] In the defence of 'tests', then, Newman's stance in this controversy is in continuity with the rhetoric of *Arians*. However, his theological responses to Hampden have a complex history, notable for their indirectness, while the pamphlet he eventually wrote specifically concerned with Hampden, the *Elucidations*, is one of his slightest works. The ramifications of the Hampden controversy extend to all Newman's activities from late 1834 to early 1836. Like an atmosphere, Hampdenism pervaded and conditioned his patristic research and his public rhetoric.

The course of the controversy was protracted and bitter.[2] It centred at first upon Hampden's *Observations* and the issue of admission to Dissenters. Newman saw the threat to Anglican hegemony at Oxford as a threat to Christianity itself and, in late November 1834, wrote to Hampden telling him that it tended 'altogether to make a shipwreck of Christian faith'.[3] It became a peculiarly claustrophobic feud: they were, after all, Fellows of the same Common Room. Hampden's feelings flared to fury on the occasion of a little pamphlet war about him, involving Newman's protégé, Henry Wilberforce. In March, 1835, Newman had suggested that Wilberforce write a pamphlet on 'Socinianism at Oxford' as a counterblast to one by Edward Hawkins, who had come out on Hampden's side over subscription.[4] The pamphlet eventually emerged as *Foundations of the Christian Faith Assailed* which, Wilberforce told Newman, was 'really yours'.[5] This pamphlet announced an important theme for the whole controversy – and for the critique of liberalism which eventually sprang from it: that liberal positions adopted within Christianity conceal Socinianism.

Hampden, enraged at what he regarded as a personal attack – he found it difficult to distinguish between exegesis of his tenets and *odium theologicum*[6] – demanded of Wilberforce that he acknowledge what was rumoured, that he had written it, and, moreover, publicly reveal the name of his suspected accomplice.[7] That Newman should have brought the pamphlet into the Oriel Common Room aggravated Hampden's grievance.[8] By June 1835, Hampden was addressing another angry reproach, this time directly to Newman, about his anonymous editing and compilation of a *Collection of Pamphlets*[9] against him; he expresses 'disgust' at Newman's behaviour, 'for no other feeling I am sure, is so due to the conduct of a person who can act with the dissimulation, and falsehood and dark malignity, of which you have been guilty'.[10] One sentence in this letter was even interpreted (by Froude) as meaning that Hampden would have challenged Newman to a duel.[11] The picture of the two men exchanging pistol shots on Christ Church Meadow is a bizarre one indeed. The humour of the situation was not lost on Newman – he was privately amused.[12] But his icy third-person reply to Hampden's rage was not conciliatory.[13]

Nine months later, in February 1836, the controversy moved into a second stage, when Hampden was proposed as Regius Professor. There was a Tractarian outcry.[14] But by then a host of important events had intervened, conditioning Newman's perspective. It will therefore be necessary briefly to return to Hampden at a later stage in the narrative.[15]

In the meantime, Newman had been scrutinising Hampden's works. We may assume that he had read *Observations on Religious*

Dissent by late November 1834.[16] Hampden's pamphlet was based upon his *Bampton Lectures* of 1832, published in 1833 as *The Scholastic Philosophy Considered in Its Relation to Christian Theology*.[17] These made no impression on Newman when they were delivered, for he neither attended nor read them at the time. It was not until 31 March 1835, that he 'looked into Hampden's *Bampton Lectures* for the first time' – that is, only after the controversy about the admission of Dissenters was well under way.[18] He was, no doubt, looking for signs of Socinianism and collecting examples. During this period he was amassing the evidence of the virtual Socinianism of his opponent's theology, evidence which eventually appeared in *Elucidations*, his chrestomathy of Hampdenism, written at high speed in early 1836, but drawing upon this earlier reading.[19]

Beneath the university politics provoking the *animus* of the controversy was a theological issue. For Newman and his Tractarian allies, the whole issue of subscription was theological, because the position taken over articles implied a view about their status and authority. Moreover, lying behind the issue of the *39 Articles*, there was the more general issue of the articles of faith of the ancient creeds, the Nicene and the 'Athanasian'. Where did Dissenters stand over these – and what about the Unitarians? Newman's point about Socinianism reveals the premiss of all his arguments: that a dissolution of precise dogmatic tests would initiate a slide into denial of the Trinity.

Hampden's position, too, was theological. *Observations* was not just an ecclesiastico-political pamphlet: his practical conclusion, that Dissenters should not be made to subscribe, was supported by a *theology* of the nature of revelation and its relation to articles. This theology profoundly influenced Newman by reaction: his own theology of revelation in the mid-1830s cannot be understood without reference to it, nor can his critique of liberalism as 'Sabellian'.

What, then, was Hampden's theology? He regarded revelation as a collection of facts *only*, contained in the Bible. These facts are a narration of events providentially disposed by God to affect men morally. On the other hand, ecclesiastical *definitions* of doctrine are not themselves revealed. It therefore follows that creeds and articles, being essentially *human* formulations, are open to adjustment: Dissenters need therefore only to subscribe to the Bible as a collection of facts to be upholding what has been revealed.

Pamphlet though it is, the *Observations* is a precisely worded and closely argued document. It contains a clear statement of his characteristic line:

the whole revelation contained in ... [the Scriptures] so far as it is revelation, consists of matter of fact ... there are no propositions concerning God in Scripture, detached from some event of Divine providence to which they refer and on which they are founded.[20]

Conclusions drawn from Scripture are *not* revealed.[21] However, Hampden qualifies his position here carefully. He does not mean that we must restrict ourselves only to scriptural phraseology, and he *would* include as revealed conclusions by Christ or His apostles about the Old Testament.[22] Hampden's exclusion only applies to 'intellectual', or speculative, or theological truth.[23] Yet, despite his rider, he appears to be excluding from the status of revealed both the Church of England articles and – more important – the dogmatic, as opposed to the narrative element in the creeds.

Moral conclusions, on the other hand, *are* allowed because incitement to duty is the very purpose of revelation, 'Every intimation of the Holy Spirit conveyed by the word of God is, in its strict and proper application, an appeal to the heart of man; and each appeal is an argument and incitement to duty.'[24] Man can make moral inferences from Scripture because there is an analogy between his natural moral knowledge, and the enlarged and elevated form of revealed morality.[25] The revealed facts are, then, intended by God as stimulations of innate moral instincts, rather than disclosures about the divine nature. This shift of emphasis, from the dogmatic to the ethical, attenuates what Newman would have called the mystery. Scripture has, indeed, become an 'open book' – open to what human beings already know about themselves as 'men in the world' – a phrase likely to provoke instant hostility in Newman.

Hampden's anthropocentrism emerges even more clearly in the discussion of revelation in the *Bampton Lectures*, upon which his position in *Observations* is based: 'Scripture-arguments are arguments of inducement addressed to the whole nature of man – not merely to intellectual man, but to thinking and feeling man living among his fellow men; – and to be appreciated therefore in their *effect* on our *whole* nature.'[26] There is no element in revelation transcending the human: revelation is a human *mode* of divine manifestation, 'If now we regard the Scriptures in the way of the Schoolmen, as having God for their proper subject, instead of reading them as a divine history of man, we naturally neglect the analogy of times and circumstances.'[27]

Hampden does, however, have something positive to say about speculative doctrine, which in his view separates him from latitudinarians.[28] There *is* an issue of truth in the case of such articles, but opposing views need to be argued out by persuasion, in an atmosphere of mutual respect and tolerance – that is, without a bar being compulsorily imposed upon Dissenters applying to study at seats of learning.[29] This is a long-term process. Meanwhile dogma has a twofold function within each Christian denomination:[30] 'as guarding the depository of divine truth and as moderating between conflicting opinions'.[31] First, then, dogma acts as a hedge around the revealed facts of Scripture.[32] Secondly, it has a social function, in curbing the natural human impulse to form theological opinions, which would logically result in as many theologies as there were people, by imposing terms of communion.[33] Both functions involve a relativity in relation to dogma: dogmatic formulae had an historical evolution and a sociological context. Although the truths dogmas guard are eternal, the dogmas, being relative to culture, may in the future be altered, without destroying their 'guarding' and 'moderating' function:

our doctrinal system as it now stands expressed, cannot be more than a declaration of terms of communion on the part of the Church, subject to revision and alteration, as expediency may suggest – expediency I mean, in regard to the fundamental interests of *Christian truth*; since the very existence of separate communions professing certain theological opinions is relative to this.[34]

But if dogma is relative to the eternal truths of revelation, and if these eternal truths are no more than facts producing a moral impression, then it is difficult to avoid the conclusion that the doctrines of the ancient Church about the Trinity and the Incarnation are relative only to human culture and therefore, in principle, adjustable. Newman certainly interpreted Hampden's drift to be

that the articles of the Nicene and Athanasian Creeds are merely human opinions, scholastic, allowing of change, unwarrantable when imposed, and, in fact, the produce of a mistaken philosophy; and that the Apostles' Creed is defensible only when considered as a record of historical facts.[35]

Hampden's contribution to an issue of university politics, then, involved a challenge to credal and patristic orthodoxy. It also challenged, quite specifically, Newman's sense of the importance of heresy, and its history, as applicable to the early nineteenth-century English scene. Just as Newman, quite radically, had re-asserted patristic heresiology, so Hampden proposed an equally radical re-interpretation of traditional formulae. Both were attempting to re-draw the boundary-lines in the highly contested atmosphere following the Reform Act.

Hampden's treatment of heresy, in the *Bampton Lectures* arises from a temper of mind, ironically, not far from Newman's own: a mistrust of the reduction of revelation to system, 'the fetters of a systematic theology'.[36] Perhaps they were both – Newman in *Arians* and Hampden in his *Bamptons* – reacting against the 'Noetics', and the logic of which their Common Room was reputed to stink.[37] Systematisation, for Hampden, as for Newman, was a form of rationalism,[38] arising from 'the pure exertions of the mind within itself, conscious of its own powers, and struggling to push itself forth against the constringent force of the spiritual government'.[39] Hampden's theme is 'the evil of a Logical Theology'.[40]

His application of this anti-rationalism to heresy and dogma also has affinities with Newman's. Just as Newman in *Arians* blames rationalistic heresy for the Church's unwilling introduction of Creeds and technical vocabulary, so also Hampden:

Orthodoxy was forced to speak the divine truth in terms of heretical speculation: if it were only to guard against the novelties which the heretic had introduced. It was the necessity of the case that compelled the orthodox, as themselves freely admit, to employ a phraseology, by which, as experience proves, the naked truth of God has been overborne and obscured.[41]

Again, as Newman, Hampden laments the spread of dialectic, from defence against heresy, to the mainstream of Christian theology.[42] This regrettable process culminated in medieval scholasticism, the residual effects of which he would root out of the Church of England. Scholasticism, pretending to 'perfect science',[43] was really imposing upon revelation *a priori* categories extrinsic to it:[44] it is a false systematisation resulting from the fact that 'the human intellect supposes a greater regularity and equality in things than it actually finds'.[45] Inadequacy before the revealed is not something the mind itself is naturally prepared to accept, so that it 'eagerly seizes on the truths contained in these [Scriptures], to recast them in the mould which its own imaginations have formed'.[46]

So much for the affinities between the two men, but what of the differences? How did two such determined opponents of 'the fetters of systematic theology'[47] end up as such irreconcilable enemies? Part of the answer, no doubt, lies in the *political* dimension of the row: Newman wanted Dissenters kept out of Oxford: Hampden would have them in. But Hampden's theological position is also much more radical than Newman's, even in the latter's 'Romantic' phase in *Arians*. Newman had indeed regretted the fixing of the faith in creeds as a descent from mystical communion to the exigencies of a public, imperial church, often nominal and shot through with heresy, but he also regarded the creeds as *preserving* the faith by fixing its terminology.[48] Hampden, on the other hand, extends the scope of 'rationalism' and 'systematisation' to the doctrines themselves of Christian Antiquity, which he opposes to scriptural 'fact': 'The only ancient, only Catholic truth is the Scriptural fact.'[49]

Moreover, while Newman accepted the *insufficiency* of language to describe the depth of divine realities, by calling it *economic*, he nevertheless saw words as, in some sense, containing, or participating in, the realities they inadequately describe – the economy rooted in the mystery. But Hampden was radically anti-propositional: for him, it seems, all verbal formulations are dangerous scholasticisations of revelation. What, then, of Scripture, which, after all, contains propositions? No, says Hampden: Scripture is 'a *record* of the divine dealings with the successive generations of mankind'.[50] It was scholasticism which treated Scripture 'not simply as the living word of God, but as containing sacred *propositions* of inspired wisdom'.[51] It must be remembered here, for the effect of such a statement on Newman, that Hampden saw as 'scholastic' not only medieval but also patristic theology. Newman had no brief for, and scant knowledge of, the former, but was, of course, an urgent defender of the latter. Hampden accepts Scripture – and Scripture *only* – as revealed in a *narrative* sense: it is a story of human experiences of God through history, 'a divine history of man'.[52]

Hampden's understanding of the Doctrine of the Trinity, and of the heresies traditionally regarded as opposed to it, follow from his experiential, non-propositional concept of revelation. He does himself profess belief in a 'factual' form of the Doctrine, that is as 'a Theory of all revealed truth . . . the combined result of all the Scripture facts', but attacks its conversion into 'a speculative *a priori* principle, a logical basis, from which all other facts of Scripture, rationalised in like manner might be demonstratively concluded'.[53] Such rationalisations stem from analogies perceived between the working of the human mind and God's nature. One such analogy was particularly baneful to Hampden: the consideration of the 'Being of God' according to the laws of causality, the rigorous distinction between cause and effect,[54] and the conception of God as 'the principle of Efficiency'.[55] Hampden's indictment of 'Logical Theology' goes beyond a condemnation of medieval divinity to Trinitarian orthodoxy itself: 'The orthodox theory of the Trinity, accordingly, consisted in an exact scientific view of the principle of causation.'[56]

While being critical of the over-logical nature of orthodoxy, Hampden is sympathetic to the heretics who fell foul of it. Heretics were not so by intention: they became heretics by the inferences of their enemies. Trinitarian heretics, for example, 'set out with a trinitarian hypothesis'[57] – but fell victim to the logic of orthodoxy; treating of the Sabellian heretics, he declares: 'If the opinions of Praxeas, and Artemon, and Theodotus, of Paul of Samosata, Noetus, Sabellius, and others, amounted to Unitarianism, it was in the way of *consequence* or *inference*.'[58] Hampden, in fact, distinguishes between two kinds of logic: first, 'consequence', the inner logic of their own intellectual history, by which their developing speculations concluded in an evacuation of the truth they intended to uphold: 'they explained it away themselves by their speculations'.[59] Secondly, there is 'inference': they 'had the consequences of their theories forced on them by their adversaries, as the principles of their belief'.[60]

Like Newman, then, Hampden observes the tendency in orthodox Fathers to infer consequences from the propositions of their opponents, but he brings to it a different set of premises about the authority of Antiquity. It is possible, indeed, that the potential polemical value of 'inference' was impressed upon Newman by Hampden's treatment of heresy in the *Bampton Lectures*. Little did Hampden know, as he peacefully wrote them before the subscription controversy had broken out, that he would himself be made a heretic by inference and stand accused by Newman of virtual Socinianism from the logical consequences of his own principles!

The significance of Hampden for the ramifications of Newman's theories of heresy is all-important. He presented an occasion. His writings had ideas in them which would be advantageously turned to Tractarian use. He forced Newman to consider what might be meant by 'revelation' and how the particular heresies he was studying could be made to relate to this. He touched a nerve.

CHAPTER EIGHT

Blanco White

In the midst of Newman's struggle against Hampden, Blanco White became a Unitarian: Newman heard the news on 20 March 1835.[1] Newman and Blanco White had, before 1833, been close friends and, although they had drawn away from each other,[2] and Blanco White had thrown in his lot with the liberals under the patronage of Whately,[3] Newman retained a warm and lasting affection for him.[4] It was with genuine personal anguish that he contemplated Blanco's embracing of what he was coming to see as 'a deadly heresy, full of lasting evil to its wilful professors, and influential moreover on their moral character.[5] He wrote to try to dissuade his friend 'in great pain and much affection'.[6] Blanco's reply reflects the poignancy of the situation, 'I must follow the light that is in me. If that light be darkness, it is so without my being aware of it: without the slightest ground for suspecting that it is wilfully so . . . I would give anything to have it in my power to relieve the pain you suffer on my account.'[7] This apostasy was for Newman a horrible aberration in a friend he loved – he even came to see it as mental derangement.[8] The trauma of Blanco's loss effected a change in Newman's perspective: he saw in Blanco a heretic acting in good faith, falling through delusion into involuntary error. Accordingly, Newman's treatment of heresy in terms of 'consequences' – to use Hampden's vocabulary – took on a sympathy, even a tenderness, in the face of a tragic concept of the heretic's course.

On the other hand, the defection of Blanco White provided a useful debating point, as Martin Murphy has pointed out:

Blanco himself provided the Tractarians with one of their most powerful weapons against Hampden, for they adopted the line that Blanco's Socinianism (i.e. Unitarianism) was simply the logical outcome of the liberal theology of his own associates, Whately, Hampden and Arnold –

a group which Newman described as the 'advanced guard of a black host'.[9]

Blanco White could be used as a 'beacon':[10] by comparing the teaching of a frank Unitarian with that of Hampden, liberalism could be shown up for the crypto-Socinianism that it was. The rumours which had circulated, that Blanco White had had a part in Hampden's *Bampton Lectures*,[11] and that Whately might have had a hand in Blanco White's *Second Travels of an Irish Gentleman*,[12] suggesting a complex web of mutual influence,[13] would have strengthened Newman's view about the real direction of liberalism.[14]

It was not until four months after the news of Blanco White's apostasy that Newman began to study the book in which Blanco publicly announced his change of church allegiance,[15] *Observations on Heresy and Orthodoxy*, that is, just over one month before he wrote *Tract 73*. The sentence which Newman adopted from Blanco White's book, and which he did not tire of repeating in his letters, was that 'Sabellianism is but Unitarianism in disguise'.[16] It was during this period, in early August, 1835, that Newman realised that ideas in Blanco's book could be used against the very liberalism out of which his approach to heresy and orthodoxy emerged: 'It strikes me his work might be very usefully turned as a witness for the tendency of certain opinions.'[17]

The *context* of Blanco White's use of 'Sabellianism' throws light upon why Newman found the idea so significant. The term occurs in the 'Preface' to *Observations on Heresy and Orthodoxy*, where Blanco White describes his spiritual journey. He arrived at Unitarianism, not by reading Unitarian theology, but, significantly for Newman, from 'systematic study of the Scriptures',[18] 'I never read any defence of Unitarianism till, in 1818, the study of the New Testament *alone* had made me a Unitarian.'[19] In isolating the Bible from Tradition and credal affirmations, and studying it concentratedly, Blanco White had, by as early as 1814, while at Oxford studying theology, begun to doubt.[20] His example provided powerful confirmation of Newman's view that ultra-Protestantism and liberalism were, for all their apparent differences, somehow all of a piece, and on the way to infidelity.[21]

Although, by 1818, Blanco White had arrived at Unitarianism, he did not make any public avowal. By 1824 he had come round again to orthodoxy, not from intellectual conviction, but from the human warmth and influence of those he met at Oxford. But, eventually his reason 'resumed its operations against the system I had thus wilfully embraced'.[22] His conscience was driving him unwillingly to accept the conclusions of his own reason, while his emotions held him to the Church of England. At this point, he introduces Sabellianism:

in my anxiety to avoid a separation from the Church by deliberate surrender of my mind to my old Unitarian convictions, I took refuge in a modification of the Sabellian theory, and availed myself of the *moral* Unity which I believe to exist between God the Father and Christ, joined to the consideration that Christ is called in the New Testament the Image of God, and addressed my prayers to God as apparently in that image.[23]

This passage, which later played an important part in *Tract 73*,[24] is full of pathos: clinging to a Church he loved, Blanco found in Sabellianism a way of deceiving himself, of concealing from himself the real direction in which his reason was taking him – but it was a 'flimsy veil':

the *devout* contrivance would not bear examination. Sabellianism is only Unitarianism disguised in words; and as for the worship of an image in its absence, the idea is most unsatisfactory. In this state, however, I passed five or six years; but the return to the clear and definite Unitarianism in which I had formerly been, was as easy as it was natural.[25]

His friend's story was, for Newman, full of warning.

Blanco's presentation of heresy and orthodoxy, confronted Newman with a clearer – and, one might say, a more honest and forthright – form of the theology of revelation which he found in Hampden. Blanco White held that the Bible only is the source of all religious truth, but that the only *certain* conclusions we can draw are those assimilable in sense experience.[26] The 'facts' of the Bible are, in the latter sense only, objective. This is pure Hampden. However, in this assessment of the nature of doctrine, Blanco goes a little further – far enough, Newman of course argued, to show the 'consequences' and legitimate 'inferences' touching Hampden's similar theology. For Blanco, a *doctrine* about the nature of God is not open to empirical experience – it is not part of common public language as are facts and events – but it is a purely *private* interpretation of the one who holds it, 'an impression which exists in his own mind'.[27] Each person has a duty, Blanco argues, to convince others of his own interpretation. But the condition of 'orthodoxy' only arises when a particular interpretation agreed by a group ('sect', 'church', or 'Christian party') is imposed as 'objective Christian truth'.[28] The true interpretation of the Bible is only *certainly* known by 'the Divine mind'.[29] Heresy is the name given by a *party* to the opposite of the opinion it is trying to impose.[30] Both Hampden and Blanco, then, see doctrine as unrevealed, but whereas the former tries to accord it nevertheless a regulating function of sorts in the Church, Blanco asserts frankly its subjectivity.

Blanco White denies that the Bible can be interpreted in credal or dogmatic propositions. What does he affirm? The answer is that idea of the Bible as moral instruction which we have seen in Hampden. He separates doctrinal orthodoxy from 'saving faith'.[31] The former is a 'logical act', identifying by the powers of the mind certain propositions deduced from Scripture as essential – but this is to make salvation a matter of chance, because it would then be conditional upon congenital intellectual power, or upon the education needed to perform the 'logical act'. 'Saving faith' is, on the other hand, centred in will and trust, rather than intellectual assent, and hangs upon one point, 'belief or trust in Christ as the moral king and instructor of mankind'.[32] This is the 'essential principle'[33] of the Gospel. Genuine 'moral' heresy is possible because some moral positions may interfere with the Gospel, but a latitude of doctrinal stances may be tolerated within Christianity. Therefore the 'way of salvation, through the Gospel, must be that which remains after the removal of all the doctrines which have been constantly disputed, between the Orthodox and the Heterodox'.[34] What remains is obedience to the moral law revealed in conscience, and trust in Christ as moral exemplar.[35]

Blanco's very original concept of 'Sabellianism' provided Newman with a bridge between his section on the *ancient* heresy in *Arians* and the possibility of using it to designate a *modern* heresy – liberalism – which was concealing its essential Socinianism under the form of Sabellianism, Father, Son and Holy Spirit being 'revealed' only in the sense of being images, manifestations or modes of expression of the *One* God's moral will for humanity. Blanco's apostasy took him, to Newman's sadness, into a sect his one-time friend abhorred above all others: 'I would not sit down to dinner with a known Socinian.'[36] But there were others, like Hampden, mildly disclaiming any imputation of Socinianism, happy to occupy the benefices, stalls and professorships of the Church of England and to diffuse their influence. Might not 'Sabellianism', in Blanco's sense, be an instrument to root them out?

The influence of Blanco upon Newman's terminology may be clearly discerned only a week after his first perusal of *Observations on Heresy and Orthodoxy*, that is, in early August 1835. Newman has come almost to identify as Sabellian the liberalism within the Church of England which calls for the waiving of tests and creeds:

A cry is raised that the Creeds are unnecessarily minute . . . Thus, e.g., Sabellianism has been spreading of late years because people have said 'What is the harm of Sabellianism? It is a mere name', etc. . . . Well, what is the consequence? We just now have a most serious and impressive warning if we choose to avail ourselves of it. Poor Blanco White has turned Socinian, and written a book glorying in it. Now in the preface of this book he says: 'I have for some time been a *Sabellian*, but the veil is now removed from my eyes, for I find *Sabellianism* is *but* Unitarianism in disguise'.[37]

Newman is here inveighing against the poisonous influence of the recently published correspondence of the popular evangelical writer Hannah More, who writes 'slightingly' of the Niceano-Constantinopolitan creed and by her 'scoffing' strengthens 'a system of doctrine which ends in Unitarianism'.[38] 'Sabellianism' has evolved a sense quite different from its strictly patristic sense – the opponents of a Niceano-Constantinopolitan orthodoxy were Arians not Sabellians – as a general term of broad contemporary significance.

Yet the story of this term's origin is, ultimately, even more complex and tortuous. Why was Newman so swift to discern the *usefulness* of Blanco's self-declared 'Sabellianism', if not because a vaguer form of the same idea had been forming in his *own* mind? Six months before Newman had read Blanco's *Observations*, and even before he had heard of his 'fall' or of the 'instructive' idea of Sabellianism, he preached a sermon on 8 March 1835, *The Humiliation of the Eternal Son*.[39] One section of this Christological[40] sermon discusses the relation between doctrinal terminology and the spiritual life. There is a form of orthodoxy, Newman tells us, which consists merely in adhering to an imprecise form of words –

such as to call Christ 'God' – which is not rooted in the 'object of faith' behind the words. So superficial is such a faith that a 'subtle disputant' could rob them of 'the sacred truth in its substance, even if they kept it in name'.[41] This is already quite close to Blanco's analysis of his own conversion to Unitarianism: a form of words conceals a shift which has *already* taken place without the subject's conscious knowledge. The 'substance' of a truly orthodox faith is preserved only by communion with God, so that words then 'light up' 'the image of the Incarnate Son on our hearts'.[42] Then Newman turns to 'the theology of late centuries' which he argues has facilitated the erosion of true orthodoxy by providing vague Christological formularies, and neglecting Nicene theology; so that 'when we merely speak first of God, then of Man, we seem to change the nature without preserving the Person'.[43] Newman's thought is not entirely clear in this passage. His drift seems to be that the terms of patristic orthodoxy preserve the *unity* of Christ, divine and human in one person, while modern theology oscillates in its way of speaking of Christ and falls into a kind of Nestorianism. This argument is, however, not integrated with the view that it is experience of God – 'communion' – which preserves the orthodoxy. At this point, Newman abruptly introduces Sabellianism, in the company of a number of other heresies. He is discussing the dangers of modern theology to the literate and learned, (the illiterate being happily immune from temptation): 'they begin by being Sabellians, they go on to be Nestorians and . . . they tend to be Ebionites and to deny Christ's Divinity altogether'.[44] It is clear that here Newman already has in mind Sabellianism as a resting-place on the road towards Unitarianism.

Moreover, two weeks later, writing to Henry Wilberforce when the news of Blanco's defection was only just out in Oxford, and preoccupied with the virtual Socinianism of his liberal opponents there, Newman again touches on Sabellianism. He prompts his friend with headings for a pamphlet and eggs him on with regard to the targets: Thomas Arnold, Richard Whately and his domestic chaplain Samuel Hinds, N.W. Senior, another ally of Whately, and Blanco White. Sabellianism is introduced with tantalising imprecision: 'Hinds, his notions about Inspiration and his Sabellianism and Nestorianism . . . Whately, Sabellianism, Nestorianism.'[45] The bringing together of Sabellianism and Nestorianism shows Newman's growing sense of the underlying identity of all heresies, no matter how far separated in place or time; he may also have seen both as denying the hypostatic union of divine and human in the one Person of the Word, which his sermon on the *Humiliation of the Eternal Son* had so recently defended. The consistent feature of this passage, however, is the association of the Whatelian circle with Sabellianism, Hinds and Whately being considered as an identical fount.[46]

This association of Sabellianism with Whately originates in a disturbing voice from the past, when the White Bear and the unfledged young Fellow took sweet counsel together and walked as friends. Whately had criticised the young man's sermon, *On the Mediatorial Kingdom of Christ* (1828) for its Arianism. It was seven years later – they were friends no more – and Newman remembered that his critic tended towards an opposite extreme, Sabellianism.[47] Newman had a long, if selective, memory. It is just possible that it would have been jogged by controversy surrounding the elevation of Whately to the Archbishopric of Dublin in 1831. Protests were raised about his unconventional views, and particularly that he verged on Sabellianism.[48] But, if so, there is no sign of it in Newman's correspondence. His one letter upon the subject of Whately's promotion considers what he might do, if invited to accompany him to Dublin.[49] Relations between them were still very cordial – dining and walking together.[50] Whately offered him a college vice-Principalship.[51] There seems little evidence that Newman was much troubled by Whately's 'Sabellianism' in 1831. By 1835, it was, of course, another matter. By then, they were definitely in opposite camps.[52]

In conclusion, Blanco White's theological justification of his conversion introduced the term 'Sabellianism' into the *public* discourse by which the issue of liberalism and dogmatism was being debated. Blanco had walked into the Unitarian church in Liverpool with his eyes open. He had taken a path in which the break with the traditional formularies of Christianity was *overt*. He had turned his back upon his own Sabellianism and faced, without self-deception, what it had been concealing. Newman saw and lamented this as a private, individual tragedy. On the public stage, however, he took the term 'Sabellianism' up, for rarely did he fail to press into his own service the material which came his way. Sabellianism's previous association with Whately and Whately's recent patronage of Blanco made easier his adoption of the term.

Always impressed by coincidence, Newman must have read Blanco's narrative and been struck by 'Sabellianism' with the force of a revelation. He was to use it to strip away the delusion, as he saw it, that liberalism occupied a reasonable middle ground – not, of course, to make ambiguous waverers into Unitarians, but rather to frighten them back into the ancient fold.

CHAPTER NINE

Apollinarianism

Meanwhile, Newman had not given up his scholarly aspirations. The edition of Dionysius was proceeding, if with interruptions. His letters and diaries suggest there may have been a *hiatus* in his work, between the inception of the Subscription Controversy in November 1834, and July and August 1835, when there are renewed references to his being 'hard at it' again.[1] Thus he attempted a spurt of energetic patristic research just before and during his reading of Blanco White's *Observations on Heresy and Orthodoxy*.[2]

His work took a new turn just at the time when Blanco's book was in his hands, that is, in early August 1835. Suddenly, there appear, throughout that month, references to Apollinarianism in connection with his edition of Dionysius: 'At present I am hard at Dionysius – i.e. at the Apollinarian controversy.'[3] Newman writes as if there is an obvious connection between the edition of Dionysius, where the heresy concerned is Sabellianism, and Apollinarianism. In fact, there is no historical connection between them. Nevertheless, throughout August 1835, he continues to write as if there were: 'Dionysius . . . is taking me, as I expected he would, into a consideration of the Apollinarian controversy.'[4] But why does he 'expect' this? It is no casual reference, for, in his first reference to the papers on Apollinarianism which he compiled in August 1835, he sees his account as emerging directly from Dionysius: 'Dionysius is nearly done – i.e. as far as it can be till I read more. I have used up all the documents on the Apollinarian Controversy and have written an account of it with references.'[5]

The answer to this puzzle must be sought in Newman's own theorising, rather than in the sources he was handling. His theories are fully expounded in his 'Apollinarianism' papers, but a *theory* of heresy is clearly already implied in the link he perceives between two such apparently unrelated heresies as Sabellianism and Apollinarianism: that is, that all heresies are particular forms of an identical underlying rationalism, and therefore, have hidden relations with one another, which may be drawn out. Newman writes to his friends in August 1835, as if this hardly even needed arguing amongst his inner circle.

Did such a theoretical understanding of heresy emerge *purely* from his research into the Fathers, only later being applied – for example, in *Tract 73* – to contemporary liberalism? Or did Newman's already existing conviction of the underlying Socinianism of Oxford liberalism, and Blanco White's 'Sabellianism' condition his research, so that he found in the Fathers what he was looking for – an authoritative basis in Antiquity for the method he was employing in his critique of his opponents? Chronology suggests the latter alternative as the most likely one. The Hampden controversy had been raging for nine months before his research on Apollinarianism, the badge of Newman's party being that liberalism over tests conceals Socinianism. The news of Blanco's Unitarianism was four months old. Six days *before* Newman saw the transition from Sabellianism to Apollinarianism, he had begun to perceive the importance of Blanco's thesis that 'Sabellianism is but Unitarianism in disguise' – he had 'seen'[6] Blanco's book, but it is not clear whether he had yet read it thoroughly: perhaps he had only perused the *Preface*. Three days later, referring again to Blanco's book, he was beginning to see its value 'as a witness to the tendency of certain views'.[7] Then, on 9 August, came the first of his declarations that study of Dionysius *leads* inevitably to Apollinarian controversy.[8] In this letter to Hurrell Froude, he also adverts to Blanco and Sabellianism: that it is 'a *witness* of the tendency of certain opinions' and that the idea may be 'turned'.[9] On the same day, he wrote to his sister, Elizabeth, about Blanco, Sabellianism, Socinianism and creeds.[10] Here, he also refers to his Dionysius edition and his patristic reading, declaring that his research has 'far graver objects in view' than merely a scholarly edition, in view of the 'flood of scepticism'[11] he expects to pour over the land. Doctrinal truths are being abandoned because people 'do not *understand their value*'.[12] It is, therefore, clear that Newman's patristic research had merged with his public struggle against liberalism by the time he began to study Apollinarianism.

The first attempt to treat systematically of Apollinarianism occurs in a rough draft written on 15 August 1835 on the 'defection of Apollinaris'.[13] It is an incomplete, abbreviated and much crossed-through document, with Newman's theses about the heresy written on the left, and references on the right. The first sentence, however, is written in full: 'The defection of Apollinaris from the Catholic Faith excites feelings of especial pain and [regret], both from his high character and former services to the Church and the particular cause to which it may be traced.'[14] The stress upon the personal tragedy of the heretic and the pain and anguish his fall occasions in orthodox circles perhaps has its source in that other 'defection' which touched Newman so nearly, that of Blanco White. The tone of this sentence will be characteristic also of many of his statements on heresy in August and September 1835. It is almost as if, while the Hampden affair ran to its bitter close, Newman was striving to break free from the toils of *odium theologicum* and strike a note of universal pathos.

This draft is shot through with the theory of the underlying identity of all heresy. Despite its incomplete and tentative form, the logic by which Apollinarianism may be seen as running into Sabellianism is clearly traceable, and gives a picture of the state of Newman's speculations as he was making the transition from the Dionysius edition (and Sabellianism) to the two weighty and carefully written papers on Apollinarianism which were soon to follow.

According to Newman, Apollinaris' position was grounded in opposition to Arianism. Now, Arians held that Christ – whatever else he was – was 'a perfect man'. But Apollinaris' 'great object' was 'to ascertain and secure the doctrine of Christ's divinity' – so much so that he ended up denying His humanity.[15] Apollinaris' reasons for this imbalance disclose what Newman is beginning to think might be rationalism, for all the heresiarch's high Christology: Apollinaris was unwilling to accept that the human *nous* was compatible with the Divine Logos in Christ. His 'badge' was 'one person' and he considered 'human soul, or . . . perfect man' as 'superfluous'.[16] Newman asks himself here, 'qu[estion], whether he objected to the *mystery*'.[17]

Apollinaris cannot only be shown in this roundabout way to be rationalist. Newman's phraseology in describing his teaching also shows why he could see Sabellianism and Apollinarianism as so obviously connected:

All manifestation of a perfect human nature seemed to him to destroy that literal manifestation of the Godhead which the Incarnation implied. The object being *manifestation of the Unseen* . . . this meant that the Word had but taken to him an outward form by which he might be seen, or as Scripture itself expressed it, *Flesh* (John).[18]

Newman's presentation of Apollinarianism here makes it out to be virtually Sabellian: the person of Christ manifests God and is identical with Him. There are no subsistent distinctions within the Trinity, and the only difference between 'God' and 'Christ' is the addition to the latter of a human body: 'accordingly he considered the body of Christ but as the medium of displaying Him – and the *eikon* of the Invisible'.[19] But Newman does not yet come out with what he is already hinting: his route to the conclusion that Sabellianism and Apollinarianism have a hidden similarity is still more circuitous.

Having outlined Apollinaris' position, Newman announces his method of analysis of the heresy – a method we have already seen challenged by Hampden: 'he [Apollinaris] had entailed on himself certain consequences which he could not avoid'.[20] The heresy has, as it were, taken on a life of its own, and its 'consequences', logical or historical, can truly define its hidden nature, despite the sincere disclaimers of the heretic himself. A list of 'consequences' follows. The body of Christ, by its unity with the Word and lack of a human soul, is so divinised as to be 'unearthly', not a human body at all. But, conversely, the Word itself as long as united to a body was itself changed into 'some third', neither God nor man. Then, there was the problem of Christ's sufferings: Apollinarianism would have to maintain either that the divine nature suffered[21] or that no Passion, and no Atonement took place. This consequence is even more alarming in the case of Christ's death – did the *Word* die? At the end of his list of consequences, comes Sabellianism. Newman has been considering Apollinaris' response to the problems presented by his view of the relation between flesh (σαρξ) and Word (Λογος): 'Ap[ollinari]s went so far in simplifying his system as to consider the σαρξ as a more mysterious development of the divine essence'.[22] He moves to his final point, 'Lastly they were led to Sabellianism as making human nature His εἰκων.'[23] The phraseology is very significant here. Firstly, in 'they', Newman considers the heresy's development in the sectaries following Apollinaris – its succeeding history clarifies its original nature.

Secondly, they are '*led*': the slide into Sabellianism is inadvertent, they are borne along as the heresy takes its inevitable course.

Only four days after this draft, Newman embarked upon two substantial documents on Apollinarianism, which remain unpublished in their original form. First, dated 19 August 1835, is a continuous manuscript of nineteen sheets, written on both sides, entitled *Apollinaris' history*.[24] On the first page, above the text, in red ink, is written a declaration of the paper's purpose:

NB The object of these papers I intend to be this – to have somewhere where my *authorities* for facts and opinions are brought together which want so much in the *Arians*. The *matter* of this may be, if it so happens, cast into quite another shape, or contracted, or alluded to, or scattered here and there over another subject, in anything which I may actually publish.[25]

The textual complexity promised by Newman's intention to re-cast according to as yet unforeseen demands upon him was indeed fulfilled: substantial edited portions of this paper appear in a *British Magazine* article for July 1836, which was reworked for the 1840 *Church of the Fathers*, but is familiar to readers of the collected works as part of another redaction, a chapter in *Primitive Christianity* (1872). A second paper entitled *Apollinarianism* is dated 22 August 1835. It is part of the privately printed booklet[26] also containing a paper from 1839 on Monophysitism. It bears a direct relation to the *Heresy of Apollinaris* which Newman published in 1874 in *Tracts Theological and Ecclesiastical*, but there are important changes to the 1835 version, as the old man, always tinkering, put in a new sentence here[27] and conflated a paragraph there. The two 1835 papers are somewhat different in character. *Apollinaris' history* has more of a historical and narrative quality, while *Apollinarianism* is more analytical and theological, but this distinction is not clear-cut: the former also has a highly theoretical and analytical quality, while the latter does not omit history and characterisation.

Apollinaris' history opens with a rich and complex paragraph, reverberant with the newly acquired sense of the heretic's tragedy:

The fall of Apollinaris into heresy is a passage of ecclesiastical history, very painful and very instructive, from his high repute for learning and virtue, his intimacy with the great Catholic teachers of his day, his former services to the Church and the particular circumstances which led to it. He had suffered and laboured for the truth's sake in a time of persecution; he had been a vigorous and successful opponent of Arianism during the ascendancy of that heresy; and he seems to have at length been betrayed into an opposite error by the unguarded zeal with which he encountered it.[28]

There are here, perhaps, echoes of the 'painful', yet 'instructive' 'Fall' of Blanco, but equally there are hints of a parallel between Apollinaris' and Newman's own position: was he not, too, labouring for the truth's sake? Did he not aspire to 'learning and virtue'? And might there not be a hidden danger in orthodox 'zeal', that even a champion of Catholicism might be taken unawares and 'betrayed into an opposite error?' The heretic is no longer – as so often in his portrayals in *Arians* – lucre-loving, shifty, shallow and base, but learned, profound, heroic. His theology has a fatal flaw but he does not see it, and it takes him he knows not where.

After this opening flourish, the document narrates Apollinaris' upbringing and early education.[29] Then follows a detailed account, with long patristic quotations, of the course of the heresy. Newman dates its first appearance at AD362: while Athanasius was still living, it was discussed at the Council of Alexandria,[30] although it was not yet associated with Apollinaris' name.[31] Citing a long passage from Athanasius' *Tomus and Antiochos*, Newman works towards a definition of the heresy: 'the opinion of Christ's soul being destitute of mind is the characteristic tenet of Apollinaris'.[32] The heresy, repressed by the weight of Athanasius' authority, 'slept' for seven years, then emerging in Syria and Greece, by which time, 'it had run into those logical consequences which make even a little error a great one'.[33] Athanasius never suspected his ally's error – it was only after the patriarch's death (in 371 or 373) that Apollinaris came out. Then a sect was formed, and the Catholic Church condemned it. After the heresiarch's decease, many of the sectaries applied to the Church for reconciliation.[34] There follow illustrative passages from the heresy-collector, Epiphanius.[35] The document ends with a long passage about the development of the heresy in its sects.[36]

Parts of the document eventually found their way, with modifications, into the collected works: Apollinaris' biography and the narrative of the heresy's progress, the doctrinal passages considerably abbreviated, appear in *Primitive Christianity* (1872).[37] However, completely absent in any form from this later redaction, and, indeed, from any of the published works, are the remarkable last three pages, which treat of Apollinarian sects. Here, Newman speculates most fully about the nature of heresy and articulates a theory of its development in its generality, going far beyond the Apollinarian dispute, and echoing the debates of his own contemporary situation.[38]

The discussion of the reconciliation to the Church of certain Apollinarian sects vibrates with Oxford associations. Newman warns of the dangerous long-term effects of too readily re-admitting sectaries to the Catholic body, without a very strict examination of their beliefs. At the beginning of the fifth century, the rump of Apollinarianism, now restricted to Antioch, begged re-admittance to the Great Church. He finds the history 'instructive':

Being many of them at least scarcely sincere in their recantation, they cherished and gradually propagated those notions in the Church which before they had failed in spreading externally to it. The evil increased; it infected the Catholic body and the dissentions [sic] [the evil] followed which developed itself in the heresies of Nestorius and Eutyches, the schisms and prostrations of the Eastern Church, a gradual preparation for the triumphs of Mohammedanism and the establishment of heretical doctrines which continue within the Church to this day.[39]

The imaginative and allusive character of this passage is strong, the very phraseology shaped by the subscription controversy and the imminent 'pollution' of Oxford by Dissent. Newman universalises his anxiety into a theory: heresy admitted by latitudinarian laxity, is a canker *within*, which, when through course of time, it develops into its mature form, will so weaken the Church as to make it vulnerable to dissolution. As in the early Church, Newman implies, so now, as heresy makes its way within the Church in the guise of liberalism. He even discerns a link between Apollinarianism, via Nestorianism and Eutychianism, and modern heresy – 'to this day'. We may only guess *who* – he is not specific – but it is certain that, however tortuously, Hampden and Blanco White form part of the answer. In this passage, Newman goes beyond the limits he set himself in his declaration of intent. No longer is he merely gathering 'authorities', 'matter' to be deployed as the occasion arises. He has slipped into making comparisons between modern rationalism and ancient heresy, as he did in *Arians*.[40]

In his consideration of the Apollinarian leaders, such as Vitalis and Valentinus, who succeeded the heresiarch, Newman expounds his theory of the development of heresy. The fragmentation of Apollinarianism was caused by the 'dissensions' which are a 'common result of separation from the Catholic body'.[41] Newman's point is conventional enough – often made by big churches against little ones.[42] He follows it with something startling:

> In truth every novelty in religion, to speak in general terms, starts with a doctrine short of that to which it legitimately leads and in process of time results; and in the interval it is necessarily inconsistent and variable, making statements in different times and persons more or less advanced towards its final development, or explanations only experimental and perhaps temporary with a view how best to overcome difficulties as they arise, or to adjust its tenets with such principles, whether scriptural or philosophical, on which it has engaged to rest them at the outset.[43]

Newman's expression is clumsy – the sentence had yet, no doubt, to be polished. Nevertheless, the 1845 idea of the development of doctrine is in some respects here strikingly anticipated – only in relation to *heretical* doctrine. Apollinarian doctrine is seen as developing through history, and the development takes place 'legitimately', so that the final expression of the heresy more fully and truly defines the nature of the original, earlier doctrine. As in the *Essay on Development*, something new is learned as a result of the process: development is not only greater accuracy of words, but a clearer and fuller *idea*. Again, as in the *Essay*, a period of confusion and debate precedes the final development, though there are some isolated 'early anticipations' too.

There are, however, important differences also. In the *Essay*, the development of revelation into ever-greater fullness and precision impresses Newman with its *unity* and coherence: what has gone before is consolidated, not overset, and ever more firmly integrated into the *one* body of truth. But heresy's development is destructive and fissiparous, mercilessly exposing the initially imperceptible contradictions of its original formulation. It is what he would, in 1845, call 'corruption'. The sects are embodiments of these inner contradictions: 'Had Apollinaris given birth to as many sects as there seem to be distinct doc[trinal] theories in his own writings, there probably would be more divisions among his disciples than there really were.'[44]

Touching the doctrines of the sects, Newman will 'notice' two only. These he chooses because they dramatise an essence-of-Apollinarianism debate, arising out of the opposing tendencies originally embedded in the heresy: the two schools of thought 'seem to be drawn respectively from the two chief professions which his writings contain, attachment to the ancient Fathers, and maintenance of a novel doctrine'.[45] This oscillating quality, this inner chaos, was, of course, what the detractors of the ante-Nicene faith had been, since the late seventeenth century, attributing to the age of the early Fathers. Newman is naturally opposed to such a view of patristic *orthodoxy* – but happy to deploy it against *heresy*.

Newman discerns a conservative and a radical wing. The party of Vitalis and Valentinus consisted of rather static traditionalists who 'professed to adhere to the tradition of the Church, [and] protested against the interpretations by which their rival division carried out their common master's language'.[46] They eventually rejoined the Church. Their 'rivals', whose leader was Polemius, were both more open to development and 'more vigorous in the propagation of their views' – they had more *'life'*, as the later Newman might have said. Therefore they 'embraced' the consequences of the original heresy, 'all the more detestable doctrines which have been above enumerated',[47] conveniently for orthodox heresiologists such as Newman who may thereby define the true nature of the heresy by its extravagances. If Newman is more sympathetic to the conservative Apollinarians, he is nevertheless grateful for the radicals, because it was all too easy for the heresy with its 'subtle distinctions' – one thinks of Hampden's slipperiness – to cloak its nature, and even to 'shelter' behind the names of orthodox writers. Not surprisingly, Newman discerns the possibility of a *slide* from the more 'orthodox' to the more radical form. As an example of this, he cites the case of bishop Timotheus, once an intimate of Apollinaris himself, who was first inclined towards Vitalis, but 'after a while' joined sides with the 'adventurous divine', Polemius.

The paper ends. Newman had been scribbling for two days. The last sentence marks a transition: 'But it is time to turn to an [internal] consideration of the heresy itself which has been the subject of this outward survey.'[48] History and narrative are over: now analysis of the inner dynamics of Apollinarian doctrine is to follow. This was almost certainly *Apollinarianism* of 22 August 1835, commenced only two days after *Apollinaris' history*. Newman's distinction between 'outward survey' and 'internal consideration' does not quite work – he has already started to examine the inner logic of Apollinarianism in his first paper, while his second is not devoid of psychological interest.

Apollinarianism appears in the collected works in a much later redaction, entitled *The Heresy of Apollinaris*.[49] They share a similar structure: both are an examination of Apollinarian doctrines, in numbered paragraphs, moving from Apollinaris himself, through a consideration of the logical consequences of his teaching, to its confirmation in the theology of its sectarian developments. However, the later work expresses Newman's theories with clipped and scholastic precision, while the 1835 paper contains both powerful rhetoric and subtle psychological analysis, which is excised from the later published work. The 1835 *Apollinarianism* therefore stands as a distinct work in its own right, which was never published.

Newman immediately plunged into his most explicit statement so far of the underlying identity of all heresy. *Apollinaris' history* had tended to stress a particular heresy's fragmentary and incoherent quality. Now, Newman turns to the question of the one essence of heresy, beneath the forms, the theory by which he explains to himself how Sabellianism merged, in his perception, with Apollinarianism, and how Arianism reveals its cloven hoof beneath the skirts of both. It would seem that Apollinaris' error, in view of the 'unguarded vehemence with which he attacked the Arians', arose out of 'a reaction from Arianism'. Newman quickly dismisses this as only a superficial view – the heresy's 'formal characteristics'; he is

not forgetful the while, that all heresies may be made upon paper to look contrary to each other, while in fact, when analysed, all will rather be found to run together into one, for they are all really opposed to the Truth and The Truth alone, which seems at first sight merely to lie in the middle between them.[50]

Radical and extreme indeed is Newman's denial that the heresy, even partially, participates in truth. Apollinaris is only *apparently* (or formally) anti-Arian – really he is an enemy of truth *and truth alone*. The essence of heresy is, therefore, opposition to truth. But what is the nature of this 'opposition'? Clearly it is not the content of a particular heresy's teaching which Newman relegates to the *formal*. An answer begins to emerge, even in this opening paragraph, when he explains, by way of example, how Arianism and Sabellianism are really identical: 'though diametrically opposed in a drawn out scheme of doctrine, [they] substantially agree together, and are at variance with the Catholic Faith, in that the latter asserts the mystery of a distinction of Persons in the One divine Substance and both heresies deny it'.[51] His argument has two layers. The first draws its strength from his familiarity with patristic sources:[52] the orthodox tendency is always to hold to subsistent distinctions within the very being of the Godhead, while heresy tends to confuse person with divine essence. This view is crucial, as will be seen, for his later work on contemporary error, which he accordingly characterised as 'Sabellian'. A Christological point bolsters the Trinitarian one: in a note, Newman debates whether or not Arians denied that Christ had a human soul, and concludes that they did: Apollinarians, too, then may be shown to 'run into' Arianism, for they had an Arian Christology![53] Newman is all the while professing that he is treating of heresies more *really* than those who 'make them look different on paper' or who 'draw them out into a scheme of doctrine'. He is, of course, – at least in this first level of argument – himself being highly theoretical, drawn-out and schematic.

The occurrence of the word 'mystery' announces a second layer, hinting at the underlying rationalism of Apollinarians. This implication is pursued in the terms in which he couches his opening summary of Apollinaris' teaching:

Apollinaris opposed to Arianism a strong and (what may be called) intelligible doctrine, asserting with more or less clearness, as the case may be, but always with a necessary implication, not merely that Christ was more than man, but that he was simply the Eternal Son, either without the addition of a human nature at all, or with only its nominal addition.[54]

Apollinarianism's appeal streamlines Christology, sidesteps 'mystery', makes 'intelligible', strives for 'clearness'. This appealed to 'those who had wearied themselves with speculations upon the mystery'. They found in Apollinarianism 'relief'; they could take 'refuge' in it. It was 'a plain and broad view of the subject which, while rescuing them from Humanitarianism, saved them also from the irritation of mind occasioned by that subtle orthodox phraseology which had been rendered necessary by Arianism itself'.[55] There are echoes of *Arians* in this passage. Those embracing Apollinarianism are one with the Newman of 1832 who lamented the enforced *reduction* by heresy of the orthodox faith to creed and system. Moreover, the phrase he uses to describe their attitude – 'a plain and broad view of the subject' – closely parallels the words actually used in *Arians* to describe the qualities lacked by heretics: a 'broad and commonsense view of an important subject'.[56] Did Newman see himself ominously mirrored in the 'irritation of mind' of Apollinarian converts? He certainly wished to be rescued from 'Humanitarianism'. His diction suggests that he sensed the dangers of such an attraction.

The sympathy continues. He warms to Apollinarians as his analysis proceeds: they 'seemed to have some countenance for the line of doctrine which they were about to adopt, in the received teaching of the Church'.[57] They began by emphasising what Newman sees as the Church's 'great article': that the Personality[58] of God is his Divine Essence, so that his manhood is 'but an addition to his real nature'. The high Christology of Apollinaris strikes a chord in Newman's bosom:

'His human nature . . .', they said, and truly too, 'must not be looked at by itself or rested on by the mind as having a substantive, or in itself independent or individual character; as it was indissolubly connected with, so it necessarily depended on and rested in the Essence of the Eternal Word.'[59]

Newman identifies strongly enough with the heresy to dramatise its argument in his own terminology. His identification of what was 'not so defensible' in Apollinarianism is equally instructive: Apollinarians disliked describing Christ as 'man' because it suggested an 'independent and individual nature', 'and interfered with the literal and actual manifestation of God in Christ'.[60] Apollinarianism is not wrong in its dislike of describing Christ as a human being, but in its tendency towards Sabellianism.

Newman moves towards ever more precise and technical definition of the heresy, demonstrating a control of sources independent of the current manuals. Apollinaris denied that Christ had a human intellect for fear of introducing 'a new being or person, or thinking principle, into the Sacred economy'.[61] He could not accept *pneuma* in Christ, for this could mean divine nature. He could accept ψυχη, the animal soul or principle of motion (hardly in principle distinct from living flesh). But he denied νους, the intellectual principle. Again, there is a flash of fellow-feeling on Newman's part: 'Apollinarianism, then, was a denial of the intellectual principle, or *nous*, in Our Lord's human nature, and that maintained with a view of guarding against the doctrine of a double personality, or what was afterwards called Nestorianism.'[62] Newman can see Apollinaris as a prophet against Nestorianism, a heresy Newman always categorised as of the 'humanitarian' type.

What, then, is the positive orthodox response to Apollinarianism? To this question Newman now addresses himself, not without ambivalence. He makes a striking start – not a reasoning out of orthodoxy but the 'thrill of horror and indignation'[63] experienced by the early Christians upon their first encounter with the heresy, a shudder 'which it is difficult for us, with blunted feelings, to enter into'.[64] Newman identifies himself with an imagined audience as he depicts the insouciance with which the modern mind first makes acquaintance with this heresy. The error seems 'at first sight' but 'slight': 'a foolish fancy or conceit, rather than a heresy'.[65] Over against this stands the record of an ancient orthodox *frisson* challenging modern assumptions. Newman's method is dramatic and rhetorical.

Rhetoric is, indeed, freely employed as Newman attempts to engender appropriate horror in his readers, and, possibly, to stimulate it in himself. It works upon Apollinarian 'difficulties', that is, upon the consequences of presenting the Incarnation as a union of divine Word and soulless flesh: the criticism that the union of Word and animal nature (*psyche*) implies change and modification in the divine nature. However, Newman's manner of presentation of this 'difficulty' is rhetorical rather than logical:

what an impiety it was to suppose that [the non-rational body] could mingle with the Eternal Essence; that the Lord of Glory should clothe himself in perishable dust and ashes, after the manner of the Avatars of the Oriental Deities, and be acted upon by all the gross influences of a material tenement?[66]

Newman finds even the orthodox position, that the Eternal Word 'should take up his residence within a human soul' to be 'an incomprehensible humiliation'. But to dispense with soul is 'a far different degradation of the Eternal essence'.[67] He finds it difficult at this point effectively to argue quite *why*. It is, he urges, unwarranted by Scripture, but he has also shown that Apollinarians had a few problems coping with Scripture. It is moreover, 'without any benefit to man'. This hint of a soteriological argument, which does get another chance a little later, is presently overwhelmed by another wave of rhetoric: 'If we must argue about what needs no argument, better it would be that He should have shown Himself in vision or angelic shape, as the Patriarchs, than that He should assume a mode of manifestation, no more adequate, and far less gracious to man.'[68] Apollinarianism is attacked in its *underlying* tendency – the 'mode of manifestation', virtually Sabellian, which will slide into Arianism – but Newman's own preference for 'vision or angelic shape' gives away a Docetism, more extreme even than that of Apollinaris himself. The passage is overwrought, reflecting deep-seated uncertainties on Newman's part with regard to the full humanity of Christ. He was a happy Trinitarian theologian, but at times a somewhat uneasy Christological thinker. These ambivalences remained and emerged in his 73rd *Tract for the Times*.

With the phrase, 'far less gracious to man', the vessel, perilously close to a capsize, rights itself, taking on the ballast of a sound patristic principle: that what was not assumed cannot be deified. At the same time, Newman's attention shifts from the humanity of Christ to the indigence of humanity, and especially of the human soul:[69] the divine assumption of a soulless body would be an 'incomplete tabernacle' not truly 'our representative', since it would be ineffectual to a *complete* restoration of human nature: 'How is this to be done if the soul be omitted in the work? Does the soul need no cleansing? Is it to be left as it was before, in the darkness and weakness of unassisted nature?'[70]

The voices, the accumulated questions, the 'horror', the hubbub of arguments – has served its purpose to re-create in the mind of an early nineteenth-century reader the perplexities of fourth-century Christians: 'Such as these were the reflections which crowded on the mind of a Christian on hearing the ground which Apollinaris had taken up for his intellectual warfare with the Arians.'[71] Now Newman moves to a consideration of the heresy's development in its sects. But before this, he takes a last look at Apollinaris himself: 'Apollinaris did not, and could not stop at the point at which he began. He had already turned aside into the by-paths of heresy, and he was hurried on by the pressure of argument to far deeper and more extravagant errors.'[72] Heresy develops with frightening speed: it hurries the heretic on – he cannot pause or call a halt – it is swifter than thought – and 'already', before he has caught up with his own creation, he finds entailed upon him the grotesqueries of unimagined but inevitable consequences, the degradation of the Logos into a monster neither divine nor human. Thus does Newman take leave of this most congenial of heresiarchs. It is an anguished farewell.

As with *Apollinaris' history*, *Apollinarianism* concludes with a discussion of the sects, in which the latter duplicates many of the points made in the former, with, however, some new refinements. The two main parties of Apollinarianism are distinguished according to the degree to which they will accept development: 'if they varied, it was only by such differences as arose from their difference of acuteness or unscrupulousness in developing their original tenet'.[73] Newman's choice this time to discuss the sects against the background of party expediency lends the discussion a vividness and political complexity perhaps derived from his own experience of Oxford party groupings. It also introduces some confusions: he identifies 'unscrupulousness'[74] as a characteristic of the 'developmental' party, that of Timotheus, although it is the 'more cautious' sect of Valentinus which was 'unwilling to renounce the shelter of an orthodox profession, however nominal'.[75]

His technique of analysis of the doctrine of the sects is by now familiar: he considers the logical consequences to which their respective positions may be drawn out. While the moderate Valentinus argued that Christ's human body was not changed into the *substance* of the divine, although its properties were affected by the presence of the divine nature, the radical Timotheus argued that through the union with the Logos, Christ's body became consubstantial with the Godhead.[76] The consequence to be drawn from this, Newman summarises in the words of Gregory Nazianzen: 'Christ did not die, or else the Trinity suffered.'[77] Not surprisingly, Apollinarians wriggled upon the hook of this imputed consequence. The means of escape they sought was twofold: first, to say that only the animal soul (*psyche*) suffered in Christ – a denial of Christ's fully human and rationally expressed mental agony on the Cross; or, secondly, to deny that the passion took place.[78] In the latter case, the Incarnation was reduced to one 'simple object', 'the manifestation of God'.[79] However, Newman anticipates a 'third means of escape', the ultimate consequence of Apollinarian Christology by which the unseen interrelatedness of all heresies might be revealed: 'that the Word was not God; and this they could not really escape from the first, violently opposed, as they considered themselves, to Arianism'.[80] Apollinarianism has passed into its opposite. This development Newman associates with a long passage upon 'the more presumptuous side of the heresy',[81] identified with Timotheus, whose slide from moderate to radical Apollinarianism he has already analysed in the preceding document, *Apollinaris' heresy*. The route to his conclusion is tortuous, involving the most extreme employment so far of his method of 'drawing out' the essence of heresy. He finds Timothean Apollinarianism to be tending, successively, towards Docetism, Nestorianism, and 'Arianism or Sabellianism it matters not which'.[82] Heresy is all one – this he eventually asserts – but, first, analyses the strands within Apollinarian discourse which may be drawn out into the other heresies. It is a twisting course, and, especially in the citation of Nestorianism, one which leapfrogs chronology.

The first imputation, that Apollinarians are Docetists, though no doubt unwelcome to the Apollinarians themselves, is hardly unexpected, since both heresies are a consequence of an unbalanced stress upon the divine nature in Christ. Newman thinks Apollinarians are Docetists because, although, unlike the original Docetists, they held that Christ *had* a human body, their view that it changed its substance by union with the divine into what is 'increate and everlasting' makes him wonder 'in what sense it [could] be considered a body at all', as opposed to a 'phantom or *dokesis*'. Newman is happy to make the leap, on Apollinarians' behalf, from 'increate and everlasting' to 'never . . . in existence at all'.[83]

Newman's leap to Nestorianism is surprising. How is the Nestorian insistence upon the co-existence of two distinct principles – the divine and human persons in Christ linked only by a moral union – to be compared with Apollinarian stress upon the *divine* Logos as the principle of unity in Christ? Even Newman admits that Nestorianism is 'apparently a very opposite heresy'.[84] But by now he has warmed to his theory. He derives a 'Nestorian' consequence from Timotheus' profession that, while Christ's body had been originally human, it ceased to be so, once united to the Divine Word: 'This implied that it had an existence previously to its conception and birth in the womb of the Virgin Mary, which was a tenet closely connected with what was afterwards called Nestorianism.'[85] Newman, then, finds what, to adopt the terminology of the *Essay on Development*, may be called an 'early anticipation' of Nestorianism. He admits that *no* Apollinarian would ever have dreamt that his theology entailed such a consequence. His analysis is pursued 'whether or no any adopted this conclusion'.[86]

The Fathers' criticism of Apollinarian consequences – along very similar lines to Newman's – eventually pushed Apollinarians[87] into an *intentional* development, a simplification of their system:

seeing at length that the notion of a human body really meant nothing in their mouths, [they] simplified their view of the Incarnation still further, by relinquishing it altogether; and taught, that Christ's body, instead of being born of the Virgin Mary, was but a development from the internal essence of the Divine Word, as if thrown out round about it for the purpose of a manifestation to the eyes of men.[88]

Just as, ten years later in the *Essay on Development*, Newman showed how heresy stimulated ever more precise definition in orthodoxy, so here he presents the *converse*: heresy stimulated into development by an orthodox critique.

It gets more complicated still. This deliberate development upon the part of the Apollinarians had as its consequence a further – but this time *unintended* – development:

Lastly, it is obvious how easily this last opinion might pass into a sort of Arianism or Sabellianism, (it matters not which) by identifying the Word with this mere development, which was external to the Godhead; in accordance with which they had already taught that he was the *eikon* of the Father, not in His Divine Substance, but in his earthly.[89]

The slide of Apollinarianism into Arianism or Sabellianism is 'obvious' to Newman, but the line pursued here by his critique of heresy, working as it does against the grain of the surface testimony of history, requires further exegesis. Apollinarians, then, were driven to present Christ simply as a manifestation of the Father, His earthly image or icon. If they saw this icon as not of the Divine Substance, one can understand Newman's concurrence with the accusation, made at the time, of Sabellianism.

Since Newman envisaged, as early as 1832, a slide from Sabellianism to Arianism, the way is open also from Apollinarianism to Arianism. His method of getting from Apollinarianism via Sabellianism to Arianism is particularly intricate! Having slid as far as a form of Sabellianism, some 'scrupled' to go even further, as Praxeas was supposed to have done, and say that 'the Divine Nature suffered on the Cross'.[90] Since they 'denied' to Christ a human soul

– the badge of all Apollinarians – they would have to find another way whereby Christ suffered, than either in His Divine nature or as a fully human being. Thus they could be 'easily persuaded to believe that the Word was not strictly God, and *therefore* could suffer'.[91] Apollinarians, then, have ended up like Arians with a Christ neither fully divine nor fully human, perhaps as a consequence of an ultimately rather similar Christology. He does not bring out this latter point fully: the paper is coming to an end, and even Newman's capacity for discerning analogies and resemblances is perhaps wearing thin.

Newman's heresiological method is constantly drawing upon a consistent general feature of patristic polemic – the drawing out of heresy's consequences in order to affiliate it with other, already existing, heresies. For the link between Sabellianism and Arianism, Newman's notes on the opposing page provide specific information as to his source: 'Vid. on the subject Tertull[ian] in Prax[ean]'.[92] Tertullian's treatise is directed against the 'Praxean' variety of Sabellianism which confounded the distinction between Father and Son in *one* Person. Tertullian traces the logical consequences, as he sees it, of their position. He understands Praxeas to hold that the Word *became* flesh in a total identification, rather than by uniting flesh to Himself. For Tertullian, this entails the flesh ceasing to be flesh (it has become the Word) and the Word ceasing to be divine (it has become flesh): a change in substance has occurred in both cases, in flesh and divinity.[93] Tertullian saw as a consequence of this the ultimate denial of Christ's divinity:

Jesus, therefore, cannot at this rate be God, for he has ceased to be the Word, which was made flesh; nor can he be Man incarnate, for He is not properly flesh, and it was flesh which the word became. Being compounded, therefore, of both, He actually is neither; He is rather some third substance, very different from either.[94]

Tertullian preceded Arius by 150 years, but it was easy for Newman to see this passage as a prophecy of Arianism.

The contemporary application of all this was never far from Newman's mind. In a note to the passage on the 'Arianism or Sabellianism' of Apollinarianism, he cites the writings of Athanasius as the subject: the phraseology of his paraphrase shows how Blanco White was haunting him: 'Athan . . . hints they were Unitarians like Paul S'.[95]

The document ends with a view of heresy openly dispensing with history; as to the sects of Apollinarianism and their developments, he declares:

Which party held which tenet, it would be impossible to decide without historical evidence; for, as all heresies run into one, when a speculator has once departed from the narrow path of orthodoxy, it is a matter of accident which error he takes up with, as well as how long he will be contented with it.[96]

The lack of historical evidence about the sects did not prevent him from boldly proclaiming his *general* theory: all heresies run into one, and the specific forms ('which error') are now a matter of pure chance. But so far has Newman run, that he is in serious danger here of undercutting his own arguments: if the developments to which heresies eventually run are in the end accidental, how can the orthodox argue with such confidence that a heresy's *logical tendency* may be discerned? It is hard to avoid the suspicion that it is the orthodox *imputations* which are arbitrary, and that the whole argument is circular. Newman's adaptation of patristic polemic here undermines his pretensions to logical analysis. His phrase 'matter of accident', indeed, suggests that, at the end of this paper, he was not entirely confident in the rationality or power to convince of his own arguments. In his later public expressions of his theory of heresy's development, particularly as applied to contemporary figures, Newman was more careful to keep concealed this Achilles' heel.

These papers show Newman developing, against a background of contemporary heterodoxy, a general method of criticising heresy which scores its points by illustrating the relationship between heresy and infidelity. Its rhetorical possibilities are enormous, because they can be used as part of a strategy re-asserting patristic theology against contemporary liberalism, exposing proposals to modify ancient dogma as part of a vast process of secularisation. The equation of heresy and infidelity is not, in itself, a new stage in Newman's thinking. However, the *method* is new, in its subtlety and acknowledgment of complexity. Most important is the separation of a heretic's *intention* from the tendencies embedded in his language which have a life of their own. It is not therefore necessary for Newman to argue, baldly, that heretics are always in some sense, wicked. Rather, the real nature of a heresy is only made clear in its *developments*. The infidelity which he argues is inherent in *any* heretical position is tragically unintended. We may see this distinction between heretic and heresy as a result of Newman's strenuous and unsuccessful efforts to extricate theological issues from personal acrimony in the Hampden dispute. We may also think of his personal affection for Blanco White and his horror of the Unitarianism which his friend had in good conscience embraced. On the other hand, Newman has not completely broken with the arguments from *ethos*: the heretic has, in some sense, failed personally: there is a weakness somewhere, although he does not perceive it in himself. The heretic has opened a Pandora's box, and the dark forms emerging will spread and mutate, beyond the control of any theologian.

CHAPTER TEN

Tract 73: 'On the Introduction of Rationalist Principles into Revealed Religion'

I NEWMAN AND REVELATION: THE THEOLOGICAL BACKGROUND TO 'TRACT 73'

(i) *Rationalism, 'Liberalism' and Heresy*

Newman wasted nothing: the bitter feud and little pamphlet war against Hampden, his friend Blanco White's heartrending apostasy, his own theorising as he pored over the patristic accounts of Apollinarianism – all were sucked in by the sheer force of his obsessive sense of their contemporary application. Everything Newman touched confirmed his apocalyptic view of Christianity's imminent internal collapse, as intellectuals seemed to disparage the ancient creeds, only to replace them, in the name of toleration, with comprehensive formulae acceptable to the premises of the present age. This process was for Newman not only a *trahison des clercs*: it also included the busy preachers of popular Protestantism.

In *Tract 73*, Newman brought together an analysis of the tendencies of popular Protestant pietism with a critique of systematic theologians, in order to suggest that *both* were reducing the transcendant in divine revelation to human standards of judgment. While systematic theology was reductive in making mystery too clearly intelligible, popular evangelicalism brought it down to mere feeling. Newman saw *both* as forms of rationalism, because they presented revelation as something comprehensible, whether that comprehension be intellectual or emotional. Newman caught what has since been called the 'turn to the subject'[1] – the post-Enlightenment atmosphere in which religion was perceived as being about how human beings understand themselves, rather than about what God has revealed.

This atmosphere Newman portentously describes as a 'Spirit

abroad'. He equated this rationalistic spirit with *liberalism*, a term now used in its broadest possible application. The party-political sense of the word falls into the background – not that the specifically party sense of liberalism no longer threatened him: the controversy about the admission of Dissenters to Oxford was still in full swing. But in *Tract 73*, the most subtle of Newman's tracts, he played it down. He came at his opponents indirectly, by implying that they might be fitted into a universal framework of significance: they were playing out in modern dress roles played long ago in Christian Antiquity.

Tract 73 used the idea of the third-century Sabellian heresy in a uniquely personal way. In his writings previous to this tract, Newman has retained the historical sense of Sabellianism as a trinitarian heresy: the erroneous view that the three persons were only names for, or modes of, the one God's activity. Blanco White had come, via Sabellianism, to a denial of the Trinity. Hampden, too, seemed to be approximating to Socinianism – and so to a denial of the Trinity. But Hampden's virtual Socinianism (as Newman saw it) arose from his *general* understanding of revelation and dogma. In *Tract 73*, Newman consequently broadened the terms 'Sabellian', 'Sabellianism', to apply not only to a defective trinitarianism, but also to an inadequate, and ultimately infidel, theology of revelation. Just as early Church Sabellianism was modalist, in seeming to deny that the three persons really existed in the Godhead, so Newman identified as modalist certain theologies of his own age – those which presented revelation as an expression of human states and aspirations, rather than as a breakthrough of the divine into the empirical structure of human understanding.

Newman defended 'mystery' and 'reserve' in communicating religious knowledge,[2] because he saw revelation as intractable to human understanding. It was, he thought, heresy to suggest that we might recognise an authentic revelation simply because we perceive its excellence by the light of our human reason: this is to confound the natural and the supernatural, reducing the latter to the former. Newman's view is, of course, an extreme one, and one which his opponents would hardly have accepted as true of themselves. But this is precisely Newman's point: since the very essence of Christianity was threatened, a sharp distinction between natural theology and revealed theology has to be maintained, whereas intellectual apologists and popular preachers alike were blurring this distinction. Without realising it, they were contributing to Christianity's erosion, when they seemed to be advocating it.

(ii) *Newman and 'Evidencing'*

The task of the Christian apologist – to prove the truth of his religion – had never been more difficult than in the early nineteenth century. One method traditionally relied upon miracles, the fulfilment of Old Testament prophecies and the supposed veracity of witnesses to prove the truth of the New Testament. This method came to be called 'external evidencing', because it advanced proofs from *outside* the New Testament as to its authority and truth. However, confidence in such external evidencing had been shaken by the late eighteenth century, not least by the persuasive scepticism of Davis Hume.[3] Consequently, a new apologetic method arose, characteristic of Scottish theologians such as Thomas Chalmers and Thomas Erskine of Linlathen. They argued that the content of the New Testament had its own authority: the moral goodness of the message would itself convince the judgment of the enquirer and so convert him. This method was called 'internal evidencing'; it relied upon 'the intimate relation, or "fittingness", which inheres between the mode of being recommended in the Bible and the moral, physical and mental constitution of human beings'.[4] Particularly important to Erskine's case was his assertion of a 'point of contact' between moral insight and the knowledge of God.[5]

The first part of *Tract 73* (1835) is a sustained attack upon such internal evidencing. Newman's critique of Thomas Erskine's *Remarks on the Internal Evidence for the Truth of Revealed Religion* addresses an established trend in liberal Protestant theology, which was widely influential.[6] First published in 1820, Erskine's *Internal Evidence* had made a sensational impact, going into nine editions in as many years and being translated into French (1822) and German (1825).[7]

Newman was, of course doing something very similar to Erskine in his own apologetic. Erskine's view of the moral imperative as an existential encounter between God and Man resembles Newman's argument from conscience to the existence of God.[8] Moreover, like

Erskine, Newman was repelled by the rather glib reliance upon miracles as proofs, as his remarks upon William Paley's apologetic show.[9] Newman, however, restricts his moral proof to natural theology, that is, to proving God's existence. He saw Erskine as wrong in applying his moral proofs to revelation itself. Erskine seemed to Newman to be arguing that human reason, with its sense of right and wrong, could form a judgment about the truth of revelation. This Newman saw as reducing the revealed to the merely human. While, then, Newman thought that arguments from conscience could be used to convince an unbeliever of God's existence, he denied that anyone could come to *full* acceptance of Christianity, with all its revealed doctrines, without external evidence.

(iii) *'Critical Remarks Upon Dr Chalmers' Theology'*

Newman's disquiet about internal evidencing was not based only upon a theoretical disagreement about the respective spheres of natural and revealed thology. He also saw a link between internal evidencing and the evangelical emotionalism of revivalist preachers, who proclaimed the saving doctrine of Christ's sacrifice for sin in order to pierce the heart and effect conversion. Newman consistently regarded this as a sort of affective utilitarianism, because it reduced the content of revelation to its emotional usefulness. Preachers who strove to stir the affections of their audience[10] were but the popular manifestation of a liberalism which found its intellectual outlet in internal evidencing.

In 1834, Newman wrote an important paper, still extant though unpublished, on this theme – the *Critical Remarks upon Dr. Chalmers' Theology*,[11] which he may have read to a clergy meeting that year. Although it does not discuss internal evidencing, it provides valuable background to *Tract 73*. Newman identified a school of thought of which Chalmers is 'the most moderate and sensible'[12] exponent; it is 'a religious system exerting a considerable influence among us', and exemplifying a tendency, which in the later *Tract* he calls 'rationalism' and 'liberalism'.

The paper is, however, more than a critique. It contains a positive statement of Newman's 'own view'.[13] It is a more definite statement of his underlying position in *Tract 73* than we find there and may be used to complement it. Particularly useful is its exposition of the distinction between natural and dogmatic theology and its strictures upon the practical ills of the conflation of natural and revealed in the preaching strategy of evangelical Protestantism. Newman's comments upon *limits* of the theological task go some of the way towards explaining why in *Tract 73* he is more of an effective critic than a positive theologian.

Newman's 'own view' is an exposition of the relation between the natural and the revealed in relation to *conversion*. He sees factors external to revelation – 'conscience, tradition and the visible world moral and physical' – as bringing before man 'a certain creed, whether he obeys or neglects it'.[14] By 'creed', he means a belief-system derived from nature, and *preceding* the reception of revelation. It excites in those who heed it – for all have it in some form or another – 'chiefly fear, yet some hope' and a desire to do one's duty[15] before God. When the Gospel, 'Christ and his satisfaction' is proposed to such a one, he receives it, but this effects *no* change in the 'kind' of his religion. He is, as it were, *already* converted *before* the reception of revelation. His natural state accounts for the fact that he receives what is revealed: 'He cannot but pass from one to the other – not by a *revolution* of sentiment, but a *completion*.'[16] It follows that the Gospel should not be used to effect conversion, for this is the job of natural theology:[17] there is 'nothing' in the Gospel-doctrines 'to *convert the heart*': 'a man who does not obey God under natural religion, will not under the Law, nor under the gospel'.[18]

Newman's emphasis upon natural religion seems to leave little for revelation to do. He is happy, in this mood, to put it on a high shelf where it cannot be easily taken down and used:

> Should it be inquired what the peculiar message of mercy in the gospel has done for him, I reply it has given him *encouragement* – encouragement sufficient to outweigh the preponderating fears of nature, and the new disclosures which the Bible gives of sin.[19]

Newman is not entirely convinced even about this: over the final words, he adds, 'scarcely here?'[20] Nevertheless, his overall drift is clear enough: the Gospel initiates the believer into a higher level of 'degree and excellence',[21] where 'hope and joy' predominate over fear, but this is not a conversion different in kind from nature. He is most happy for the Gospel to be 'unreservedly' proclaimed to infants in the rite of baptism.[22] The Gospel, then, is best proclaimed where it can have least effect.

It is particularly in relation to the Doctrine of the Atonement that Chalmers offends:

He maintains that till a man receives the gospel he cannot love God – that the message of pardon is that in the gospel which makes him love God, opens his heart etc. – so that an appeal to the affections, not the conscience, is the characteristic and sole instrument ordinarily by which the Christian religion is heartily embraced . . . that the peculiar doctrine of the gospel, the love of God in sending His Son to die for us, the economy of the Atonement, is the doctrine exciting this gratitude – i.e. The instrument of conversion.[23]

Precisely this view will re-appear in the examination of Erskine and Abbott in *Tract 73*: that the presentation of the Atonement as persuasive device dangerously humanises revelation and evacuates its transcendent quality. This Newman associated with 'Sabellianism'.

(iv) *The link with Sabellianism*

The Chalmers document does not make the link with *heresy* as such. In March 1835, however, Newman did establish a relation between (internal) evidencing and heresy, in a fleeting reference in his letter to Henry Wilberforce, to 'Hinds, his notions about Inspiration (?) and his Sabellianism and Nestorianism'.[24] The reference is to Samuel Hinds' *An Enquiry into the Proofs, Nature and Extent of Inspiration and into the Authority of Scripture* (1831).[25] Hinds was a progressive clergyman, in the van of liberal Anglican theology, a client of Whately (his domestic chaplain in Dublin), who was eventually rewarded with the episcopal throne of Norwich. Newman had associated Whately's view of the Trinity with Sabellianism since 1827.[26] Hinds' book was concerned with revelation generally, not the doctrine of the Trinity. Reading it may have provided Newman with the link between Trinitarian Sabellianism and the liberal theology of revelation. 'Nestorianism' remains, however, a puzzle.

Hinds' treatise begins with a very old-fashioned ring for such an apparently *avant-garde* theologian: in setting out to counter 'slow-corroding scepticism',[27] he declares the only proof to be expected from any writer pretending to divine revelation is authenticating *miracle*.[28] This is warmed-up Paleyism – he even later in the book invokes proof from Old Testament prophecy – but it is *not* internal evidencing. Hinds' appeal is, in fact, external: he refers to the 'chain of external evidence',[29] and relies upon miracles to authenticate the authority of the New Testament.[30] Internal evidencing soon comes in, however, although Hinds is throughout cautious about its use. The task of establishing whether or not there *is* miraculous attestation amounts, in practice, to examining 'numerous links of proof'[31] – which is impossible for all but the most scholarly. If 'external evidences' are 'the boast and bulwark of Christianity', nevertheless 'it is to the internal that the Christian most appeals in secret for his own satisfaction and bosom comfort. Here he is at home'.[32] Internal evidencing has a more direct appeal to the ordinary person at a time when 'the mechanic and day-labourer'[33] are, through the spread of education, beginning to question the authorities for things. He thinks it possible, and he invokes St Paul's authority for it, for Christians to exercise judgment about what Scripture is: in I Corinthians, Paul, Hinds argues, appeals to the 'prophets and spiritual persons' to decide 'whether Paul had written the uncontrolled suggestions of his own mind; or the commands of the Lord – in other words, whether the Epistle was or was not in Scripture'.[34] This sounds 'rationalist', in Newman's sense, but this is not quite Hinds' drift: he is calling attention to the testimony of the Christian community, living in the 'spirit' and 'power', and particularly of those pneumatic individuals who are 'conscious of performing the very like miracles'.[35] They are qualified to recognise the supernatural or transcendent character of the apostle's message.

From this position, Hinds drifts into one which could with greater accuracy be described as a reduction of revelation to human preconceptions, in Newman's sense. He points to the purity and perfection of 'the moral instruction contained in Scripture [as] a proof of inspiration'.[36] Hinds does not see this as reductionist. Indeed, his point is that New Testament morality cannot be explained as a product of merely human powers.[37] However, it might be suggested that the decision that New Testament morality *is* of an excellence beyond human power to devise draws upon an already existing human standard of moral excellence, against which moral codes, including that of Scripture, may be judged. Hinds comes close to this:

The estimate we form of the authority of the Gospel as evidence depends, for example, on the view we take of man's intellectual powers – of the character, age and country of the individuals who wrote Scripture – of the contemporary progress of ethical knowledge elsewhere.[38]

Nevertheless, Hinds' position is very moderate. He does not wish to rely entirely upon the psychological authority of internal evidencing. He rather advocates a combination of both.[39] The inquirer 'should place before his mind, not only the separate result of any one process of proof but the combined result of all'.[40] In view of this, Newman's identification of him, albeit hesitantly, as heretical requires explanation. In fact, Hinds was indicted by association – as an ally of Whately. Moreover, Hinds, like Hampden, held that the *only* authority being Scripture, doctrinal 'tests' were merely 'judicial' matters, and the 'Fathers' 'human authorities'.[41] He therefore belonged to the theological party at Oxford, directly opposed to the Tractarians against whom Newman was egging Henry Wilberforce to write a pamphlet.

There is little evidence that Newman had read Hinds' book carefully or with discrimination. No notes or papers on it exist. The lack of material here suggests that Newman's somewhat tentative conclusion that the author was in some way heretical does not arise from a systematic working through of his treatise. It is more likely that the idea arose as part of a whole series of intuitive, highly speculative remarks made on the wing – for the private consumption of his inner circle of friends. Nevertheless, the reference to Hinds is very important, because it is the first occasion when Newman associates Sabellianism with a theology of revelation, rather than considering it, classically, as a Trinitarian heresy. Blanco White had shown how Sabellianism concealed Socinianism from its deluded adherent. Hinds' book, with its combination of internal evidencing and latitudinarianism, may have been the first step towards the idea, only clearly expressed in *Tract 73*, that the slide to infidelity via Sabellianism is not only a matter of *Trinitarian* error, but that, beneath the latter and accounting for it, there lies a more general, pervasive heresy regarding *revelation*, which is also, in some analogous sense, 'Sabellian'.

II THOMAS ERSKINE'S HERESY

Newman presents Erskine as the most noble of all the liberals: a good man, victim of a bad method. For Newman, Erskine's tragedy was that he had unwittingly accommodated his theology to the spirit of the age. Newman presented liberalism as a modern way of being religious, which sacrificed ancient truths to modern prejudices and was preparing the ground for outright atheism. Erskine, in swimming with the stream, was, Newman argued, contributing to the process whereby revealed religion would eventually be swept away altogether.

Newman's use of the term 'liberalism' has now become so broad as to be classified, by Lee Yearley, as a 'type of religiosity'.[42] Yearley omits to mention that Newman identifies this 'religiosity' with aspects of early Church heresy. Especially important is Yearley's description of one of the underlying principles of liberalism as 'Revelation as a Manifestation not a Mystery', the view that

any particular revelation indicates an ever-present situation; that revelation's encasement in ambiguous historical events makes its meaning dependent on the observer's ability to perceive; and that particular revelations need to be criticized and systematized because revelation's object is, at least in theory, completely understandable.[43]

As we have already seen, the word 'Manifestation' had appeared in his *Notes on Apollinarianism* as a description of the way Apollinaris presented Christ as a 'manifestation of the Godhead' – a step in the slide from a high Christology, via Sabellianism, to Arianism. Newman's definition of 'manifestation' in *Tract 73* marks a development: it is 'a system comprehended as such by the human mind',[44] and his reference is not just to patristic Trinitarian and Incarnational formulations, but, more inclusively, to the whole question of *revelation*: 'the revelation' of the 'truths' found in Scripture. He has effected a transition to a critique of theological liberalism by a broadening of his patristic heresiology. The assumption behind the liberal 'manifestation' theology is that revealed truths are by their very nature fully comprehensible, and that the intelligibility of the revealed object is a condition of belief in it. It is thus that Newman paraphrases Erskine's 'tendency': 'That is, I cannot believe anything that I do not understand.'[45] Newman will eventually, not without caution, lead on to the conclusion that this is a modern version of Sabellianism: just as the ancient heresy explained the persons of the trinity as aspects of God's activity in the world, rather than as eternal distinctions in God, so modern theologians such as Erskine explain revealed truths as comprehensible rather than mysterious, modes of God's self-expression to humanity, behind which He hides unknown.

Against this manifestation-theology, Newman advocates his own theology of *mystery*. There *is* a disclosure[46] to humanity of the hidden life of God, but it is not cognitively assimilable – it becomes problematic at the moment of its unfolding.[47] Human *language* is the medium of the revelation, but it cannot express clearly what it carries hidden within it: 'a doctrine lying *hid* in language, to be received in that language from the first by every mind, whatever be its separate power of understanding it; entered into more or less by this or that mind, as may be'.[48] Newman's negative theology here – that we must hang on to the language no matter how unintelligible to us for the sake of what is hidden in it – is a development of what will be familiar from his treatment of Chalmers: revelation is closed to human enquiry, it comes to us and we must accept it in obedience.

Newman's extreme conservatism here makes him identify systematic theology with heresy[49] in theology. Here he lay down a challenge to the systematic trends in the theology of his German and Caledonian contemporaries, to that impulse towards a presentation of Christianity coherent in terms of modern philosophy and scientific theory, which was flourishing in Schleiermacher, and which found such a powerful expression, in English, in the theology of Erskine. Newman presents revelation as dissonant, rather than harmonious in its interaction with man. Although there may be a relation between revealed truths, that relation has not itself been revealed, and, Newman suggests, perhaps could not have been:

> Revelation . . . is not a revealed *system*, but consists of a number of detached and incomplete truths belonging to a vast system unrevealed, of doctrines and injunctions mysteriously connected together; that is, connected by unknown media, and bearing upon unknown portions of the system.[50]

The rationally coherent coordination of these 'detached' elements, involves the introduction of governing principles derived from human understanding, not themselves revealed, so that the result is a *reduction* to system: 'Arrange and contrast them we may and do; systematize (that is, reduce them into an intelligible dependence on each other, or harmony with each other) we may not.'[51]

Newman's polemic against systematic theology merges with an

attack upon the emotionalism of popular Protestantism. Both intellectual apologists and evangelical preachers have in common the fact that they make central human experience rather than God. Consequently, Protestant preaching foregrounds the one revealed truth which seems to affect Man most, the Atonement of Christ on the cross for human sin. Newman would keep it as a 'wonder in heaven'.[52] He laments that it is broadcast because of 'its experienced effects on our minds, in the change it effects when it is believed'.[53] Although it seems at first fanciful to discern a link between systematic theology and sentimental preaching – and then to see them as both in some way 'Sabellian' – the example of Friedrich Schleiermacher suggests that Newman had, albeit intuitively, discerned a trend: the Father of modern protestant theology produced the first great post-Enlightenment system based on the idea of *feeling*. Moreover, he considered the classical doctrine of the Trinity to be so unimportant as to relegate it to an appendix. He also wrote a sympathetic account of Sabellius' theology.[54] Newman loved to draw conclusions from coincidences of this kind, and – as we shall see – when he had acquired a superficial knowledge of Schleiermacher, he found all his suspicions to be confirmed.

Contemporary apologists and popular preachers were, no doubt, all honourable men – Newman does not deny it. He presents them, rather, as unwitting victims of their partial and anthropocentric views. They have become heretics without really *meaning* to. For Newman,this is all grist to the mill: in his papers on the Apollinarian heresy he had already worked out a theory that can accommodate this paradox, the idea of the development of heresy. He can apply to Erskine the idea of a distinction between deliberate intention on the one hand, and, on the other, the tendency which may be drawn out of his theological discourse. This enables an oblique attack against liberalism which can, at the same time, disclaim any interest in *personal* polemic. It lets Newman out of some of the difficulties he got into over attacking Hampden. Thus, it is the direction of Erskine's approach, the ultimate logical consequence of his theological method that Newman is concerned to identify. At no point does he impugn Erskine's personal orthodoxy. Newman argues that there are two attitudes to revelation which, though distinct, are so close, that a transition is possible between them. First, there is Erskine's own method, of examining truths of revelation in relation to their conformity with what is humanly perceived as true and good, in order to recommend revelation as very likely to be true. Secondly, there is the more radical position: whatever is not in conformity with what we regard as true and good is not revelation. Newman's procedure here is familiar, both from his early treatment of Sabellianism, and his papers on Apollinarianism: there are two positions, the first more orthodox – even, apparently, innocuous, and the second a definitely heretical or rationalist position which can be arrived at by holders of the first. The two reasons given for the *slide* from the first to the second positions are also by now familiar. The first is to suggest a subtle modification from the argument of *ethos*: the 'slide' takes place because of a rationalism so deeply embedded that it is concealed from the heretic. The second is to argue the autonomous power of heretical discourse to develop uncontrolled. In Erskine's case, Newman advances *both*. Erskine exemplifies the rationalism of a well-intentioned theologian deploying a revisionist scheme with regard to the traditional orthodox formulae:

But it is the way with men, particularly in this day, to generalize freely, to be impatient of such concrete truth as existing appointments contain, to attempt to disengage it, to hazard sweeping assertions, to lay down principles, to mount up above God's visible doings, and to subject them to tests derived from our own speculations.[55]

The more radical tendencies of a theological discourse thus established will develop, Newman predicts, in a way unforeseen by their originator: 'Mr Erskine has been led on'. He is using the theory of heresy which he expounded in his treatment of the Apollinarian sects.[56]

It is in this context – of the application to contemporary liberalism of his theories about patristic heresy – that we find Newman's first very cautious employment of the term 'Sabellian'. On both the occasions that he associates Sabellianism with Erskine, he presents it as a development or consequence of Erskine's theology, rather than a consciously held tenet. On the first occasion, Newman is considering the *influence* of Erskine's 'leading idea', the 'habit of thought' engendered by 'the silent influence of such books as this of Mr Erskine's'. At this point, Newman uses the term 'Socinian' in harness with 'Sabellian': he does not clarify his view of their *relation* until later in the *Tract 73*.

He declares that Erskine's method will lead 'pretty nearly to Socinianism', and will render smooth the path to 'Sabellianism': 'Now, I would ask – do we never hear it asked, – have we never been tempted ourselves to ask, – "What is the *harm* of being, for instance, a Sabellian?" '[57] This is a subtle variation upon his theory of heresy's development: he imagines the state of public theological language after an injection of liberalism of Erskine's kind, and envisages it as facilitating or encouraging dangerous habits of mind. It shews his sense of theology as rhetoric, operating in the public sphere and moulding public opinion. His analysis in *Tract 73* moves beyond that of his Apollinarianism papers, where the argument takes place between theologians, the logical consequences of whose tenets may be drawn out, to the seething world of early nineteenth-century religion, with its voracious appetite for pamphlets, sermons, journals and religious literature of all kinds. Language is, as it were, the atmosphere breathed by believers – and Erskine's 'tendencies' have changed the quality of that atmosphere. Newman is, indeed, obsessively concerned with the purity of the air. His own attitude is not reactionary, however: he sees the process unconsciously engendered by Erskine as irreversible. Newman's aim is, rather, to stimulate awareness of the subtle, unconscious workings of religious self-understanding as it is affected by the currents of the times. One might say that he was attempting to bring liberal *ideology* to self-consciousness.

So far, in *Tract 73*, the terms 'Socinianism' and 'Sabellianism' have not been employed in any *special* sense: he is alluding to them as Trinitarian heresies. Socinianism would, of course, be a familiar enough term – often one of abuse – to the reader of the 1830s. 'Sabellianism' would have been a somewhat more mysterious term to all but those versed in the history of doctrine.[58] It is, indeed, probably for this reason that he uses the two terms in conjunction – 'Socinian' as it were, glossing the more unusual 'Sabellian'. On the second occasion when he describes Erskine as 'Socinian' and 'Sabellian', the point of departure is, still, the classical doctrine of the Trinity. Newman is considering a passage in which Erskine contrasts what he regards as the abstract formulations of the Doctrine of the Trinity, which makes 'no address either to our understandings, or our feelings, or our consciences', with the moral effect of such texts as 'God so loved the world that He sent his only-Begotten Son'.[59] Erskine's antithesis, as Newman describes it, derives from his experiential or affective theology of revelation. Newman is, therefore, now pointing towards an underlying cause for Erskine's exaltation of Atonement at expense of Trinity. Needless to say, this 'tendency' in Erskine is neither deliberate nor foreseen, but arises in its consequences. Newman exposes the 'tendency' by placing theology in a rhetorical context – demanding *how* Trinitarian orthodoxy may in practice be *advocated*, in the light of Erskine's 'developments':

Now I do not say that such a passage as this is a denial of the Athanasian Creed; but I ask, should a man be disposed to deny it, *how* would the writer refute him? Has he not, if a Trinitarian, cut away the ground from under him? Might not a Socinian or Sabellian convince him of the truth of their doctrines, by his own arguments? Unquestionably.[60]

Erskine's apologetic principle whereby doctrines are advocated leads him to seem to be saying, Newman argues, that revelation must always be perceived as reasonable – and that, by 'reasonable', is meant 'morally useful', so that, for Erskine, the Trinity 'is only influential as it exhibits the moral character of God'.[61] Here Newman finally identifies the broader 'Sabellianism' of Erskine's theology of revelation which underlies and accounts for his treatment of Trinity. The persons of the Trinity are reduced to modes or manifestations exhibiting God's 'moral character', the depth of the Trinity, rooted in the infinity of the Godhead, is rendered shallow, and the persons are cut off from any intrinsic relation to the essential divine life:

He has cut out the doctrine by its roots, and has preserved only that superficial part of it which he denominates a '*Manifestation*', – only so much as bears visibly upon another part of the system, our moral character – so much as is perceptibly connected with it – so much as may be comprehended.[62]

Newman's use of 'Manifestation' here moves beyond his identification of its historical use by Sabellians in patristic sources, and the approximation to this sense by some Apollinarians. He now employs it to describe a systematisation of revealed truths which, by the application of the *moral* as a principle of organisation and explanation, subsumes revealed to natural knowledge, thus destroying the transcendent element which, Newman argues, will always remain epistemologically intransigent.

Newman's treatment of Erskine has been notable for its tentative and sensitive probing of a liberal position. But Newman is not himself systematic. Indeed his technique is almost impressionistic as he picks a sentence here, a paragraph there from Erskine's book. The term 'Sabellianism' which he uses to establish the subtle connection between modern Trinitarian heresy and liberal theologies of revelation is introduced with a diffidence appropriate to his informal, experimental method of analysis: Newman floats an uneasy question and urbanely passes on. The mentions of Sabellianism have the calculated casualness of the throw-away line. Perhaps for this reason, the important place of the concept of Sabellianism in the rhetorical strategy of *Tract 73*, unifying Erskine's tendencies, diagnosing them, and distancing them from the immediate context, has gone unnoticed by commentators upon this *Tract*. This impressionism and diffidence of tone in the handling of Erskine shows Newman modifying polemic into a critique which sounds not unfriendly, and avoiding the imputation of Tractarian bigotry which some of his less equivocal contributions to contemporary debate had provoked.[63]

In *Tract 73*, then, the method of analysis derived from his Apollinarian papers enables Newman to make an advance on what was, in his treatment of Arianism, often a crude identification of heresy with personal moral weakness. He can now come to terms more adequately with the tragic dimension of heresy as a destructive error elaborated in good conscience by the heretic. This is a theme to which he returns more fully, in the second part of the *Tract*, in his treatment of Jacob Abbott.

III JACOB ABBOTT AND POPULAR EVANGELICALISM

The Corner Stone by Jacob Abbott,[64] the prolific American writer of popular religious books for the young, was a new arrival on the English scene. The Congregationalist theologian, John Pye Smith,[65] in his preface to one of the three editions of *The Corner Stone*[66] published in London in 1834, received favourably the work of an author previously unfamiliar to him.[67] It was this edition which attracted a hostile review in the Tractarian organ, *The British Critic*,[68] in 1836, and to which, in 1835, Newman referred in *Tract 73*, following his analysis of Erskine with a section on Abbott.

The Corner Stone is addressed to the 'young Christian',[69] employing a combination of narrative, poetic description of nature, homiletic and argument, to inculcate virtues such as hard work, abstemious habits and obedience to parents.[70] The later part of the book might be termed 'revivalist', aiming to stimulate an emotional conversion experience, describing in extended narrative one such revival, at Amherst College.[71] Although the book is frankly popular, it has a systematic dimension, treating of the main themes of Christian theology: God, nature, evil, providence and punishment, Christology, the Atonement and salvation, and the work of the Holy Spirit.

Newman presents Abbott as 'applying'[72] what is only a 'Sabellian' *tendency* in Erskine 'bringing out the tendency of Mr Erskine's argument',[73] so that 'Sabellianism' may be seen as a true development of what Erskine has not *explicitly* taught:[74] 'They are evidently of the same school.'[75] There *is* an historical link between Erskine and Abbott, albeit tenuous; in a letter to Erskine from Professor Noah Porter of Yale, in 1866, Erskine's *Internal Evidence* is acknowledged as a direct influence over the theology of the Andover school.[76] Since Abbott attended Andover in the early 1820s,[77] it is not improbable that the *Internal Evidence* directly influenced him. This may be Newman's meaning, although his scant knowledge of other details of New England theology makes this unlikely.[78] A more plausible explanation is that he is speaking more loosely: Erskine's tendency has entered theological discourse and been absorbed and developed by Abbott. Abbott and Erskine are 'of the same school' in the sense of participating unwittingly in the underlying movement of thought and sentiment, for which 'liberalism' is Newman's collective term. Abbott, then, stands in relation to Erskine, as the sect of Timotheus to Apollinaris. Abbott is the more explicit development of the spirit to which Erskine has given a more orthodox expression. A modern heresy has been 'unchained', and, as it develops, it progresses ineluctably towards infidelity.

Abbott's more explicit heresy arises from a radical application of revelation as 'a Manifestation of the Divine Character'. He regards revelation as 'a collection of facts'[79] considered entirely as a history providentially designed for their moral effects on human beings. Erskine, as we have seen, admitted a transcendent or irreducible element into his system; but Abbott, Newman argues, eliminates this altogether, limiting his discussion to the 'witnessed history of Christ upon earth'.[80] For Abbott, the *facts* themselves only, considered as events affecting human hearts, are separated from doctrines about them. Newman's presentation of Abbott's teaching is conditioned by his previous encounter with Hampden's distinction between revealed biblical facts and unrevealed ecclesiastical doctrines. Yet Hampden is not mentioned. This is skilful rhetoric – Newman can glance at Hampden without disturbing the pretension to be pursuing an enquiry of more universal relevance.

It is in relation to Abbott's revelation-as-facts that Newman catches him making a 'Sabellian' statement in his reference to 'the three great *Manifestations* of Himself to man which the one Unseen All-pervading Essence has made and exhibited to us in the Bible, and in our experience and observation'.[81] Newman's comment accords with what has already been shown about his use of the term 'Sabellian', that it can be applied not only to false teaching about the Trinity but also to certain views of revelation, and that the one goes with the other:

This sentence, be it observed in passing, savours strongly of Sabellianism; he has spoken of what he calls three Manifestations of Almighty God, as our natural Governor, as influencing the heart, and as in Jesus Christ, without there being anything in his way of speaking to show that he attributed these Manifestations respectively to Three Persons.[82]

Even here, Newman is tentative ('savours'): it is the result of his 'way of speaking', rather than of the contumacy of the heretic.

Newman finds *Socinianism* lying hidden beneath the Sabellian forms of Abbott's expressions. The distinction between orthodoxy and Socinianism is, in any case, according to Newman, a fine one: the difference between presenting the 'Economy' as containing otherworldly elements, and limiting it to 'the witnessed history of Christ upon earth'.[83] Abbott's approach, like Hampden's, concentrating upon the latter aspect, would, in the case of the Incarnation, naturally stress the humanity of Christ, rather than his Divinity. Newman argues that a Christology which *begins* from the statement, 'Man is God', will – although this is in itself orthodox – slide into the view that the Trinitarian persons mean no more than certain characteristics or dignities of God, that is, into Socinianism.[84] The Socinianism which Newman discerns arises as a consequence of Abbott's radical and untrammelled employment of a manifestation-theology which is also to be found in a less uncompromising form in Erskine. Erskine taught a 'double manifestation',[85] that in the Incarnation, its history and circumstances, although there is manifested primarily the mercy of God, there is also a divine breakthrough, 'of the Son of God personally in human nature',[86] even though he underplays this latter element at the expense of the former. Newman argues that Abbott, by contrast, eliminates the divine breakthrough and presents the person of Christ *entirely* as an expression of God's mercy, so that Christ was 'not more than a man aided by God, just as the conversion of the world was a human work aided and blessed by God'.[87]

Newman is now beginning to clarify his view of the relation between Sabellianism and Socinianism, along the lines of his patristic theory of heresy's development. Just as Erskine tends towards Sabellianism without consciously embracing it, so Abbott, definitely Sabellian, tends towards Socinianism: he is 'within a hair's breadth of Socinianism';[88] his manifestation-theology is 'a poorly concealed Socinianism'.[89] Newman suggests along lines familiar from his work on Apollinarianism, both that Abbott's Sabellianism *conceals* Socinianism, and that the former has in itself the capacity to develop into the latter. Although, therefore, Sabellianism at first hides its real Socinian essence, it also ultimately discloses it. The slide or development from a specious, or moderate, position into an infidel one is an inevitable feature of heretical discourse – and, Newman warns, may drag down its unwitting exponent, and those influenced by him, into something very close to atheism.

Thus Newman, although establishing a firm distinction between a heretic's intention and the meaning of his discourse, nevertheless is able to re-introduce a personal element, in the unwitting – and potentially tragic – fall of the heretic. Here he uses the passage from Blanco White's *Observations*, which had so struck him when he first read the book, in which it is declared that 'Sabellianism is only Unitarianism disguised in words.'[90]

Newman had been eager to *use* this idea as soon as he had heard about it, but its deployment seems, initially, feeble, in view of the fact that he has already declared Abbott's Socinianism to be 'poorly concealed'; Sabellianism can hardly be an appropriate designation for the hidden dangers of liberal theologies, if the disguise is so transparent. But Newman's point is subtle: Sabellianism conceals one's *own* infidelity from *oneself*, deluding one – as

Blanco deluded himself when an Anglican – that one is at least subscribing to something like orthodoxy, when one has in fact already departed from revealed Christianity: 'This passage of Blanco White proves this much, not perhaps, that the philosophising in question *leads* to Socinianism but may *be hid*, even from a man's own consciousness.'[91] Newman's 'turning' of Blanco's testimony of Unitarianism into a warning against the Sabellian tendency of liberalism involves a shift of perspective upon the idea of the development of heresy: he presents Socinianism, not so much as the next stop on the road leading from Sabellianism, as an already present but unperceived condition: the apostasy has *already taken place*, without the consent, or even the consciousness, of the apostate.

This 'turning' of Blanco is a powerful rhetorical instrument against liberals within the Church of England. The explicit profession of orthodoxy on the part of such theologians may, of course, be discounted – for they may be deluded. And this leaves free a large field of inference for the Tractarian critics. It is a strategy designed to engender unease.

Up to this point, Newman's picture of the stages in the liberal heresy's development has been relentless: internal evidencing to Sabellianism, Sabellianism to Socinianism, and thence to Unitarianism. Of these depths there is yet a lower, as Newman edges nearer to the conclusion that this *nexus* of heterodoxy will lead to an almost complete evacuation of revealed Christian theism. Newman does not call Abbott, or his tendencies, 'atheistic', but he does impute to *The Corner Stone* something close. He discerns 'pantheism'[92] in Abbott's concept of God: God's nature is so closely associated with the manifestation of His qualities in creation that Abbott's language, at any rate in Newman's understanding of it, seems to identify God and Nature, 'he speaks of God in pantheistic language, as an Anima Mundi, or universal essence, who has not known existence except in His works'.[93] God, thus diffused throughout the whole, acts 'impersonally' through nature, that is by means of 'laws' and 'provisions'.[94] The impersonation of God in Christ expresses in personal *form* the various energies whereby God is manifested in nature, concentrating them in Christ; they are 'condensed and exemplified in a real personal being'.[95]

Newman sees Abbott's Christology as part of the popular 'tendency to explain away Christ's divinity', beginning from the *human*, stressing *first* that 'Man is God', while the 'Catholic' and 'orthodox' tendency is to begin from the *divine*: 'God is Man'.[96] Therefore, to speak humanly of Jesus is a mark of heresy, as far as Newman is concerned: 'we must never speak, we have utterly no warrant to speak, of the person of the Eternal Word as thinking and feeling like a mere man, like a child or boy, as simply ignorant, imperfect and dependent on the creature, which is Mr Abbott's way'.[97] Newman's own 'Apollinarian' tendency[98] here emerges as an issue in his discussion of Abbott. If he did, indeed, slip into Apollinarianism, this would be a remarkable turn, an extraordinary lapse, in view of the depth with which he had surveyed this very heresy only weeks before! Moreover, his Christological sermons during the preceding months between March and May 1835, expound a classically orthodox position upon the unity of Christ. In, for example, *The Humiliation of the Eternal Son*, he declares of Christ that 'He took into His own Infinite Essence man's nature itself in all its completeness, creating a soul and body, and, at the moment of creation, making them His own.'[99] Before the Incarnation, the Word 'had thought and acted as God', but now it 'began to think and act as a man, with all man's faculties and imperfections, sin excepted'. Christ therefore experienced joy, grief, fear, anger, pain and 'heaviness' as fully as we do.[100] On the other hand, Newman is anxious to locate the *identity* of Christ in the person of the Divine Word. In *Christ the Son of God Made Man*, he presents Christ as 'in nature perfect man' but not in the sense that we are: 'He was not, strictly speaking, in the English sense of the word, *a* man . . . He was man because he had our human nature wholly and perfectly, but His person is not human like ours, but divine.'[101] It would therefore be inappropriate to speak of Christ as 'governed' by a 'human intelligence'. Christ *can*, at choice, act sometimes as God, and sometimes 'through the flesh'. He 'was not a man made God, but God made man'.[102] Newman is here arguing for the anhypostatic humanity of Christ, by no means formal Apollinarianism in the patristic sense.[103] In *Bodily Suffering*, although he sees the cry of anguish upon the cross as 'recorded for our benefit', he nevertheless accepts that Christ did genuinely experience, if only for a moment, something approaching despair: 'For one instant a horrible dread overwhelmed Him, when He seemed to ask why God had foresaken Him . . . the trial of sharp agony, hurrying the mind on to vague terrors and strange inexplicable thoughts.'[104]

Christ's human experience of mental suffering is real enough, although the manner of its occurrence is 'inscrutable' since He was 'all along supported by an inherent Divinity'.[105]

Compared with such passages in the sermons, Newman's treatment of Abbott appears to verge upon a position which may, with greater accuracy, be described as Apollinarian. However, even initially, one may observe that Newman's point here is subtle – an assertion, not so much about what the human Jesus felt, as about how we should *speak* of Him, in other words, the theological issue of the need for precise Christological formulation. He attempts to criticise the phraseology of the popularist Abbott, with the measured prudence of the theologian.

Unfortunately, much of Newman's analysis at this point is marked by a stridency which causes to slip the subtle, probing, analytical persona, possibly because he is concentrating more upon the authorial *personality* than was the case in his criticism of Erskine. In his treatment of Abbott, the gap which he has established between author and text is narrowed. However, this still does not amount, for all his irritation, to a personal attack upon Abbott, who is still presented as an *unwitting* heretic, although in the 'if you will', only just:

I have neither wish nor occasion to speak against him as an individual. For we have no concern with him. We know nothing of his opportunities of knowing better, nor how far what appears in his writings is a true index of his mind. We need only consider him as the organ, involuntary (if you will) or unwitting, but still the organ, of the spirit of the age.[106]

Newman will not 'reprobate' the man, but he *will* criticise the 'feelings' he expresses. This is, in fact, a re-introduction of the argument from *ethos*. Abbott's character is representative of a certain kind of piety engendering the text, which text, in turn, contains dangerous tendencies unforeseen by the author: 'Mr Abbott's theological system may be fitly followed by some specimens of the temper and tone of his religious sentiments. In this way we shall be able to ascertain the character of mind which such speculations presuppose and foster.'[107] We may expect that Newman, in exposing Abbott's heretical *ethos*, will also disclose his own: the question of his 'Apollinarianism' will also revolve around his 'temper' and 'tone', as well as his formal profession.

Abbott's fanciful description of Jesus as a human person is

something of a period piece: Jesus the Romantic enthusiast for the beauties of nature, who, storing his imagination therefrom, fashioned an oratorical style of powerful and original metaphorical impact. This was no rough and untutored peasant, but a civilised man, an elegant dresser and, indeed, something of an aesthete, an appreciator of good architecture.[108] The public success of Jesus' teaching ministry commands Abbott's admiration: it was wonderful how He did it all, without the benefits of modern communications, the postal service and the press.[109] His courage before suffering and adversity reminds Abbott of Napoleon.[110] His recreations from public life are such as we might expect from such a sensitive and poetic figure: lone rambles in the moonlight, communing with God and nature.[111]

Newman is more than provoked by this picture of Jesus, and his analysis is punctuated by expostulations which stab at the humanistic assumptions underlying it: '"There was no press!" What notions does this imply concerning the nature, the strength, and the propagation of moral truth!'[112] Newman sees Jesus as labouring under no 'disadvantage' through his lack of access to modern communications, for He is, primarily, divine, and therefore miraculously and inevitably successful: 'Under no disadvantage, if he were God'.[113] Newman's attitude towards the history of post-revolutionary France, the impact of which was in conservative circles still being felt in England, contrasts sharply with Abbott's easy republicanism. The patriotic Englishman and Tory bristles: 'Who could have conceived that there was any possible category under which the image of our Lord could be associated with that of Napoleon?'[114] He is also affronted by Abbott's picture of Jesus as Romantic communer with nature: 'Could the Creator of nature "stop to *examine*" and "enjoy the grace and beauty" of His own work?'[115] Newman does not think so; it is, rather, 'evidence of an earthly and Socinian bias in his view of the Saviour of mankind'.[116]

Newman's acid *ripostes* to Abbott's gushing enthusiasm are effective in pointing to the drawbacks of this popular theology. A doubt, however, lingers regarding his own Christology: Jesus, being God, was under no human 'disadvantage'; His was no human struggle and He experienced none of the wonder of a human mind in the presence of nature. Newman opposes any comparison between Jesus and other human beings: 'The Son of God made flesh, though a man, is beyond comparison with other men; His person is not human; but to say "most of all men" is to compare.'[117] Newman does not *deny* that Jesus *had* a human psychology but cannot bring himself to show how His Saviour used it. He was, emotionally, if not formally, Apollinarian, if we are to judge by his accumulated reactions to Abbott's presentation of Jesus.

To counteract this impression, however, there is also a finely drawn theological argument. Newman gives us more than outraged exclamation, and rhetorical enquiry: he also expounds post-Chalcedonian Orthodoxy, which, while taking account of Apollinarianism and Monophysitism, nevertheless locates the unity of Christ in the Person of the Divine Logos:

His [Christ's] personality is in His Godhead, if I may express myself in theological language. He did not undo what he was before, He did not cease to be Infinite God, but He added to Him the substance of a man, and thus participated in human thoughts and feelings, yet without impairing (God forbid) His divine perfection. The Incarnation was not a conversion of the Godhead into flesh, but a taking of the manhood into God.[118]

Newman, then, accepts Christ's full humanity – at any rate theoretically. He is not, however, interested in the reconstructed psychological experiences of a supposedly historical Jesus. Imbued with the Eastern Fathers, his eyes fixed upon a vision of the glorification and deification of humanity,[119] he stresses that the Word constitutes the unity of Christ's person.

To this classical expression of orthodoxy, Newman juxtaposes another *way of speaking*, which has been formulated in the modern age because of the demand for apologetic against the background of spreading unbelief. This latter – which, of course Abbott exemplifies – is a dangerous habit to which everyone has become more or less addicted.[120] He goes much further than his strictures upon Erskine, to present *any* apologetic which takes seriously the presuppositions and arguments of unbelievers as moving dangerously close to infidelity.[121] A slide from apologetic to infidelity may take place, he warns, when the slant upon revealed Christianity, necessitated by dialogue with unbelievers, becomes second nature, engendering 'an habitual disrespect towards what we hold to be divine, and ought to treat as such'.[122] And by 'treat as such', he seems to mean, 'not to touch at all'. For Newman, revelation has become the privileged language of faith, an hermetic discourse.

Newman may, then, be defended against the charge of *formal* Apollinarianism, in the patristic sense. His phraseology is the result of reaction against an opposed way of speaking – the low Christology of Abbott, a consequence of *beginning* from the human. Moreover, Newman's irritated rhetoric is balanced by the cooler, 'classical' statement of ancient and traditional Christological ortho- doxy. On the other hand, just as Abbott's 'rationalism' is a *consequence* of his way of speaking – which derives from his *ethos*, though is unintentional – may we not also declare that a form of 'Apollinarianism' is an unforeseen consequence of Newman's own way of speaking?[123] It is his own principle that an heretical tendency may be undiscerned by the heretic himself. It therefore seems not inappropriate to apply a 'tu quoque' to Newman, touching his final remarks about Abbott.

Several years after *Tract 73*, in 1843, Abbott and Newman had a surprisingly amicable meeting.[124] Later still, in a Note to the *Tract* in the Collected Edition, Newman recalled how Abbott 'met my strictures with a Christian forebearance and generosity which I never can forget', 'I think he [Abbott] felt what really was the case, that I had no unkind feelings towards him, but spoke of his work simply in illustration of a widely-spread sentiment in religious circles, then as now, which seemed to me dangerous to gospel faith.'[125] The generosity of his tribute to Abbott suggests that Newman suspected the *persona* he was affecting in *Tract 73* had slightly slipped. Nevertheless, this later statement is a good account of Newman's rhetorical purpose in the *Tract* as a whole.

Newman's striving for polemical restraint is all the more remark- able in the light of two characteristic prejudices of his class and party.[126] First, there was his ambivalence towards the 'popular': although he saw the *Tracts for the Times* as themselves a popular appeal over the heads of the powers that be,[127] nevertheless, popular revolutions and social upheavals were associated in his mind with the great apostasy which would take place before the apocolyptic arrival of Antichrist.[128] Secondly, Newman's attitude to America, occupied, it must be remembered, by republicans and secessionists, was often hostile.[129] He does identify the explaining away of Christ's divinity as a popular mode of speech but does not, on the whole, subject Abbott to the hostile rhetoric of which he was capable.

Only at the very end of the *Tract*, does he issue a severe, blunt and dramatic condemnation, extending not only to Abbott but also to Erskine. As individuals, indeed, he will exonerate them from the harshness of his conclusion – 'the good will be separated from the bad'.[130] He will not spare 'the School, as such'. To this he applies that 'ancient phrase' he borrowed, via Bull, from Eusebius, and describes Sabellianism as a stage in a tragic, predestined journey: 'the School . . . will pass through Sabellianism to that "God-denying Apostasy", to use the ancient phrase, to which in the beginning of its career it professed to be especially opposed'.[131]

IV 'POSTSCRIPT': NEWMAN AND SCHLEIERMACHER

Newman's analysis in *Tract 73* was restricted to two outsiders to academic theology.[132] Six months later, however, on 2 February 1836, he wrote a short but wide-ranging 'Postscript' upon 'the Sabellian tendencies of the day',[133] in which he extended the discussion to continental and American theology, in particular to Friedrich Schleiermacher, who had, by the early 1830s, published the works[134] which were to establish his reputation.

On the face of it, Schleiermacher's theological method opens him to the criticism that he is, in Newman's peculiar sense of the term, a 'Sabellian'. *The Christian Faith*, first published in 1821–2, attempts to order the doctrines of Christian revelation in terms of a human feeling or state of consciousness,[135] which is the universal basis of all religions, 'the feeling of absolute dependency'.[136] Christianity is for Schleiermacher the most perfect form of religion, because it enables the God-consciousness[137] latent in all human beings most effectively to be released from bondage. This release, effected by a revelation in Christ which is certainly new and which cannot be exhausted by historical explanation,[138] is what Schleiermacher calls redemption – and it is in terms of this that Christianity is systematically presented.[139] Although, then, the original impetus of the Founder of Christianity is more than merely human, most of Schleiermacher's re-statements of Christian doctrines present them as expressions of human states of mind.

Most important in relation to Newman are, first, Schleiermacher's redefinition of the divinity of Christ in terms of human psychology,[140] and, second, his criticism of the classical doctrine of the Trinity's insistence upon *eternal* relations within the Deity, for not being 'an immediate utterance concerning the Christian self-consciousness.'[141] Schleiermacher is, indeed, preoccupied almost exclusively with the 'economy' of salvation, 'we have no formula for the being of God in Himself as distinct from the being of God in the world'.[142] The doctrine of the Trinity is presented as due for revision,[143] because it does not directly relate to human 'god-consciousness', and is relegated to the very end of his systematic theology.

Moreover, Schleiermacher's use of a priori categories – philosophical, sociological and psychological – is open to Newman's critique of 'system'. It may be that, as S.W. Sykes points out, the 'crude objection that Christianity is being evaluated in the light of some prior notions about religion' is disposed of by distinguishing methodologically the matter of revelation from the categories used to clarify and systematise it, and by saying that such categories are only 'over' Christianity in a 'formal' sense. The doubt, however, remains that Schleiermacher's approach has far-reaching consequences 'for the form of any subsequently articulated Christian doctrine of humanity'.[144] To attempt to put this into Newman's terms might be to say that, even if Schleiermacher did not intend to sit in judgment upon revelation, his method would lead to a theology appearing to be dangerously close. A Newman might argue that Schleiermacher, like Erskine, has been 'led on'.

How, exactly, Newman's concept of 'Sabellianism' may be applied to Schleiermacher can only partially be expounded. Newman did not read German, although he toyed with the idea of learning it,[145] and therefore did not have access to Schleiermacher's principal works, which were untranslated. Pusey's study of German theology,[146] which he did read, with considerable bewilderment,[147] does not expound the principles of Schleiermacher's systematic theology, although it does convey admiration for him, and seems to have absorbed a not dissimilar experiential approach.[148] Perhaps Newman and Pusey discussed Schleiermacher together, but, if so, there is little evidence that Newman got to grips with the latter's theology of religious feeling. Must we, then, conclude, with Lee Yearley, that 'Newman never really faced the more weighty Liberal alternative'[149] of Schleiermacher?

It is not true to say, as Yearley does, that Newman 'knew Schleiermacher ... only through a second-hand report on his Trinitarian ideas'.[150] In fact, the document in Newman's hands was a weighty and detailed translation of, and commentary upon,

Schleiermacher's treatise upon the Sabellian heresy. In the 1836 'Postscript', Newman refers to an 'American periodical' which has come into his hands since the writing of *Tract 73*. It contains 'an account of Dr Schleiermacher's view of the doctrine of the Holy Trinity'.[151] This was *The Biblical Repository and Quarterly Observer* for April and July, 1835, which contained a full translation, with notes, of Schleiermacher's 'On the Discrepancy Between the Sabellian and the Athanasian Method of Representing the Doctrine of the Trinity.'[152] The translator was Moses Stuart, Professor of Andover Seminary, who makes an extensive contribution to the discussion, both elucidating Schleiermacher's position, and making his own, somewhat different, view clear. The two articles amount to 200 pages. Schleiermacher's treatise analyses in detail the evidence for a historical reconstruction of Sabellius' teaching, and places him against the background of his precursors, Artemon, Praxeas, Noetus and Beryll. Moses Stuart had also translated a section of *The Christian Faith* concerning the doctrine of the Trinity.[153] Although, therefore, Newman's understanding of Schleiermacher's theology of feeling would have lacked depth, because he had not read the works which fully expounded it, it is untrue to say that he had 'a second-hand report on his Trinitarian ideas'.[154] The material at his disposal was first-hand, full and specific.

Schleiermacher's account of Sabellianism is conditioned by an attitude towards the ancient Church, and towards heresy and orthodoxy, antipathetic to Newman's. He contrasts Sabellianism with the 'Athanasian view', which he also confusingly refers to as the 'Athanasian symbol' – he does not mean the Athanasian Creed, but the theology promoted by Athanasius which triumphed at the councils of Nicea and Constantinople, and issued in the Niceno-Contantinopolitan Creed.[155] Schleiermacher's declared aim is to correct this latter orthodox Trinitarian formulation, which has reacted too far 'in opposition to Sabellianism'.[156] The problem of the Trinity is presented as the need to steer a course between Judaistic monotheism on the one hand, and Hellenistic polytheism on the other; reaction against heresy on one side led to a closer approximation to the opposite error.[157] Sabellianism was a valuable expression of an essentially orthodox insight, which, because of the bitterness of controversy, was not allowed to develop into full balance and precision, to the cost of ancient orthodoxy.[158]

The positive value of Sabellianism for Schleiermacher is that it distinguishes between the Divine Monad or Godhead on the one hand, and *all* three persons of the Trinity on the other. Rejection of Sabellian theology prevented this distinction from being made clearly enough in orthodox Trinitarianism. The 'oscillation' or instability in the orthodox doctrine[159] derives from a fundamental mistake: to regard the persons of the Trinity as subsistent distinctions within the Deity introduces, in the terms 'Father' and 'Son', relations of dependency and inequality into the Deity.[160]

Schleiermacher gives us an essay in the history of dogma, reconstructing in detail Sabellius' teaching and carefully distinguishing it from the heresiarch's cruder predecessors. While the latter often seemed to say that the persons of the Trinity are merely names of different divine activities, Sabellius declares them to be real distinctions. However, for Sabellius the persons did not *always* exist in God. They were, rather, creative developments of God, expansions of His being, which came into existence as a result of God's interaction with the world. God *became* Father in Creation, Son in redemption, and Spirit in bestowing charisms on humanity. The three persons will abide for as long as it takes for the world to be saved.[161] Schleiermacher approves of this theology because it is based on the economy of salvation and avoids pointless prying into the unknowable essence of God.[162] Of course, to allow change within God would hardly satisfy the Fathers of the Church, or a modern advocate of neo-patristic theology like Newman. But this does not concern Schleiermacher, who is committed to a radical re-statement of ancient dogmas.

When one turns to Newman's use of Schleiermacher's treatise, one is struck by the perfunctory quality of his remarks.[163] Schleiermacher has raised important *historical* questions about the nature of orthodoxy in relation to Sabellianism, which Newman makes no attempt to meet. Moreover, Newman makes no distinction between the theologies of Erskine and Abbott, and that of Schleiermacher and of Moses Stuart, 'The American publication above alluded to is a melancholy evidence that the theologians of the United States are bringing the learning and genius of Germany to bear in favour of this same (as the writer must call it) spurious Christianity.'[164] In three short sentences, Newman identifies three underlying assumptions or tendencies which he holds are found, not only in Erskine and Abbott, but also in Schleiermacher and Stuart. They are, first, that the object of revelation 'is to stir the affections and soothe the heart', secondly, that revelation 'really contains nothing which is unintelligible to the intellect', and, thirdly, that 'misbelievers, such as Unitarians, etc. are made so, for the most part, by Creeds, which are impediments to the spread of the Gospel, as being stumbling-blocks to the reason and shackles and weights to the affections'.[165]

Only a caricature of Schleiermacher's thought could be made to harmonise with all three of these statements. As we have seen, his treatise on Sabellius does not provide an exposition of his theology of feeling, which is only to be found in untranslated works. Moreover, although it is clear that Schleiermacher identifies revelation with the 'economy', he does not go so far as to say that it is totally intelligible to the intellect, nor does Newman provide us with any analysis to show that he implies it. Schleiermacher does, it is true, suggest that the difficulties of Unitarians are caused by creeds: it is part of his case that the inadequacies of traditional Trinitarianism have caused such divisions. He does not regard Unitarians as 'misbelievers': 'in point of fact their piety is by no means lacking in the specifically Christian stamp'.[166] It is here that Newman and Schleiermacher face one another most directly: for Schleiermacher, membership of Christianity is defined by a psychological canon – Christianity is a certain quality of religious feeling or 'piety' – whereas for Newman acceptance of the creeds is an important part of any definition of what it means to be Christian.

All this is not to say that Newman may not have identified a tendency in Erskine and Abbott – a tendency in Newman's own peculiar sense 'Sabellian' – which may not also be applied as a critique of Schleiermacher. The point is, rather, Newman's apparent unwillingness to provide a fuller and more precise critique, even on the basis of what was translated into English. This is all the more surprising in view of the full and sensitive treatment of Jacob Abbott, a comparatively minor figure.

Perhaps, Newman's concern is not so much Schleiermacher as developments on the American religious scene. His use of quotation suggests this: all his references to the *Biblical Repository* articles are to the translator's, Moses Stuart's, contributions.[167] With regard to the 'Sabellian tendencies of the day', Newman concludes, 'These extracts are perhaps sufficient to justify the apprehensions above expressed, as far as the more religious part of Protestant America is concerned.'[168] Newman adds that 'Protestant France also would afford similar evidence'[169] of the Sabellian tendency. Germany, for all its 'learning and genius'[170] is, perhaps, seen by Newman as too far gone to elicit concern.

Newman, however, substantially misunderstands Stuart's own position on the Trinity, as well as the North American context of Trinitarian debate. A full and careful reading of the *Biblical Repository* articles would have provided the information on the first point at least, but Newman's selective use of quotation presents a picture of Moses Stuart's theology which is the exact opposite of the truth.

Stuart does agree with Schleiermacher that patristic theology needs reformulation and accepts his German contemporary's point that the familial language of the doctrine of the Trinity misleadingly implies either subordination of the Son, or tritheism.[171] He is impressed by Schleiermacher's 'economic' Sabellianism because it keeps us rooted in the tangible realities of church life: in a passage cited by Newman, Stuart approves of Schleiermacher's question, 'What more can further the interests of practical piety?'[172] However, Stuart does not go along with developments within God as part of the economy of salvation, 'God must be *in seipso* what he has revealed himself to be.'[173] For Stuart, the three persons existed in God from all eternity. What *are* constituted, however, as part of the 'Economy' are the *names* themselves of these distinctions, so that, for example, the second person of the Trinity *became* 'Son' in the Incarnation, although the Incarnation had a pre-existent, ontological basis.[174]

Moses Stuart, then, is seriously misrepresented by Newman, even on the basis of the information Newman had in front of him. Moreover, when Stuart is seen in his own American context, there are still stronger grounds for the view that he has been unfairly treated. In New England, Unitarianism had been growing since the eighteenth century. It took two forms: first, the 'Arians', influenced by Samuel Clarke's *Scripture Doctrine of the Trinity*, who held that Christ was less than God but more than man; secondly, the 'Socinians' or 'humanitarians', who held that Jesus was no more than a man with a special divine mission.[175] The anti-Trinitarian movement was associated, in Congregationalist circles, with a liberal revolt against Calvinist orthodoxy. After bitter controversy over the appointment of two 'liberals' to Harvard professorships, in 1808, Andover, the seminary of which Stuart four years later became a professor, was formed as a breakaway movement to be the rallying-point for Trinitarian orthodoxy.[176] It was Stuart who entered into controversy against the leader of the Unitarians, William Ellery Channing.[177] In 1819, Stuart prophesied that Unitarianism was a halfway house on the road to infidelity[178] – a view close to Newman's own. Stuart refers to his controversy with the Unitarians in the *Biblical Repository* article[179] – and, surprisingly, Newman quotes this reference as his last in a series of quotations to prove the 'Sabellian' tendency in North American theology: 'It may be proper for me to say, that the results of this re-examination of the Doctrine of the Trinity are, in their essential parts, the same which I some years since advocated in my letters addressed to the Rev Dr Channing.'[180] But, as we have seen, Stuart's line could hardly be called 'Sabellian'. One can only assume that it was the word 're-examination' which attracted Newman's, at this point, undiscerning, hostility. Newman's failure to read Moses Stuart accurately cannot be explained by saying that he had perhaps omitted to read the Translator's final section where Stuart makes his own view clear, because Newman's final quotation, in reference to the Channing controversy, belongs to this very section. Therefore, his reading must have been careless, skimming through Stuart's pages to find quotations to fit a preconceived view formed during the analysis of Erskine and Abbott.

Perhaps Stuart's enthusiasm, albeit critical, for a German theologian would have implicated him with what was, as far as Newman was concerned, a major source of heresy and unbelief. Hostility to German critical theological scholarship was apparent in Newman's pre-Tractarian period: for example, his 1832 description of Gesenius, Professor of Theology at Halle, as 'an unbelieving Hebraist'.[181] Moreover, earlier still, in 1829, when Newman was being consulted by Pusey about his controversy with H. J. Rose,[182] he would have come across Rose's thesis that, in German theology, rationalist unbelief had taken over in the guise of Christianity.[183] His impression of Schleiermacher's treatise would only have confirmed this attitude. By 1841, after he had read Milman's footnote about Schleiermacher's silence on the resurrection,[184] Newman was referring as a matter of course to 'the sceptical and infidel writers of Germany'.[185] By 1845, 'Germanism and infidelity' had become synonymous.[186]

It was prejudice, then, which compounded Newman's linguistic limitation, prevented him from offering a worthy critique of Schleiermacher and even distorted his understanding of fellow theologians writing in America in his own language. It is a measure of the narrow parochialism of early nineteenth-century Oxford that it was no very damaging admission for Newman to reveal such *lacunae* in his theological understanding, in his 'Postscript'.

The 'Postscript' rounds off the process by which Newman came to discern a modern form of Sabellianism in his liberal contemporaries, in which an experiential or moral theology of revelation underpins a mildly heterodox Trinitarianism (Sabellianism) concealing Unitarianism: it is the 'Socinianism of Sabellianism'. Having evolved this 'Sabellian' critique, Newman will return to it fitfully in subsequent years, although we have to wait until 1841 before he again uses the idea of Sabellianism on a large scale, in his review of Milman's *History of Christianity*.

CHAPTER ELEVEN

The 'Elucidations' on Hampden

The inception of the process leading to the evolution of this idea of 'Sabellianism' was, it will be remembered, the controversy surrounding Hampden about Oxford matriculation. Only a week after Newman had completed the 'Postscript', he again returned to the subject of Hampden, when the controversy moved into a second phase. On 8 February 1836,[1] it became known that Hampden's name had been put forward to the King for the Regius Professorship. There was just time for a last improvised protest to avert Hampden's occupation of the Chair. Newman made his contribution on the night of Wednesday, 10th February, he 'sat up all night at pamphlet against Hampden'.[2] The *Elucidations* had, in fact, a limited function: to demonstrate overwhelmingly, from Hampden's own works, that the professorial nominee's theology was indistinguishable from Socinianism – and to do so with the minimum of comment, so that the pamphlet might act as a reference-work, providing quotable ammunition at a moment's notice. He demands: 'Now, supposing hearers of his were to take up with Socinianism would he be *earnest* in reclaiming them or not?'[3]

Hampden's theology of revelation-as-facts could easily be made to fall into Newman's category of 'Sabellian'. Was not the controversy over the Regius Professorship a further opportunity for Newman to deploy this critique, especially since it was fresh in his mind from the 'Postscript' written only a week or so earlier? Yet there is not a single reference in *Elucidations* to Sabellianism.

One possible explanation may lie in the *function* of the pamphlet: Sabellianism as Newman uses it, is a complex, subtle, many-sided and, indeed, sometimes elusive concept. He may have judged it inappropriate for immediate need on this occasion: to drum up support by a clear and uncomplicated appeal to the lower clergy. It was not an occasion for theological subtlety. Still, this does not explain why, in the numerous letters Newman wrote about

Hampden, he *never once* called him 'Sabellian'. There is a deeper answer than the exigencies of a localised controversy.

The conflict between Newman and Hampden had been particularly acrimonious in its first stage concerning matriculation. Newman, for his part, had in 1834–5 attempted to distinguish between his opponent's personality and his teaching. However, by January 1836, Hampden had assumed a shape more awesome than any ordinary heretic: it was no use any longer to 'mince matters' – he was the 'Forerunner of Antichrist'.[4] In a revealing letter, commenting upon the publication of the *Elucidations* in the *British Critic*, of March 1836, by which time Hampden was *in situ* as Regius Professor, Newman provides some evidence about why he never called him a 'Sabellian' – he is far too *bad*. Newman tells his correspondent that he could not possibly 'picture anything a quarter so bad as he really is'.[5] He is *worse* than a Socinian, and much worse than the other heretics of the day,

There is no doctrine, however sacred, which he does not scoff at – and in his Moral Philosophy he adopts the lowest and most grovelling utilitarianism as the basis of Morals – he considers it as a sacred duty to live to this world – and that religion by itself injuriously absorbs the mind. Whately, whatever his errors, is open hearted, generous, and careless of money – Blanco White is the same, though he has turned Socinian – Arnold is amiable and winning – but this man, *judging by his writings*, is the most lucre-loving, earthly minded, unlovely person one ever set eyes on.[6]

The qualification, 'judging by his writings', scarcely offsets the *animus* of this passage. While the *British Critic* reviewer of *The Corner Stone* had not hesitated to fling the charge of 'utilitarian' at Abbott, Newman had forborne.[7] However, he now brings it in to describe Hampden, though in a somewhat different sense. Hugh James Rose had, in January 1836, called his attention to Hampden's moral philosophy as 'worse than the Bamptons'.[8] Newman's interpretation of its consequences is applied directly to Hampden's 'unlovely' personality: his acceptance, without scruple, of the Chair, despite the outcry at Oxford, is the result of a worldliness born of his utilitarian ethics. The sarcasm of 'sacred duty' is stinging. It is therefore easy to see why Newman could not bring himself to introduce Sabellianiam into his discussion of Hampden, for he reserves this term, in his own peculiar use of it, to describe an unconscious tendency in thinkers, who, though erroneous, are accorded respect and sympathy.

CHAPTER TWELVE

Apollinarianism revisited

Newman returned to the subject of Apollinarianism in late June 1836, five months after Hampden's appointment to the Regius Professorship. Liberalism had triumphed at Oxford – at any rate in the matter of 'canonries and stalls'. Meanwhile, Newman had been continuing his imaginative re-drawing of the authentic Christian *ethos*, in his *Letters on the Church of the Fathers* for the *British Magazine*, continued with interruptions from 1833 until 1837.[1] The sixteenth *Letter* is entitled 'Apollinaris'.[2]

Letter XVI bears a close literary relation to Newman's long unpublished manuscript of 1835, *Apollinaris' history*, which he had originally declared was a bringing together of material to be eventually re-cast, as the need arose.[3] *Letter XVI* is one such re-casting. Newman's awareness of the needs and limitations of a popular, rather than a learned, readership, against the background of a continuing struggle against theological liberalism,[4] accounts for the nature of his very considerable redaction of the original paper.

The character of *Letter XVI* is most readily defined by what is *omitted* from *Apollinaris' history*: his theory of the development of heresy, and the connected theological discussion of Apollinarian sectaries. His *theories*, though not the doctrinal details by which he arrived at them, found their way, as we have seen into his discussion of Erskine and Abbott, under the different category of 'Sabellianism'. *Letter XVI*, however, aims at an altogether lighter and more straightforward contribution to Newman's anti-liberal strategy.

Moreover, specifically *doctrinal* discussion of Apollinaris is severely attenuated. Newman wisely does not count upon a relish for the intricacies of patristic scholarship on the part of the *British Magazine*'s readers. He restricts himself, at the outset, to a precise, but brief few sentences, freshly written, which define the Apollinarian heresy. Apollinaris' purpose was, we are told, 'to secure more completely the doctrine of the divinity of our Lord's person',[5] in the face of Arianism. This seems harmless enough – and a theological definition of it makes it appear even more harmless:

our Lord, though perfect man, as far as nature is concerned, is not a man in the sense in which any given individual of the species is such, his person or subsistence not being human, but divine. Apollinaris seemed to say no more than this, that our Lord had not that particular part of human nature in which personality seems to reside – viz., the rational part of the soul. Such is the seemingly trivial character of his doctrinal error.[6]

Newman finds himself, as an upholder of orthodoxy, very close to the heretic, not surprisingly, in view of his remarks upon Abbott. However, even this – the apparent 'triviality' of his error – will be used as a shaft against liberalism, when Newman draws the threads together at the conclusion of the article.

Newman includes from *Apollinaris' history* the material which is most vivid and least erudite or speculative. The ornate and resonant opening sentences of this document[7] appear, with only minor alterations, as the opening of *Letter XVI*. So does most of the narrative, historical material concerning Apollinaris' upbringing and education, his early apologetic work, his rise as an opponent of Arianism and ally of Athanasius, his slide into heresy unsuspected by the latter, the 'open avowal', his condemnation and death.[8]

Newman chooses material which not only tells a good, simple story, but also serves his polemical purpose. The accumulation of impressive details about the learning and zeal of Apollinaris acts as the prologue to a tragedy. Even such a man as this, Newman warns, can fall. He also draws from his original fount details that are subtly disturbing, although he tactfully avoids underlining this too heavily: Apollinaris was highly trained in rhetoric and letters, then moved into philosophy and 'began to distinguish himself by his opposition to philosophical infidelity'.[9] His refutations of paganism were 'on grounds of reason'.[10] In the light of his own reservations, in *Tract 73*, about apologetics of any kind – 'internal' or, in the end, even 'external' evidence – this is clearly intended to sound sinister.

The account of Apollinaris' orthodox phase at Athanasius' side and his degeneration, at first unnoticed, into heresy is lifted, with a few minor alterations, from *Apollinaris' history*. The detailed quotations concerning the Council of Alexandria, in 362, where the 'first intimations' arose of the heresy later associated with Apollinarianism, are curtailed. Apollinaris is absolved from dissimulation at this stage of his development, when he was moving towards heresy without openly avowing it: 'I have no intention of accusing so considerable a man of that disingenuousness which is almost the characteristic of heresy.'[11] In fact, Athanasius was exercising a retarding influence over his mind. When the great man died it was natural that 'he should find himself able to breathe more freely, yet be unwilling to own it'.[12] As with Apollinarianism's 'Sabellians' – Blanco White and Erskine – self-deception takes place. Here, he indulges in some editing of the original fount: *Apollinaris' history* reads: 'While indulging the speculations of a selfwilled and presumptious intellect, he still endeavoured to persuade himself that he was not outstepping the range which Scripture prescribed and Athanasius had observed.'[13] This could almost be Blanco White: the rationalism, though the outcome of an unregenerate *ethos*, is tragically concealed from its exponent by delusion. In *Letter XVI*, he slants the phraseology in the direction of the contemporary debate initiated by Tractarianism: 'While indulging the speculations of a private judgment, he might still endeavour to persuade himself that he was not outstepping the range which Scripture had prescribed, and the Church Catholic witnessed.'[14] Apollinaris' dilemma is no longer portrayed as that of an individual character, sloughing off unwillingly the influence of a loved and revered spiritual father: he has come, in Newman's redaction, to stand for the typical Protestant liberal, for whom the exercise of 'private judgment' – almost always an opprobrious term in Newman, virtually synonymous with 'heresy' – is the real, though still concealed, impetus. And 'private judgment' is, in a classical expression of the Tractarian position, opposed to the witness of the 'Church Catholic'.

This 'outline of a melancholy history',[15] drawn from *Apollinaris' history*, leads up to an entirely *new* piece of writing which brings the *Letter* to an end:[16] five paragraphs, the first two being closely argued justification of the Tractarian position on dogma, for which the biography of Apollinaris has served as an attractive introduction predisposing the reader towards a sense of the *need* for precise doctrinal distinctions.

Newman begins by taking the line to which one has now become accustomed in his 'Sabellian' critique: the road to heresy is paved with good intentions. His already established connection between Sabellianism and Apollinarianism in the expression of this theme emerges starkly – not only as a logical necessity, but an historical fact: 'It is a memorable and very solemn fact that of the zealous opponents of Arianism and friends of Athanasius, two of the principal fell into heresy – Apollinaris into the heresy above spoken of, and Marcellus into a sort of Sabellianism.'[17] The 'lesson' of this need not be drawn out, Newman declares – but he draws it out anyway: 'the "straitness" of the true faith, and the difficulty of finding and keeping it, in the case of thinking and speculative minds'.[18] Newman's procedure implicitly acknowledges the complexity of a modern apprehension of patristic orthodoxy: it has first to be *found* before it can be kept – it cannot be absorbed as part of the atmosphere, he seems to be suggesting, as in days of old; both finding and keeping are difficult in an age of intellectual self-consciousness. Newman is a subtle advocate: he invites identification with Apollinaris, who was both zealous and intellectual and does not exclude *himself* from the danger. The reader, thus both flattered and warned, is then explicitly confronted: 'at this day a reader may ... be tempted to question the necessity of such exactness in doctrine, in order to possess the title and hopes of a Christian'.[19] The contemporary issue raised by Hampden, by latitudinarianism, by liberalism, of the *necessity* of dogma for salvation is announced. Newman will say 'a few words', consisting of two tightly packed paragraphs of argument, three of application to the history of Apollinarianism, and one of conclusion.

Newman's argument is best summed up by a sentence in the final paragraph: 'while there is no antecedent improbability in the notion that the Christian faith is exact and definite, or what liberalists call *technical*, there is, on the other hand, a great body of testimony from the earliest times to prove that so it is'.[20] His argument is twofold: first, a general argument from probability, and, second, from the testimony of the early Church. He is in defence of the 'technical' and his target is 'liberalists', a unique coinage in Newman for the more usual 'liberals'.[21]

First, Newman's argument on behalf of dogma tries to establish antecedent probability. His entirely typical rhetoric here – the appeal to *eikos* drawing on Butler – is to the 'analogy of the other parts of religion'.[22] Dogma is argued to be at least not improbable by the analogy of similar 'appointments' in the 'whole system of religion'.[23] Newman's meaning is, simply, that all religion operates by means of precise and definite actions or symbols, in order to communicate spiritual blessings, rather than at the level of generalised rationality: 'the use of a little water, the utterance of a few words, the imposition of hands, and the like'.[24] In the realm of belief, the precision, the particularity of dogmas is analogous to these 'appointments', which are 'as formal and technical as any creed can be represented to be'.[25] His argument is, however, very considerably complicated by a play upon the Aristotelian *mean* of virtue, ('a point between indefinitely extending extremes'[26]) and the *means* of salvation. Now, a *means* by which grace is communicated is also a particular point. Newman equates particularity with 'technicality': 'In a word, such technicality is involved in the very idea of a *means*, which may even be defined to be a something appointed at God's inscrutable pleasure, as the necessary condition of something else.'[27] The very possibility of mediation – of encounter between God and humanity – entails, at every level of religion, particularity, concreteness, individual points of meeting, the form of which, in the area of belief is the technicality and precision opposed by 'liberalists'. But Newman sees each particular point – the 'mean' or 'means' – as arbitrarily or inscrutably imposed. On this occasion, his argument from probability and analogy has a markedly irrationalist tinge. Dogma is a *means* coming down upon us – we must obey it. One wonders what his readers would have made of all this: the density of the argumentation must have come as a shock, after Apollinaris' informative biography.

Newman's second string – the testimony of the early Church – reads more straightforwardly. The issue, once antecedent probability has been disposed of, is whether the Christian faith 'involves the reception of certain definite truths conceived in certain definite forms of words?'[28] To decide on this is, as Newman re-iterates, a matter of 'fact',[29] which may be decided by 'catholic tradition'.[30] His introduction of the latter is another appeal to *eikos*, for he treats 'catholic tradition' as the *accumulated* evidence of the early Church's 'unanimous' state of belief: 'multiplied, concordant testimonies to one and the same doctrine bring with them an overwhelming evidence of apostolic origin'.[31]

At the end of the article, Newman returns to Apollinaris, in order to make clear the application of his biography to his more general remarks. This is an interesting moment, for Newman has the task of relating the case of a particular heresy to his general statement about what orthodoxy is, rather than, as so often, using it to attack his opponents. Heresy is brought face-to-face with orthodoxy. How, then, will he on this occasion make them define one another?

Newman condemns Apollinaris for failing to comply with the 'unanimous tradition of the churches', a convergence of testimony more certain than 'that of witnesses to certain facts in a court of law'.[32] This was, as a matter of history, the 'plain' 'ground' on which Apollinaris was condemned. Newman is not yet sceptical about the possibility of arriving at a decision about what the *consensus patrum* was,[33] and Apollinaris is blithely excluded from a place in this *consensus*, for all his closeness to the orthodox position. Needless to say, Newman ignores the Apollinarian claim to be doing no more than articulating the ancient tradition of the Church.[34]

Apollinaris is also uncomfortably integrated into Newman's argument on behalf of precise and 'technical' dogma, advanced against the 'liberalists'. Apollinaris was hardly one of those who questioned the necessity of 'exactness in doctrine'.[35] Indeed, his theology was as exact and technical as that of any orthodox Father – as Newman knew perfectly well from his detailed 1835 researches into Apollinarianism. Where, then, does Apollinaris fit into Newman's antithesis between 'technical' orthodoxy and liberalism? He was clearly *not* a liberal – yet he *was* a heretic. Newman's application of early Church history falls back upon the fine line between Apollinarianism and orthodoxy: the condemnation of Apollinaris is an indicator of the radical difference of *ethos* between liberals and early Christians to whom dogmatic intolerance of an exact and technical kind came quite naturally.

Newman is, then, less successful in integrating his material on Apollinarianism into a defence of dogma, nor does he very satisfactorily define heresy's relation to orthodoxy. This is – as Part III will endeavour to show – hardly surprising in view of the unresolved tensions of the 'Via Media' argument, which, in any case, collapsed by the 1840s as far as Newman was concerned. If, however, the effectiveness of the sixteenth *Letter* is considered in the context of the general strategy of the *Letters to the Church of the*

Fathers, then Newman may be regarded as more successful. The *Letters* cumulatively present the *ethos* of early Christianity as radically different from the assumptions prevailing amongst early nineteenth-century liberals: Christianity was ascetic and dogmatic, rather than rational and latitudinarian, and its intolerance of even the slightest of errors, as in the case of Apollinaris, presents a challenge to his own understanding of Christianity.

Newman's returns to Apollinarianism after this occasion were infrequent, until the resumption of his preoccupation with this heresy in 1839, which initiated the work on Monophysitism. It is possible, however, that he read a form of his *Apollinarianism*, which had been privately printed in 1835, to the Theological Society on Friday 3rd November, at Pusey's house.[36] This would have been an occasion when the detail of Newman's scholarship would have been relished; there was no need of simplification. On the other hand, his speculations upon the contemporary application of heresy would also have been welcome, for this was not only a learned society but a cell in which the Tractarians hammered out their ideology.[37] Newman also returned to Apollinarianism when he was compiling the book-version of *The Church of the Fathers* in 1840, when he incorporated material from the *British Critic Letters* from 1833 onwards, and wrote some new material. He included a chapter on 'Apollinaris' – an only slightly edited version of *Letter XVI*.[38]

The rich promise held out in the note prefacing *Apollinaris'* history, that Newman's 1835 work was to act as a fount for a stream of theological rhetoric, is, at first sight, disappointing: the only work on Apollinarianism to find its way into public discourse was *Letter XVI*, which omits entirely Newman's theory of the development of heresy. In fact, it is under the category of 'Sabellian' that we find the speculations of his Apollinarian papers bearing fruit. The transfer of a theory about one heresy, to another, was, of course, easy enough, if one was working with Newman's assumption of one essence of heresy – its hidden infidelity – of which particular heresies were only the outward and deceptive forms. It was Blanco White who brought Sabellianism into public debate. Newman, with his own speculations ready to hand, poured them into a ready made mould.

CHAPTER THIRTEEN

Sabellianism revisited

Sabellianism, and the related forms of the word, entered Newman's vocabulary as a shorthand way of referring to the anthropocentric basis of both evangelical Protestant piety and ecclesiastical liberalism. Soon after writing *Tract 73*, in October 1835, he could write to Froude about what was now fixed in his mind as an established trend, the 'Socinianism of Sabellianism'.[1] In September 1837, writing to Lord Lifford, he recapitulates the line of the *Tract*, with regard to Abbott and his evangelical editors: 'Mr Jacob Abbott's works, which Sabellianize to the very verge of Socinianiam have been edited by Mr Blunt, Mr Cunningham and Dr Pye Smith.'[2] Newman, in this letter, associates Sabellianism entirely with the 'Evangelical System'. Henry Blunt[3] and John William Cunningham[4] were popularisers and popular preachers, like Abbott, but Pye Smith was, even in Newman's eyes, a respectable scholar, who, in *Tract 73* is reproached for his recommendation of Abbott.[5] The 'Evangelical System' tends, Newman argues, towards Socinianism, or some analogous form of infidelity: 'That system has become Rationalistic in Germany, Socinian in Geneva – Socinian among English Presbyterians and Arian among Irish – Latitudinarian in Holland – it tends to Socinianism among our own the Evangelical Party.'[6] He has a little trouble fitting Hampden in, who is 'neither Socinian or Evangelical', but he 'speaks like both at once, and is received by both'.[7]

The letter to Lord Lifford identifies Newman's use of Sabellianism as a component in a strategy directed against what he calls adherents of 'Protestantism' or '*popular* Protestantism'.[8] Three characteristics recur in his description of Protestantism: its restriction of teaching authority to the Bible only, its vaunted right to – really an abuse of – 'Private Judgment',[9] and its stress upon psychological states in the believing subject as the guarantee of authentic faith.[10] All three – in similar ways – are destructive of revealed Christianity as Newman understands it. Biblicism leads to indifference to early Church doctrines, a vague profession of allegiance to the Bible being thought of as enough.[11] Here, Newman reacts strongly against the Hanoverian latitudinarian Protestantism which, after the English Revolution, had overlaid the Church of England.[12] Private Judgment, often a synonym for 'heresy', is claimed as a right: the individual may, according to his own conscience, interpret the Bible in his own way, uncorrected by external authority.[13] This, in practice, results in a multiplicity of mutually tolerated though contradictory views, concealing, Newman suspects, indifference and scepticism. Protestant piety, too, for all its emotionalism and zeal, approximates to infidelity, for it *begins* from the human.[14] Against all this, Newman opposes 'Catholicism': the external objective witness of the first five centuries to the fundamental faith.[15]

Newman had articulated, in classic form, his polemic against Protestantism in his *Lectures on the Prophetical Office of the Church*. Of the three parties constituting the Church of England, 'the Apostolical [or 'Catholic'], the Latitudinarian and the Puritan,' Newman is clear that the latter two 'have been shown to be but modifications of Socinianism and Calvinism by their respective histories, whenever allowed to act freely'.[16] Latitudinarianism is associated with the divinity flourishing between Charles II and George II, coming to its climax in Bishop Hoadly. Such Protestantism did not seem so bad to Anglicans of former generations: it was a bulwark against Romanism, and there was always the hope that it might eventually become more 'Catholic'.[17] However, the course of history revealed the true development of Protestantism to be quite otherwise: only in the nineteenth century, was its real essence, its tendency towards infidelity, revealed with 'fearful clearness'.[18] Drawing on H.J. Rose,[19] Newman declares,

Before Germany had become rationalistic, and Geneva Socinian, Romanism might be considered as the most dangerous corruption of the gospel; and this might be a call upon members of our Church to waive their differences with foreign Protestantism and Dissent at home, as if in the presence of a common enemy. But at this day, when the connexion of foreign Protestantism with infidelity is so evident, what claim has the former upon our sympathy?[20]

Newman's theory of the development of heresy is thus ruthlessly and uncompromisingly applied to Protestantism.

(a) NICHOLAS WISEMAN AND ROMAN CATHOLICISM

Newman returned to the idea of 'Sabellianism' on two further occasions. The first is very surprising, in view of the overwhelming association of Sabellianism with Protestantism: he sees certain tendencies in Roman Catholicism – and especially in the theology of Nicholas Wiseman – as comparable with the method of Erskine and Chalmers!

Newman attacked Rome for adding to, or 'corrupting', the faith, but was careful not to accuse Her of heresy, or of heresy's ultimate development, infidelity, as he consistently does in the case of 'Protestantism'.[21] There is, however, a strand of Newman's critique of Roman Catholicism which draws upon the method by which he analysed Erskine: Rome is systematic in its presentation of revealed truth, and 'Satan ever acts on a system'.[22] Newman repeats the view of *Tract 73* that revealed truths come to us as 'detached portions of a complicated system'.[23] We do not know how they hold together in the 'whole Dispensation'.[24] This is a version of *Tract 73*'s 'vast system unrevealed'.[25] In the *Prophetical Office*, Newman similarly declares the limitation of the human capacity to systematise, and the modesty and humility which behoves us; the 'supernatural gift' of Christianity is 'a vast scheme running into width and breadth, encompassing us round about, not embraced by us. No one can see the form of a building but those who are external to it.'[26] To go beyond such limitations is to slide into a 'spirit of rationalism': 'Rome would classify and number all things. She would settle every sort of question, as if resolved to detect and compass by human reason what runs out into the next world or is lost in this.'[27] Romanists are 'ever intruding' into and 'growing familiar' with 'mysteries'. They stretch out their hands to touch what should not be touched, as did irreverent Israelites who touched the Ark of God![28] The pretension to a completeness of theological system – a scientific certainty – opens the way to pride, and constitutes the exponents of the system as judges of what is revealed. 'He who considers himself fully to understand a system, seems to have sway over it.'[29] Theological systematising arises from the Roman Catholic clerical system, at the apex of which is Papal

Infallibility. Doctrines infallibly decided may, moreover, be subjected to a further rationalism: the organisation of doctrinal elements within the system, according to their relative importance. Newman admits that there are revealed both greater and lesser truths, but 'it is only one thing to receive them so far as Scripture declares them to be so, quite another to decide about them for ourselves by the help of our own reasonings'.[30] But it is 'not wonderful' that Rome should do so: its system is 'the work of its own hands'; the system it has 'framed', it proceeds to judge.[31]

As in *Tract 73*, Newman holds that such rationalistic systematisation works by reducing revelation to one intelligible principle extrinsic or alien to it. In the case of Roman Catholics, this principle is 'present expediency' which is 'the measure of its excellence and wisdom'.[32] Newman does not mean this to be quite as bad as it sounds: 'I do not say they are forced, but they are easily betrayed into doing this.'[33] Like the internal evidencers, Roman Catholics have been 'led on'.[34] What Newman considers to be Roman Catholic 'expediency' is not gross political intriguing or shady casuistry, but a tendency to want to consider the 'experience of the results' of a doctrine: 'They ask what is the use of this doctrine, what the actual harm of that error; as if the experience of results were necessary before condemning the one and sanctioning the other.'[35] In this respect – in the utilitarian attitude towards doctrine (although Newman does not directly accuse them of this) – Roman Catholicism is comparable with 'the religion popular among us at the present day', that is, Protestantism, which only admits 'so much of the high doctrines of the Gospel . . . as is seen and felt to tend to our moral improvement'.[36] Newman introduces a quotation from Erskine's *Internal Evidence* and criticises the assumption that 'the understanding has a right to claim an insight into the meaning and drift of the matter of Revelation'.[37] He does not want revelation to be *used* – he would preserve it inviolate from *any* definable function – and the corollary of *use* is systematic intelligibility.

Newman turns to Nicholas Wiseman's recent Moorfields Lenten lectures of 1836, *Lectures on the Principal Doctrines and Practices of the Catholic Church*,[38] as an example of this rationalist tendency in Roman Catholicism. In reference to this work, Newman hopes to demonstrate that there is 'agreement of temper and character'[39] between 'popular Protestantism' and the 'religion of Rome'.[40] This surprising and regrettable[41] identity of *ethos* produces an identical rationalism: 'this peculiarity in the religion of Rome, which it has in common with some other modern systems – its subjecting divine truth to the intellect, and professing to take a complete survey and to make a map of it'.[42] He finds Wiseman's apologetic for the Gospel draws upon the idea of it as a 'system'; Wiseman declares himself ravished by the beauty of the intelligible order of revelation.[43] The *Lectures* also recommend Christianity for its moral effect, its tendency to promote social cohesion.[44] Wiseman and Erskine are so close, as far as Newman is concerned, that he can refer to them both in the same breath, 'the Roman and the Scotch Divine'.[45]

In the *Prophetical Office*, Newman devotes to Wiseman about one page. Many could be written demonstrating the partiality and distortions of Newman's treatment on this occasion of the Moorfields *Lectures*. A few, however, must suffice to assess the hits and misses of the Parthian shafts directed at his great contemporary. He makes Wiseman into a sort of internal evidencer, who advocates Christian truth by pretending to expound it in terms of a systematic coherence assimilable by the intellect. In fact, Wiseman's concept of evidencing is by no means this. On several occasions, he repudiates internal evidencing, on similar grounds to Newman, as a form of Protestant rationalism.[46] His own view of evidence is subtle: the fullness of revealed truth – identical, of course, for Wiseman with the dogmatic teaching of the Roman Church – is open to many different ways of being evidenced. 'Systems of evidencing' will vary from age to age, for example, as historically conditioned attitudes vary.[47] Wiseman therefore, sees nothing alarming in the very new grounds for conversion to Roman Catholicism in Germany, via the aesthetics of Schlegel.[48] Even the new science of Political Economy might conceivably form the basis of a Christian apologetic![49] The truth is one, but the proofs are many: 'Truth may be compared to a gem without a flaw, which may be viewed in different lights.'[50] Wiseman, therefore, cannot justly be accused of *reducing* revelation to one particular system. Revelation and its systematisation are not identified. Rather, he establishes a duality: on the divine side, there is revelation, inexhaustible but not opaque – it is open to a multiplicity of systematic approaches, lending it an aesthetic[51] appeal; on the human side, the possibility of multiform systematisations of revelation make possible an apologetic appropriate to culture and historical evolution. Wiseman has a simple metaphor to explain the relation between truth and evidences: the one truth is like a key which opens a lock – the force of the discovery that the lock is opened effects conviction.[52] It is, perhaps, necessary to extend Wiseman's metaphor here: the one truth is a pass-key, opening a variety of locks, and thereby validating itself in a variety of circumstances.[53] However, Wiseman does not suggest, nor is it necessary to his argument, that the human mind can *fully* understand what is revealed.

On the other hand, there are times when Wiseman's own evidencing operates at a much cruder level than his own declared methodology.[54] He sounds as if he is making Roman Catholicism into a kind of utilitarian body, when he compares its 'practical success'[55] with Protestantism, in converting the heathen. It is on these practical grounds that Wiseman advocates his Church's 'rule of faith'.[56] Wiseman has done his sums. He shows that the Bible-only principle of pure Protestantism has failed: the number of Bibles purchased and circulated to the heathen has produced a ludicrously small number of converts, considering the expense. The Bible Society has spent £2,121,640 in 30 years. During a comparable period, Roman Catholic missionaries have done much better in numbers of converts – and all for only £30,000![57] There is undoubtedly here a considerable difference of *ethos* between the Roman prelate, exuding confidence and clarity, addressing his audience as a sound man of the world and ecclesiastical business executive, and the fastidious[58] Anglican, the asserter of mystery, tormented by the early modern slide into secularisation and loss of God.

Newman's passage about Wiseman in the *Prophetical Office* is an extreme example of the way in which the critique evolved in *Tract 73* can become a catch-all, the picking out of rationalistic tendencies becoming more and more arbitrary. In any case, Newman had it both ways over Wiseman. In his *British Critic* review of the Moorfields Lectures, in January 1836, he used *Wiseman*'s arguments against the 'ultra-Protestant' party. Wiseman had argued that such Protestantism was rationalistic, because its 'essential ground' was 'that each one is to be considered responsible to God for every particular doctrine which he professes'.[59] Therefore, each individual Protestant must be 'internally convinced' that the Bible is the Word of God, by the principle of 'individual research, individual satisfaction'.[60] Newman declared himself 'not displeased' with this exposure of ultra-Protestant rationalism. He manages, however, to agree with Rome while still making it sound sinister:

Well, then, let us see whether these more clear-sighted religionists (as they think themselves), these pure Protestants and rigid Scripturalists, will make a better and more satisfactory fight when they come into close contact with their foe, that crafty foe which shelters its errors under the truths which such adversaries wantonly, unreluctantly surrender to it as its own.[61]

Wiseman's 'tendencies' exemplify a broader trend in the Church of which he is the advocate. Back again on general ground, Newman pursues his attack with greater success. It is a subtle blend of sympathy and censure. He argues that Roman Catholic clarity and system stem from the desire to control people: the rigour of its theology forecloses a full personal and individual response, the *venture* of faith, by 'setting a limit to their necessary obedience, and absolving them from the duty of sacrificing their whole lives to God'.[62] The Roman Catholic system is 'a minute, technical and peremptory theology'. 'Technicality'[63] – which Newman now finds himself attacking – underpins Romanism's political spirit: 'She [Rome] has in view political objects, viable fruits, temporal expediency, the power of influencing the heart, as the supreme aim and scope of her system.'[64] Newman here also points to the popularist dimension of Roman Catholicism: like Evangelicalism, it wants to affect the heart. Yet he admits that the 'expediency' to which the Roman system adheres is born of motives of which he thoroughly approves: 'It is an effort to stem the tide of unbelief.'[65] The rationalism, then, lies below the surface of conscious deliberation: the purposes of the Roman clergy are, on the face of it, irreproachable. Roman Catholicism takes revelation down from the shelf, where Newman would have it left untouched by human hand, and ruthlessly *exploits* it for the expansion and consolidation of its empire. Rome sees revelation as something visible, a mode capable of human absorption and use: 'They who are resolved that the Divine counsels and appointments should be cognizable by the human intellect, are naturally tempted to assign some visible and intelligible object as the scope of the whole Dispensation.'[66] It is Newman's 'Sabellians' all over again!

With all the characteristics of Newman's 'Sabellian' heresiology in place, the expected does not happen: the terms 'Sabellian', 'Sabellianism', and 'Sabellianise' do not make an appearance. Nor is there any suggestion of a slide from 'Romanism' into Socinianism, despite the fact that Newman sometimes implied a resemblance between these two extreme limits of the tolerable. And after all, Blanco White had, in fact, started as a Roman Catholic and ended up as a Unitarian.[67] Moreover, especially in the detested Daniel O'Connell, 'Romanism', democracy, republicanism, and the destruction of Anglican hegemony in Ireland coalesced.[68] Newman contents himself with pointing to Rome's rationalism without making explicit the implication to be drawn by a reader of *Tract 73*: that Rome was 'Sabellian'.

The reasons for Newman's restraint here may only be conjectured. One possibility is that he had to find a form of rationalism coinciding with *explicit* evidence of Trinitarian modalism – as he could easily do with Erskine, Abbott and Schleiermacher – before he was prepared to bring in Sabellianism, and that Roman Catholic theology provided no such evidence. However, in the case of Milman's *History of Christianity*, Newman was, as we shall see, capable of using the term 'Sabellian' while ignoring, or not even noticing there, any evidence of specifically *Trinitarian* heterodoxy. A more likely reason, then, is Newman's general unwillingness to describe Rome as heretical, or to convict Her of the hidden tendency towards infidelity which heresy conceals: Rome has corrupted or overlaid the 'foundation' of the Christian faith,[69] but still holds to it: it tends, therefore, not towards 'infidelity' but to 'superstition'.[70]

(B) HENRY HART MILMAN AND THE LIBERAL ANGLICAN IDEA OF HISTORY

It was not until five years after the 'Postscript' to *Tract 73*, that Newman returned explicitly to the theme of 'Sabellianism', in his 1841 review[71] of H. H. Milman's *History of Christianity* (1840). Here Newman declared to be disappointed his hope for a Church history to replace the impressive but infidel Gibbon.[72] In explaining his dissatisfaction,[73] Newman now applied his idea of 'Sabellianism', previously elaborated only in relation to apologetic, to historical method.

Newman's use of terminology has undergone modification since he was examining Erskine: there the orthodox tendency was to accept, on external authority, the *revelatum*, while the heretical tendency was to decide whether or not something was revealed on the basis of its internal character.[74] However, in his review of Milman's *History*, it is the word 'external' which takes on heretical connotations.

Milman's declared aim is to present Christianity purely as an historian, that is, dispassionately, eschewing polemics,[75] considering only the external facts. This Newman calls 'the external view he is taking of the subject'.[76] The heretical direction of such an 'external view', is, however, a characteristic of the independent life of Milman's method, rather than of the conscious purpose of the author. This distinction, which has been a feature also of Newman's treatment of Erskine and Abbott, is even more strongly stressed in the case of Milman. Milman 'does not mean any harm'.[77] It is, rather, his 'peculiar *manner*, and the facility with which he may be taken, not unnaturally, but still over-hastily, to be saying what he does not say',[78] that worries Newman. He disclaims that he intends 'to draw up for ourselves his doctrinal notion of Christianity'.[79] He will not expound Milman's doctrine, but only 'those momentous principles, which he has adopted indeed, but which are outside of him, and will not be his slaves'.[80] The distinction between text and author could not be more sharply presented.[81] A text takes on a life of its own: 'Principles have a life and power independent of their authors, and make their way in spite of them.'[82]

This apparently sophisticated way of interpreting a text is in fact a debating tactic, allowing Newman great freedom in the interpretation of the text. He can thus apply his 'Sabellian' critique flexibly to the ultimate tendencies he discerns in that particular strand of the text which he selects. Such a procedure, it must be said, is a subjective one. Who, after all, can judge objectively of the ultimate direction of forces operating in the text which are hidden even from the author, not to mention the difficulty of establishing the *effect* of a text upon any mind other than one's own? Newman is, in any case, heavily reliant upon ironic raillery in order to bring the reader over to his view as he relentlessly contrasts Milman's liberal restatements of Gospel events with their starker originals. The 'persona' of Milman's text, rather than Milman himself, one supposes, is being thus rhetorically engaged,[83]

He says respecting the incident in John XII., that what 'the unbelieving part of the multitude heard only as an accidental burst of thunder, to others . . . *seemed* an *audible*, a *distinct*, – or, according to those who adhere to the strict letter, – the' – (it avails not to delay, out with it!) – 'the *articulate* voice of an Angel.')'. Yes, the real articulate voice; how painful to our 'subtle and fastidious intelligence.'[84]

It is to Milman's 'external' approach, and its consequences, that Newman applies the related heretical categories of 'Socinian' and 'Sabellian'. He discerns heresy in the effect of Milman's style of presentation, 'For the fact is undeniable, little as Mr Milman may be aware of it, that this external contemplation of Christianity necessarily leads a man to write as a Socinian or Unitarian *would* write, whether he will or not.'[85] Socinianism, the denial of Christ's divinity, is the inevitable result of Milman's 'external' method. Some elements of Christianity, such as Christ's human nature and crucifixion, are susceptible of 'external' presentation in a history, but others, such as Christ's Divinity and the Atonement, are not. Milman's history will inevitably 'dwell on the latter' and 'slur over the former'.[86] His own methodology has him in thrall. Now, to deny Christ's Divinity and the Atonement, but to confess his humanity and crucifixion, is Socinianism.[87] Moreover, 'moral improvement', which can be examined and presented 'externally', will, in Milman, predominate over the empirically unverifiable doctrine of the forgiveness of sins. Therefore, as with Erskine and Abbott before him, revelation is reduced to a particular interpretation of the moral, 'consequently he will make the main message of the Gospel to relate mainly to moral improvement, not to forgiveness of sins'.[88]

Inevitably for Newman, Milman, because he is 'speaking mainly of what is externally seen',[89] will be 'Sabellian'. He will present the persons of the Trinity as manifestations of characteristics of God, especially moral traits recognisable as such by human understanding, 'what is "*manifested*" in Him, is not, cannot be, more than a certain attribute or attributes of the divinity, as, for instance, especially love'.[90] Therefore Milman's method, because of what it cannot but omit, will bring him to 'Sabellianism'; he 'will be led to speak almost in a "Sabellian" fashion, as if denying, because not stating, the specific indwelling which Scripture records and the Church teaches'.[91]

The relation between Socinianism and 'Sabellianism' is not

clarified, as it is in *Tract 73*. The picture is further blurred by the introduction of Nestorianism. In commenting upon the Christology which Milman's method 'obliges' him to arrive at, that is, Christ as 'man with a presence of divinity',[92] His person being 'by this very theory nothing more than a man', Newman asserts, 'The . . . doctrine is Sabellianism, Nestorianism and Socinianism.'[93] What unites these diverse heresies for Newman is that by subjecting Christianity to analysis in terms primarily of human phenomena, they initiate a slide into atheism, 'If we indulge them [such principles], Christianity will melt away in our hands like snow; we shall be unbelievers before we at all suspect that we are.'[94]

Newman reworks his *Tract 73* idea of heresy as 'reduction to system'. Milman's intention *appears* to be the very reverse of the systematic, his purpose being 'merely' to state 'the *facts* of Christianity'.[95] But Newman is quick to point out that this approach is itself 'a theory of the facts'.[96] This is because the 'principles' which are the 'life' of the facts are omitted.[97] The supernatural, which underlies and sustains the facts, is artifically repressed by a principle of selectivity which amounts to an 'external system'[98] distorting the 'higher and invisible system' of revelation, the inner life of the supernatural which has its own mysterious coherence.[99]

Newman is prepared to say more about this mysterious coherence than the highly condensed expression 'a doctrine lying hid in language', which is found in *Tract 73*. Revelation, he argues, has an inner logic all of its own, a logic quite different from that of human reason. The human language points towards a vision. The history of dogma has a sacramental quality: 'The Christian history is "an outward visible sign of inward spiritual grace".'[100] Milman's fault is that he has detached the outward signs, that is, the external researchable data of historiography from its divine, hidden inner reality. In Milman's defence, it is difficult to see how else he could have operated – and remain a historian! By contrast, Newman's assertion of the symbolic quality of Christian history seems to have absorbed the other-worldliness of the Alexandrian Platonist Fathers, in that 'it neglects chronology, and objective consistency . . . as though history were but a veil or a phantom across the face of the unchanging Eternal'.[101]

But Newman does not just see Milman as the wrong kind of historian: he also implies that he is heretical, too. In other words, Newman's point is theological: theology and the history of dogma cannot be separated from faith. Newman is not so much neo-platonic as incarnationalist: his vision of Christian history derives from the two natures of Christ, which, though distinct, are hypostatically united. As A.M. Allchin has pointed out, a theological vision centred upon the Incarnation implies the transfiguration, but not the destruction of, the human.[102] It is this vision, encompassing but going beyond history, that Newman opposes to Milman's 'theory of the facts'.[103]

This 'theory of the facts' is, as we have seen, only 'Sabellian' in the subtlest of fashions. For all the sharpness of Newman's strictures upon the *History*, he is only prepared to say that Milman has been 'led to speak almost in a Sabellian fashion'.[104] It comes, therefore, as a surprise to find that he does not refer to a passage in the second volume in which Milman declares himself to be sympathetic to a modern form of Sabellianism. In discussing the teaching of Sabellius, Milman states,

A more modest and unoffending Sabellianism might, perhaps, be imagined in accordance with modern philosophy. The manifestations of the same Deity, or rather of his attributes, through which alone the Godhead becomes comprehensible to the human mind, may have been thus successively made in condescension to our weakness of intellect. It would be the same Deity, assuming, as it were, an objective form, so as to come within the scope of the human mind; a real difference, as regards the conception of man, perfect unity in its subjective existence.[105]

His sympathy with Sabellianism arises from his ideology of history. Like that of his fellow Liberal Anglican historians, Milman's relativistic[106] presentation of history, in terms of cycles from childhood, through maturity to decay,[107] with its stress upon the alien quality of the mental worlds of the past,[108] is balanced by belief in the application of a universal standard of morality, as an interpreted fixed point.[109] Therefore, Milman is provided with a means by which to evaluate the universal in relation to the party torn world of the Fathers. It is the moral impression upon men, wrought by Christ's example, which, now dimly, now clearly, is to be discerned in the records of the Christian past. Christ is

the Goodness of the Deity, which, associating itself with human form, assumes the character of a representative of the human race; in whose person is exhibited a pure model of moral perfection, and whose triumph over evil is by the slow and gradual process of enlightening the mind and softening and purifying the heart.[110]

Milman's second volume, in which he shows such frank sympathy towards historic Sabellianism, applies the moral ideology of history of the Liberal Anglicans to early Church history in such a way as to challenge the Tractarian view that Antiquity contained doctrinally normative interpretations of the revelation contained in Scripture. Again, surprisingly, Newman only very briefly interacts with this challenge, when he declares that Milman speaks the truth despite himself in characterising the early Church as marked by 'the principle of dogmatism', opposed to 'ecclesiastical liberty'.[111] Milman's words, lifted from the context of his argument, form part of a carefully worked out theory of heresy and orthodoxy. Milman sees the imposition of purely speculative tenets for acceptance by the faithful, through creeds, as oppressive.[112] Dogmatism has become divorced from love.[113] There are, in fact, two kinds of heresy. First, there is 'heresy of opinion', which, being easy to identify and attack, was the target of too much attention to the patristic age. Second, there is the 'darker and more baleful heresy of unchristian passions'; this was more difficult to detect, and being a matter of Christian behaviour, was much more difficult to eradicate.[114] Antiquity concentrated upon weeding out the more easily identifiable doctrinal heresy, to the neglect of the moral variety. Christianity became distorted by the usurpation of the dogmatic (concerning 'Faith') upon the moral (concerning 'religion').[115]

As in the case of Schleiermacher, then, Newman appears unwilling to interact with specific *historical* challenges to his own concept of Antiquity. This causes him to omit references providing powerful confirmation of his own position about 'Sabellianism'. Even when Milman's historical method challenges the idea of mystery, there is no response from Newman. Milman presents mystery as having a purely historical evolution.[116] He argues that Christian ceremonies excluded outsiders through fear of persecution,[117] but when Christianity became a state religion, the secrecy surrounding sacraments was retained,[118] so that, after a certain point in the liturgy, outsiders were excluded. Eventually, under the influence of esoteric mystery-religions,[119] doctrine taught to catechumens also became associated with secrecy. Finally, after the Trinitarian disputes with heretics, there were even more powerful reasons to withdraw doctrine from the gaze of the profane.[120] Here, then, Milman gives a purely historical explanation of what Newman considered to be an unconditioned fact of the religious attitude of Christian Antiquity. Yet Newman presents us with no counter-arguments – indeed his review shows no awareness of the existence of this passage in Milman.

Newman's interest, in fact, lies elsewhere. It is not Milman's presentation of the early Church which has attracted his attention, so much as that of the New Testament. Of the 23 full-length quotations from Milman, for example, only 6 are from Volumes II or III which deal with Christian Antiquity, while 17 are from Volume I, which deals with the New Testament period. It is in relation to Milman's depiction of Jesus' life and teaching, especially, that Newman makes his strictures about the effect of the 'external' 'Sabellian' method.

Milman's presentation of the life of Jesus would, at first sight, seem to present much less to provoke criticism, than his more tendentious chapters on Church history. In the area of the New Testament, he could be shown to be constructive and conservative, striving to preserve historic Christianity against the 'ultra rationalistic' life-of-Jesus school of such as D.F. Strauss, in Germany.[121] Milman's historical approach has been formulated against Strauss' radical distinction between the abstract universal truths of Christianity and the supernatural events of the life of its Founder, which are open to historical scepticism, the view that 'The supernatural birth of Christ, his miracles, his resurrection and ascension, remain eternal truths, however their reality as historical facts may be called in question'.[122] Milman attacks Strauss for describing the gospel-events as 'mythic', the imaginative creations of early Christian communities.[123] This thesis Milman attacks on four grounds: that Strauss has dogmatically assumed the question in dispute – i.e. that supernatural events are myths; that he ignores the fact that *some* of these supernatural events are essential to Christianity and must therefore have been the belief of earliest times, e.g. the resurrection; that the Biblical evidence shows that supernatural events were part of the strata of earliest belief; finally, that Strauss' handling of New Testament evidence is uncritical in failing to discern the early material in the Gospels contradictory to his thesis.[124]

Milman, therefore, is trying to present Christianity as historical rather than 'mythical', and his method springs from a desire to claim the New Testament as history. The purpose of his impartial stance is to recommend Christianity for belief, in a context where critical scepticism is calling it into doubt. He narrates as *history* a large supernatural element. No attempt is made to present the raising of Lazarus as anything but an historical fact;[125] he accepts the cursing of the fig tree as *both* parable *and* event;[126] Jesus' prophecy of the Fall of Jerusalem is not merely 'political sagacity', but supernatural knowledge.[127] The healing of the High Priest's servant's ear is flatly and factually narrated, 'The man whose ear had been struck off, was instantaneously healed.'[128]

Particularly important is Milman's strong assertion of the physical resurrection of Jesus, as the basis for the doctrine of the immortality of the soul,[129] a position made polemically in contradistinction to his understanding of Schleiermacher.[130] This contradicts Newman's argument that Milman favours the outward facts about Jesus which are human, as opposed to internal realities, which are divine: the resurrection is an outward fact for Milman, but it is also by its very nature supernatural. Confronted by this, Newman is forced, first, to respond that Milman is nevertheless reductionist in *reducing* the supernatural to *essential* supernatural events,

He thinks it is a sign of an acute and practical intellect to pare down its supernatural facts as closely as possible, and to leave its principal miracles, the multiplying of bread, the raising of Lazarus, or the Resurrection, standing alone like the pillars of Tadmor in the wilderness.[131]

But, as we have already seen, Milman allows a greater latitude to the supernatural than this. Secondly, Newman suggests that Milman is inconsistent with his own method, 'Mr Milman of course insists, though we see not with what consistency, on the doctrine of the Resurrection as proper to Christianity.'[132] The circularity of Newman's reasoning must be observed here: he is interpreting the tendency and effect of Milman's method in the light of Milman's text: it is hardly conclusive to suggest that a strong counter-indication is inadmissible because inconsistent with what, after all, is Newman's interpretation of these tendencies and effects.

Newman's characterisation of one of the most distinguished liberal Anglican historians as 'Sabellian' indicates his attitude to a school which was both near, and far, from Tractarianism. Like

Newman, the Liberal Anglicans were opposed to the sceptical, static rationalism of the Enlightenment;[133] like Newman they opposed the glib optimism of the 'march of mind' mentality,[134] and like Newman they saw that Christian civilisation had come to a crisis.[135] But they offered a middle way, an accommodation with the apparently destructive inroads of the new historical sciences, which would provide a way foward without obscurantism,[136] to avert the collapse of the 'house of authority'.[137] It is precisely this middle way that 'Sabellianism' is made to symbolise in Newman: it obscures what he sees as the real crisis of the early modern period, the stark choice between God and atheism. To accept Milman's view is to take the first inadvertent step towards unbelief, to make 'a sort of irenicon or peace-offering, to reconcile the faith of eighteen centuries, and the infidelity of the nineteenth'.[138]

CHAPTER FOURTEEN

Heresy, typology and the encodement of experience

Newman was, by the mid-1830s, undertaking something more sophisticated than an imposition of his own preoccupations upon the patristic age. He moved beyond the satiric parallelism of *Arians* towards what, in his treatment of Apollinarianism and Sabellianism, may be described as the encodement of experience.[1] Searching for a pattern of universal significance beneath the surface features of his own situation, he found in the Fathers' presentation of the patterns of interaction between heresy and orthodoxy a code to bring out the *hidden* significance of early nineteenth-century debates about doctrine, while distancing them from the localised polemic of England and Oxford. He took from the Fathers a sense of inner logic by which all heresies either have developed, or will develop, into the 'God-denying apostasy' which is their concealed essence. This he brought to bear upon his England. An extraordinary fusion was the result: on the one hand, his treatment of ancient heresy is tinged with a very English preoccupation, the growth, challenge and toleration of heterodox Dissent; on the other, contemporary debates take place *sub specie antiquitatis*.

Putting present experience into code: this does not seem, at first sight, a very happy way of describing Newman's efforts to illuminate the present by the past. Yet 'code' does catch the *indirectness* of his use of heresy as a description of the forms of liberal theological discourse. In fact, encodement is no esoteric procedure: it simply describes Newman's use of what is a very ordinary Christian activity, the tendency to see one's own experiences, sufferings and dilemmas, paralleled in the Bible's stories, to journey with Abraham, to cross the Red Sea with Moses, with Peter to confess or to deny the Christ; to find in that 'Great Code'[2] a censure or a condemnation, and, in the end, a key to the chaos of experience. Moreover, the patristic Church had, in typological exegesis, encouraged Christians so to encode their experience; this was to some extent retained in Calvinism.[3] Newman's patristic study only reinforced it. The encodement upon which his treatment of heresy is based only extends the typological or figurative principle from exegesis of the Bible to interpretation of Christian history, ancient and modern, and makes the Doctrine of the Trinity the code by which the significance of all theological disputes may be understood. Accordingly, controversy in the 1830s about tests, doctrines and the nature of revelation is encoded by means of analogies between the underlying dynamic of the liberal approach to dogma and that of ancient Trinitarian heresy.

Encodement brings the ancient uncomfortably close: aspects of Fathers and heresiarchs live again in contemporary figures and situations. Conversely, the uncomfortable present is glorified: the unlovely Hampden, the apostate Blanco, the pollution of the Regius Chair, the hostility of Heads of Houses, the accusations of bigotry – all may be played out somewhere else as part of a grand and perennial drama. We have seen how the personal acridity of the Hampden controversy drove Newman, in *Tract 73*, towards a generalisation of the issue of Socinianism at Oxford by projecting it into the texts of Scottish, American and German divines, remote from his acquaintance. This is already, by the very *choice* of Erskine, Abbott, Schleiermacher and Stuart, a form of encodement.

It was not just other people, the pain of apostate friends, the abrasion of liberal enemies, which made the present uncomfortable for Newman: there was the problem of theology itself. He feared the appeal to human experience. He asserted a gulf between revealed and natural theology and would keep the former inviolate – yet, in his own apologetic, he constantly argues from human phenomena: conscience, probability, history, introspection. Newman's own 'phenomenalism' and 'psychologism'[4] may be seen as close to the 'Sabellianism' he criticises. It has been argued that, in moving from heresy hunting, to the construction of an *a priori* on behalf of revelation, Newman failed to avoid a kind of reductionism himself.[5]

For all his strenuous efforts to the contrary, a sense that he, too, was close to what led to modern Sabellianism may account for the subtlety, sympathy and poignancy of his analysis: 'have we never been tempted ourselves to ask – "What is the harm of being, for instance, a Sabellian?"'[6] The use of heresy to typify his present situation therefore serves as an important function in his own self-definition as a theologian. The patristic presentation of heresy checks and balances the egotistical hypersensitivity to the intricacies of the mind's operations, which strikes such a 'modern' note, providing him with a means of distancing himself from the assumptions of the age of which he was a part.

Yet the urge for personal self-definition cannot easily be separated from Newman's rhetorical impetus: both come together in his way of doing theology. He encodes the present, certainly, in order to categorise his experience, but rarely does he neglect, at the same time, the *public* use of the code. Encodement of facets of the present in terms of Antiquity is also a rhetorical strategy. The rhetoric's power derives from the tradition of the *normativeness*, embedded in Anglicanism since the seventeenth century, of the first five centuries of Christianity.[7] In equating liberalism with heresy, Newman imposes a framework upon one ecclesiastical party of his time, in such a way as to dictate the conclusion, for the normative framework of the patristic age imposes its own implicit judgment of value. However, *consensus patrum* was the ideology of the Apostolicals – and, before then, the 'Z''s, not of Anglican Evangelicals, nor of Dissenters. Newman is doing a little more than preaching to the converted, but his rhetoric has a limited appeal – to the waverers in the Anglican fold in a time of re-alignment after the Reform Act. The deployment of 'heresy' precludes the universality to which his rhetoric aspires.

PART THREE

Retreat and re-alignment: Monophysitism and the collapse of the 'Via Media'

Things fall apart; the centre cannot hold
(W. B. Yeats)

CHAPTER FIFTEEN

Construction

(A) TENSIONS IN THE CLASSICAL CONCEPT OF ORTHODOXY

In the period leading to his conversion, Newman underwent a revolution in his understanding of the nature of orthodoxy. The *Apologia* (1864) presents this revolution as the collapse and replacement of a paradigm.[1] Its account of 1839–43 describes, in language full of violent and painful images, his anguish as his 'stronghold' was demolished: the 1839 brush with Wiseman which 'pulverised'[2] the 'Via Media'[3] then in 1841 the 'three blows which broke me' – the Athanasius translation, *Tract 90*'s condemnation, and the farce of the Jerusalem archbishopric, and finally his Anglican 'deathbed'.[4] By December, 1841, the collapse was complete: the 'Via Media' had fallen to pieces 'and a Theory, made expressly for the occasion, took its place'.[5]

In his autobiographical narrative of the 'Via Media's' collapse (1839–43), Newman brings the analogy of ancient heresy (1831–41) to bear upon his own concept of orthodoxy. The former corrodes and, finally, dissolves the latter, itself surviving and, indeed, flourishing in the *Essay on Development* (1845) and *Difficulties of Anglicans* (1850) as a means of describing the very position to which he had formerly adhered. This analogical method was compulsive: he never abandoned it.

This revolution in Newman's concept of orthodoxy suggests that, beneath the confident surface of his Tractarian rhetoric, unresolved problems were lurking. This is not surprising if we regard him as having inherited a classical concept of orthodoxy which was already riddled with tensions. It has been described as 'static'.[6] It is rooted in the anti-sectarian polemic of the seventeenth century, which saw the true faith as immutable. To concede development was to admit, with the sects, that Christianity had been corrupted.[7] This position was shared by both Anglican theologians, such as Bull, and 'Gallicans', such as Bossuet.[8] They did not, of course, necessarily agree about particular doctrines – transubstantiation, images, the Blessed Virgin would have been contested – but they were arguing on identical assumptions about what orthodoxy and heresy were in general: orthodoxy had always been everywhere the same – heresy was novelty.[9] They also shared the assumption that early Christianity was normative, and that a study of it would vindicate their respective positions.[10]

This view could find ample confirmation in the statements of early Fathers, who, from the second century onwards, saw the orthodox faith as temporally prior to any heresy. To hold the latter is for St Irenaeus, 'setting aside the truth'.[11] It is innovation, hence its variety and inconsistency, as contrasted with the one truth. He can appeal to a self-evident *sensus communis*: once the heresies have been given an exposition, no refutation will be necessary, for their novelty will be manifest to all.[12] Similarly, Tertullian in his *De Praescriptione Haereticorum*: the true faith was given by Christ to the apostles; seeking ends when we have found it; we must thenceforth hold to it; heresy is a departure from the already-existing truth.[13]

The idea of the temporal priority of orthodoxy may, however, be challenged, on historical grounds, as the view of an ecclesiastical hierarchy which had, with considerable difficulty, been establishing itself from the second century onwards, and which only attained unquestioned hegemony in the fourth. Such a challenge is associated, in the twentieth century, with Walter Bauer, whose *Orthodoxy and Heresy in Earliest Christianity* (1934) actually *reversed*, on historico-critical grounds, the classical view of the chronological priority of orthodoxy.[14] This provoked an Anglican reply from H.E.W. Turner, who, while accepting that the 'classical' view was, historically, untenable, nevertheless advocated 'an interaction of fixed and flexible elements'[15] in early Christianity, placing among the 'fixed' 'the Creed and the Rule of Faith'.[16] The Bauer-Turner debate is not so foreign to Newman's world as might at first appear: an analogous controversy had been proceeding since the mid-seventeenth century, associated with the work of the great Jesuit patristic historian, Petavius.[17] It passed into eighteenth-century England, and Newman revived it in his arguments for a 'Via Media'!18 Indeed, Turner is himself probably the last in a line of Anglican theologians who have attempted to reconcile the subversive implications of the variety and 'fluidity'[19] witnessed by historical scholarship, with a fixity in the rule of faith.

Newman was introduced to this problem by George Bull's *Defence of the Nicene Faith* (1685).[20] This he first read and used as a reference-work, when he was writing *Arians of the Fourth Century*, in 1831.[21] When he looks back upon his Anglican period, Newman invariably identifies Bull as the most important influence upon him.[22] Yet at the time of *Arians'* composition, he could refer to Bull, somewhat disparagingly as a 'Doctrinist', rather than a historian.[23] One can easily see why: voluminous and erudite, crammed with patristic influences, painstakingly taking the reader, century by century, Father by Father, through the labyrinth of pre-Nicene Trinitarian debates, the *Defensio* is disappointing as a model for the vivid and readable narrative to which Newman was then aspiring.[24] His retrospection is, nevertheless, not necessarily mis-leading, because he presents Bull as affording, not a narrative model, but a *'principle'* upon which an orthodoxy may be con-structed: 'that Antiquity was the true exponent of the doctrines of Christianity and the basis of the Church of England'.[25] It was upon this principle that the 'Via Media' was constructed. When, in 1845, he took his leave of this 'great theory, which is so specious to look upon, so difficult to prove, and so hopeless to work', he associated it with 'Bp Bull's theology' as 'the only theology on which the English Church could stand'.[26]

Bull brought to Newman's attention the most formidable extant scholarly challenge to a static concept of orthodoxy, in the Jesuit historian, Denys Pétau's (Petavius') account of early Church doctrine. The motivation for the latter's analysis is as obscure as his ultimate conclusions.[27] What made him the object of Bull's hostile attention was his presentation of variations of teaching amongst the pre-Nicenes, in an analysis which seemed to contra-dict the immutability of orthodoxy and to suggest 'a concept of evolution which until that moment had been almost totally unknown' (Paul Galtier).[28] Particularly controversial was his argu-ment that Arianism was no new invention, but that it came straight out of earlier orthodox Fathers' subordination of the Son to the Father: 'they thought He [the Son] had a beginning, as do creatures, that is that He was a distinct person by no means existing from all eternity'.[29]

In defending the pre-Nicene Fathers, Bull stolidly presents the

Church's understanding of the *revelatum* as always having been the same: 'orthodoxy' is fixed and immutable, no new ideas or developments being possible. When confronted with heresy, the Church always knew what this orthodoxy was – it had a clear idea of it – although it may, initially, have been stuck for the best way of putting it into *words*. This sharp distinction between on the one hand, words or terms, and, on the other, things, ideas, or realities was all-pervasive in Bull[30] as the main means of reconciling the Fathers' variations with a fixed and static orthodoxy. The problem, for Bull, is manufactured by the heretics: really, there is no problem of *knowledge* for the Church when it gives expression to its orthodoxy. Armed with this rudimentary mode of explanation, Bull may argue for the temporal priority of orthodoxy over heresy which he has acquired from the Fathers themselves: the apostles handed down a pure, unmixed expression of the *revelatum* to the bishops succeeding them.[31] Thus may heresy be demonstrated to be innovation by pointing to the previously existing condition of orthodoxy: 'But which of the Catholic doctors before his time taught this?'[32] We must add – in substance, if not in *words*.

Bull tries very hard at a specific level, to vindicate pre-Nicene doctrine. This raises, indirectly, the general issue, the relation of orthodoxy to heresy, which forces itself upon a scholar reluctant to treat of it. If orthodoxy is an expression of the *revelatum* which is immutable and temporally prior to heresy, how may the origination of particular heresies be explained? Bull answers that any heresy may be demonstrated to derive from another, earlier, heresy.[33] This only puts off the problem: for, working on Bull's premises, the temporal regression must come to a halt at a point *later* than the uncorrupted apostolic teaching. A further shift is necessary: heresy is *perversion* of orthodoxy, heretics preceding from right belief to a distorted form of it.[34] But, as his distinction between words-and-things has already conceded, it is not possible to point to a homogenous form of *expression* which may act as a prior norm against which the perversions of heresy may be identified: if the variations of the pre-Nicenes are diverse verbal expressions of the one orthodox faith, on what criterion are the similarly diverse expressions of heretics excluded as inauthentic expressions of the faith? Why, indeed, was it so *difficult*, when heresies arose, adequately to exclude them? Bull's explanation – it is not original – of why Arianism gained such wide acceptance within the Church is that many were *deceived*[35] by Arian language into believing it orthodox. This only highlights the difficulty of deciding *which* expressions of Christian revelation are authentic. Moreover, even Bull has, on a few occasions, to concede that, in a sense, orthodoxy had been on the move, as it underwent distortion in striving to re-express the true faith in contradistinction to heresy.[36] The distinction between words-and-things is therefore ultimately of no avail to defend a static concept of orthodoxy – indeed the former calls attention to the untenability of the latter.

Bull escapes into particulars; learning is his *forte*, not systematic analysis. Sometimes, however, even in specific cases, he has to admit that orthodoxy and heresy were not as different as he thought they were. Bull's argument cracks open when it collides with the fact that both Tertullian and Justin say that, in the burning bush, it was the Son, not the Father or Spirit, who called to Moses, because only the Son, as His Incarnation shows, was materially circumscribable! Bull sounds a rare note of personal anguish and alarm:

Who indeed, but must be utterly amazed at these surprising statements of the Fathers? Are we to suppose that these writers were so dull and inconsistent as to suppose that the Son of God, whom they every where else declare to be very God of very God, was at any time circumscribed within the narrow bounds of one and that a small space, or that He was in His own actual nature visible? Far be it from us to think so of men so distinguished. By what clever expedient, then, you will say, can such words of theirs be set right?[37]

Bull brings in his words-things apologetic, but it has worn very thin. He is whistling in the dark. Although 'quite of the opinion' that the Fathers concerned stated a view 'most true', he has to concede that they expressed themselves 'somewhat harshly', and 'in a manner unsuitable and incorrect'. It is all the heretics' fault, for their obstinacy drove the orthodox into 'unguarded expressions'.[38]

Newman, then, inherited from Bull much to be unthankful for. Yet the *Defence of the Nicene Creed*'s significance in Anglican ideology was such that it could hardly fail to recommend itself to Newman. On one front, Bull was defining his position against the Roman Catholic assertion of a living papal magisterium, which appeared to claim the ability to expound Tradition without respecting the Fathers.[39] On the other, he was defending the dogmas of the

Nicene creed against burgeoning anti-Trinitarianism in England: the Socinian Christopher Sand's *Nucleus Historiae Ecclesasticae* used a Petavian style of historical analysis to demonstrate that the pre-Nicene Fathers' subordination of the Son to the Father brought them closer to Socinianism than post-Nicene orthodoxy.[40] This dual threat to Bull's conception of the fixed faith of Antiquity is similar to the two extremes of sectarian Protestantism and Roman corruptions against which Newman was in the 1830s attempting to define his 'Via Media'. Indeed, Newman identifies *all* popular Protestantism as virtually Socinian.

The polemical discussion of arguments about the nature of orthodoxy was, by Newman's time, no longer restricted to disputations in Latin between the learned. Socinianism had grown steadily in popularity, and the English Unitarians were pressing for a theological and social acceptance in accord with their influence.[41] Moreover, the historical issue of variations in pre-Nicene doctrine had been popularised in Edward Gibbon's brilliantly sardonic account of the age of the early Fathers, which argued that Trinitarian orthodoxy was fundamentally incoherent.[42] Newman deplored, admired and used the *Decline and Fall of the Roman Empire*.[43] In justifying the Anglican Church's patristic authority, he could hardly fail, once again, to have the problem of variations forced upon him.

(B) 'THE ARIANS OF THE FOURTH CENTURY' AND THE PROBLEM OF THE NATURE OF ORTHODOXY

Newman's estimation of Bull's influence in the *Apologia*, and the number of citations of the *Defensio* in *Arians* might lead one to anticipate a strong imprint of the static concept of orthodoxy in his first work on heresy. It is, indeed, true that Newman deploys the connected idea of the temporal priority of orthodoxy. In his section upon 'Variations in the Anti-Nicene Theological Statements',[44] he discusses the historical fortunes of the *Homoousion*, – the view that Christ was of one essence or substance with the Father – and argues that it was *first* used in the orthodox sense – 'a Being, real, living and individual'[45] – to mean the revealed God of Scripture, distinct from and beyond Creation. It was applied to the Son as early as Justin Martyr, Newman argues, in order to express His identity with the Father and to protect His divinity: for Justin, the

Son is 'inseparable from the substance of being, $ov\sigma\iota\alpha$, of the Father'.[46] Heresy perverted this established meaning by imposing the alien Gnostic usage, which denoted the sharing in the essence of the Supreme Intelligence by aeons or spirits emanating from It. This is alien to what Newman regards as the basic principle of revelation – 'the incommunicable character and individuality of the Divine Essence'.[47] The *Homoousion* once tainted, the orthodox could not insist on it. Consequently, at the Council of Antioch, Paul of Samosata was able successfully to object to the term, when proposed as a test.[48] The orthodox had to give way and withdraw the term, lest 'weak minds'[49] be perplexed. Having extorted this concession from 'Catholics', heretics began a wholesale onslaught upon the established language of orthodoxy, with the result that 'they were gradually silencing the Church by the process which legitimately led to Pantheism when the Alexandrians gave the alarm and nobly stood forward in defence of the faith'.[50]

Newman's narrative of the *Homoousion*, then, implies throughout a distinction between the fixed and prior condition, 'orthodoxy', the 'thing' itself, and the words used to express it, the variety and fluctuating meanings of which explain the supposed 'variations' of the pre-Nicene age. However, Newman cannot, any more than Bull, adequately explain why, if a prior orthodox meaning had been so firmly attached to the term, it was so readily corrupted.

Yet Newman's absorption of Bull was in *Arians* a more complex procedure than this, and he cannot really be said to have followed the *Defensio* slavishly.[51] Rather, he transformed both concepts and material from the *Defensio*, and, while glancing at the infidel and Roman threats defended by Bull's 'staunch polemic', is altogether more subtle and ambivalent. At the outset of Newman's section upon 'Variations', there occurs a highly ambiguous passage where conflicting tendencies are being held in tension: on the one hand, there is allegiance to Bull, but, on the other, an understanding of ecclesiastical dogma which is redolent of Romanticism, in its appeal to the affective and experiential. Newman only *just* comes down on the side of the priority of orthodoxy. His opening sentence shows the glimmerings of an idea of dogmatic evolution, competing with the 'classic' view:

There will, of course, be differences of opinion, in deciding how much of the ecclesiastical doctrine . . . was derived from direct Apostolical

Tradition, and how much was the result of intuitive spiritual perception in Scripturally informed and deeply religious minds.[52]

He concludes, in phraseology suggesting a degree of hesitation, that 'it does not seem too much to affirm' that the language of ecclesiastical dogma may be found, or found to be implied, in the New Testament. He uses a form of the words-things distinction, arguing that the language of ecclesiastical orthodoxy expresses in a systematic form the truths unsystematically and imprecisely expressed in Scripture.[53]

This brings him before the problems of the pre-Nicene Fathers. He sees them as distorted by the exigencies of a post-Nicene orthodox perspective: they have to be accommodated to this later picture and – while Newman does not deny that such accommodation is possible – it is clear that such a process involves loss and impoverishment. The warm and unselfconscious familiarity of the early Fathers with the object of their reverence had to be sacrificed in the interest of clarity: 'it is we in after times who systematize the statements of the Fathers, which, as they occur in their works, are for the most part as natural and unpremeditated as those of the inspired volume itself'.[54]

Newman announces a *tension*, between the preciser Trinitarian language of the era of the ecumenical councils ('Creeds'), and the looser language of pre-Nicene Christianity, where words are organically integrated with the worshipping life of a community ('doxologies'): 'We count the words of the Fathers, and measure their sentences; and so convert doxologies into creeds.'[55]

This antithesis between 'doxologies' and 'creeds' introduces a note of complexity into the discussion absent in Bull, who defends orthodoxy on the assumption that its varying verbal expresssions are rooted in one, clear, common idea which was present in the Fathers' minds. Newman, however, sees language as part of the life-form[56] of a community and interests himself in the political, social and psychological factors behind the evolution of dogma. His theory is that credal, propositional dogma was a *secondary* stage beginning in the fourth century. From this secondary condition, to which Newman sees himself as belonging, he looks back to an earlier, *primary*, stage with unconcealed nostalgia, the later stage being an attenuation of *life*. Here, in a sense, Newman accords with the Socinian historians' theory of 'corruption' – something, indeed, had gone wrong after Nicea! But he blames heretics for it: the lamentable constrictions of the secondary, credal stage were caused by the heresies which forced the Church into unwonted and unwelcome clarity; of dogmatising he declares, 'That we do so, that the Church has done so more or less from the Nicene Council downwards, is the fault of those who have obliged us, of those who, "while men slept", have sowed tares among the wheat.'[57]

Newman does not use the word 'orthodoxy' in this discussion. What, then, may be drawn out of this passage which applies to the problem of orthodoxy's relation to heresy? Two answers are possible. First, if by 'orthodoxy' Newman means *only* the secondary stage of credal expressions, then he conceives orthodoxy, not as prior to heresy, but subsequent to it. Alternatively, he may be proposing as his concept of orthodoxy something very complex, that it is a historically layered expression of the *revelatum*, the earlier stratum operating according to different socio-linguistic rules from the latter. Indeed, there is a resemblance to the position eventually adopted in the *Essay on Development*, in the dichotomy between the impact of the *revelatum*, itself a mysterious object, upon our experience, and the evolving ideas we form of it.[58] If so, this passage contains some original and pregnant suggestions.

Yet, Newman's very next paragraph falls back from this many sided apprehension of what 'orthodoxy' might be, to a position unequivocally derivative of Bull. He faces the fact that when the pre-Nicene Fathers – for the most part sunk in the doxological mentality – did make their occasional forays into precise dogmatic theology in 'more intentional systematising', then they appear closer to what was later seen as heresy, than to orthodoxy: their statements are 'ambiguous, and in consequence afforded at times an apparent countenance to the Arian heresy'.[59] He defends them by the well-worn distinction between *ideas*, clearly and commonly understood, and *words*, ambiguous and needing clarification:

It often becomes necessary to settle the phraseology of divinity, in points, where the chief problem is, to select the clearest words to express notions in which all agree; or to find the proposition which will best fit in with, and connect, a number of revived doctrines.[60]

Eventually, the right idea becomes associated with a defined term, after a process of 'scrutiny': 'they are variously expressed during the process . . . they are consigned to arbitrary formulas, at the end of it'.[61] But even this goes beyond Bull: 'arbitrary formulas' betrays awareness that something new comes into being even with a verbal development.

Scarcely a ripple of epistemological anxiety disturbs the even surface of Bull's *Defensio*: Newman's *Arians* is riddled with tensions, ultimately traceable to the pervasive antithesis between the credal and the doxological. This is particularly apparent in Newman's manner of describing the delicate balance between the *disciplina arcani* – the secret life of faith – and the *economy*.[62] This balance was upset by the disclosures of apostasy and the assertions of heresy, impelling the church to publish creeds. According to Newman, the pre-Nicene Church jealously guarded its saving doctrines from all but the initiate who knew them in an atmosphere of worship, mystery and secrecy. On the other hand, the Church also wanted to articulate some of its beliefs so that those outside could at least begin to understand them, by 'adapting their sentiments and even their language as far as they could'.[63] The *economy* provided flexibility of expression, while the *disciplina arcani* protected the *revelatum* from corruption. This balance is, perhaps, a version of Bull's words-and-things, but modified radically: the *economy* is, indeed, words, but the *thing* is not seen as *just* a clear body of ideas which may be expressed in one way or another, for the *disciplina arcani* is a pattern of believing activity, bound up with participation in the Christian mysteries or sacraments, in a corporate atmosphere of reverent feeling. Newman declares the *disciplina arcani* to have conceptual content – he describes it as 'doctrines'[64] handed down from the apostles – but does not explain precisely what he means: he is probably thinking of the private, catechetical instruction to initiates, which was eventually taken over by the Church's public, credal doctrine.

the secret tradition soon ceased to exist even in theory. It was authoritatively divulged, and perpetuated according as the successive innovations of heretics called for its publication. In the Creeds of the early Councils, it may be considered as having come to light and so ended.[65]

He appears unwilling to open the *disciplina arcani* to epistemological analysis: it is the numinous dawn of faith which heretics have caused to be replaced by the stark day of adulthood.

All that is holy, all that is beautiful or Romantic, is broken down by heresy. In two intense metaphors, Newman conveys his nostalgic yearning for the Church's childhood, 'trailing clouds of glory'. First, a very English image of the love between friends and family is used to describe the *reserve* of the *disciplina arcani*: as in a profound relationship, the emotions are so strong as to preclude their expression in outward feeling, so in the piety of early Christians.[66] Secondly, he draws an analogy with literature: great works are 'composed freely' and only later 'subjected to the rules of grammarians and critics'.[67] Heresy has driven the Christian to a lower level of existence, transforming him from poet to grammarian.

On occasion, Newman strives to ease the tension between doxological and credal by positing the inevitability, given the human intellect's dynamic structure, of a natural movement from one to the other:

As the mind is cultivated and expanded, it cannot refrain from the attempt to analyse the vision which influences the heart, and the Object in which that vision centres; nor does it stop till it has, in some sort succeeded in expressing in words, what has all along been a principle both of its affections and of its obedience.[68]

The transition is not a little tinged with regret: it is unavoidable, and our choice is only to do it well or badly. We 'murder to dissect' and cannot help it.

The ambivalence and hesitation of Newman's attitude to the problem of orthodoxy is epitomised in his description of the 'systematic doctrine of the Trinity'.[69] The doctrinal expression of Trinity is secondary to the rich but undefined immediacy of religious life; it is 'the shadow, projected for the contemplation of the intellect, of the Object of Scripturally-informed piety'.[70] Doctrine 'tranquillize[s] the mind,' giving it rest from perplexity, by limiting the scope of speculation,[71] but it is always 'a representation, economical; necessarily imperfect', and expressed in a 'foreign medium', that is, in the language of human experience, which imposes the 'seen' upon the 'unseen'.[72] It involves 'inconsistencies or mysteries'. For a deeper, predominantly emotional satisfaction, the believer will always turn from doctrine to 'the text of Scripture', which, 'being addressed principally to the affections', is 'of a religious not a philosophical character'.[73] In order, however, to counteract the impression of early orthodoxy as purely an emotional experience, later replaced by dogma, Newman introduces a cognitive element into his treatment of the pre-Nicene period, in order to balance the affective. He therefore asserts that the 'systematic doctrine of the Trinity' was 'given to the Church by tradition' contemporaneously with Scripture.[74] With the epithet 'systematic', Newman runs into contradiction, for, as has been shown, he elsewhere in *Arians* argues that the systematic only marked the *later* credal stage which developed from doxology. His attempt to get around this causes further confusion: he argues that the 'systematic' doctrine was, in earlier centuries 'kept in the background', and only 'brought forward' when 'reason . . . disproportionately developed' strove for mastery over 'religion'.[75] Much hangs on the sense of 'brought forward', but Newman does not help one to decide if the 'bringing forward' is from implicit to explicit, or from private to public, or from ideas to words, or from impressions, via ideas, to words.

On the whole, the heretics are the systematicians. They intellectualise and demand explicitness, while orthodoxy is maintained – notably by 'uneducated men' – practically and implicitly. It is to make this point that Newman undertakes a further subtle modification of Bull's words-and-things antithesis, when he declares that heresy 'put[s] upon us words for things.[76] The heretics are always mistaking 'arrangements of words, which have no existence except on paper, for habits which are realities'.[77] Bull's antithesis is transformed: the 'things' to which the words refer are patterns of behaviour ('habits'), rather than ideas or objects, while Newman reserves for words an assessment verging upon the sceptical or nominalistic. For Newman, in *Arians*, then, the *life* is all, the speculative or analytical usually empty.

Newman found himself, in his earliest work, being pulled in contrary directions. His heroes were Bull and the early Fathers. He wanted to be their disciple and to revive and defend the classical idea of orthodoxy, to assert the ancient and unchanging in a world in process of rapid dissolution, to re-create it imaginatively in the minds of his readers, just at the time when, in society, the 'old ways' were crumbling. On the other hand, Newman was the child of British empiricism, hypersensitive to epistemological issues, concerned with the psychology of impressions and ideas, agnostic about their object.[78] His presentation of heresy–orthodoxy therefore has a more sophisticated and modern air than that of Bull, who had not passed through the philosophical revolution of the eighteenth century. Moreoever, Newman's empiricism is overlaid with Romanticism, his nostalgia for the primitive, and an exaltation of feeling over reason. This mixture of influences accounts for the haunting and ambivalent quality of *Arians*. It must be admitted that his account of orthodoxy remains unsatisfactory, largely because of confusion about, or even unwillingness to expound, the relation between the *revelatum*, its assimilation by humanity, and its expression in doctrine. Nevertheless, he was beginning to grapple with problems of which the seventeenth-century patrists had never dreamed. He comes to us as a modern.

(c) THE PROBLEM OF DEFINITION: A SURVEY OF THE 'VIA MEDIA'

Newman's 'Via Media' was the persuasive re-creation of an orthodoxy. The Church of England's situation after the Reform Bill precluded the unselfconscious mediation of its Catholic tradition to *all*. The first stage of Newman's rhetorical response to this suddenly unfamiliar situation was the popular appeal, in his depiction of the Milan of St Ambrose, to the 'irrefragable'[79] nature of the Christian Church's Apostolicity and Catholicity. But, of course, no such spontaneous recognition of the ancient heritage of Anglicanism necessarily sprang up in the generality of the English people. It was divided: the *sensus communis* had not so much to be sought for as to be constructed. Newman therefore had to *re-invent* 'Antiquity'.

In his 'Via Media', Newman posited a form of Christianity in continuity with Antiquity but distinguishable, not only from the various forms of 'Protestantism' which – as he saw it – had broken with the past altogether, but also from Rome's additions to, and corruptions of, the authentic Christian tradition. His method may be described as rhetorical. From Joseph Butler, Newman acquired the idea of probability, a method of argumentation calling upon patterns of understanding drawn from practical everyday experience.[80] Butler's distinguished place in the history of philosophy should not, however, obscure the fact that he was an apologist, nor that probability (or εἰκός) has been, since classical times, *par excellence* the method of the rhetorician.[81] Newman applies this method to history by an appeal to converging evidences, cumulatively constructing a picture of the faith and practice of the early Church. What, he asks, are the broad outlines, the essentials of the

Christian faith, as illustrated by the age of the Fathers? Translations of the Fathers themselves – the *Records of the Faith* and, eventually, the *Library of the Fathers*[82] – strengthened the broad outline of the nature of patristic Christianity. This approach to the historical appeals frankly to the ordinary person of sense, rather than to the intellectual whom Newman castigates, as requiring an unreal and abstractly theoretical certainty before assent. Moreover, the heritage of the past, Newman argues, could easily be grasped and epitomised in the *Creeds*,[83] known by heart since childhood and constantly recited in Church.

It was always, however, a troubled vision. Newman could never entirely repress snags in the detail of his argument about how orthodoxy and heresy may be defined in relation to each other. Especially problematic was the need to define a position simultaneously anti-Roman and anti-Protestant. This raised complications inhibiting the freedom he had occasionally brought to his treatment of the problem in *Arians*. His own remarkable tendency to *raise* difficulties touching his own position explains the crisis at the end: a decade of tension and unease exploded in the move towards Rome.

Newman's two tracts, of July and August 1834, launching his 'Via Media' of the Church of England as lying 'between the (so-called) Reformers, and the Romanists'[84], or between 'Protestantism' and 'Popery'[85] immediately suggests an insecurity underlying the grandiose programme of a 'second Reformation'[86] to re-Catholicise the Church. The discussion inevitably moves, via the problems of the status of Reformation articles, to the nature of the unchanging apostolic faith with which such articles are contrasted. When heresy comes up, a fearful tangle ensues.

The problems of the relation of development to fixity is raised in the dialogue in *Tract 38* between Clericus, an ardent 'apostolical' and Laicus, a dubious but sympathetic enquirer. The former declares that 'Age after age, fresh battles have been fought with heresy, fresh monuments of truth set up.'[87] This is not what it seems: Clericus is not arguing evolution of *dogma*. The 'fresh monuments' are, however, in some sense, 'additions' made to the Apostolic Faith. Such are the *39 Articles*, the other continental Protestant articles, and for that matter, 'Tridentine articles' (which differ from the Anglican only in being 'unsound').[88] All these articles were framed 'against certain errors of a certain period of the

Church'.[89] They do not constitute a coherent statement of the Christian faith in its wholeness ('a body of divinity'),[90] and are therefore to be distinguished from 'rule of Faith', the 'Apostolic' faith, 'whole Gospel of Christ' or 'whole counsel of God', which may be identified by its *priority* to the Reformation, and by the fact that 'Romanists and Reformers' alike agreed upon it.[91]

Tract 41, continues the conversation. Here, Clericus further defines the prior, unchanging Apostolic Faith as *saving*. He explains additions as being of two kinds: either 'Romish' corruptions or reforming protests, the latter of which aimed to return the Apostolic Faith to its original purity. Laicus attempts a summary of the 'apostolical' position:

> that, as time goes on, fresh and fresh articles of faith are necesssary to secure the Church's purity, according to the rise of successive heresies and errors. These articles were all hidden, as it were, in the Church's bosom from the first and brought into form according to the occasion.[92]

The Roman Catholic Newman, in a note to the Collected Edition, declared this account – which Clericus accepts[93] – to be an early admission of 'the principle of doctrinal development . . . as true and necessary for the Christian Church'.[94] But Newman is reading his earlier self by the later. In fact, Laicus confuses the issue considerably by failing to distinguish between essential 'articles of faith', such as 'the Nicene explanation against Arius', and local, disciplinary 'articles of religion', such as 'the English articles against Popery'.[95] Yet Clericus, the Tractarian mouthpiece, fails to disabuse him, and himself seems unaware of the distinction. Further to confuse the matter, Laicus in another summary, equally readily accepted by Clericus[96] defines 'the doctrines of the Catholic Church' as what 'we are clearly bound to believe, and all of us do believe, as essential, doctrines which nevertheless are not contained in the Articles'.[97] The essential 'doctrines', then, are not articles. But is the Nicene definition a 'doctrine' or an 'article'? The drift seems to be that, insofar as it is a *verbal* expression, then it is an 'article', and so *not* essential.

This ambiguity about articles was to haunt Newman's presentation of orthodoxy in the 1830s. It was a difficulty which others had already encountered in the discussion of fundamental articles, in the seventeenth and eighteenth centuries.[98] It was forced upon Newman when he was pulled into a debate initiated by his friend

Benjamin Harrison with the Abbé Jager.[99] The systematic clarity required to defend Anglican claims against the often uncomfortably acute enquiries of the tenacious Abbé was uncongenial to Newman and the translation into French inevitably diminished the effectiveness of his style. The result is a 'rather confusing'[100] argument. But there is a *structural* incoherence too, pointing to a basic uncertainty about the definitions of heresy and orthodoxy. Newman's other Tractarian writings more skilfully conceal it, but the Jager correspondence exposes the cracks, before, as it were, the cosmetics were applied.

The terms of the initial discussion between Jager and Harrison had been complicated enough: they both accepted Tradition in some sense but disagreed about *how* it was to be found, and about how Vincent of Lerins' *Commonitorium*[101] – the *quod ubique, quod semper, quod ab omnibus*[102] – was to be applied. For Harrison, the Vincentian Canon is an invitation to make a judgment about what Tradition is, on the evidence.[103] Jager, on the other hand, argued that, since no one can read *all* the Fathers and make scholarly judgments on them, the *Commonitorium* upholds ecclesiastical authority and recommends obedience: Vincent meant that, when new heresies arose, *if* they had not been condemned by the Church, then one could have recourse to the *quod ubique, quod semper, quod ab omnibus* as a rule of thumb by which to gauge Tradition – but if the Church *had* defined, then obedience was all that was required.[104] Jager, then, asserted the role of the *magisterium* in *defining*[105] what had always been, while Harrison upheld historical judgment against Roman authoritarianism. Moreover, they differed not only about the *nature* of Tradition, but also about its relation to Scripture. For Harrison, the latter was the sole authority, Tradition being a guide to its authentic interpretation. Jager, however, saw *both* Scripture and Tradition as sources of revelation.[106]

Newman further complicated the terms of the debate by introducing for the first time, the subject of fundamental articles, hitherto unfamiliar to Jager.[107] Newman's exposition is marked by a grotesquely elaborate precision, which only serves to magnify the confusion about how *heresy* is to be placed. He defines fundamentals as 'doctrines . . . necessary for Church Communion', identical with 'the articles of the Creed'.[108] They are 'ultimately' grounded in Scripture, though we may receive them 'immediately' from Tradition.[109] There are other traditional doctrines, not based on

Scripture, which are only points of discipline, not terms of communion and not fundamental. Newman, then, distinguishes between two kinds of Tradition. There is, first, and most important, 'the authority of tradition based on Scripture in fundamental points' which is 'imperative'.[110] There is also secondly, and much less importantly, Tradition 'in matters of doctrine not fundamental and of discipline', which it is only 'pious'[111] to believe. The latter, which Newman, unhappily, calls 'pure Tradition'[112] is what Rome wrongly imposes as fundamental. In contrast, Newman sees as fundamental a static deposit, 'ever one and the same, admitting of no addition and imperishable'.[113] It is 'the ground of communion' – but it *precedes* the Church and is hidden, as it were, in Scripture. Only one strictly limited form of Church Tradition, Apostolic Tradition, is capable of finding it, and expressing it in what Newman calls the 'fundamental creed'.[114] Newman does not clarify its relation to the various Creeds which came into existence in the Early Church – the Nicene, Athanasian and Apostles'. Is the 'fundamental creed' an expression, in articles, or the deposit? Does this imply a form of doctrinal development? Indeed, does the 'fundamental creed' consist of verbal propositions at all? Obviously the answers to such questions will dictate where heresy is to be placed in relation to fundamental orthodoxy.

Aware of these difficulties, Newman makes a distinction between the 'fundamental creed' and its development by various communities into 'Articles of religion' which are not fundamental and have a disciplinary usefulness. These 'voluntary developments' are, indeed, 'additions', but the essentials of the faith are prior to them, remaining static and unchanging.[115] However, Newman has not settled whether the 'fundamental creed', too, consists of articles. When he comes to give examples of 'Articles of religion' this problem intensifies. As 'Articles of religion', which are *not* fundamental, he lists infant baptism, the double procession of the Holy Spirit, and the *Homoousion* of Nicea.[116] His explanation of the function of 'articles of religion' in relation to 'fundamental creed' makes it obvious that he considers such dogmatic definitions as the *Homoousion* to be equivalent to Anglican articles, rather than articles of faith: 'The object of these additions is either to secure the fundamentals, as was effected at Nicea by the *Homoousion*, or to fortify the Church itself, as our article denying the jurisdiction of the Roman See in England.'[117] But if the *Homoousion* isn't fundamental, then the Arian heresy was not a *denial* of the fundamental faith. In what, then, does heresy consist?

Newman's answer hardly supports his characteristically strong sense of the perniciousness of heresy: he sees the 'voluntary developments' of the fundamental creed which were made in the first five centuries as having 'great weight to all Christians in every age' because agreed by an undivided Church. Thus the first four Ecumenical Councils act as 'the rule of orthodoxy against heresy'.[118] His explanation has odd consequences: heresy is not a direct denial of the fundamental creed, but, even more surprising, Newman will not impose the dogmatic definitions of Ecumenical Councils 'as terms of communion'.[119] It is, however, improbable that he intended to present heresy as only a local or disciplinary infringement, for this would contradict the stress he lays elsewhere upon the danger posed by heresy to the survival of Christianity, and his vigorous defence of the ecclesiastical anathema.[120] Indeed, Newman is trapped: to concede a development of dogmatic definition as fundamental, essential or 'of faith', would be to throw in the towel to Tridentine Rome, but to cling to a static concept of the fundamental faith makes the Church's response to heresy incomprehensible. Why all the fuss, if essentials are not at stake?

Jager shrewdly and ruthlessly pressed this weak point in Newman's argument: the issue of *fundamental error*. If Roman errors are fundamental, then a branch of the church has failed – and the branch theory falls.[121] But if Rome's errors are not fundamental, why has the Church of England broken with it? Newman's failure to clarify the relation between terms such as 'fundamental error', 'heresy', 'addition' and 'corruption' is understandable: he needs Rome to justify a form of Catholicity against Protestantism, which he is always happy to call heretical. On the other hand, Rome has to be, in some sense, wrong, though not radically *enough* to lend weight to the ultra-Protestant claim that, by 1500, the Christian faith had been corrupted. Moreover, Jager identifies Newman's difficulty over the *content* of the 'fundamental creed', which would seem not to include Original Sin or Baptismal Regeneration. Newman was, of course, vigorously advocating such doctrines, in his polemic against Protestantism – it is hard to imagine that he did not regard them as essential. But he did not need to with Rome – here was agreement. Newman's expression of the essential content of the Christian faith has a shifting – and, indeed, an almost shifty – quality, as his articulation varies with the polemical context. Jager's blunt demand for him to spell out what the fundamentals are is therefore a pertinent one.

Newman's second letter, however, continues the wire-drawn distinctions of his first, bringing his difficulty over heresy to preternatural clarity. He distinguishes between fundamentals, 'necessary for Church Communion', and doctrines 'necessary to profess in order to be saved',[122] so that he can justify, by means of the latter, submission to ecclesiastical doctrines which are not fundamental. It is, of course, difficult to imagine how a doctrine can be 'saving' without also being fundamental. Newman uses this dubious distinction to prove that heresy is a bad thing even though it does not directly threaten the fundamentals. He defines a heretic as a *public* teacher ('doctor'), promulgating what is contrary to the 'teaching of the Church'.[123] By this latter phrase, he does *not* mean the fundamentals, but their developments. This is clear from his distinction between heretic and private individual: both may hold the same opinion but the latter should not be excommunicated provided he keeps quiet.[124] In both cases the doubt or error concerns 'certain developments of doctrine', not fundamentals.[125] The heretic is excommunicated, not because he denies fundamentals, but because he *teaches* developments at variance with the Church.[126] He is, in fact, cast out from the Church without ever violating the 'terms of communion'. This is how Newman would keep 'Socinians, Pelagians and others' out of the Church, even though the truths they deny may not necessarily be found in the Apostles' Creed.[127] It is a real difficulty that, to protect his flank against Rome, Newman has to make heresy a non-fundamental error. He is driven to locate the culpability as disruption in the public sphere, reverting to the line pursued in defence of *ancien régime* which identifies as 'tests' both ancient dogmas and modern articles:

The laity of the upper classes have a great power in the Church of England: I mean the Privy Council, the law officers, the members of Parliament etc. Just as the Council of Nicea imposed its belief on the Clergy, so we impose our articles on certain laymen, namely on the members of the universities.[128]

The second letter re-iterates that the *Homoousion* of Nicea is only an article of religion, not an article of faith. Newman averts the consequence – that even Arianism was a non-fundamental error, by the words-things distinction. St Athanasius, he argues, did not excommunicate those semi-Arians who baulked at the *word*, provided they believed the same *thing* as himself.[129] On this basis, Newman distinguishes between the 'general doctrine'[130] of Nicea and the *Homoousion* which was used to express it. As *word*, the argument seems to run, the *Homoousion* is non-fundamental, but if the *thing* it denotes be meant, then it *is* a fundamental. It therefore may, or may not, be heresy to deny it.

Finally, Newman articulated for the first time in this letter a distinction which was to become celebrated when he re-used it in his *Lectures on the Prophetical Office of the Church*, that between 'Apostolic Tradition' and 'Prophetical Tradition'. Here the tension between stasis and fixity attains its clearest expression: while 'Apostolic Tradition' is immutable, fundamental, hands down articles of faith and is virtually synonymous with the Apostles' Creed, 'Prophetic Tradition' is the development of the Apostolic into a vast system of interpretation 'permeating the body of the Church like an atmosphere', out of which non-fundamental 'articles of religion' arise.[131] However, 'to develop is not to create'[132] – not for the Newman of 1834 – and heresy cannot stimulate the 'fundamental faith' into a new understanding of itself. Heresy is opposed, not to the Apostolic, but the the Prophetical Tradition. Since this latter is non-fundamental and contains within itself truths 'entitled to very different degrees of credit',[133] Newman's recommendation of it as a standard for orthodoxy can only be tentative: 'This is that body of teaching which is offered to every individual according to his capacity and which . . . must be received with trust and affection, and not be said to err, although it be not necessary to submit to it without proof.'[134] This is hardly a clinching dissuasive against heresy, and even suggests, in its mention of the need of 'proof', a means by which the heretic may legitimise his dissent.

The argument with Rome about the Rule of Faith continued on the soil of England where a formidable antagonist, the urbane and plausible Nicholas Wiseman, had disembarked, to deliver, at St Mary's Moorfields, an engaging set of Lenten public lectures in defence of Roman Catholicism (1836).[135] Newman had, in the previous year, in the Brome Chapel, been drawing upon his exchange with Jager to justify the 'Via Media'.[136] The presence of

Wiseman so preoccupied him from March 1836 onwards that he could list as one of the events of that 'cardinal time' when a 'new scene gradually opened'[137] his 'writing against the Church of Rome'.[138] His new association with the *British Critic*[139] produced two articles pursuing the argument over the Rule of Faith: in July, *Apostolical Tradition*,[140] and in September, his review of Wiseman's *Lectures*.[141] Finally, in late 1836, he worked over the ground again and brought his position to classic expression in *Lectures on the Prophetical Office*.[142] In all these works, Newman matched the suavity of Wiseman with a polished and attractive style very different from the turgidity of his letters to Jager. Yet the inconsistencies apparent there with regard to heresy may still be discerned beneath the surface sheen.

Apostolical Tradition, written in the wake of the Hampden controversy,[143] argues the latitudinarian, and ultimately infidel, consequences of the Protestant principle of Private Judgment and sole reliance on Scripture. He places 'Apostolic Tradition', the assertion of Trinity and Incarnation, in direct opposition to the line of virtual Socinianism running from Locke to Hampden.[144] In contrast to his argument with the Abbé Jager, he suppresses distinctions between immutable, fundamental creed and articles, articles of religion and those of faith, or apostolic and prophetic tradition. He wants to bring the full weight of the Ecumenical Councils to bear upon such as Hampden: it would weaken his position to suggest that ancient definitions, such as the *Homoousion*, were neither fundamental nor terms of communion. He only needed to argue in this latter way when resisting developments of the fundamental creed in controversy with Rome. The shift from Catholic France to Protestant England provoked a jarring shift of strategy.

The review of Wiseman's Moorfields *Lectures*, written three months later,[145] presents a somewhat different argument for the Rule of Faith, in its placing of heresy and orthodoxy. Significantly, of course, the rhetorical context has changed: Newman is still arguing on behalf of Tradition as an authoritative interpretation of Scripture, but, this time, has to protect himself against the Roman understanding of Tradition as in itself a *source* of revelation, in addition to Scripture.[146]

Newman has tidied up his terminology, possibly in response to criticism.[147] 'Fundamentals' and 'fundamental faith' give way to terms more immediately communicative – 'necessary' or 'essential'.[148] Moreover, he has dropped the distinction between 'essential' and 'saving'. While, then, Rome defines 'points of faith *beyond* Scripture' and adds to what Tradition draws out of Scripture, the 'points necessary to be believed in order to salvation',[149] Anglicanism holds to 'what is agreeable to Scripture doctrine, and gathered thence by the 'Catholic Fathers and ancient Bishops'.[150] His definition of necessary or essential doctrine brings in the branch-theory to validate Anglicanism: the Anglican Church is described as being one of the branches of the ancient Catholic Church, because it holds to its essentials. The introduction of 'fundamental doctrines' is carefully glossed with the word 'essential'.[151]

Fundamentals – now popularised into the distinction between saving essentials, and non-essentials – play a vital role in Newman's anti-Roman defence.[152] The *static* quality which has been a consistent feature of his characterisation of the fundamental faith may, moreover, be clearly seen, in his response to Wiseman, as a consequence of the need to hold Church authority and fundamental doctrine as far apart as possible, in order to avert the Romanist inference 'that the Church may create articles of *necessary* belief; that what was not necessary to be believed in order to salvation before her decision, becomes so afterwards'.[153] Newman argues the faith to precede the Church, which merely guards what has been immutably given to it: 'Both parties consider "the faith" to be *necessary to salvation* but we say that the faith is prior to the Church; they, the Church is prior to the faith.'[154]

This distinction presents the problem for the placing of heresy which has already been observed: heresy, arising later than the deposit, cannot contradict the essentials of Christianity. There is *something* wrong with heresy, but Newman is not sure what it is. In attacking Wiseman's position of an infallible defining Church, he brings in 'heresy and schism' to demonstrate that the Church is by no means as perfect as his opponent has suggested; they are 'spots and wrinkles in the Church during the time of their growth, and an enfeebling of her when they were cast out'.[155] This is perhaps sufficient to refute Wiseman's argument that the Roman Church had always maintained doctrinal purity. It is not, however, sufficient to explain why heresy was ever so vehemently condemned, if, despite it, there was always, unimpaired, 'perfect maintenance of *fundamental* doctrine'.[156]

Four months after Newman's initial response to Wiseman, he reworked much of his anti-Roman material into *Lectures on the Prophetical Office of the Church*, written in November, 1836.[157] An immediate asymmetry arises in Newman's treatment of the two extremes to which the 'Via Media' is equally opposed. The two distinct polemical strategies, against Rome and against popular Protestantism, necessitate two different methods of placing heresy. That against Protestantism *extends* the definition of heresy to cover rationalism and crypto-infidelity. That against Rome *restricts* it to denial of the fundamentals, and castigates Her for unwarrantably extending her criterion of heresy to her additions to the fundamentals: 'We are at peace with Rome as regards the essentials of faith; but she tolerates us as little as she tolerates any sect or heresy.'[158] Moreover, while Protestant error is heresy, the Roman is *not*, for Rome '*holds the foundation* or *is the truth overlaid with corruptions*',[159] and lacks the tell-tale mark of heresy, the tendency to unbelief.[160] It is, of course, indispensable to the argument on behalf of the Catholicity of his own communion that there be certain irrefragable fundamentals, shared by Anglican, Roman and Eastern Orthodox Churches. In the division between belief and unbelief, he would have Rome on *his* side, but Protestantism against him.

Newman's attempt to construct a pattern of orthodoxy, while resisting what he sees as the Roman claim that additions or corruptions are really developments, results in additional problems of definition. He presents orthodoxy as a fixed deposit, which the Church has no authority to alter, and joins Bull against Petavius, who

consents that the Catholic doctrine of the Holy Trinity should so far rest on the mere declaration of the Church, that before it was formally defined, there was no heresy in rejecting it, provided he can thereby gain for Rome the freedom of making decrees unfettered by the recorded judgments of Antiquity. [161]

Newman defines the fixity by reference to the fundamentals: the 'essentials' do not change, only the 'superstructure' develops. He enforces this distinction throughout the *Lectures* with a battery of antitheses, drawn mainly from the Jager controversy between essentials and non-essentials,[162] articles of faith and articles of religion,[163] terms of communion and disciplinary precepts,[164] 'saving' faith and local, or particular, traditions,[165] and the basic outline of the Apostles' Creed and its developments in the technical definitions in the Nicene or Athanasian.[166] The antithesis is, however, blurred by the introduction of *quinquesaecularism*,[167] for even the *Prophetical* Tradition of the first five centuries of the undivided Church has an authority going beyond mere articles of religion, and approximating to what is of faith. As in 1834, Newman proposes the Vincentian *canon* as a means of identifying the Catholic essentials, so as to distinguish them from the articles of religion of particular national Churches. Newman seems to mean by 'orthodoxy' the deposit of apostolic tradition expressed in articles of faith. One might expect that he defines heresy as the denial of this, but he by no means adopts such a consistent definition.

His uncertainty about the exact *content* of the fundamentals and their relation to Antiquity is so persistent as to imply a chronic inability to declare what orthodoxy is. In the following passage, from his first *Lecture*, Newman epitomises 'the relation which Romanism bears to Catholic Truth', as confirmed by a comparison of 'the doctrinal articles of our own and of the Roman faith':

> In both systems the same Creeds are acknowledged. Besides other points in common, we both hold, that certain doctrines are necessary to be believed for salvation; we both believe in the doctrines of the Trinity, Incarnation and Atonement; in original sin; in the necessity of regeneration; in the supernatural grace of the Sacraments; in the Apostolical succession; in the obligation of faith and obedience, and in the eternity of future punishment.[168]

Newman's drift is familiar: Rome, though corrupt, holds to the fundamentals – it is 'substantial truth corrupted'.[169] His allusion to 'Catholic Truth' suggests that he is itemising here what he thinks fundamental orthodoxy is. But it is a highly ambiguous passage. It is not clear, for example, if he identifies 'the same Creeds' with 'certain doctrines . . . necessary to be believed for salvation', or even whether he means that Anglicanism and Romanism agree about the latter. Moreover, Newman's list of doctrines cannot *all* be identified with the 'essentials' or fundamentals, or the articles of the Creeds – sacramental grace and Apostolic succession are particular difficulties – but it is not certain, anyway, if he intends them to be. He is, in fact, appealing 'to the common opinion of the world'.[170] But this sits uneasily with the distinctions about fundamentals which he has also imported directly from the Jager debate. Common sense, indeed, could only with difficulty be described as a characteristic of this more theoretical strand of the *Lectures*: a sentence such as, 'Scripture is the foundation of the Creed, but belief in Scripture is not the foundation of belief in the Creed',[171] is hardly an appeal to 'common opinion'. About generalities, Newman is precise but arcane. Yet when he comes to *specify* the content of orthodoxy, he attempts to evade, with bluff practicality, the tighter distinctions he has elsewhere established.

Nowhere is this difficulty about the nature of orthodoxy more apparent than in the treatment in the *Lectures on the Prophetical Office*, which have inherited all the unresolved *conundra* of the Jager controversy, about whether heresy is to be placed in opposition to articles of faith, or articles of religion. Newman's oscillation on this point emerges starkly. On the one hand, he can declare heresy to be a denial of the essentials, the fundamental faith:

> The Creed commonly so called, not in its mere letter, but in its living sense, is this Faith, 'the engrafted word, which is able to save our souls', to deny or resist which, is no lawful use of Private Judgment, but heresy or scepticism. We find it declared . . . by the Church in the beginning; we find it actually maintained by all its branches even in this day of division.[172]

On the other hand he can declare that the Church may rightly exclude those who oppose its teaching even as it goes beyond the essentials:[173] 'Let this maxim be laid down concerning all that the Church Catholic holds, to the full extent of her Prophetical Tradition, viz. that her members must either believe or silently acquiesce in the whole of it.'[174]

This is how Newman meets 'the difficulty of drawing the line between essentials and non-essentials':[175] the Church demands an uncritical assent even for teachings that are, confessedly, non-fundamental. She will tolerate those who keep quiet, but may legitimately crush persistent critics, that is, the 'hopelessly contumacious'.[176]

Yet Newman has to confront the fact that, in the face of evolving theological terminology, it was not always easy to decide who was being contumacious. A day arrived when the *Homoousion* became a test of orthodoxy, when it had not been so before: were all those who refused to accept it heretics? Although Newman would have all who failed in acquiescence, obedience and passivity in their demeanour towards the church – all troublemakers, in a word – to be heretics, yet he shrinks from the idea that the Church *defines* the essential Faith, in reaction to heresy, by adding fresh articles – for to admit this would be to play into the hands of Rome. He *dare* not therefore place defined dogmatic articles, such as the *Homoousion*, in direct opposition to heresy, lest a defining *authority* be conceded: the 'Rule of Faith' is, for Newman, '"sole, unalterable, unreformable;" not a hint being given us of the Church's power over it. To guard and to transmit it, not to remodel it, is her sole duty'.[177] Newman explains the relation between new articles, such as the *Homoousion*, and the static, fundamental faith, by borrowing Bull's defence of the Nicene dogma based upon the distinction between words and things. The *Homoousion*, Newman argues, was an *explanation* of what was already *known* unambiguously;[178] it was 'merely in explanation of a great article of faith, held from the first, but then needing, from circumstances, a more accurate wording'.[179]

Dogmatic articles, then, are the clearer articulation of what had always been understood by the Church, necessitated by agitation on the part of heretics for a re-definition ('a new sense')[180] of the Creed. The Church learns nothing new about its understanding of the *deposit*, in its encounter with heresy. It is the heretics who desire development of doctrine; it is in sticking out for this that their contumacy consists. Newman argues that the *Homoousion* was not a development in this sense: rather, its function was 'to fix and perpetuate'[181] the unalterable *meaning* that had always been held by the Church. Nevertheless, there were some 'who repudiated the Homoousion with an unaccountable violence' who yet were not really heretical, because they held to an orthodox meaning, and only choked at the word. Newman cites with approval St Athanasius' toleration of such 'semi-Arians' as these, admitting them to communion.[182]

To keep the essential Creed static by recourse to the re-description, as 'explanation', of dogmatic definitions which appear as additions to the creed is a desperate shift. It does not cover many dogmas which Newman thought it heresy to deny. In a passage recounting what he thinks St Athanasius would have said had he met Pelagius, for example, Original Sin is made an explanation of 'forgiveness of sins' in the Nicene Creed. This stretches 'explanation' as far as development. As the Roman Catholic Newman remarked many years later, in one of the numerous glosses upon this text: 'Surely this is giving up the point in dispute. Original Sin is as much external to the Creed as the Immaculate Conception.'[183]

Newman's attack upon this aspect of his earlier self is rejoined in his commentary upon a passage in *Lecture X* where the *Homoousion* is expounded as a verbal explanation of an eternally immutable reality.[184] The Tractarian Newman argues that the 'article of *Homoousion*' is 'true but not necessary'[185] and characterises it very much as an article of religion – disciplinary, not fundamental and imposed on pain of anathema only upon clergy and theologians. The placing of heresy is crucial: 'the mass of Christians [were] left as they were before, neither pledged as if teachers, nor expelled as if heretics'.[186] On 'heretics', the later Newman demurs: 'This is not quite the point. It was not a difficulty of doctrine at Nicea, but of a word; the doctrine was both true and necessary, and the mass of Christians were so zealous for it as not to need to be pledged.'[187]

Here, he sees the 'word' as vital to the Nicene faith. He is, accordingly, in his account of those 'parties' who 'refused the word', much harder on the Semi-Arians than in the *text* of the *Lectures on the Prophetical Office* – he now sees them as 'pious but subtle-minded and perverse'.[188] Perhaps, over the abyss of years, Newman is glancing critically at his earlier self.

The *Lectures*, then, fail to surmount the problems of defining orthodoxy which Newman had encountered in the Jager controversy. This is not surprising – in the interim, he has become less reflective and even more obsessive, feverishly hacking out a clearing in which to stand. The obstinate presence of heresy refuses to fit his scheme, and he, with equal obstinacy, refuses to modify his scheme to place it. In the end, his frankest reaction to heresy is exasperation:

If, after all, persons arose, as they would arise, disputing against the fundamentals, or separating on minor points, let them go their way: 'they went out from us, because they were not of us'. They would commonly be 'men of corrupt minds, reprobate concerning the faith'.[189]

Unwilling to decide if heresy be a fundamental or a non-fundamental error, Newman falls back upon his earliest, and most obvious characterisation of it as personal inauthenticity ('corrupt', 'reprobate'), yet in his approximation of heresy to *schism*, he reveals how much *public* ecclesiastical order is on his mind: the heretic is essentially a trouble-maker. That the dissident is – here almost by definition – reprobate is a maxim more extreme than any adopted even at the apogee of his defence of *ancien régime*. His succeeding sentences betray a flicker of unease, as he faces the possibility ('extraordinary cases') that 'better men' may be heretics, but he would still have them 'put out of the Church for their error's sake, and for their contumacy'.[190] This is a problem for God to sort out, providing 'in His own inscrutable way for anomalies which His revealed system did not meet'.[191] In practice, Newman invokes the authority of the Church. He will not call this 'infallibility', but rather 'the confidence and obedience of her members'.[192] This benign phrase, however, introduces a procedure which emerges, only a few lines later, as something altogether more brutal: 'the proud and self-willed disputant' will be 'discarded without the perplexed inquirier suffering',[193] once ecclesiastical power is exercised. In the end, then, Newman hoped that all dissidents would either go away of their own accord to start a sect, or that the Church would be able to throw them out. It is unlikely that he was expressing such hopes with any conviction: experience would already have adequately disappointed him.

Newman was more effective when he avoided exposing his weaknesses by drawing out all the implications of his position. It is, perhaps, for this reason that his *Preface* to the translation, made by R.W. Church, of the *Catecheses of Cyril of Jerusalem*,[194] written a year later than the *Lectures*, has not even today lost its power to convince.[195] Many of the features which have been prominent in Newman's treatment of 'Antiquity' so far – necessary doctrine or fundamentals, *consensus patrum*, Scripture and Tradition, and, of course, heresy – reappear. The placing of heresy in the argumentative pattern is, however, markedly different from what has gone before, for, after all, this time Newman is arguing the writings of a Father, who was, in some sense, heretical, to be, in some sense, normative. It was a confident performance, at the high point of Newman's Tractarianism, just before he began to falter.[196] It belongs to the most ambitious of all Tractarian enterprises, the *Oxford Libary of the Fathers*,[197] in which Newman and his allies launched into translation, passionately believing that the ancient past could be shown to be on their side – as much a rhetorical as a scholarly effort, in its desire to bring over the English people by imbuing them with a particular vision of the meaning of Antiquity. The *Oxford Library* at least began with pretensions to impartial

autonomous scholarship, in that interpretative notes accompanying the text were deliberately eschewed.[198] But even in its second
publication, Newman's *Preface* to the plain text directs the reader's
attention towards what is significant for the contemporary debate
about 'the religion of the day'.

Newman argues that 'necessary' or 'apostolic' doctrine is contained in Scripture but that the broad testimony of the early
centuries of Antiquity is Scripture's interpreter. If we are to
understand Scripture aright, therefore, we must betake ourselves
to the Fathers.[199] Yet the Father whom Newman here introduces
belonged to that school of opinion called 'Semi-Arian', which,
disliking the *Homoousion*, occupied an uneasy middle ground,
'disinclined both to the friends of Athanasius and to the Arians'.[200]

The first task of the *Preface* is to explain this paradox: how an
apparent heretic may be a witness for orthodoxy, against 'the
religion of the day'. Newman uses a familiar strategy – the
'words–things' distinction – but it is more carefully integrated into
his argument, and avoids the air of desperate special pleading, so
evident in his specifically anti-Roman apologetic. A mild-man-
nered 'lover of peace', he was imposed upon by *words*, by the subtle
argumentation of the Arian Acacius, without, however, being, in
any respect, 'an Arian or an Arianiser' himself.[201] Cyril's orthodoxy, then, goes deeper than mere technicalities; 'doctrine' is not
words:

> Here is a writer, separated by whatever cause from what, speaking
> historically, may be called the Athanasian school, suspicious of its
> adherents, and suspected by them; yet he, when he comes to explain
> himself, expresses precisely the same doctrine as that of Athanasius or
> Gregory, while he merely abstains from the particular theological term in
> which the latter Fathers agreeably to the Nicene Council conveyed it.[202]

How Cyril's doctrine could be '*precisely* the same' as Athanasius'
without using identical terms tormented Newman four years
later.[203] For the moment, his appeal is, once again, to a kind of
common sense: it is possible to be technically and even theologically wrong, yet still in touch with the authentic voice of Christian
tradition: of such as these,[204] Newman declared, 'Their judgment,
which was erroneous, was their own; their faith was not theirs
only, but shared with them by the whole Christian world.'[205]
Newman's principle here announced is not without relevance to

his stance towards his own contemporary audience: the essential faith of Antiquity is a broad outline, witnessed by the unanimous convergence of Fathers. It does not require a trained theologian to discern it. Just, then, as Cyril could fail on a technicality, while being essentially orthodox, so may a modern man of sense discern the mind of the primitive Church. Newman intends the *Library of the Fathers* to take patristic writings out of the realm of scholarship and into the area of popular debate.

Newman can capitalise upon the experience of every zealous Christian who attempts to argue with another Christian who does not agree with him: invoking Scripture texts never seems quite to clinch it. As in the 1830s – so in the fourth century; but the latter age, by relying upon Tradition in the first instance, had at least a means of finding, hidden in Scripture, the texts to answer their difficulties:

The Arian and other heresies obliged them [the Fathers] to appeal to Scripture in behalf of a certain cardinal doctrine which they held by uninterrupted tradition; and thus they have been the means of pointing out to us particular texts in which are contained the great truths which were assailed.[206]

Newman bypasses the question of the heretics' relation to the 'uninterrupted tradition' – he implies they stand outside it, and are out of touch with the *sensus communis*, yet they provoke those within to find it. Finding the grounds of truth in Scripture, as 'elicited' by controversy, is, then, a mysterious, but not a special-ised task, – it comes within the ambit of a communal, if not an everyday, experience. In a transition of feathery lightness from Antiquity to Reformation, Newman introduces 'our Divines', and in an audacious feat of legerdemain re-presents the English Refor-mation, and all its tomes, as a sort of patristic revival:

our Divines at and since the Reformation have betaken themselves to the extant documents of the early Church, in order to determine thereby what the system of Primitive Christianity was; and so to elicit from Scripture more completely and accurately that revealed truth, which though revealed there is not on its surface, but needs to be *deduced* and *developed* from it.[207]

But Newman cannot conceal an uneasy sense that such divines' reflection upon revelation had a remote and theoretical quality – his very phraseology ('betaken themselves to the extant documents,' 'system') suggests that the 'Divines' are hardly eliciting from the 'uninterrupted tradition' of the patristic age: they are trying to find out what it was, or even to re-create it; they seem as much outsiders as the Arians.

Newman's attempt to construct, out of his patristic reading and the controversies of seventeenth- and eighteenth-century divinity, a rhetoric of orthodoxy with a common appeal to the person of ordinary intelligence is unconvincing – and failed ultimately to convince even Newman himself. He appeals to the obviousness of how it was in the first five centuries but never quite extricates himself from the theoretical difficulties lurking at the corners and margins of his discourse. Having committed himself to a view of both history and Tradition which presupposed consensus on the part of sensible people, he confronted the fact of heresy presenting an obstinately irreducible disagreement about the nature and significance of both, a fact he was forced to marginalise. But, in the end, he was both too honest and too perceptive not to be tortured by these difficulties. In his *85th Tract, Holy Scripture in Its Relation to the Catholic Creed*[208] (1838), he argues, along lines now familiar, that Tradition as manifested especially in the first five centuries, points to the truths hidden in Scripture. But he is no longer confident, too aware of difficulty for his own happiness:

Doubt and difficulty, as regards evidence, seems our lot; the simple question is, What is our duty under it? Difficulty is our lot, as far as we take it on ourselves to inquire; the multitude are not able to inquire and so escape the trial; but when men inquire, this trial at once comes upon them. [209]

Ironically, it was in the same *Tract* that Newman had declared – already, perhaps, more in hope than certainty – that 'What is right and what is happy cannot in the long run and on a large scale be disjoined. To follow after a truth can never be a subject of regret; free inquiry does lead a man to regret the days of his childlike faith; therefore it is not following after truth'.[210] Indulging in that syllogistic manner absorbed from Whately, Newman exposes his characteristic duality with regard to theological reflection: on the one hand, he is a critical thinker, an adept even at the *sorties* of scepticism, on the other, he refuses, by an act of will, to embrace 'the kind of seeking which begins in doubt'.[211]

It is this duality which explains why the years 1839–45 saw, unavoidably, both collapse, and, equally inevitably, reconstruction and reaffirmation. The collapse of the 'Via Media' did not happen just because events turned against him, but also because he found his position inadequate to an ever-increasing, erosive, inner criticism: the *experimentum crucis* to which he refers in the *Apologia* was the pain of a religious being who, though he flinched from it, could not shut out the implications of his own intellectuality. Yet he would not allow himself the full scope of autonomous choice – the *hairesis* – of following wherever criticisms might lead – he feared the despair of scepticism: he yearned for authority and wholeness: 'we may seek some heresy or sect: true, we may; but are they more sure? are they not a part, while the Church is whole? Why is the part true, if the whole is not?'[212]

CHAPTER SIXTEEN

Collapse

(A) MONOPHYSITISM (1839–40)

Newman had used *analogy* between past and present as polemic, subjecting his opponents to a hostile interrogation in which the pattern of the past laid bare their hidden tendencies. When he came to portray his *own* period of doubt and self-questioning from 1839 to 1843, he presented the analogical and critical structure of his own rhetoric as *turning back upon himself,* as he found his own position the subject of an inner inquest, in the same style of interrogation to which he had subjected his opponents. In his 1839 study of Monophysitism, the analogy *turned*:

My stronghold was Antiquity: now here, in the middle of the fifth century, I found, as it seemed to me Christendom of the sixteenth and nineteenth reflected. I saw my face in that mirror, and I was a Monophysite. The Church of the 'Via Media' was in the position of the Oriental Communion, Rome was where she now is; and the Protestants were the Eutychians.[1]

And, quoting from *Difficulties of Anglicans*:

It was difficult to make out how the Eutychians or Monophysites were heretics, unless Protestants and Anglicans were heretics also; difficult to find arguments against the Tridentine fathers which did not tell against the Fathers of Chalcedon; difficult to condemn the Popes of the sixteenth century without condemning the Popes of the fifth.[2]

Newman's doubts are here depicted as taking on a rhetorical structure – 'difficult to find arguments'; he is always thinking of how to persuade, how to justify, imagining an audience. Indeed, he perceived, in 1850, his 1840s experience of the bankruptcy of the 'Via Media' as a bankruptcy of rhetoric: 'What was the use of continuing the controversy or defending my position, if, after all, I was forging arguments for Arius or Eutyches and turning devil's advocate against the much-enduring Athanasius and the majestic Leo?'[3]

These sources of Newman's picture of 1839–43 – his fiercest anti-Anglican polemic written in his Roman Catholic honeymoon period (1850)[4] and his own eloquent self-vindication against Kingsley (1864)[5] – might lead one to suspect that the exigencies of later rhetorical strategies shaped the expression of remembered inner states. What, then, appears to be the internalisation of the rhetorical might, equally, be a later rhetoricisation of past experience. Newman's later accounts need therefore to be considered in relation to the evidence of the time.

Newman remembered Spring 1839 as his Anglican apogee: 'I had supreme confidence in my controversial *status*.'[6] By Summer, things were starting to go wrong. The underlying unease about whether or not the 'Via Media' really was so straightforward and sensible, hints of which are observable even in 1838,[7] has become explicit: he now finds the debate between Roman and Anglican divines about Church and Catholicity to be 'a tangled and manifold controversy . . . not easy to sum up and settle'.[8] Then came Monophysitism, studied between 13 June and 30 August 1839, when 'for the first time a doubt came upon me of the tenableness of Anglicanism'.[9] Newman's reminiscence is very precise: Monophysitism was the *very* first thing to worry him, before Wiseman's Donatist comparison, and long before the 'three blows' that broke him of the summer of 1841. He presents the inception of the 'Via Media''s collapse as an inner revolution, born of reflection, rather than as a consequence of public events. The *Apologia*'s presentation is only to be expected: the purpose of Newman's narrative is to counter Kingsley's thesis that Roman Catholics are invariably shifty,[10] by the powerful evocation of himself as a conscientious man inwardly moved – to his great cost – by the inconvenient voice of truth.

According to the *Apologia*, Monophysitism did not disturb him because he thought he was, in his Christological doctrine, a Monophysite. What he presents as unnerving him, as he looked into the 'mirror' of Antiquity,[11] arises from a flash of imagination, a sickening intuition: he places his own 'Via Media' position in an analogical relation to the spectrum of ancient theological opinion, and finds in his own espousal of moderation, and of a conservative view of Tradition resisting development, the very qualities of the

Monophysites, who, giving up the extremes of Eutyches, harked back to Cyril and Athanasius, but resisted the present voice of the Church in the Chalcedonian definition. As Martin Svaglic rightly comments: 'It is not the doctrines themselves which are significant for Newman's point here, but rather the mode in which a solution was reached.'[12]

Newman's own dating of this inner experience at 1839 is, however, open to a number of difficulties. The rhetorical purpose of the *Apologia* has already been remarked. But what particularly provokes suspicion is that Newman does not support this splendid piece of self-dramatisation by any corroboration of letters or memoranda of the time – something he always does in the *Apologia* when he can – by drawing upon what was by 1864 a large personal archive. He gives a lengthy quotation from *Difficulties of Anglicans*, 'the account which I gave in 1850, of my reasonings and feelings in 1839'.[13] This work is, of course, dedicated to the public demolition of the cause he once espoused. It is in this much later context that his reminiscence first appears as 'a key to the different parties and personages who have figured on the Catholic or the Protestant side at and since the era of the Reformation'.[14] *Difficulties* is, in turn, drawing upon the rhetoric of the *Essay on Development* (1845), which used the analogy of the Monophysites to undermine the 'Via Media',[15] in order to advocate the extreme of the Roman Catholic position as, in the light of Church history, the authentic inheritor of Antiquity. What Newman does *not* draw upon to substantiate his reminiscences are the papers on Monophysitism which he actually wrote in 1839, even though he had carefully kept them, along with his notes. This is not surprising, for they present a very different picture of Monophysitism from that which he put forward in 1845, 1850 or 1864, and which only his Roman Catholic writings project back to the Long Vacation of 1839.

Newman compiled three papers on Monophysitism in 1839, none of which ever appeared in published form. The manuscript entitled *The Monophysite Heresy*, dated 23 August 1839,[16] is the longest paper Newman ever wrote which has remained unpublished. Running to eighty-three pages, a meticulous and detailed examination of the patristic evidence about Eutychianism, and the relation of this extreme position to Monophysitism, it also contains an important strain of generalisation about the nature of heresy. Then there is, secondly, a private printed paper, fourteen pages long, which Newman describes as 'an abstract . . . with Notes and References' of the long manuscript.[17] Its style of presentation is comparable with that of the printed paper, *Apollinarianism*, based on the 1835 manuscript. Lastly, there is another untitled manuscript,[18] of only eleven pages, dated 1839, which ends abruptly. It is possibly part of something Newman read, or intended to read, to the Theological Society. Its character is somewhat different from *The Monophysite Heresy*, and contains material peculiarly its own. In none of these papers do we find the *method* of placing heresy which the *Apologia* describes as originating in 1839.

It is, however, possible, in the light of Newman's autobiography, retrospectively to discern in the 1839 papers the stirrings of a profound unease, which only some years subsequently developed into a method of describing heresy, a ghostly, but nevertheless genuine, memory which he later expressed in the forms of his distinctively Roman Catholic rhetoric. The sense that Newman might have been, as early as 1839, beginning unhappily to find points of correspondence between himself and the Monophysites emerges most clearly in the opening pages of *The Monophysite Heresy*. Here, he considers Monophysitism as the result of a zealously orthodox reaction against the Arian tendency: 'It may be observed that, as Syria was the especial seat of Arianism, so Egypt which had resisted it, was the seat of Monophysitism, the counter error which succeeded it.'[19] That a defence of Christ's divinity – and such a defender was Newman himself – could ultimately result in one of the Church's greatest heresies was, no doubt, a disturbing thought. Newman's topology hints at a frightening sense of closeness here: if Syria was the seat of rationalism and humanitarianism, then did its antithesis, 'Egypt' – he cannot quite bring himself to write 'Alexandria' – the home of Clement, Athanasius and Cyril, eventually spawn the most perduring and divisive heresy in the history of the early Church? Newman implies a certain sympathy with the Monophysite *ethos*: 'As the Monophysite heresy is contrary to Arianism in doctrine, so, as might be expected, is it in its ethical character. It was far more subtle, specious and attractive to pious minds.'[20] While the Arians were 'able partizans and intriguers; men of the world', unscrupulous and 'clear' (or – as he first wrote – 'clever') 'disputants', the Monophysites are unworldly, unskilled in polemic (or 'seem' so), motivated, in their rejection of the two natures in Christ, by reverence for the Son of God: 'they did not dare to use such a word as human *nature* of Him who had a divine nature'.[21] Or such, at any rate, was the zeal and reverence they professed: Newman's passages of sympathy with Monophysitism are usually accompanied by disclaimers ('seemed', 'specious', and, most notably, 'they had at first sight not little to say for themselves').[22] Nevertheless, an ominous, though dim, recognition of the face in the mirror has been registered.

Moreover, in Newman's meticulously fair distinction between Eutychianism and Monophysitism, there emerges a quite new sense of the danger of a moderate position – of a 'Via Media' – in dogmatic controversies. Eutyches maintained two tenets, Newman argues, in his extreme emphasis upon the divine nature: that is, both that 'Christ was of only one nature after the incarnation, and that he was not of our substance'. When pushed, he persisted in the former, for which he had Cyril's authority, but 'wavered' in the latter.[23] Now the 'Semi-Eutychians' – after some vacillation, Newman concludes they actually existed[24] – embraced the proposition from Cyril, but condemned what Eutyches 'wavered' about.[25] Newman identifies Monophysitism as this moderate 'Semi-Eutychian' position, holding Christ to be human, but denying He had a human *nature*, after the Incarnation. Christ's humanity was present, but *not* as *nature*: 'They held that the Divine Nature of the Word had the addition of what viewed by itself was a human nature, but viewed in the Word thereby ceased to be a separate nature, but formed one nature with his Divine.'[26] In this they held to Cyril's horror of Nestorianism – of introducing two distinct but irreducible principles of unity into Christ – and their determination was reinforced by their understanding of 'nature' ($\varphi \upsilon \sigma \iota \varsigma$) as synonymous with 'person' (hypostasis).[27] Newman, then, was confronted with a moderate position eschewing both Eutychianism proper and Chalcedonian orthodoxy, which maintained itself by the highly self-conscious and theoretical adoption of fine distinctions. He *may* have seen a parallel between this and his own 'Via Media' but, if so, he did not remark on it, still less use it to 'place' the 'Via Media' as he did in 1845, 1850 or 1864.

Finally, Monophysitism presented a disquieting challenge to the view of heresy as innovation, which Newman so often expressed between 1833 and 1839. The Monophysites, far from being innovators, were traditionalist and conservative, resisting the apparently new 'two natures' of Chalcedon with the *one nature* of their

Father, Cyril: 'They claimed but the use of what was already received, what had already been determined against heresy. They wished to add nothing, they said, they were contented with what had been [they found] already provided for them.'[28] But, again, although we may imagine that this may have disturbed Newman, he makes very little of it. Indeed, Newman describes Severus, 'head of the Monophysite school', as distorting earlier tradition, in the interests of party spirit,[29] much as Bull accused Sandius and Petavius.[30]

If, then, there is at times a vague unease, there occurs, in *The Monophysite Heresy*, none of the stark and terrifying self-recognition, as Newman tells it in 1850 – and, again, in 1864. Nowhere is the rhetorical method of the *mirror* – placing modern theological parties against the spectrum of early Church opinion – deployed, or applied to Monophysitism, in the long 1839 manuscript. The explicit argument of this paper is quite otherwise: its method of describing and schematising the heresy is, in fact, a revival of the heresiology of the 1835 Apollinarianism papers. In the Long Vacation of 1839, he did not cook up a new method of treating Antiquity: he merely warmed up an old one.

Newman sees his Monophysitism papers as containing a story he left off when treating of Apollinarianism: indeed he opens *The Monophysite Heresy* by declaring the date of the enquiry to commence with Apollinaris in AD 361 and to end with the VIth General Council, AD 681.[31] Apollinarianism he considers to be an early form of Monophysitism. The same methods of analysis are deployed in 1839 as in 1835: an apparently high Christology conceals an infidel tendency, which is revealed in its developments, as elicited either by logical inference or by the course of history:

Though the Monophysite heresy is the contradictory of Arianism, yet strange to say, it comes round, when reasoned out, to somewhat the same result, letting slip the great doctrines of Christ's Divinity, which it seems to be defending, equally with the vicious who impugned it.[32]

Although the *detail* of the process by which Monophysitism 'comes round' to infidelity differs from Apollinarianism, the underlying principle which accounts for the development is, in 1835 and 1839 alike, made out to be rationalism. Thus he declares in 1839, that, for all their antipathy of *ethos* and language, Monophysitism shares with Arianism 'an allowance of abstract reasoning, in other words, that is, maintenance of intellectually conceived first principles in a matter which was purely of faith'.[33] Later in the paper, Newman admits that it 'may seem unfair to press upon the party who held it the conclusions which *we* draw from it as if such conclusions were [are] but our own'.[34] Especially so – he frankly acknowledges it – since the 'Form of words may in certain cases be an accident and the character of mind represented be the *real* d[ire]ction for a c[er]tain principle'.[35] He is aware of the force of such an objection, in the light of the Monophysite *ethos* of 'especial . . . reverence and devotion'.[36] He 'presses upon' them nevertheless because of his strong sense of the uncontrollable power of speculative reason, once let loose: whatever a moderate heretic may have *meant* to say, wherever he fixes his own sticking point, – 'thus far and no further', – the 'form of words' he has created takes on a life of its own, developing, by laws of iron necessity, to the very edge – thus Newman's scholarship purposes to show – of atheism:

considering what a wakeful, operative, persevering principle our reason is, how the mind is ever anticipating knowledge by means of it, ever darting forward to conclusions spontaneously, how instinctive and strong and certain it is that, after all the differences of private judgment, yet on the long run and ultimately all men from the same premisses arrive at the same conclusions.[37]

Newman's handling of his patristic sources is dominated by this distinction, between the intentional features of a heretic's discourse, which lie on the surface but are of deceptive appearance, and the real, unintended, 'conclusions' which may be drawn out of tendencies hidden, or embedded, in the language. The bulk of *The Monophysite Heresy* is dedicated to showing that the sources bear out this theory. His demonstration of the logic of heresy aims to show how Monophysitism tends ultimately towards its very opposite, the denial of the Divinity of Christ which it appears so vehemently to be upholding. This is because 'Opinions apparently very opposite, or rather those which are apparently most so, agree in the major premiss or principle of which they rest, and differ in the minor. Hence they are much more connected than at first might be supposed.'[38] Newman's manner of expressing this idea shows that, if he has sloughed off the Noetics' theological liberalism, he has retained their predilection for the syllogism. He even regards the Fathers as having divined instinctively what he will elicit logically: 'the Fathers often condemn the most opposite heresies at once'.[39]

First, Newman considers Eutychianism, out of which the more moderate Monophysitism or 'Semi-Arianism' eventually arose. He finds that Eutyches was 'running into the heresy he most hated, Nestorianism'.[40] Drawing upon the critiques of Eutyches 'was maintaining the impiety of Nestorius'.[41] Newman elicits the implicit Nestorianism of the Eutychian understanding of 'nature' ($\varphi\upsilon\sigma\iota\varsigma$) and its relation to person ($\upsilon\pi o\sigma\tau\alpha\sigma\iota\varsigma$). Eutyches was unable to see how a nature could exist without personhood. This is the identical premiss adopted by Nestorius, so that 'while here was an agreement in fundamental principle at once, there would moreover be no great difficulty in their actually passing over from their own party to the opposite'.[42]

Newman's analysis immediately proceeds to elicit further, more radical and damaging consequences. He sees two possibilities: first, that the humanity of Christ is absorbed into the Divinity so as to be of one substance with it, and, in this case, 'nothing is left of Christ but the original Divine Nature; or, in other words, there is no incarnation at all'.[43] Secondly, that 'Christ was *perfectus homo*, though not consubstantial with us.'[44] Eutyches, who wanted to hold to the Incarnation, drew back from the first but embraced the second. The orthodox ('Catholics'), however, 'insisted' that even this second position entailed a consequence: 'a change of the Godhead into flesh, or at least into some third new nature'.[45] The Eutychians, themselves, 'resisted this conclusion', maintaining their own language that the Word was 'changed into flesh without change'.[46] Pressed as to how this could be, 'they answered that they were not bound to explain the manner *how*, that it was a mystery'.[47] Newman's self-inconsistency here, in the way his analysis tries to push the Eutychians out of 'mystery' into rational explicitness, is difficult to palliate, when his own defence of Trinity and Incarnation so often takes a similar refuge.[48]

As *The Monophysite Heresy* proceeds, we find Newman pushing the heresy further and further outside the circle of authentic Christianity, into the realm of infidelity. In a passage where he discusses what he sees as the crux of the controversy, he most forthrightly dismisses Eutychian pretensions to 'mystery', by coining the startling phrase, 'the mystery of unbelief in the Eutychian party', which he finds to have been 'working out, by degrees and in diverse manners, through its various sects and champions, even when they seemed furthest from such a result'.[49] Here, Newman deploys the idea, familiar from the 1835 Apollinarianism papers, of a heresy developing *historically* from a high Christology, via its sects, to the real unbelief underlying it. The 'unbelief' of which Newman argues Eutychians were guilty was that they could not accept the human life and death of the Logos. Their strategy for evading this was ultimately destructive of the Incarnation – as much, and for the same reasons as Nestorianism: 'What the Nestorians had avoided by separating the man from the God, Eutychianism had evaded by denying the reality of the manhood.'[50]

The remoter deductions, however, of Eutychians' 'stumbling' at Christ's humanity bring them to consequences they would never have even imagined. In the end, Newman sees them as implicit Socinians! These remarkable and radical conclusions occur at the very end of the long section on 'Eutychianism Proper'. They are what he has been working up to all along. Newman considers the Eutychian inability to accept the human nature of Christ as an implicit denial of his sufferings and death *as man*.[51] This entails, ultimately, denial of 'the Atonement made for the sins of the world, the great revealed purpose of the whole Economy'.[52] But they do not fall into this at once: there is a mediate consequence – if Christ had one divine nature, then God suffered. They could hardly rest long in this 'Theopaschism'; in the end it was too 'shocking' and 'repulsive'.[53] Beyond this halfway house lies an unavoidable alternative: 'either . . . a denial of Christ's sufferings or of His Divinity'.[54] The route to the first conclusion lies through a retreat from Theopaschism, to a Gnostic–Docetic position, that the sufferings of Christ were only apparent. Thus, 'A denial of the Atonement was the necessary consequence.'[55] Finally, Newman brings Eutychianism round to a denial of what the heresy was so strenuous in upholding, the Divinity of Christ. Here, Newman's argument is highly scholastic: by denying a human nature in Christ, the Eutychians had to locate His priesthood, and therefore his suffering, in His divine nature. Christ, then, was 'not man and yet passible', a supernatural being distinguishable from God by the fact that he suffered.[56] Thus Eutychianism and, by implication, Monophysitism, make Christ inferior to the Father and approximate to Arianism: 'the Monophysite doctrine, denying the proper humanity of Christ, made him Mediator and High Priest according to his Divine Nature, which was notoriously a Platonic & semi-Arian tenet, and favoured the idea of His inferiority to the Father as God'.[57]

Although Newman ruthlessly reduces the heresy to a form of virtual Socinianism, he initially admits a degree of ambiguity about the heretic: *ethos* is held in tension with logical consequence. He ends his section on 'Eutychianism Proper' with a meditation upon 'the view' which 'ecclesiastical history' gives of 'the personal character of heretics', a view than which 'perhaps there is nothing . . . more awful'.[58] The 'awfulness' consists, not as one might expect, in the baseness of heretics, but in the tragic contrast between the frequent excellence of their characters and gravity of their error:

I mean there is so much about them good, interesting, at least exciting our compassion. The case of Eutyches is more to the point here perhaps than others, for the clear and awful condemnation with which his doctrine is mentioned in 'Every spirit that confesseth not that Jesus Christ is come in the flesh is not of God, and this is that spirit of Antichrist.'[59]

Newman's evident sympathy for Eutyches makes him steel himself: 'To say that perhaps Eutyches did not hold this doctrine really, is scarcely in point. We can but judge from appearances. He seems to hold it and he *seems* a harmless innocent man – one appearance is likely to be as wrong as the other.'[60] The ambiguity of the situation thwarts Newman's natural tendency to argue from *ethos* to truth or error ('We know of course that evil is joined with evil – not evil with good'[61]). But he pulls back ultimately from the paradox – good *ethos*: false doctrine – and re-states what the 'awfulness' consists of: 'it is awful that *our* view of things is so untrustworthy; and that good and evil are so mixed together that we must not [dare not] rely on our judgment'.[62] Thus is ambiguity too much to bear, and he resolves it in characteristic manner, scepticism anaesthetising the judgment, that authority may be unquestioningly embraced: 'we . . . must act in all things singly from what God's word commands'.[63]

When Newman moves to the Monophysites or 'Semi-Eutychians', we may suppose that his sympathy is even greater. This does not, however, exempt them from having similar consequences drawn out from their teaching: Monophysites, too, are infidels by inference. As the Monophysite position is both more subtle and moderate than the Eutychian, so is the logical procedure by which Newman elicits his conclusion more finely drawn and elaborate. In seven pages of close analysis at the end of the paper,[64] he essays a demonstration of how Monophysitism may be logically brought round both to Arianism (denial of Christ's Divinity) and to Docetism (denial of his humanity), so that this most 'orthodox' of heresies entails a total destruction of the Incarnation.

The analysis commences from a refutation of the 'philosophical grounds' upon which Monophysites' Christology was based, the denial that a nature may exist without an hypostasis or person, which led inevitably to their inability to see that the unity of Christ could be affirmed without maintaining only *one* nature.[65] Although it is true that 'every nature, if it really exists & and is not a mere word expressive of a generalization of the mind, must exist in an individual', it is not true that a nature must always have an hypostasis of its own, for a nature may exist as individualised in another hypostasis. Here Newman is arguing along the lines of the orthodox Fathers he was reading:

the Catholics distinguished between *hypostasis* and *enhypostaton*, individual & individualized or in individuality. They allowed that no *physis* or *ousia* could exist except at least individualized, but they denied that it need be an individual, since it might belong to an individual.[66]

Thus the Word 'had taken to Him a manhood, but so that it became attached to his individuality as a part of Him'.[67] There was, therefore, one person of the Word, but two natures, the human nature being in itself impersonal but taking on personal individuality from the Divine.

Newman's analysis of the Monophysite position, in contrast to which he has so carefully drawn the orthodox stance, proceeds by way of inference, 'A participation in the principle involved a participation in its consequences.'[68] The Monophysite equation of person with nature leads, Newman argues, logically to Sabellianism, if the one divine nature is considered, or to tritheism, if the three persons in God are held to.[69] Next, Newman sees the Monophysite formula μια φυσις συνθετος, ('one nature of the union') as leading to a denial of Christ's Divinity, because if two natures divine and human 'went to make up one nature', then the 'result, thus gained' must be seen as 'more perfect than the parts of which it is composed'.[70] It follows – this is the 'drift of it – that the Eternal Word went on to perfection by the Incarnation'[71] – which derogates the Word's eternal perfection. Finally, Newman would have the Monophysites to destroy the humanity of Christ also. Indeed, he regards the μια φυσις as totally destructive of the Incarnation:

Then again as this tenet of the *mia physis* derogated from our Lord's Godhead, it could not but impair the doctrine of His manhood ... In order that God might certainly be received as man, and man held to be God, it seemed to teach that Christ came short of being God in that He was man, and of man in that He was God.[72]

The Monophysites, then, are subjected to all the severest censures of the 'Eutychians Proper'. Both, in fact, are brought round to a virtual Arianism.

Although Newman's line on heresy remains, despite the *Apologia*, overwhelmingly in continuity with that of the mid-1830s,[73] the subtle linguistic distinctions of the Monophysite–Eutychian controversy – so confusing that even the clear-headed Leo at first hesitated to condemn Eutyches – have brought out a sharper awareness than before of the cruciality of dogmatic *language* (*words*, as opposed to things), and of its capacity for creative development. *The Monophysite Heresy* contains an eloquent passage on the dynamic manner in which the Church uses human language, and even the terms of pagan philosophy, to formulate its doctrines, transforming such words in the very process of their appropriation: 'the Church forms its own language, it remodels the tongues of earth, it creates associations. No theology could be formed without allowing the Church this power, which indeed every philosophy assumes in its own particular province'.[74]

At this point, Newman creates for himself an alarming objection: a *tu quoque* is possible, for as the Church has framed a language – in this case that of Chalcedonian orthodoxy – so has Eutychianism. They are both equally contestable: 'Was the language used by Christian theologians in the doctrine of the Incarnation open to objections nearly so plausible as must be brought against their [Eutychians'] exposition of the Eternal Sonship of the Word?'[75] But having seemed to concede – albeit 'for argument's sake'[76] – a legitimate pluralism in ancient Christological formulations, he will not pursue its implications for the placing of heresy. Rather, he deploys political and psychological description to demonstrate the

Eutychians' personal inauthenticity. They are, firstly, found guilty of a schismatic mentality: even if valid, their objections to Chalcedonian orthodoxy were 'a poor ground for causing a schism in the Church'.[77] They held out, moreover, because of 'some real peculiarity of temper, which was likely to go, and in the event did go, much further'.[78] If the Eutychians' conscious intention was to defend a particular *theology*, the very pertinacity with which they maintained it argued the covert operation of sinister forces, deeper and more powerful than any dialectic:

> Their real objection lay, not against the word nature, but against the humiliation which the assumption of that nature implied; and whether consciously or not, they objected to the word nature, in order to mask the force of the shock which the humiliation itself gave to their feelings.[79]

Thus they 'stumble' at the very Incarnation itself. The moment has passed – and Newman is back on familiar ground, having psychologised, characterised, rhetoricised heresy for all he is worth, as he swerves from a systematic and reflective examination of the confrontation of Monophysite with Chalcedonian language.

Newman's second piece of work on Monophysitism[80] is different in character from *The Monophysite Heresy*: it is less logical and analytical, with an interest in the psychological and political origins of heresy. However, it no more bears out Newman's later descriptions of 1839 than the longer manuscript. Nowhere is Monophysitism compared with the 'Via Media'. There are, indeed, fewer hints of unease in this paper than in the other. Newman holds the heresy disdainfully at arm's length, and minimises the difficulty of the evolution of orthodox language. Concerning the dispute over the natures in Christ, he demands, 'Who could have supposed that any difficulty could arise on so plain a point; or, if a difficulty, more than a difficulty of words?'[81]

Newman's theme is the rise of heresy, a subject he admits is 'very obscure and can seldom be investigated without theorizing'.[82] His opening aetiological flourish imitates the pronouncement of so many ancient writers: the origin of heresy is the Devil, that father of lies.[83] But Newman's own first theory is a speculative, psychological one: heresy originates in the labyrinth of 'subtle minds', of those who, having obscured what was originally quite clear, fall into a state of chronic perplexity: 'They cannot view the subject in the plain straightforward way they did at first.'[84]

Common-sense meaning is lost in a proliferation of 'strained' or 'unnatural' senses. Unaware of the disorder of their 'critical powers', they 'persist, at a time when they should fall back upon authority, to decide, under so great a disadvantage, by their private judgment',[85] and so become committed to a heresy, which once embarked upon, 'deviates further and further from the way of Truth'.[86]

This description has much in common with the writings of the 1830s, and especially *Tract 73*, where heresy is closely associated with the abuse of private judgment. There is a fresh nuance here, however: whereas, in 1835, heresy is seen as the result of a rationalistic simplification, a 'reduction to system' of the boundless mystery of the *revelatum*, here, in 1839, it obfuscates the essentially plain and simple truth. Yet the view is itself in touch with a marked feature of Newman's earlier Tractarian rhetoric – the appeal to commonsense. His 1839 theorising also implicitly draws upon the static concept of orthodoxy which has prevailed since 1832, for he supposes that a pure and simple truth preceded a corrupting intellectualism.

The rise of Monophysitism is also explained by reference to an elaborate historical theory, which traces the origin of the heresy back to fourth-century Apollinarian factions. Newman's explanation of how this can be, in view of the ninety-year gap between Apollinaris and Eutyches, is ingenious. He dates the rise of Eutychianism from 428, when the rump of the Apollinarian secession applied for re-admission to the Great Church. They were received 'without a real abandonment of their heretical opinions, the circumstances of the times favoring [*sic*] such an oversight. No wonder that in consequence the controversy had to come over again'.[87] The 'circumstances' were favourable because of the reaction against Nestorianism: 'the necessary resistance to it would both clothe and foster the opposite error'.[88] Nestorius tended to push into Monophysitism those whom 'he did not persuade'. As a result of Nestorianism, there was an 'existing or rather pre-existing disposition of the Church towards Monophysitism', so that its 'outbreak' was 'inevitable', once Nestorius was overthrown.[89] Once the heresy broke out, the form of Apollinarianism, from which Eutychianism, and then Monophysitism grew, was a more tenacious and subtle one, which had the advantage of being able to invoke Cyril's language (one nature or hypostasis) on its side: 'It had learned to state its errors more guardedly, and to defend them more speciously; and it claimed the especial sanction of that portion of the Church, which, under Cyril of Alexandria as leader, had fought with its own adherents against the Nestorians.'[90]

This theory is a projection into the ancient past of a contemporary preoccupation which had been with Newman since the late 1820s – the urgent and almost obsessive desire, in the wake of an *ancien régime*'s collapse, to shore up the established Church's visible order and coherence, as it fragmented into parties, and was challenged by Dissent. Just as, in the 1830s, it was proposed that tests, statutes and anathemas be waived so as to admit alien elements, so in the early 400s, a Church alarmed by Nestorianism was too liberal in its re-admission, on insufficiently stringent terms, of Apollinarians, whose residual heresy was the seed of a later, indissoluble dispute. Indeed, Newman's choice of phraseology shows that the underlying motivation dictating his characterisation of Monophysitism in 1839 is not new: it still belongs to the overall strategy, commencing in 1832, of which the 'Via Media' was a part.

There is nothing new either in his understanding of dogmatic definition in the face of heresy. Newman, while admitting the extreme subtlety of the distinctions between Chalcedonian, Eutychian and Monophysite, betrays less anxiety about the complex issue of dogmatic *language*, than is the case in his longer paper, *The Monophysite Heresy*. Indeed, the final pages rely[91] rather heavily upon the words–things distinction he so often makes in the Tractarian period to get himself out of difficulty. Here, it is 'not a difficulty of argument as to the doctrine itself and its importance but as to the measures to be taken, or the test adopted for defending the doctrine'.[92] The Church's 'difficulty' was not that it did not know what the true doctrine was, and had always been, but only which word to choose to express it, in such a way as to safeguard it: 'Leo alone and his section of the Church was clearsighted enough to see where the danger lay and how to obviate it.'[93] Newman remains committed, in Summer 1839, to the static concept of orthodoxy to which he had adhered since the late 1820s.

An examination of the unpublished material on Monophysitism suggests several possible conclusions about the importance of Summer, 1839, as the first point in the collapse of the 'Via Media'.

The first possibility has already been raised: that Newman rhetoricised his earlier self, so that 1839 might serve a place in his Roman Catholic polemic, that is that, what was, at most, a seminal unease was massively expanded, and expressed from a later perspective as the 'face in the mirror'. Such a conclusion has the advantage of taking fully into account the rhetorical nature both of the *Apologia*'s account and of the passage in *Difficulties of Anglicans* which it cites. It is to suggest that so dominant was the rhetorical in Newman's mentality that the very act of remembering was also a rhetorical procedure, and that his understanding of himself was caught up in the elaborate structure of self-justification, which his prominent public position could almost be said to necessitate.

Such a view, however, leaves no room for a more conventional, and on the face of it, common-sense, view that individuals have private access to their own experiences, which they, and they alone, can remember. If this be accepted, then Newman's Roman Catholic reminiscences about August, 1839, are uncriticisable: one would have to conclude that he did indeed so early recognise himself as 'Monophysite' in the special sense recounted in *Difficulties of Anglicans*, even though there is very little trace of any such experience in the writings of 1839 on that heresy – we must, as it were, take his word for it! To do this entails seeing Newman omitting from his writings any reference to a major anxiety destructive of his whole 'Via Media' position. This would have been either a massive act of suppression, or again, a rhetorical necessity, for, although the Monophysitism manuscripts were never published, it does not follow that they were private, or secret, reflections. Indeed, all the evidence indicates that they were intended to form a part of his public discourse: they are shot through with the rhetorical procedures deploying heresy, that are entirely characteristic of all his other Tractarian writings. To include the parallel between Monophysites and Tractarians in his 1839 writings would have been to turn his guns on his own friends, allies and disciples, and on the position which he still publicly stood for. He was not yet ready to do that.

There is, however, another, more probable interpretation, mediating between these two extreme solutions. It may be argued that Newman *did*, in fact, form an analogy between the 'Via Media' and Monophysitism in *1839* – but *not* until about a month after he had completed his studies of it, when, in September 1839, he read

Nicholas Wiseman's *Dublin Review* article on the 'Anglican Claim'.[94] This acted as a catalyst in the formation of the image which fixed what had been, a month earlier, a vague unease. The idea of the Monophysite 'face in the mirror' arose out of the turmoil provoked by Wiseman's adept public challenge, rather than the scholarly researches of his closet some weeks before. But it remained a private ghost. Newman did not deploy it rhetorically until the desperate rearguard action of 1839–41 had conclusively failed. Such an interpretation is implied by the *Apologia*'s narration of the initial alarming effect upon Newman of Wiseman's challenge, but unlike the immediately preceding account of the Long Vacation, this reminiscence is borne out by corroborative evidence from the period in question.

In the *Apologia*, Newman tells us that he was unmoved by Wiseman's comparison between Anglicanism and Donatism, but that it helped him to see that Monophysitism *was* a disturbingly apt analogy:

It [Donatism] was a case of Altar against Altar, of two occupants of the same See, as that between the Non-jurors in England and the Established Church; not the case of one Church against another, as of Rome against the Oriental Monophysites . . . 'Securus judicat orbis terrarum' . . . were words which went beyond the occasion of the Donatists: they applied to that of the Monophysites.[95]

This description of Monophysitism resembles that of the *Essay on Development* raising the problem of *national* secessions against which, as he later argued, papal supremacy developed. However, the 'application' of Monophysitism does not have any *doctrinal* dimension, as one might expect when the attention is shifted from schisms to heresy. Newman's 'placing' of the heresy is entirely *political*: Monophysitism's *schismatic* quality is uppermost in his thinking, not its distinctive theology. In this, he follows Wiseman, whose application of Donatism is applied especially to the break with Rome in the reign of Henry VIII.

The 'stomachache'[96] which Newman contracted on this occasion was perhaps caused by the fact that, for the first time, he had received a dose of his own medicine: Wiseman is no less inventive in the analogical rhetoric which he applies to 'Via Media' Anglicanism, than Newman himself on the subject of liberalism and ultra-Protestantism. Wiseman is often wickedly particular and unsettling: Anglican and Donatist schisms were occasioned, he tells us, by the pique of two powerful women, Anne Boleyn and Lucilla, respectively;[97] both involved the theft of Church property – here he brings together the dissolution of the monasteries and the issue of lost church plate in Donatist Africa;[98] both Donatists and Tractarians insisted on being called 'Catholics';[99] Donatists justified themselves, like Anglicans, by supposing the corruption, at a particular instant of time, of the universal Church.[100] Wiseman even finds Donatists to possess a Branch Theory of their Catholicity, and to have had a 'High Church party'.[101] These are debating points. But Wiseman's placing of Donatism argues a way of discerning the judgment of Antiquity which brutally cuts through the elaborate distinctions of Tractarian argument:

by the Fathers, who combated [sic] the Donatists, the question was essentially considered one of fact rather than of right; that is to say, the very circumstance of one particular Church being out of the aggregation of other churches, constituted these judges over the other, and left no room for questioning the justice of the condemnation.[102]

Wiseman has invoked common sense, just as Newman, in his use of Antiquity. But whose common-sense interpretation was to be chosen?

Newman's correspondence at the time indicates strongly that he felt the pull of Wiseman's, and had begun to doubt his own. Here, for the first time, a month after he wrote on Monophysitism himself, appear the first expressions of anxiety about the threat the case of that heresy presents to his own position. Donatism and Monophysitism *equally* haunt him. Monophysitism has only become a threat *after* he has read Wiseman. Thus, writing about Wiseman's 'Anglican Claims' in late September 1839, to Frederick Rogers, Newman declared 'we have sprung a leak . . . It is no laughing matter'.[103] At about this time, according to a reminiscence of Henry Wilberforce, Newman, in a walk in the woods with his friend, confided a doubt if Rome might not, after all, be right: 'the two examples which had inspired the doubt – the position of St. Leo in the Monophysite controversy, and the principle *securus judicat orbis terrarum* in that of the Donatists'.[104] The Monophysite analogy here is a secret anguish, confided to a friend, provoked not by his own studies of the heresy, but by Wiseman's article.

Newman's unreadiness publicly to make the Monophysite – 'Via

Media' parallel is confirmed by his response to Wiseman in his *British Critic* article of January 1840, a vigorous re-assertion of Tractarian ecclesiological principles[105] which suppresses the inner anxiety. In a reminiscence of November 1843 – by which time, of course, the rhetorical usefulness of the Monophysite analogy to his new position had become apparent – Newman told J.B. Mozley of the destructive effect of Wiseman's challenge, and the way he tried, in 1839, to write his way out of it:

> Last summer four years (1839) it came strongly upon me, from reading first the Monophysite controversy, and then turning to the Donatist, that we were external to the Catholic Church. I have never got over this. I did not, however, yield to it at all, but wrote an article in the 'British Critic' on the Catholicity of the English Church, which had the effect of quieting me for two years. Since this time two years the feeling has gradually strengthened.[106]

This remarkable piece of introspection postulates two rhetorics, two patterns of argument proceeding coterminously: the one, centred on Monophysitism, is submerged, an erosive inner inquest, Newman's own rhetoric turned upon himself; the other is both a public argument to justify the continuing viability of Tractarianism, *and* an attempt, only partially successful, to quieten the working of the inner counter-pattern of argument, which he only embraced unreservedly after 1843.

Newman's treatment of *heresy* in *The Catholicity of the Anglican Church* (1840), shows this rearguard action going on. Passing from the 'parallel' between Donatism and Anglicanism, to that of Monophysitism, he dismisses the latter with an argument which, in earlier years, he has used many times: 'The Monophysites got possession of whole districts, and might seem, if any men, identified with the local Churches in those districts. Yet they are named from Eutyches, from Severus, from Jacob, from Gaianus and from Theodosius.'[107] The particularism of Monophysitism is revealed, Newman argues, either in being 'formed upon a certain doctrine' (the μια φυσις), or begun 'in a certain leader'.[108] But of Anglicanism, he can declare, with apparent confidence, 'We have none such.'[109] Yet it is notable that, albeit fleetingly, Newman raises the 'might seem' of the Monophysites – after all, Wiseman had not. He does not succeed entirely, then, in repressing the ideas in his public discourse. It slips out, even when it is not necessary for an engagement with Wiseman.

How far Newman's *public* discourse was from the position he eventually adopted in the *Essay on Development* regarding heresy is evinced by two passages on doctrinal development, where he dismisses what, after 1843, became his own distinctive position: 'that the Church held in the first age what she holds now; only that heresy, by raising questions, has led to her throwing her faith into dogmatic shape, and has served to precipitate truths which before were held in solution'.[110] But he invites us to imagine the Apostles as 'implicit Tridentines',[111] or behaving in a way even remotely to suggest that they believed in Purgatory or the intercession of Our Lady.[112] The Romanist concept of developing articles of faith is 'all very well in the abstract', but becomes absurd *in concreto*: he demands of the Romanist, 'did he or did he not hold that St Peter could give indulgences to shorten the prospective sufferings of the Corinthians in purgatory?'[113] This would, of course, not be a conclusive objection to the Newman of the *Essay on Development*. But, even in 1840, the appeal to what is or is not imaginable seems strained, almost desperate: 'we cannot imagine an Apostle saying and doing what Romanists say and do; can they imagine it themselves?'[114] This is hardly the point. In any case, Newman's *own* sense of what *is* imaginable – 'We can imagine them administering extreme unction or wearing copes'[115] – calls attention to the arbitrariness of this criterion.

Contemporary with the parallel of Monophysitism, between 1839 and 1842, Newman began a project which also played an early part in inducing the 'Via Media's' collapse, that is the translation of Fleury's *Ecclesiastical History*: 'that simple representation of the early centuries had a good deal to do with unsettling me in my Anglicanism'.[116] Newman notes the irony of this. Hugh James Rose, that pillar of High Anglicanism, had urged him to translate it.[117] Moreover, though a Roman Catholic, Fleury was 'of the Gallican school',[118] so that his line reduced the points of antipathy between his position and that of Anglicanism. In his 1864 memory of Fleury's effect, Newman uses a word – comparatively new to the language – which declares he found in Fleury's history more than congenial support for his party's position: 'it presented a sort of *photograph* of ecclesiastical history'.[119] He is alluding to his *Advertisement* of 4 June 1842, where he declared 'Fleury's work is a minute and exact narrative of the course of ecclesiastical events as they occurred.'[120] In a manner markedly different from the self-consciously sophisticated approach to histo-riographical method of the *Essay on Development*, the Newman of only three or four years earlier could recommend Fleury in preference to Mosheim, Milner or Neander, as an unbiased historian, who self-effacingly told it as it was: 'one who does not prominently put forward the characteristics of his Church, but mainly contents himself with setting before the reader facts, opinions, characters and writings without comment of his own'.[121] The metaphor of a 'photograph' is, indeed, different from that of 'mirror': in the former there is less of a sense of disturbing self-recognition. But both invoke Antiquity as an immediate and disturbing visual image, the impression of which is difficult to remove.

Newman commenced the translation-project in July, 1839.[122] It was a concerted venture, various disciples revising an eighteenth-century English translation,[123] while Newman composed most of the notes,[124] many of which were very extensive. He saw it as fitting well with his shift of interest towards the fourth and fifth centuries:[125] the dates chosen, AD 381–456, coincided with his incipient study of Theodoret, Cyril, Nestorius, Leo, and, of course, Monophysitism.[126] The work on Fleury commenced just as he began to take an interest in the material which he incorporated in his Monophysitism papers. On July 12th, in a letter announcing the inception of the Fleury translation, he declares that he has 'got up the history of the Eutychian controversy, got hold of the opinions of Eutyches . . . have got up St. Leo's works . . . now that I am in the Monophysite controversy, I think I shall read through it, and then back to the Nestorian'.[127] The translation and notes proceeded between 1839 and 1842, when the first volume, AD 381–400, was published, with the *Advertisement* and the long *Essay on Ecclesiastical Miracles*, which served as an introduction to the work, the completion of which, by the end of July 1842, exhausted him.[128]

There would have been sufficient material in Fleury to disturb the 'Via Media', if one were to assume that Newman was already familiar with the material for translation at the inception of the project in 1839. Particularly in the matter of the third volume (429–56), he would have found heretics such as Nestorius and Eutyches to be conservatives, defending themselves by reference to Nicea, to which they would have no addition; they appealed to past Fathers; they held to the faith as it had been delivered to them.[129] No doubt this was disturbing, in view of the manner in which, as we have seen, Newman presented 'Via Media' Catholicity as static, resisting the additions or corruptions of Roman Catholicism.

However, the notes to Fleury make no reference whatever to this Monophysite parallel. In any case, Volume I, which was being compiled between 1839 and 1842, dealt with the period *before* Monophysitism arose (AD 381–400), so that there would have been no occasion to comment upon this heresy. Nor is there any reference to the 'face in the mirror' in Volumes II and III. Even at this point, Newman eschews any rhetorical strategy centred on Monophysitism, reserving it for the later public justification of his conversion, in the *Essay on Development*,[130] and even here there are only gentle hints. On the whole, he remained loyal to his allies right to the last moment, in such joint, public projects as the Fluery translation.

Newman felt the loss of 'a distinctive plea for Anglicanism', unless he 'would be a Monophysite'.[131] He felt his position open to what he imaginatively anticipated as a devastating counter-rhetoric. His understanding of Monophysitism is therefore dominated by the demand for self-justification in terms of a distinctively West European argument about which of the several conflicting polities is the 'True Church'. His contribution was the capacity to frame imaginative analogies, which worked well, until they were turned upon himself. This affected, as we have seen, the theoretical structure which he applied to the examination of his sources. It also affected his perspective upon the *living* communities – the Monophysite churches in the Near East – inheritors of the anti-Chalcedonian tradition. The personal and artificial character of his preoccupation with Monophysitism emerges nowhere more clearly than in his remarks a little later during the controversy over the Jerusalem Bishopric: 'It seems we are *in the way* to fraternise with Protestants of all sorts – Monophysites, half-converted Jews and even Druses.'[132] Newman described the Druses as 'Socianian–Mohammedan'.[133] To speak of Monophysites in the same breath as them argues a man putting together a picture of Antiquity from his Oriel study: a nineteenth-century Englishman's view of Palestinian religion. But, then, it is hardly *Palestine* that really interests him.

(B) SEMI-ARIANISM (1841)

1841 was the year Newman broke. He had published *Tract 90*: this and the connected writings were his last attempt to argue for the Catholicity of the Church of England.[134] The almost universal condemnation of the ecclesiastical authorities followed, in the succeeding months.[135] In July, the project for a Protestant Bishopric in Jerusalem further shook his confidence in the Church of England: he saw it as a fatal compromise with heresy, whether Western or Oriental.[136] By the end of the year, he was finished: he was on his 'Anglican death-bed', and 'A death-bed has scarcely a history.'[137]

In the midst of these events, Newman went back to re-examine Arianism. The *Apologia* tells us that, despite the *Tract 90* affair, he was able to withdraw to Littlemore, 'without any harass [*sic*] or anxiety on my mind'.[138] Heads of Houses had criticised, but the bishops had not yet come out against him. Nevertheless, there is a close link between *Tract 90* and his translation of the works of Athanasius.[139] Newman told his Bishop in April 1842, that the adverse criticism surrounding *Tract 90* made him withdraw from public controversy to scholarship.[140] It was yet another Oxford summer, and Newman was again reaching down his lexicons and thesauri. As the *Apologia* tells it, there then occurred another decisive imaginative reversal, in which heresy was 'placed' in such a way as to shatter the 'Via Media': 'I had got but a little way in my work, when my trouble returned on me. The ghost had come a second time. In the Arian History, I found the very same phenomenon, in a far bolder shape, which I had found in the Monophysite.'[141] This comes to him as a 'providence' – he 'has not sought it out', and finds it 'wonderful'. The allusion to the appearance of Banquo's ghost in *Macbeth* adds to the dramatic and mysterious atmosphere. He declares that he was 'reading and writing in my own line of study' – and, here, we may doubt him! – 'far from the controversies of the day'. He was never that 'far' – as his placing of heresy shows only too clearly: 'I saw clearly, that in the history of Arianism, the pure Arians were the Protestants, the semi-Arians were the Anglicans, and that Rome now was what it was then. The truth lay not with the *Via Media*, but with what was called "the extreme party".'[142] The sympathy which his earlier Tractarian writings evinced for a portion, at any rate, of the semi-Arians has, by this account, evaporated. Moreover, Rome has now become the party of unchanging fixity – but it is a fixity of overall disposition, an uncompromising rigour and precision, rather than adherence to a static body of doctrines. This presentation of heresy and ortho-doxy, in terms of various forms of moderation and rigour, is found in the *Essay on Development*, but Newman declares it to originate in a flash of insight which took place as he was translating and annotating St Athanasius, in 1841.

There is, however, no sign of any such understanding of Semi-Arianism in the numerous and often extensive annotations to the translated text of Athanasius' works. Newman frequently expounds the static concept of orthodoxy, 'setting forth in writing what has ever been held orally or implicitly in the Church'.[143] The fixed faith was only expounded more clearly – and more technically – when heresy challenged, but there had never been any doubt about the *thing* itself. Difficulties might, however, arise over the terms: some might stumble at the orthodox terminology, though they held to an orthodox meaning. Such were the Semi-Arians, in Newman's mid-Tractarian portrayal of them. In the Athanasius footnotes, there is no reversal. Newman re-iterates the words–things distinc-tion: 'it should be observed how careful the fathers of the day were not to mix up the question of doctrine, which rested on Catholic tradition with that of a certain term which rested on Catholic injunction'.[144]

The mention of semi-Arianism is, moreover, anything but hos-tile: he distinguishes two elements in the moderate 'Eusebian court party': 'the more religious or semi-Arian which tended to Catholi-cism, and ultimately coalesced with it, and the other the proper Arian or Anomaean which was essentially heretical'.[145] St Hilary receives praise for his discernment of this distinction: 'Hilary, wishing to commend the hopeful semi-Arians to the Gallic Church, makes excuses for them of the *necessity* of explanations of the Nicene formulary.'[146] Athanasius too 'does justice to the semi-Arians',[147] but is not as well informed as Hilary.[148] There is, certainly, no sense that the 'truth lay . . . with what was called "the extreme party".'[149] Newman has not yet abandoned the Vincentian canon of the Rule of Faith, in which the very idea of convergent testimonies is sympathetic to moderation.[150]

The *Apologia*'s narration cannot, then, be taken straight-forwardly as a picture of heresy's role in the collapse of the 'Via

Media'. As with Monophysitism in 1839, so with Arianism in 1841. We must suppose an anguished tension between Newman's private experience and his public position. This would have been especially the case with the *Library of the Fathers* translation; here he was committed to a party-venture, and it is not surprising that he excluded any doubts from the annotation to the text. His pretensions to pure scholarship were here at their highest, and the scholarly footnote was not, in any case, the ideal vehicle in which to write himself into a problem such as the Semi-Arian/Anglican parallel. Moreover, as in the *Apologia*'s account of 1839, the pages on Semi-Arianism may be considered as also heightening and dramatising experience in conformity with his later distinctively Roman Catholic rhetoric.

CHAPTER SEVENTEEN

Rhetoric refashioned (1843–1845)

(A) THE 'ESSAY ON DEVELOPMENT': ANGLICAN OR ROMAN?

The rhetorical 'placing' of Anglicanism against the spectrum of theological parties in Antiquity may, or may not, as we have seen, be traceable back to 1839. What is certain is that this strategy first *appears* in Newman's public discourse only in the *Essay on Development*, composed between the beginning of 1845 and October of the same year.[1]

But is the *Essay on Development* an 'Anglican' writing? J.J. Byrne's article on 'The Notion of Doctrinal Development in the Anglican Writings of J.H. Newman' includes the *Essay* in his survey, and defines 'Anglican writings' as 'all that Newman wrote in the years 1825–1845'.[2] Technically, Newman was an Anglican while he was composing the *Essay*, in the semi-monastic seclusion of Littlemore. The work was substantially complete, when Dominic Barberi received him[3] on 8 October 1845: 'As I advanced, my difficulties so cleared away that I ceased to speak of "the Roman Catholics", and boldly called them Catholics. Before I got to the end, I resolved to be received, and the book remains in the state in which it was then, unfinished'.[4] Newman's 1864 account suggests that he was working through a residual Anglicanism, and that, as the work progressed, he wrote himself into a decision.

However, the character of the *Essay* as an 'hypothesis to account for a difficulty',[5] that is, an attempt to remove historical difficulties as obstacles to a full assent to Roman dogma, hardly confirms Newman's own suggestion of its exploratory character. Indeed, the die had been cast some time before. By Autumn 1843, Newman could declare that the Roman Catholic Church was the Church of the Apostles and that the Anglican Church was in schism.[6] In September of this year, he resigned his curacy at St Mary the

Virgin, Oxford[7] and lay down gingerly upon his Anglican death-bed. At the height of his composition of the *Essay*, in the summer of 1845,[8] upon the occasion of the visit of a theological student from Oscott, he was 'attired in grey trousers – conclusive evidence that he no longer regarded himself as a clergyman'.[9] The student, on the look-out for a 'sign', reported that 'the end was near'.[10] In a sense, then, the author of the *Essay* was a Roman Catholic.

On the other hand, the *Essay* belongs to the world of distinctively Anglican ecclesiological debate, presented by Newman's 'Via Media' writings, and addresses itself specifically to the Anglican claims to a form of patristic 'Catholicity'. Pure Protestantism is, by contrast, summarily dismissed: 'What ever be historical Christianity, it is not Protestantism. If ever there were a safe truth, it is this.'[11] The *Essay* completes the story of the 'Via Media's' collapse and re-integrates into a new model the elements of the earlier, now redundant, paradigm. Newman is still speaking as an exponent of the Fathers but his method of presentation of the early Church has shifted to accommodate his new plea. But he is still speaking as an Anglican to Anglicans – as the bewilderment provoked by his *Essay* in Roman circles demonstrates.[12]

As may be expected, Newman need no longer resist some of the implications concerning the nature of orthodoxy to which his 'static' presentation was so vulnerable. He can allow a dialogue between orthodoxy and heresy and admit that the latter provokes real development of *understanding* on the part of the Church. Yet it would be a mistake to see Newman as presenting a *dialectical* relation between heresy and orthodoxy – in the truly Hegelian sense, where all oppositions conceal a *relation*, and where a higher reconciliation, a synthesis, is possible. This is clear from the fact that he uses comparisons between heresies such as Monophysitism, Nestorianism and 'Semi-Arianism', in order to suggest that the Anglican 'Via Media' position is invalid. Such comparisons depend for their effect on the assumption that heresy and orthodoxy arise from radically different underlying principles, whatever their surface resemblance may be. Newman will allow development to arise from a 'warfare of ideas', but, equally, will not tolerate pluralism: the way of truth is not only narrow but *single*. Accordingly, there co-exist somewhat uncomfortably in the *Essay* two ways of presenting heresy: first, that heresy provokes development in orthodoxy, and contributes to the evolution of Christianity's *language* about itself; but, second, that it is a form of personal inauthenticity, an existential failing. The former belongs to his philosophical discussion of the manner in which ideas develop, the latter to the literary dimension of the *Esssay*: vivid portraiture of the fourth- and fifth-century heretics, and deft glances at the present. The question of the *relation* of these two strands presents an acute problem of interpretation, and points to the weaknesses of the *Essay*, arising from its improvised character.

The idea of doctrinal development did not, of course, appear for the first time in the *Essay* but in an Anglican sermon, the XVth *University Sermon*, preached several months before the moment in 1843 when he recorded that he privately began to feel that the Roman was the Church. There are, indeed, some indications that the doctrine of development was present much earlier in Newman's thought in an either inchoate or repressed form. The *Essay on Development* (1844–5) must therefore be seen against this background (1839–44), if its peculiar character, particularly in the treatment of heresy, is to be appreciated.

(B) THE IDEA OF DEVELOPMENT AND HERESY (1839–1844)

Newman had, of course, always allowed that doctrinal terminology may develop, but when he was defending the 'Via Media', presented such development as verbal explanations of what had always been explicitly present in the mind of the Christian community as an idea. However, the idea of development breaks from the picture of believers having a clear and constant inward mental representation of the content of the Christian faith. From now on, the 'idea' of Christianity is tacit, mysteriously alive, and, in the process of coming-to-be through history, sharpening and particularising an originally vague consciousness: 'The inward idea, the impression of that truth, might be made on the mind and exist in it without the person becoming conscious of the fact.'[13] It eventually became possible for Newman to use such an approach to dogma, to explain why a Church professing teachings St Paul would hardly have recognised or even understood was still nevertheless faithful to the deposit handed down by the Apostles. It was also possible for Newman to show how it was inevitable that orthodox terminology should have affinities with heretical discourse, and that there would even be a period, before the latent

'Idea' had been drawn into explicitness, when heretic and orthodox expressions could hardly be distinguished.

Characteristically, Newman asserted that he had always, all along, believed in this idea of development. In a letter to Mrs Froude, written from Littlemore on 14 July 1844, he declared 'From the time I wrote the Arians, or at least from 1836, I have had in my thoughts, though I could not bring it out, that argument or theory, which at last appeared in my closing University Sermon.'[14] This passage shows how much the idea had become an *idée fixe* by 1844. He uses an idea of development about himself to show that he had always believed the idea of development! The problem of the relation of change and continuity was not only pressing in the realm of Church history – it presented him also with acute difficulties in the understanding of his *own* identity, which his obsessive concern to demonstrate consistency discloses.

On the other hand, there is evidence that Newman's Anglican rhetoric was always fighting off something very like the doctrine of development of the *Essay*. The gap which he announced in *Arians* between doxological and credal, for example, closely resembles the 1843 *University Sermon*'s distinction between the tacit indwelling of the 'idea' in the Christian community, and its propositional expression.[15] Moreover, Newman had been exercising a doctrine of the development of heresy in the mid-1830s,[16] and this deployed a method of analysis going far beyond merely verbal development. When he came to apply it to orthodoxy, he would have already been well practised in the art of discerning development where others saw only difference and discontinuity. Indeed the link between his work on heresy of the 1830s and the doctrine of development was in his mind when he was composing the *Essay*, for in his 1844 *Copybook on Development*, under 'In loco haereti-corum' is found: 'Sabellianism becomes Socinianism – down to *atheism*.'[17]

The idea of doctrinal development, even if traceable back to the 'Via Media' period did not necessarily always present a threat to Newman's Anglican position. For example, in 1840, he could use it, in renewed correspondence with his brother, Francis, to justify 'the Anglican *principle*', that is, 'quod semper, quod ubique'.[18] Here Newman argues that the sparse evidence concerning the nature of historic Christianity in the early centuries may be interpreted in the light of the fourth and fifth, and shown to form an organic identity with what came later. The idea of development is introduced to argue for the variations, while identity of 'temper and principles' is invoked – as later in the *Essay* – as the underpinning of the whole revealed system.

By 'development', here, Newman means *more* than explanation in words, as he so often does when discussing Bull and Petavius:

Its [the Church's] doctrines and course of conduct have developed from external and internal causes; where by development I mean the more accurate statement and the varied application of ideas from the action of the reason upon them according to new circumstances.[19]

From what immediately follows, it is clear that Newman is thinking along the lines of the XVth *University Sermon* (1843), rather than repeating Bull's idea that the Church merely explains what it already explicitly knows: 'All systems which have life, have a development, yet do not cease to have an identity though they develop e.g. Locke and Luther have done far more than they themselves saw.'[20] What is latent or tacit is drawn into explicitness through the conflicts of history. Newman's examples are significant: Locke and Luther are important figures in his heresiology, unconscious originators of infidelity and heresy respectively. Again, the detail contributes to the impression that Newman's rhetoric of the development of heresy of the 1830s eased him into the idea of the development of orthodoxy.

Completely lacking from this letter, however, is any sense that development of doctrine is a *threat* to Anglicanism. Even by 1843, when Newman's Anglican nerve had almost snapped, it is by no means certain that he saw development of doctrine as incompatible with Anglicanism. He was, for example, still overseeing the translation of Fleury, originally part of the programme of translations to be published to bolster the 'Via Media' position. In a note to the text of the third volume, he accommodates the rise and prevalence of heresy to a scheme of divine providence: some of its 'best ends' are 'to promote humility – to try our faith – to rouse the careless to an attentive study, and the religious to a more earnest realization of the Christian verities – and to subserve the evolution of these verities in a dogmatic form'.[21] This note can with some certainty be dated at 1843, for it refers to a work published in that year, the German edition of Möhler's *Einheit in der Kirche*. Newman, of course, did not read German and it is unlikely that he was familiar with this book's argument even when it later appeared in French translation.[22] Nevertheless, he was using the book as a handbook of references regarding development of doctrine: 'the interesting passages collected by Möhler Einheit in der Kirche'.[23]

Yet he does not understand dogmatic development to be in conflict with the static concept of orthodoxy of the 'Via Media'. Still, in the edition of Fleury, references to Möhler co-exist with the by now well-worn distinction between 'words and things'. Newman's account here of Leo's *Tome* could belong to any works of the mid-1830s on the Rule of Faith:

The letter was received, not as a final, judicial decision, but as evidence that was to be weighed, and scrutinized, and accepted only if found to agree with that which was from the beginning. And this is precisely what we meet with in every part of the history of Christian doctrine; it is not new truth that is discovered, but old truth that receives a new expression adapted to the present exigency.[24]

That Newman means by 'new expression' only a verbal expression or explanation of a truth generally agreed is clear from a note a few pages earlier on the same subject, Eutychianism: 'The truth is, that in the contest with diverse forms of error the words became more fixed and definite in their application. "Had Eutyches never appeared", says Leontius to the Acephalus, "you and I had perchance been using the same terms in common".'[25]

It is, perhaps, unfair to require systematic consistency between the footnotes of a work in which he was collaborating with others. Nor would this project – part of a distinctively Anglican apologetic programme – have been an appropriate place to raise anxieties about the relation of dogmatic development to ecclesiology, even supposing that Newman felt them.

In the XVth *University Sermon*, however, Newman reached his highest point so far of systematic clarity concerning the relation between dogma and revelation, and between orthodoxy and heresy. In this sermon, the epistemological sophistication is such as to make his own previous formulations in terms of words-and-things seem naive. Immediately, in discussing Mary's 'pondering', he breaks with his own earlier static model: the mark of an authentic faith is not 'acquiescing' in what is given, but in unfolding it by reflection.[26]

His presentation of the cognitional status of dogmatic orthodoxy is remarkable for its employment of the epistemology of eighteenth-century British philosophy, and, particularly, of the terminology of David Hume.[27] Newman presents revelation as a vivid inward 'impression', which is only gradually conceptualised and then expressed: 'what was at first an impression on the Imagination has become a system or creed in the Reason'.[28] In the latter, development of dogma consists: in the former consists its identity with the deposit of faith. The inner conceptualisation of the initial vivid impression is described in very Humean terms, as an 'idea', that is 'an image of what is real'.[29] On the other hand, Newman also uses 'idea' to mean the 'impression' of revelation in all its inexhaustible richness, to which dogmatic propositions are contrasted as but partial and feeble attempts to express the original: 'Particular propositions, then, which are used to express portions of the great idea vouchsafed to us, can never really be confused with the idea itself, which all such propositions taken together can but reach, and cannot exceed.'[30] The body of dogmatic orthodoxy consists, then, of shots from various angles at a mysterious entity that can never be exhausted by conceptualisation: thus, he can describe the doctrines of the Incarnation and Trinity as 'not a philosophy, but an individual idea in its separate aspect'.[31] Significantly, Newman identifies 'knowledge' in the Christian sense of knowledge of God in Christ, not with concepts, but with an inner 'impression' of an 'intimate kind', which is 'faint and doubtful in some minds, and distinct in others'.[32] By contrast, the dogmas which develop to explicitness by the action of Reason are accorded a more provisional status; they are 'the truth as far as they go, and under the conditions of thought which human feebleness imposes'.[33]

At several important points in his argument, Newman touches on heresy, although it is given much less attention than in the *Essay on Development*. He can now accord heresy a role in the formation of 'any Catholic dogma'.[34] This contrasts with the line taken in the 1830s concerning the fundamentals. But he does not concede a genuine dialectical relation between heresy and orthodoxy, for he can still place heresy outside the circle of authentic Christian discourse: it is only heretical *wickedness* which provides the irritation stimulating the exuberant forms of developing doctrine.[35] In two ways, Newman adapts his manner of describing heresy, to fit his new and sophisticated treatment of orthodoxy. Firstly, heresy is castigated not so much because it innovates, as because it *fails* to throw up what is new: 'its dogmas are unfruitful; it has no theology; so far forth as it is heresy, it has none'.[36] Heresy is sterile – 'it develops into dissolution', and grudges orthodoxy its fecund life: 'Heresy denies to the Church what is wanting in itself.'[37] Secondly, heresy is not marked by intellectual sophistication, a common feature of Newman's earlier presentations of it; rather it is epistemologically naive, embracing 'this or that proposition of the Creed' and taking this proposition logically further, but failing to discern the complex reality which concepts are struggling to express.[38]

The sermon's clarity about the nature of dogma is not, however, accompanied with any apparent anxiety about the validity of Anglicanism. Indeed, Newman can distinguish between the discussion of doctrinal development, and questions of church authority, and can postpone a consideration of the latter without anguish or sense of threat:

Nor am I here in any way concerned with the question, who is the legitimate framer and judge of these dogmatic inferences under the Gospel, or if there be any. Whether the Church is infallible, or the individual, or the first ages, or none of these, is not the point here, but the theory of developments itself.[39]

In this sermon, then, Newman was still – though perhaps only just – speaking as an Anglican. He was not trying to persuade his audience that historical objections to Romanism are surmountable. There is no hint that Anglicanism is challenged at all by the idea of development of doctrine. Indeed, the Sermon concludes with the earnest injunction to submit the reason to the teaching of God's 'Holy Jerusalem. His Church'.[40] A listener at St Mary's on this occasion would have no reason to assume that he did not mean the 'Church Catholic' in the *Tractarian* sense.

Newman reminisces that privately he was drifting ever Romewards – but it was not a drift promoted by the *philosophical* definition of orthodoxy of the 1843 Sermon. He was, rather, haunted by an *imaginative* parallel between heresy and Anglicanism – his 'ghost' of 1841, his face in the mirror of 1839. The 'principle of development' acted as 'a sort of test, which the Anglican could not exhibit, that modern Rome was in truth ancient Antioch, Alexandria and Constantinople, just as a mathematical curve has its own law and expression'.[41] But this disturbing *application* did not strike him, according to the *Apologia*, until after the composition and delivery of the 1843 *Sermon*.

The relationship between the idea of development and the treatment of heresy between 1839 and 1844 is in marked contrast to the *Essay on Development*. In the latter, heresy plays a prominent part in his rhetorical strategy, while in the former it occupies no such important role. The reason for this contrast was a change in rhetorical purpose: in the *Essay*, Newman finally changed sides: the construction of a positive case on behalf of Roman Catholicism had to be accompanied by the destruction of the case for 'Via Media' Anglicanism and, as in 1832, Newman could reach for heresy as a devastating offensive weapon.

(c) THE 'ESSAY ON DEVELOPMENT' (1844–1845)

In the *Essay*, Newman stood once again in the forum of debate, after a brief period of collapse. Although he abandoned the rhetoric of orthodoxy of the 1830s, he retained that appeal to probability upon which it was based: 'the gaps . . . which occur in the structure of the original creed of the Church make it probable that those developments, which grow out of the truths which lie around them, were intended to complete it'.[42] He is still, as Professor Lash describes him, 'fundamentally jurisprudential . . . a pleader'.[43]

However, Newman's rhetoric is necessarily more complex than that of the 'Via Media', because of the revolution in his concept of how Antiquity may be appropriated and deployed. He has moved away from the idea of a normative Christian past as a *static* entity which may, at any rate in its broad outlines, be brought to bear upon the uncertainties and ambivalences of the present, in order to codify it and prescribe for it. To find in Rome the answer to uncertainty and the resolution of ambiguity positively *required* a form of historical scepticism. Newman has, then, shifted from a strategy prescribing for a contested present by reference to an unproblematic past – 'the present is a text and the past its interpretation',[44] – to such complicated formulation as the *Essay*'s 'The event alone still future, which will bring its [a past event's] completion, will also bring its interpretation.'[45]

Newman's appeal to the 'idea' of Christianity is therefore a complex persuasive strategy, balancing several subordinate tactical procedures: it is, as Professor Lash describes it, 'at one and the

same time, an historical, descriptive claim, a heuristic recommendation (creating expectation that things would turn out this way),
and a complex prescriptive argument'.[46] Newman's 'demonstration' is not therefore theoretical: it is, rather, 'coaxing the
reader to "see" the (ambiguous) evidence in the way in which he
himself has come to see it'.[47] It is a bid for his Anglo-Catholic
reader's assent to a view of the past which simultaneously
demands also a life-decision. But such a decision demands awareness of the trickiness of all historical interpretation. In order, then,
to persuade his audience, Newman brings to explicitness the
complexity of historical interpretation and argues that any interpreter will inevitably use his own preapprehensions in re-creating
the 'text' of history. He attempts to break down an obvious
'prejudice' – which he himself shared in the 1830s – that Roman
dogmas are corruptions, while feeding the imagination with the
idea that the Roman claim to Antiquity is not really, after all, so
improbable.

It is primarily as part of such an attempt at persuasion that
descriptions of heresy are deployed in the *Essay*. Central to his
strategy is his use of Monophysitism. He proceeds subtly, avoiding
the brutal equation of 'Via Media' Anglicanism with Monophysitism, which *Difficulties of Anglicans* deploys five years later. Nevertheless, his description of Monophysitism is organised to signal
such a parallel to the patristically minded Anglican alert for
analogies. Personally 'unexceptional', Eutyches took his stand on
Tradition – on the Fathers, on the previously canonised Council of
Nicea and Constantinople. He could invoke Athanasius 'When the
Catholic doctrine was put before him, he answered, "Let Athanasius be read; you will find nothing of the kind there".'[48] Nor could
the Vincentian canon be easily applied to him: 'it is plain . . . that
there could be no *consensus* against him, as the word is now
commonly understood'.[49] Eutyches seemed to have the very things
on his side that an exponent of the 'Via Media' might invoke on
behalf of Anglicanism against Rome: 'Much might be said on the
plausibility of the defence, which Eutyches might have made for
his doctrine from the history and documents of the church before
his time.'[50] Most poignantly, Eutyches will have no *addition*; he will
adhere obediently to what has been handed down. Newman can
describe Eutychianism as 'a heresy, appealing to the Fathers, to
the Creed, and above all to Scripture . . . by a general Council,

professing to be Ecumenical'.[51] This is almost an epitome of his own position between 1833 and 1840!

By equating doctrinal conservatism with Eutychianism, Newman is undermining the 'Via Media' by invoking the normative authority of the patristic age: the suggestion that conservatism was analogous to the Eutychian position would, of course, only unsettle a reader who was himself unquestioningly *convinced* of the irreformable rightness of the Chalcedonian settlement which condemned Eutychianism. To make his analogy work, however, Newman is compelled to adjust his earlier descriptions of patristic orthodoxy. Most strikingly he stresses the innovatory character of Ephesus, the Ecumenical Council which preceded the Eutychian controversy: 'It is remarkable that the Council of Ephesus . . . had itself sanctioned the θεοτοκος an addition, greater perhaps than any before or since, to the letter of the primitive faith.'[52] Thus Eutyches in invoking Ephesus is involved in a contradiction, for his conservatism clashes with that very Council's developmental spirit. Newman can now even bring himself to describe the Council as making an 'addition' to the Creeds.

On the other hand, Newman cleaves more strongly than ever to his conception – stretching back to the 1820s – of orthodoxy as obedience. But in order to be able to characterise Monophysitism as disobedience, he has to re-define obedience. While in his 'Via Media' phase, orthodoxy was obedience to a *given* body of teaching which was distinct from the visible Church, and to which the Church must conform itself, in the *Essay* orthodoxy and Church are organically identified. It follows that Newman is now thinking of the Church as a particular communion, or even party, following Wiseman's 'argument from schism' against Anglo-Catholicism. This influence is apparent in Newman's description of the moderate Eutychians, or Monophysites, who seceded from those who upheld the Chalcedonian settlement: 'their refusal to obey the voice of the Church was an omen of error in their faith, and its secret heterodoxy is proved by their connection, in spite of themselves, with the extreme or ultra party whom they so vehemently disowned'.[53]

This is the closest Newman has come so far to the expression of that parallel between Anglicans and Monophysites which the *Apologia* and *Difficulties of Anglicans* alleged to have been influential upon him since 1839. The analogy is carefully integrated into his argument: if the idea of development of doctrine is correct, then it becomes essential to be a member of that one ecclesiastical party – the true Church – in which dwells the genius of authentic evolution, as opposed to those whose tendency is towards corruption and dissolution. But it is possible to be tragically unaware of the inauthenticity of one's own party and, by the logic of heresy's development, to be always tending unconsciously towards a more radical error.[54] Newman would have us seek a sign, a mark provided by Providence – an 'omen of error'[55] to point the way, and, in this imaginative appeal, can advocate the claim of that most imperious of communions, the Roman. The fate of the Monophysites is one such sign.

If Newman's section on 'the Monophysites' in the *Essay* is compared either with the passage in *Difficulties of Anglicans* which the *Apologia* cites, or with many of the passages in *Arians*, then it seems markedly *less* rhetorical, in the sense that analogies with the contemporary scene are not explicit. The section ends mutedly,[56] before the highly wrought conclusion, with its elaborate final twenty-four line period,[57] on behalf of the Roman claim. There is, however, another way of considering the 'Monophysite' section: that is not less rhetorical, but, rather, more skilful in its use of rhetoric, and that, consequently, it is less obvious that it is rhetoric at all. Newman is both more sophisticated than the man of 1832, but also less strident, and even less crude, than the frank polemicist of *Difficulties of Anglicans*. In the *Essay*, he is content to unsettle, to undermine, before the magnificent peroration of the fifth chapter bursts like a flood upon the reader.

The section on Nestorianism is more explicitly satirical in its deployment of analogy, than that on Monophysitism. It shares some of the malicious sense of fun of *Arians*, as Newman slips in suggestions that the Syrian school of theology out of which Nestorianism emerged bears a passing resemblance to Protestantism: he seems to be striking both at continental Protestantism, and the inheritors of the Hanoverian brand of Anglicanism. Thus Syrian Eucharistic theology was Zwinglian, 'As it tended to the separation of the Divine Person of Christ from His manhood, so did it tend to explain away His Divine Presence in the Sacramental elements.'[58] Moreover, the Nestorians introduced married clergy. Newman glances at Luther – Barsumas 'is even said by a Nestorian writer to have married a nun'.[59] One Nestorian Catholicos even used the device of extending marriage to monks, 'that is, to destroy the monastic order'.[60] The Nestorian world was a hotbed of error, on account of its loose structure of ecclesiastical authority: theologians were, not, as in Alexandria, directly answerable to one patriarch, and inhabited a 'private' world of their own 'schools', insulated from episcopal control. The result was 'diversity in religious opinion and incaution in the expression of it'.[61] Here, perhaps, is a dart at the latitudinarian Anglicanism of Hampden or Whately. All this is, indeed – unless one is the target – very entertaining. It is most probably designed to appeal to those who already have a Catholic regard to the Real Presence and for clerical and monastic celibacy, and even to suggest that papalism contrasts favourably with Anglican episcopal inertia on matters of faith. It is, however, only loosely integrated into Newman's central argument on behalf of the development of doctrine.

Most of the section on Nestorianism is devoted to demonstrating an association between the exegetical principle of the Syrian School and Nestorian Christological heresy. Newman's introductory phrases, however, show that he is also re-describing the contemporary: 'it devoted itself to the literal and *critical* interpretation of Scripture'.[62] In case the point should be missed, Newman immediately aferwards alludes to 'the connection of heterodoxy and *biblical criticism* in that age'.[63] The introduction of such anachronisms into the description of Nestorianism is, indeed, calculated. It is an oblique attack upon the methodology of Liberal Anglicanism, whose application of an historico-critical method to the New Testament Newman had already denounced in his 1841 critique of Milman. He had, in fact, not only called Milman 'Sabellian', but also declared him 'Nestorian'. In his analysis of Theodore of Mopsuestia's exegetical principles, he finds the origins of the Nestorian failure to acknowledge the *unity* of the divine and human in Jesus Christ: by interpreting the Old Testament literally and historically – excluding allegory – Theodore was opposing the idea of the interpenetration of divine and human,[64] keeping the two aspects strictly distinct; his critical principle eventually emerged explicitly in the later Christological heresy.

This attack upon historical criticism is more carefully integrated into Newman's argument from development than his more incidental sallies, for he relates it to his defence of the 'Mystical Interpretation of Scripture'[65] which he identifies as one of the constant underlying principles of authentic Christianity. The 'Mystical Interpretation' is presented as acknowledging that the meaning of the inspired text of Scripture is constantly unfolding into the future, transcending the historical context in its richness and finding its culmination in Christ. It is an essentially developmental attitude. Newman can then imply, by contrast, that the historico-critical method is static, fixing the text's meaning in its original context. It is, moreover, a clever way of casting doubt upon one of the most dangerous threats to the Roman Catholic claim to Antiquity, the patient stratifications of the historian. Imagination, Newman argues, is a necessary accompaniment of scholarship if historical data are to be united in one vision. In suggesting a modern parallel with Nestorian exegesis, he invites doubt and self-questioning in order to make room for his own hypothesis.

In characterising a rigid traditionalism as heretical, Newman was inverting his Tractarian position on the nature of orthodoxy. In the *Essay*, this reversal has two related manifestations; a general philosophical stance, regarding revelation and epistemology, and a return to a specific issue, the Bull–Petavius debate on the pre-Nicene Fathers. The accommodation of these intertwined issues to his case is one of Newman's trickiest tasks, for, in attempting to persuade his patristically minded former allies, he runs the risk of appearing a nominalist in his view of theological knowledge, and, in the acceptance of Petavius' analysis, a denigrator of the Fathers.

Newman's epistemological analysis[66] of the relation between revelation and developed dogma follows the lines he laid down in the 1843 *Sermon*, that is, an application of eighteenth-century British philosophy to the problem. In his somewhat ambiguous handling of 'idea', however, he may be seen as moving towards a Kantian apprehension of the mind's active role in the construction of knowledge – without, of course, necessarily having read, or even read about, the German philosopher. Thus 'idea' in the *Essay* means both a judgment about experience and the objective reality itself. Not surprisingly, Newman arrives at a dualism between revelation-in-itself, objectively considered, and revelation as gradually assimilated and apprehended by human minds:

Ideas are not ordinarily brought home to the mind, except through the medium of a variety of aspects; like bodily substances, which are not seen except under the clothing of their properties and influences, and can be walked round and surveyed on opposite sides and in different perspectives and in contrary lights.[67]

The rich, but occult, substratum of revelation then, is formed into a manifold, evolving body of knowledge – orthodox doctrine.

Newman's manner of overcoming the dualism between revelation as *object* and its gradual assimilation and articulation in the form of doctrine in the Church is both reminiscent of, and markedly different from, Hegel's attempt to surmount Kant's epistemological dualism. Although there is no more evidence to suppose that Newman had read Hegel, than he had Kant, the comparison is useful in placing the philosophical dimension of his argument, in order to show how its shape is tailored by his rhetorical needs.

Like Hegel, Newman argues the constructive role of *conflict*, in the coming-to-be of knowledge. This Newman applies to the Church's developing understanding of the *revelatum*, employing a dialectic of a kind – pointing to the 'warfare of ideas'[68] by which development takes place, by which the 'idea' comes to be; it is 'elicited by trial, and struggles into perfection. Nor does it escape the collision of opinion even in its earlier years; nor does it remain truer to itself and more one and the same though protected from vicissitude and change.'[69] However, while in Hegel subject and object, *Geist* and world, mutually modify – or participate in – one another as the very process of coming-to-be, in Newman, revelation, objectively considered, remains unchanged, though rich and mysterious: it does not *come to be* in the warfare of ideas and is 'protected' from the 'vicissitude and change' to which doctrine is open.

This pulling-back from a 'dialectical' understanding of subject and object emerges clearly when, towards the end of the book, Newman introduces the theme of heresy as a constructive element in the 'warfare of ideas' by which orthodoxy develops. He pursues this line at two points: in the passage on 'The Formation of Theological Science', in chapter VI,[70] and on 'Development Growing out of the Question of our Lord's Divinity', in chapter VIII.[71] In the latter, Arianism, Nestorianism and Monophysitism are reviewed touching their part in stimulating dogmatic development. These passages are separated by several hundred pages from Newman's opening epistemological discussion, 'On the Development of Ideas', where his ambiguous handling of 'idea' might make him sometimes sound Hegelian. The later treatment, however, makes clear that even if heresy and orthodoxy are in a dialectical relation, there is an immutable *tertium quid* beyond both.

In chapter VI, Newman shows how Apollinarianism and Monophysitism enabled the Church to define the distinction between the divine and human natures in Christ.[72] Arianism, on the other hand, helped the Church to develop its cult of the saints by provoking the distinction between a created mediating being and the unique, divine, mediation of Christ.[73] Indeed, it made possible Marian devotion by forcing the Church to distinguish between the *latria* due only to divinity and the *hyperdulia* due to the greatest of the saints. Nestorianism assisted further clarification of the mediating role of Our Lady.[74] Thus Newman attributes the systematic clarity of later Catholic Theology to the beneficial irritation presented by heresy:

Such was the state of sentiment on the subject of St Mary, which the Arian, Nestorian and Monophysite heresies found in the Church; and on which the doctrinal decisions consequent upon them impressed a form and consistency which has been handed on in the Church to this day.[75]

The antithesis here between 'state of sentiment' – a vivid unarticulated body of experience – and 'form and consistency' is entirely characteristic of Newman's handling of the relation between the initial impression made by revelation and developed dogma. But in making 'state of sentiment' prior both to the challenge of heresy and to developed dogma, he keeps in touch with his Tractarian position. However, he departs from it in declaring that this prior 'state of sentiment' is *modified* by 'doctrinal decisions', by having a 'form' impressed upon it: the 'impression' has – to follow Hume's terminology – become an 'idea'.

Such Humean epistemology pervades the *Essay*: a 'something', fixed, unchanging but rich and mysteriously opaque makes a vivid subjective 'impression' upon a community. The impression is clarified into distinct ideas, after a passage of conflict in which *words* in search of a mooring jostle in confusion and uncertainty. But the dialectic only takes place at the level of the subjective and communal assimilation of the *revelatum*, which latter is itself unaffected. Unlike the Hegelian dialectic, where everything is moving, Newman supposes a fixity over and above the conflict of heresy and orthodoxy. In positing this duality between fixity and change, he reaches out to his Anglican friends – and, indeed, to his former self.

The static concept of orthodoxy in fact recurs in a modified form as a component in Newman's idea of doctrinal development, as he locates the fixity of Christianity in certain underlying principles,[76] rather than in an immutable content of ideas. However, when he comes to his description of the nature of developed orthodoxy, he represents it in complex fashion as a balance between two principles naturally antagonistic: the 'dogmatic element,' which guards an immutable deposit, and the 'eclectic element'[77] which, infinitely adaptive, would accommodate all human philosophy. The former is exemplified in Tertullian, the latter represented by the Alexandrian Fathers, particularly Clement. But fixity on its own is no longer a note of authenticity: he clearly repudiates Tertullian's position as the sole criterion, by a juggling of dates whereby he can relegate that Father's conservatism to the period of his schism: 'It is chiefly in Tertullian's Montanistic works that his strong statements occur on the unalterableness of the Creed'.[78] The authentic 'idea' of Christianity, on the other hand, is a balance of fixity and flexibility: 'Thus Christianity grew in its proportions, gaining aliment and medicine from all that came near, yet preserving its original type, from its perception and its love of what had been revealed once for all and was no private imagination.'[79]

It follows that heresy can no longer be simply condemned as innovation. Its innovative tendency is, rather, a creative force, anticipating and initiating the future direction of orthodoxy:

Nay, the doctrines of heretical bodies are indices and anticipations of the mind of the Church. As the first step in settling a point of doctrine is to raise and debate it, so heresies in every age may be taken as the measure of the existing state of thought in the Church and of the movement of her theology; they determine in what way the current is moving, and the rate at which it flows.[80]

This reverses Newman's Tractarian position, where heresy is always represented as being preceded by orthodox truth. Nevertheless, he finds a way to inauthenticate heresy. His method of doing so reveals his desire to keep fixity as a component of his developmental idea: heresy is bad because it fails in 'Continuity of Principle'. Having pushed back the immutability of Christianity beyond doctrinal content to a fixed set of principles, Newman can demonstrate heresy's failure to comply with these. Thus, in chapter VII, he lists heresies against the fixed principle which they contradict: Arianism and Nestorianism opposing the allegorical interpretation of Scripture, Gnostics, Eunomians and Manichees the principle of faith, the sects the 'dogmatic principle', those who separated from the Church the sacramental principle. Like a magician pulling a rabbit out of a hat, Newman simultaneously condemns as heretical Tertullian's anti-developmental conservatism, while retaining the ancient categorisation of heresy as innovation.

Newman's attempt to reconcile change with fixity by means of the idea of development is partly the result of his characteristic craving for consistency in the face of the revolution in his interpretation of Antiquity – but it is also tact before his Anglo-Catholic audience. On occasion the argumentative structure whereby opposites are held together shows signs of strain. Nowhere is this more apparent than in his return to the issue between Bull and Petavius over the teaching of the pre-Nicene Fathers. It has been argued that Newman simply dropped Bull and went over to Petavius[81] once he was on his way to Rome, since pre-Nicene 'variations' were confirmation of his hypothesis of doctrinal development. In his section on 'Developments growing out of the Questions of Our Lord's Divinity',[82] he does indeed appear to take the Petavian line, almost taking it for granted:

No one who has looked ever so little into the theological works of the ancient church, but is aware that the language of the Ante-Nicene Fathers, on the subject of Our Lord's Divinity, may be far more easily accommodated to the Arian hypothesis than the language of the post-Nicene.[83]

But it is by no means clear that Newman here intends to abandon his former position: he mentions Bull's defence of the Ante-Nicenes against Sandius without disapproval: 'had not the fact been as I have stated it, neither Sandius would have attacked the Post-Nicene Fathers, nor would Bull have had to defend the Ante-Nicene'.[84] The Ante-Nicenes' subordination of the Son, Newman argues, was bound up with Old Testament texts concerning theophanies which they spoke of 'as if they were appearances of the Son'. It took Augustine to make explicit that these theophanies concerned 'simply angels through whom the Omnipresent Son manifested Himself'. In the light of this development, the true meaning of the pre-Nicenes is shown to be free from Arianising: this idea of angels is 'the only interpretation which could be put on the Ante-nicene statements, as soon as reason began to examine what they meant'.[85] This contrived defence of the ante-Nicenes shows Newman clinging to the idea of a *defence* of the early Fathers, and accommodating it somewhat awkwardly with his developmental hypothesis.

In a passage much earlier in the *Essay*, Newman has already adverted directly to the Bull–Petavius controversy: 'the question raised by various learned men in the seventeenth and following century, concerning the views of the early Fathers on the subject of Our Lord's Divinity'.[86] Here it is even clearer that Newman by no means regards himself as having abandoned Bull. On the contrary, he argues that *Bull* had all along been deploying the very method he himself adopts in the *Essay*: in reading the earlier Fathers in the light of post-Nicene theology and creeds, Bull was using the idea of development of doctrine as a working hypothesis, to account for a 'difficulty':

the position which Bull maintains seems to be nothing beyond this, that the Nicene Creed is a *natural key* for interpreting the body of Ante-nicene theology. His very aim is to explain difficulties; now the notion of difficulties and their explanation implies a rule to which they are apparent exceptions, and in accordance with which they are to be explained. Nay, the title of his work, which is a *Defence of the Creed of Nicea*, shows that he is not seeking a conclusion, but imposing a view.[87]

This is indeed a fantastic description of Bull's methodology. The attempt to transmute Bull's ponderous form into something fleeter shows how desperate he is to avoid giving the impression of a total reversal of his earlier 'Via Media' approach, in which the *Defence of the Nicene Faith* had been a mainstay of the Tractarian position.

The *Essay*, then, registers a complex re-adjustment of the enquiry which had since the 1830s obsessed Newman concerning the nature of Christianity's doctrinal content and its relation to the ancient past. Heresy and orthodoxy are described in very different terms from the 'Via Media' presentation. It is tempting to conclude that he has arrived at a greater systematic clarity about the nature of orthodoxy and the relation of heresy to it, which avoids the difficulties of the 'Via Media', tempting to conclude that liberation from the constraints of anti-Romanism freed him to speculate upon the problem more flexibly and imaginatively.

However, it is equally possible to view the increased complexity in Newman's position as part of a reorganisation of the elements of his rhetoric. It is not so much a new understanding of heresy and orthodoxy that emerges, as the sophisticated re-statement of well-worn adages: in its contradiction of 'Continuity of Principle', heresy is in itself both innovative and worthless. For all Newman's evocation of heresy's creative participation in the process of dogmatic evolution, he continues to share the patristic *frisson* of abhorrence at the company of heretics,[88] and can brutally consign the losing party to the dustbin of history: 'In Christianity, opinion, while a raw material, is called philosophy or scholasticism; when a rejected refuse, it is called heresy.'[89] Equally, his re-presentation of orthodoxy as development defends the Roman faith as unchanged from the beginning.

The *Essay* continues to fascinate because of the irreducible heterogeneity which an attempt to interpret it provokes. Its many sided analysis of the history of dogma is compellingly attractive to the modern sceptic in search of the elusive essence of Christianity. Yet its underlying dependence on a few very ancient assumptions – that heresy is bad and orthodoxy good, that the apostles have handed down the faith, that there *is* a True Church, the inheritor of the primitive one – warms the heart of the conservative, unnerved by modern questions. There is something for everyone in the *Essay*: not the least aspect of Newman's genius is his ability to find a way of drawing all sorts and conditions of men into the way of Rome.

Conclusion

And what you thought you came for
Is only a shell, a husk of meaning
From which the purpose breaks only when it is fulfilled
If at all. Either you had no purpose
Or the purpose is beyond the end you figured
And is altered in fulfilment. There are other places
Which also are the world's end, some at the sea jaws,
Or over a dark lake, in a desert of a city –
But this is the nearest, in place and time.
Now and in England.

(T.S. Eliot, *Little Gidding*)

Newman's Anglican writings on heresy dramatise the tensions of that anxiety about the past so characteristic of Christian reflection.[1] Such anxiety is almost a note of classical orthodoxy, which developed the notions of revelation's finality against the background of Gnostic and Montanist challenges: all its norms point to the past – apostolicity, canonicity, tradition and the rule of faith. At the same time, and despite considerable modification during the New Testament period, eschatalogy continued its hold: the future – as death and afterlife, or as salvation-in-history, or as predestination and providence – obsessively preoccupied the Christian imagination. The present became a barely isolable point on the way to the future by way of the past.

The past and the future appear to rule over the brief span of time which a Christian might call his own age. But they are as much servants as masters, for they serve to categorise the chaotic and fleeting images of the present. Just as apocalyptic may be used to judge the present age[2] against a vision of the ultimate future, so, too, may the idea of a normative past – the age of the Fathers – be turned against modernity. For such a colonisation of Christian

248

Antiquity to work, however, the inconvenient fact of early Church heresy must be accommodated to a scheme which marginalises its challenge to the often retrospective authority of patristic orthodoxy. And so the Fathers described the heretics as innovators, or pseudo-intellectuals, introducers of an alien sophistical logic, or men tragically clutching the part for the whole, or victims, or even embodiments, of Satan. What started as a problem needing explanation became a polemical weapon: an orthodoxy can use these characterisations of heresy embedded in the Tradition to describe almost any opposition. By a relentless sucking in of all otherness, such a rhetoric pillages the ancient past: whatever resists appropriation – heresy's plea for the irreducibility of difference – is ruthlessly enslaved and returned upon the present. Such re-descriptions spawn upon the occasion of a sudden, sickening jolt into self-consciousness, at a point of social, ecclesiastical or intellectual history, when the normative past, as once constructed, is no longer accepted without question. Heresiology revives as part of a mechanism for survival and preservation of identity, by which an orthodoxy struggles to marginalise the chaotic forces striking at its very heart.

Claude Welch has placed the Tractarian Newman amongst those movements in post-Enlightenment Europe which were pursuing 'Strategies of Restoration and Conservation'.[3] The peculiarly febrile fretfulness of Newman's conservative strategies, even when compared with the 'repristinators' Welch describes, arises from the influences upon him during his Anglican period. Converted in youth to an intensely patriotic and conservative form of Calvinism, he adopted apocalypticism as a response to social and political change; indeed, he never subsequently lost that Calvinist sense of the Satanic significance of contemporary events. Converted in early manhood to High Church Toryism, he suppressed his apocalypticism: underground, it dictated the course of his narration of Antiquity, merging gratefully with patristic typology. Converted in middle age to Rome, he found himself again confronting a last anxiety about the past. All these conversions were played out against the background of the growth in Europe of historico-critical studies. Its uncomfortable significance eventually dawned upon Newman: remarkably, there was no 'refusal to accept the historical question'[4] – for all the strain it put him under, he would yet take even this in.

However, Newman's acceptance of the existence of the historical question co-existed with both pre-critical and anti-critical stances. His first essay in theologico-historical scholarship, his *Arians*, was cut off from the new research taking place in Germany. The narrative itself lacks the studied disinterest of books pretending to critical scholarship: it is very much a 'tract for the times'.[5] His arguments about antiquity in his 'Via Media' phase show the same ambivalence, reflecting as they do a sense of distance from the ancient past. While constantly advocating a 'Church of the Fathers', he assumes, nonetheless, that it cannot straightforwardly be found anywhere: it is not directly to be equated with the Church of England; he polemically used the Fathers to demonstrate Rome's unpatristic corruptions; he never seriously considered the Eastern Orthodox Churches; he was certain that Protestantism was *not* the Christianity of the Fathers. But this sense of the gap between past and present is articulated in the terms of an archaic debate, stemming from the seventeenth century, between post-reformation divines arguing that their own communion was the True Church. The *Essay on Development* is, to be sure, much more sophisticated about the problem of sources – but this sophistication is subordinated to Newman's confessional argument for the newly found True Church he was about to embrace.

Newman's occupation of this no-man's-land somewhere between the critical and the pre-critical conferred an exquisite ambivalence upon his treatment of heresy. His enquiries are surrounded with the apparatus of erudition. Never a facile construer, he pored earnestly over the original texts, making his own translations of examples for quotation. But he never escaped what had by his time become the old-fashioned methods of the seventeenth and eighteenth centuries: just as he always wrote with a goose-quill, so did he rely upon the folios of a byegone age.[6] If he strikes a modern note, when contrasted with the old handbooks, then it is because, like Gibbon, he was capable of telling a story, dramatising situations and drawing characters: it is this *literary* gift which marks him off from seventeenth-century divinity. In making narrative a form of argument and a search for truth, Newman was drawing upon a powerful tradition, which began 'before philosophy' and which is still with us today.[7]

Newman's ambivalence towards the past, as he strove to play the dual role of urbane and scholarly modern, and ancient Father *redivivus*, shows up in all the heresies of which he treated. Part I has shown how Arianism was historicised and given a chronological narrative, but also rhetoricised against the political background of 1831. One little incident in the final recension of *Arians* vividly epitomises the extraordinary amalgam of the primitive and the urbane in Newman's attitude to scholarship at this time. It concerns the death of Arius. If glee were an emotion applicable to St Athanasius, then his narrative of the death of his enemy may be described as only with difficulty suppressing it: at the very moment of the heretic's triumphant return to communion with the Catholic Church, as he solemnly processed through the streets, supported by ecclesiastical allies and the imperial cohorts, he was suddenly afflicted, and, rushing to a nearby latrine, perished therein by an outrushing of his bowels. Athanasius presents his enemy's death as a providential act of God, vindicating the orthodox position. He does not shrink from drawing a comparison between Arius' evisceral demise and the fate of Judas.[8] Newman found his textbooks divided in their assessment of Athanasius' account: while Mosheim notes simply that Arius died 'in a very dismal manner',[9] Milner paraphrases the source with colourful relish.[10]

Newman did not quite know what to do. Eagerness to include the event vied with misgivings about its effect. He consulted Hugh James Rose about whether he should keep it in: 'If . . . you think it will not strike, pray strike it out.'[11] Rose was non-committal. Eventually Newman included a paragraph recounting Arius' death. His account casts a refined and delicate veil over the horror of the privy: 'the stroke of death suddenly overtook him, and he expired before his danger was discovered'.[12] Yet he does not forebear to draw out a *moral*: a 'thoughtful mind' cannot help seeing it as an 'interposition' of Providence, to show that God 'is not indifferent to human conduct'.[13] Still, he is uneasy: he pulls back from stating quite starkly that God struck down Arius to punish him and to demonstrate His disapproval of heresy, wrapping himself in fold upon fold of qualification.[14] Newman had already defended Divine 'interpositions' in his early *Essay on Miracles* (1826).[15] His application in *Arians* of the principle he had defended, however, typifies the anxiety and ambiguity with which he was appropriating an ancient perspective. He is acutely aware of the incongruity of adopting the attitudes of a fourth-century

Egyptian patriarch: yet polite, urbane, charitable and critical though he is, he yearns for some of Athanasius' toughness.

The same ambivalence marks his treatment of Apollinarianism and Sabellianism four years later. Although the reading of the texts is exhaustive and detailed, Newman moved in a consciously an-historical manner: he supports a theory of the secret correspon-dence and basic unity of heresies of widely differing provenance and theological context. It is a sophisticated re-statement of the patristic adage that all heresies are one because they were all spawned by that one Father of Lies, the Devil. Newman's attempt, historically to demonstrate an ontological structure beneath heret-ical discourse, is an early modern form of this ancient view.

Again, in his treatment of Monophysitism, the evidence of grinding study is enormous: there is little doubt that Newman was trying to find out exactly what were the teachings of all the various forms of this heresy. Yet, ultimately, the significance which he drew out from all his labours is quite unrelated to the historical *content* of Monophysite theology. Rather, he discerned a purely imaginative parallel with the 'Via Media' – the 'face in the mirror'. Similarly, the outcome of his examination of Semi-Arianism is, quite literally, fantastic – the 'ghost' which had come to him a second time!

It is this rhetorical explanation of history which has most irritated those critics of Newman who themselves prize critical, historical scholarship. A.M. Fairbairn, for example, unequivocally denounced Newman's rhetoricisation of history, declaring a 'sci-entific treatment' to be 'alien to his spirit' and calling *Arians of the Fourth Century* 'an overgrown political pamphlet, a treatise on the controversies of his own times disguised as history'.[16] Fairbairn's criticisms are, of course, the fruit of his own assumptions: that modern criticism is 'objective', that history is 'scientific'. Professor Rowan Williams' recent account of Newman's treatment of Arian-ism is less unambiguously dismissive: he describes Newman's historiography as 'eccentric, superficial and prejudiced', but admires his 'skills as a controversialist'. The latter, however, is sharply contrasted with the 'contribution to serious scholarship' so as to suggest that Newman has not rendered up to Professor Williams anything that can be called knowledge.[17]

Yet it is precisely for his rhetoric of knowledge that recent commentators have been most strenuous in claiming for Newman originality and continuing significance. Gérard Verbeke has illustrated the importance of Aristotle's rhetoric as part of the Aristotelian background to Newman's idea of informal reasoning and the illative sense, in the *Grammar of Assent*,[18] while Susan Funderburgh Jarratt has suggested that Newman's rhetoric of knowledge is comparable with that of the ancient Sophists,[19] who made the discovery of truth a matter of personal persuasion, and argues that Newman's rhetoric is a sophisticated way of dealing with the Victorian 'sense of the difficulty of establishing an authority for knowledge ... and a consequent awareness of the increased importance of language in the shaping of knowledge, given such a situation'.[20] Just as the Sophists bridged the gap between reality and perception by appealing to probability, in the *Apologia* Newman dealt with historical difficulties about the truth of Roman Catholicism by constructing a narrative which appealed to probability.[21] Most recently, Walter Jost's major study, *Rhetorical Thought in John Henry Newman*, demonstrates the importance of rhetoric for Newman's whole intellectual stance, and compares him with twentieth-century thinkers such as Hans-Georg Gadamer and Michael Polanyi.[22]

Such affirmative assessments of Newman as rhetorician appear, at first, to contradict the plain fact that he saw the *heretics* as the rhetoricians: indeed, he variously presents heresy as *both* Aristotelian and Sophistic.[23] His condemnation of heresy as rhetoric suggests that he did not see rhetoric as epistemically creative, but, rather that he thought it essentially dishonest, a view which he shares with the critics of rhetoric from earliest times. Must we not, moreover, see him as something of a hypocrite – denouncing heretics for their use of rhetoric,[24] while wielding it as his own most powerful weapon? In his embattled position in the 1830s especially, it would not, perhaps, have been wise to admit using in one's own defence the skill of making the weaker argument appear the stronger!

Characteristically, Newman was too perceptive not to anticipate these criticisms. When revising *Arians*, in the late 1830s, for a second edition, he admits that it is not only heresy that is rhetorical, but orthodoxy, too. Next to that part of the text of the first edition which read 'The skill of Arius in the art of disputation is well known',[25] he adds, 'But many of the Fathers were from the Sophists, Cyprian, Augustine, Greg. Naz. Basil, etc.'[26] More remarkable still is a pencilled annotation in which he suggests to himself an approach to be adopted in revision of the text. It appears above a passage about the theological 'economies' of the Alexandrian School:

Throw Disc. Arc. Allegory & Economy together in one calling it the principle of importing truth gradually and considerately wh. goes under different names etc.

Or qu. begin with remarks on the *Address* (wisdom of serpent) necessary for preaching gospel, give various instances of the *rhetoric* from Scripture, e.g. from St. Paul – then branch out.[27]

Newman never did 'branch out': the revision of *Arians* was never completed, nor did he ever expand these hints into his own comprehensive theory of theological rhetoric.

For all its gnomic quality, however, the annotation contains all the elements of such a theory: it expresses an assumption characteristic of his thought, the inexhaustable mysteriousness of the *revelatum* which drives the theologian to a series of shifts, as he struggles to adapt it to the capacity of his audience. However, he goes further than this, extending the application of the concept of rhetoric beyond the transmission of the faith in the early Church – to Scripture itself. In a manner which startlingly anticipates early twentieth-century German Form-Criticism, he identifies a rhetorical act – that of *preaching*[28] – as crucial to the formation of the New Testament documents.

If by the *Grammar of Assent*, he had arrived at a rhetoric of knowledge, it was the final stage in a long journey which began with the specific public occasions of the Anglican period. The years 1825–31 are crucial here. It was then that he acquired, in his collaboration with Richard Whately,[29] the detailed knowledge of the almost defunct[30] art of Aristotelian rhetoric. Whately's *Elements of Rhetoric* (1828) was the last of its kind.[31] Newman's one-time mentor, following Aristotle, distinguished sharply between philosophy ('inferring'), 'the ascertainment of the truth by investigation', and rhetoric, ('proving'), 'the establishment of [a truth] to the satisfaction of another'.[32] Whately accepts that the arguments used in inferring will differ from those used in proving, even in respect of the same truth. He nevertheless warns of the danger of confounding the distinction between investigation and persuasion, when 'those engaged in Philosophical and Theological inquiries' act as 'Advocate' as part of 'the process of *forming their own opinions*'.[33] This is, of course, exactly what Newman did in his treatment of heresy: he psychologised rhetoric into a form of investigation, and it led him where he did not expect to go. These years provided him with the occasion, which, if initially a defence of Establishment, soon developed into a journey of discovery.

Such an interpretation gives Newman's three rhetorics of heresy, for all their surface contradictions, a fundamental, strategic coherence. His rhetoric of Arianism moved from initial defence of *status quo* to ask broader questions about the Church's roots in an almost lost Antiquity. It initiated a programme of imaginative re-creation. His rhetoric of Sabellianism and Apollinarianism attacked a wide variety of opposing assumptions, including those of liberal Anglican scholarship, in order to break the ground for the reception of his 'Via Media'. His rhetoric of Monophysitism provided an existential way of apprehending the ultimate precariousness of the 'Via Media', and of supporting the sophisticated argument of the idea of development.

The question of the continuing significance of Newman's rhetoric of heresy today is a problematic one, for it is involved with the present and future absorption of 'Newman' as an artefact of the past. Just as he himself once strove to re-appropriate patristic discourse, so today the problem of Newman-interpretation inevitably encounters the use of him as a modern 'Father'. His rhetoric has the potential always to be re-rhetoricised. This process can take place in surprisingly divergent contexts: his very ambivalence provides something for all, while his empiricist epistemological framework makes him *feel* modern, even at the points he was repudiating modernity most vigorously. He has been claimed as an 'early modern', a Roman Catholic Schleiermacher.[34] In the wake of Vatican II, and the collapse of Roman Catholic neo-scholastic orthodoxy, he may be looked to as the paradigm of a new, contemporary way of doing theology.[35] Equally, he can be canonised by conservative, traditionalist theologians.[36]

The centenary of Newman's death is passing, with rumours confirmed of a more popular kind of canonisation, as his cause progresses in the Vatican. It would be a triumph for liberal and traditionalist alike. Newman encapsulated patristic attitudes in a form which resembled modernity. On the whole, his heresiology favours the traditionalists. Already, the flank of 'critical' scholarship is more and more exposed to post-critical approaches, which challenge the assumption that the meaning of the past can be objectively ascertained by impartial scholarship. If Newman only partly agreed with the historico-critical method, it was not entirely out of ignorance: an instinct, a scepticism, held him back – and it is this which brings him remarkably close to what may be termed a 'postmodern' perspective. Considered in this light, Newman's *œuvre* even now provides the framework for an intellectual repristination of traditionalism.

The very disparity of these attempts to re-appropriate Newman suggests the protean quality of the texts themselves. Newman glimpsed himself in the past, as in a mirror. He strove to gather the fragments of that past, to make just such another looking-glass for his own age. Contemporary reactions to Newman show that his writings still have the power to create disturbing reflections. In his works the image of the heretic as tragic rationalist springs up to interrogate the ideology of post-Enlightenment modernity. The secret of Newman's continuing fascination lies in the way he unleashes the creatures of imagination upon his readers, provoking an alarming personal identification with his narrative of Antiquity. The texts beckon, but in the end render up above all the reflected image of the investigator, who is startled to behold there the inescapable outline of his own obsessions.

Notes

INTRODUCTION

1 See S.W. Sykes, *The Identity of Christianity* (London, 1984) p. 251, where Sykes applies the philosopher, W.B. Gallie's 'essentially contested concept' to the problem of the essence of Christianity.

2 See Joseph Lecler, *Toleration & Reformation* (London, 1960) I for an exhaustive study of this. For Servetus, see Owen Chadwick, *The Reformation* (Pelican Books), 1964, pp. 410–12, and François Wendel, *Calvin* (London, 1976), pp. 93–9.

3 J.H. Newman, *Letters and Diaries*, II, p. 317, in calling Whigs liberals, Newman declares, 'I conceive I am saying almost as bad of them as can be said of any man.' A short definition of liberalism, from Newman's point of view is 'the anti-dogmatic principle'.

4 *Apologia*, p. 231, 'The simple question is, Can *I* (it is personal, not whether another, but can *I*) be saved in the English Church? am *I* in safety, were I to die tonight?'

5 *On Consulting The Faithful in Matters of Doctrine* (ed. J. Coulson) p. 2.

6 *Ibid.*, p. 2.

7 In *'The Trials of Theodoret'* (1860), *Historical Sketches*, II, pp. 303–62, Newman sympathises with Theodoret as a good man misrepresented to Rome by Cyril (pp. 344–5). Newman shows dislike for Cyril's personal qualities in his dealings with Constantinople: 'Cyril, I know, is a saint, but it does not follow that he was a saint in the year 412' (p. 341).

8 For example, Newman's defence of the duty to obey conscience in his *Letter to the Duke of Norfolk* (1874), presents the papal condemnation of 'conscience' in *Quanta Cura* as a condemnation only of unbridled liberty of judgment, and restricts the binding force of papal pronouncements to *general* matters, *Difficulties of Anglicans*, II, pp. 251, 256.

9 Wilfrid Ward, *The Life of John Henry Cardinal Newman* (London, 1913) Vol. II, pp. 282–3.

10 Newman does this throughout in the republication of his *Lectures on*

the Prophetical Office of the Church. In his footnotes, he is constantly taking his earlier self to task.

1. HERESY AND ORTHODOXY IN THE EVANGELICAL PERIOD

1 Meriol Trevor, *Newman: the Pillar and the Cloud* (London, 1962), pp. 18–19.
2 *Apologia*, p. 5.
3 *Ibid.*, p. 7.
4 *Ibid.*, p. 5.
5 *Ibid.*, p. 5.
6 Thomas Scott of Aston Sandford, *The Force of Truth, an Authentick Narrative.* 8th edn (London, 1808) p. 4. The first edition appeared in 1779.
7 *Ibid.*, 5: 'the mysteries of the gospel being explained away, or brought down to the level of man's comprehension, by such proud and corrupt, though specious, reasonings'.
8 *Ibid.*, p. 31.
9 *Ibid.*, p. 8.
10 *Ibid.*, p. 31.
11 *Ibid.*, p. 31.
12 *Ibid.*, p. 31.
13 *Ibid.*, p. 31.
14 *Ibid.*, p. 19.
15 *Ibid.*, p. 54.
16 in his *Early Journals*, Bk. 1, 'December 25, The Athanasian Creed', in *Autobiographical Writings* (ed. H. Tristram, 1956) p. 154.
17 *Ibid.*, p. 162.
18 *Loc. cit.*
19 *Ibid.*, p. 165.
20 *Ibid.*, p. 166.
21 *Ibid.*, p. 161.
22 *Ibid.*, p. 166.
23 Robin T. Selby, *The Principle of Reserve in the Writings of John Henry Newman* (Oxford, 1975). According to Selby, Newman began to see the value of the patristic practice of Reserve in communicating to the uninitiated the mysteries of the Christian religion, in the face of emotional Evangelical preaching of the Atonement in order to effect conversion, Selby's account, pp. 1–43. This idea appears in *Arians* pp. 47–8.
24 *Autobiographical Writings*, p. 162, *Journal* for October, 1819.
25 *Ibid.*, p. 161.
26 *Ibid.*, p. 166, *Journal* for 16 May 1821.
27 *Ibid.*, p. 167, *Journal* for 7 September 1821.

28 *Autobiographical Writings*, p. 167.
29 *Ibid.*, p. 167.
30 Meriol Trevor, *Newman: the Pillar and the Cloud*, pp. 30–1; Ward, *Life*, p. 34.
31 *Ibid.*, pp. 35–6.
32 *Ibid.*, pp. 44–5; Ward, I, p. 34.
33 *Autobiographical Writings*, p. 78. See *Apologia*, p. 35. In addition, Hawkins gave Newman Sumner's *Apostolic Preaching*, which demonstrated that Calvinistic predestination could not be shown from the writings of St Paul, see Thomas Sheridan, *Newman on Justification* (New York, 1967) pp. 75–86.
34 *Apologia*, p. 13, referring to *Letters on the Church by an Episcopalian* (1826).
35 *Autobiographical Writings*, p. 79.
36 *Ibid.*, p. 79.
37 *Apologia*, p. 13.
38 *Ibid.*, p. 13.
39 *Autobiographical Writings*, p. 81.
40 Newman distinguished between 'certitude a habit of mind' and 'certainty a quality of propositions', *Apologia*, p. 120. The former is indefectible, 'once certitude always certitude', *Grammar of Assent*, p. 221. Hence 'it is conceivable that a man might travel in his religious profession all the way from heathenism to Catholicity, through Mahometanism, Judaism, Unitarianism, Protestantism and Anglicanism without one certitude lost', *ibid.*, p. 251.
41 *Autobiographical Writings*, p. 83.
42 Newman saw the Protestant principle of 'private judgment' as essentially heretical, see Basil Willey, *Nineteenth Century Studies* (London, 1968) p. 77.
43 Newman regularly uses this term to refer to the old High Church party who exalted the power of the State over the Church. (He used 'X's to refer to the Evangelicals who exalted Church over State).
44 i.e. that it would not work in a parish.
45 *Autobiographical Writings*, p. 83.
46 *Ibid.*, p. 211.
47 This sermon is, at the time of writing, in the Birmingham Oratory Archive, to be published in a forthcoming volume of the hitherto unpublished sermons, ed., Gerard Tracey, to whom I am most grateful for access to this material.
48 All references are to the original copy, in the Birmingham Oratory Archives.
49 See Part II.
50 George Bull, 1634–1710, Bishop of St David's. His *Defence of the Nicene Creed* was published in 1685. See Part III, Ch. 15 (a) for a detailed discussion.

51 *Autobiographical Writings*, Early Journals, II, p. 211, where Newman summarises the year 1827: a note has been added, probably from a later date.
52 *Letters and Diaries*, p. 185, n. 4.
53 *Ibid.*, p. 15.
54 *Ibid.*, p. 16.
55 *Ibid.*, p. 16.
56 *Ibid.*, p. 16. It may be added that this was precisely what Newman identified as a dangerous modern heresy with regard to revelation – which he treated under the heading of 'Sabellianism', see Part III.
57 *Ibid.*, II, p. 16.
58 Here Newman anticipates his later idea of *economy*, i.e. the method of presenting religious truths 'under the nearest form possible to a learner or enquirer, when he could not possibly understand it exactly', *Apologia*, p. 270.
59 *Letters and Diaries*, II, p. 16.
60 In the unpublished sermon 'On the Doctrine of the Trinity', 1 June 1828, Birmingham Oratory, A.50.1.
61 Quoting Gerard Tracey, in the introduction to this sermon, in his forthcoming edition.

2. 'THE ARIANS OF THE FOURTH CENTURY' AND ITS BACKGROUND 1828–1832

1 David Newsome, *The Parting of Friends* (London, 1966), p. 12.
2 *Ibid.*, pp. 11–12.
3 *Ibid.*, p. 10.
4 J. H. Overton, *The English Church in the Nineteenth Century, 1800–1833* (London, 1894) p. 302.
5 *Ibid.*, p. 302.
6 *Ibid.*, pp. 306–7. See also, Edward Norman, *Church and Society in England, 1770–1970* (Oxford, 1976) pp. 71–122.
7 Norman, pp. 11–12. Repeal of Test Acts was actively supported by the Lords Spiritual.
8 Overton, *The English Church*, pp. 305–6.
9 *Ibid.*, p. 312.
10 Overton summarises the deteriorating situation between Church and State and the growing atmosphere of crisis in the late 1820s and early 1830s, pp. 296ff.
11 Overton, *The English Church*, p. 311. William Barry, *Cardinal Newman* (London, 1927) p. 113, regards Newman as one of the nineteenth-century prophets who spoke out against utilitarian ethics and economics, the other prophets being Ruskin and Carlyle.
12 Overton, *The English Church*, p. 306.
13 *Ibid.*, p. 305.

14 Overton, *The English Church*, p. 306.
15 Newman had petitioned annually *for* Emancipation until 1827/8. But in February, 1829, he changed sides, thereby passing from the *clientele* of Whately to that of Keble, via the mediation of Hurrell Froude. By contrast, Pusey consistently supported Peel, and it was he who persuaded Blanco White to change his stance, to join him, Whately and the Provost of Oriel, in support of Peel, see H.P. Liddon, *Life of Edward Bouverie Pusey*, I. 4th edn (London, 1894) pp. 189–90.
16 Sir Robert Inglis, 1786–1855, MP for Dundalk from 1824, was known as an opponent of Catholic Emancipation which he had strenuously opposed in Parliament in 1825. In 1829, he accepted the offer to contest the seat at Oxford against Sir Robert Peel, who had resigned after changing his mind over Emancipation. Inglis was returned. He remained MP for Oxford until his death, see Dictionary of National Biography pp. 443–4, where he is described as 'an old-fashioned tory, a strong churchman with many prejudices and no great ability.'
17 *Letters and Diaries*, II, p. 28.
18 *Ibid.*, p. 129.
19 *Ibid.*, p. 129.
20 *Ibid.*, p. 129.
21 *Ibid.*, pp. 129–30.
22 e.g: 'heretical and latitudinarian attempts to disparage the orthodoxy of the Ante-Nicene centuries', *Via Media*, I, *Prophetical Office* Lecture II, p. 61. See Introduction for a fuller discussion.
23 *Letters and Diaries*, II, p. 130.
24 *Ibid.*, p. 130.
25 *Ibid.*, p. 132.
26 *Ibid.*, p. 130.
27 *Ibid.*, p. 130.
28 *Ibid.*, p. 130.
29 *Ibid.*, p. 130.
30 See J.H. Walgrave, O.P., *Newman the Theologian. The Nature of Belief and Doctrine as Exemplified in his Life and Works*, trans., A.V. Littledale (London, 1960) pp. 149–50.
31 *Letters and Diaries*, II pp. 130–1.
32 *Ibid.*, p. 131.
33 *Ibid.*, p. 131.
34 See Piers Brendon, *Hurrell Froude and the Oxford Movement* (London, 1974) pp. 43–4, Keble, reacting against the intellectualism of the 'Noetics' (according to Isaac Williams) put *ethos* above intellect. See also Georgina Battiscombe, *John Keble. A Study in Limitations* (London, 1963) pp. 54–5, influenced by Butler's *Analogy*, Keble deprecated purely intellectual satisfaction in theological matters, regarding religion as something to be lived.

35 *Autobiographical Writings, Journals*, Bk 1, October 1819, p. 162: 'As a man's faith, so is his practice.'

36 The connection between truth and error, and a corresponding *ethos*, or character, is so marked a feature of Newman's thought that it has been widely observed, Gunter Biemer, *Newman on Tradition* (London, 1966) p. 116; Boekrad, *The Personal Conquest of Truth according to J. H. Newman* (Louvain, 1955) pp. 134–5, 250–1; Sean O'Faolin, *Newman's Way* (London, 1952) p. 211; Thomas J. Norris, *Newman and His Theological Method* (Leiden, 1977) pp. 101, 110, 161, 175–6; Y. Brilioth, *The Anglican Revival. Studies in the Oxford Movement* (London, 1933), points out that this is a characteristic of the *whole* Oxford Movement; Walgrave, *Newman the Theologian*, pp. 148, 162, see also p. 166.

37 Brian W. Martin, *John Keble, Priest, Professor and Poet* (London, 1976) pp. 35–6, See also Battiscombe, *Keble*, p. 55: Keble admired George Herbert's 'Country Parson'.

38 'Occasional Thoughts for 1827', in *Remains of the Late Rev Richard Hurrell Froude* (ed. J. H. Newman) Part 1, Vol. 1 (London, 1838) p. 115.

39 *Ibid.*, p. 115.

40 *Ibid.*, p. 115.

41 *Ibid.*, p. 116.

42 The subject of the relation between *ethos* and belief had been variously discussed by those in Newman's circle. In 1828, in a correspondence with Blanco White, Newman challenged Blanco 'to give me some account of the connection of speculative error with bad *ethos* – e.g. *in what is a consistent Socinian worse than an orthodox believer?* I think him to be worse, but I wish my mind clear on the subject', see David Newsome, 'The Evangelical Sources of Newman's Power', in *Rediscovery of Newman* (ed. Coulson and Allchin) (London, 1967) p. 25. Since Froude's treatment of the subject precedes this discussion, it is very likely that Newman's preoccupation with the *ethos* of heresy was sparked off by him.

43 Froude, *Remains*, 1, p. 116.

44 *Ibid.*, pp. 116–17.

45 *Letters and Diaries*, 11, p. 80. This was in early July, 1828.

46 Newman was reading the epistles of St Ignatius of Antioch on 3rd and 4th July 1828.

47 Most strongly in the epistle to the Smyrneans, which Newman read on 4th July 1828: 'Let no one do anything that pertains to the Church apart from the bishop . . . Wherever the bishop shall appear, there is the Catholic Church.' ed. and trans., Henry Bettenson, *The Early Christian Fathers* (Oxford, 1976) p. 49.

48 No. 15 of *Parochial and Plain Sermons*, 1.

49 *Ibid.*, p. 191.

50 *Ibid.*, p. 191.

51 *Parochial and Plain Sermons*, I, p. 197.
52 *Ibid.*, p. 201.
53 *Ibid.*, p. 197.
54 *Ibid.*, p. 197.
55 *Ibid.*, p. 197.
56 *Ibid.*, No. 6, preached on 4 June 1829.
57 *Ibid.*, p. 211.
58 *Ibid.*, p. 211.
59 *Ibid.*, p. 212.
60 *Parochial and Plain Sermons*, III, preached on 29 November 1829.
61 Proverbs, 4. 24–7.
62 *Parochial and Plain Sermons*, III, p. 150.
63 *Ibid.*, p. 192.
64 *Ibid.*, p. 192.
65 *Ibid.*, p. 193. The texts are 1 Cor. 11.19 and Tit. 3.10.
66 Romans 16.17.
67 *Parochial and Plain Sermons*, III, p. 193.
68 *Ibid.*, p. 192.
69 *Ibid.*, p. 199.
70 *Ibid.*, p. 202.
71 *Ibid.*, p. 205.
72 *University Sermons*, p. 21.
73 *Ibid.*, p. 29.
74 *Ibid.*, p. 30.
75 *Ibid.*, p. 28.
76 *Parochial and Plain Sermons*, I, No. 17, preached on 24 October 1830.
77 *Ibid.*, p. 222.
78 *Ibid.*, p. 219.
79 *Ibid.*, p. 218.
80 *Ibid.*, p. 219.
81 *Ibid.*, p. 221.
82 *Ibid.*, p. 221.
83 *Ibid.*, p. 223.
84 *Ibid.*, p. 224.
85 *Ibid.*, p. 224.
86 *Ibid.*, p. 226.
87 *Ibid.*, p. 226.
88 *Ibid.*, No. 18, preached on 14 November 1830.
89 *Ibid.*, p. 229.
90 *Ibid.*, p. 235.
91 *Ibid.*, pp. 237–8.
92 Louis Bouyer, *Newman. His Life and Spirituality*, trans. J. Lewis May (London, 1958) p. 184: Newman consistently denounced 'bourgeois liberalism'.
93 *University Sermons*, p. 48.

94 *Parochial and Plain Sermons*, ii, No. 16, 'Religious Cowardice', 25 April 1831, p. 181.
95 *Parochial and Plain Sermons*, i, No. 22, 'Witnesses of the Resurrection', 24 April 1831, p. 291.
96 *Ibid.*, p. 291.
97 *Letters and Diaries*, iii, p. 103. *Arians* was rejected by the editors of the *Theological Library* on 23 October 1832.
98 *Letters and Diaries*, ii, p. 323.
99 For example, *ibid.*, pp. 338, 345, 358–9, 371.
100 *Ibid.*, pp. 352–3.
101 *Ibid.*, p. 371.
102 *Ibid.*, p. 371.
103 *Apologia* (Svaglic), pp. 35–6.
104 *Letters and Diaries*, ii, p. 371.
105 It was not only tests, but also dogmatic language in the public liturgy that liberals wanted to remove. Thomas Arnold, for example, objected to the damnatory clauses in the Athanasian Creed, see V.F. Storr, *The Development of English Theology in the Nineteenth Century 1800–1860* (London, 1913) p. 110.
106 *Letters and Diaries*, iii, p. 54.
107 *Letters and Diaries*, ii, p. 321.
108 Writing to Simeon Lloyd Pope on 15 August 1830, he gives the pressing need to support the Established Church against Dissent as the reason for ceding from the Bible Society, *Letters and Diaries*, ii, pp. 264–5.
109 *Arians*, p. 373.
110 *Ibid.*, p. 264.
111 *Ibid.*, p. 266.
112 This has been touched on by H. Bremond, *The Mystery of Newman*, trans., H.C. Corrance (London, 1907), p. 108, and by Walgrave, *Newman the Theologian*, pp. 38–9.
113 *Arians*, p. 406.
114 *Ibid.*, p. 26.
115 *Ibid.*, p. 31.
116 *Ibid.*, p. 32.
117 *Ibid.*, p. 29.
118 *Ibid.*, p. 52.
119 *Ibid.*, p. 28.
120 *Ibid.*, p. 31.
121 *Ibid.*, p. 31.
122 *Ibid.*, p. 32.
123 *Ibid.*, p. 33.
124 *Ibid.*, p. 33.
125 *Ibid.*, p. 34.
126 *Ibid.*, pp. 34–5.

127 *Arians*, p. 114.
128 *Ibid.*, p. 116.
129 *Ibid.*, p. 115.
130 *Ibid.*, p. 115: 'The trinitarian hypothesis of the Eclectics was not perplexed by any portion of that difficulty of statement which in the true doctrine, results from the very incomprehensibility of its subject.'
131 *Ibid.*, p. 106.
132 Rough Notes Preparatory to *Arians* Birmingham Oratory Archive Archive, A.12.11. This definition occurs on a single sheet of paper containing notes on Ammonius Saccas, whom Newman considers an 'apostate', rather than a heretic. It is clear that he is thinking of the contemporary analogy, 'parallel of neologism'. Neologism is particularly dangerous because not easily identifiable by its language as heretical: 'its artifice is to keep within the letter'.
133 Hugh James Rose, *The State of the Protestant Religion in Germany, In a Series of Discourses preached before the University of Cambridge*, (Cambridge and London, 1825).
134 E.B. Pusey, *An Historical Enquiry into the Probable Causes of the Rationalist Character Lately Predominant in the Theology of Germany* (London, 1828).
135 For the course of the controversy, see H.P. Liddon, *Life of Pusey*, I, pp. 51ff. Rose's book was unanimously regarded as being misinformed, ibid., pp. 151, 154.
136 Newman recorded its appearance, in his *Diary* of 1828, but confessed to his sister, Harriet, that he found it 'very difficult' and had made little of it. Writing to Samuel Rickards, he criticised the style of the book, see *Letters and Diaries*, pp. 74, 98.
137 Liddon, *Life of Pusey*, I, p. 164.
138 *Ibid.*, pp. 173–4.
139 *Letters and Diaries*, II, for 8 June 1829 and 31 July 1829, pp. 147, 155. See also Liddon, *Life of Pusey*, I, pp. 164, 167.
140 Pusey *Historical Enquiry*, pp. 48, 176.
141 Newman refers to the influence of Rose upon him in *Apologia*, pp. 37–9, and alludes to his book on German theology.
142 Rose, *State of Protestant Religion in Germany*, (Part I), p. 3.
143 *Ibid.*, p. 65.
144 *Ibid.*, p. 10; see also p. 103.
145 *Arians*, p. 109.
146 Liberalism became an all-embracing concept in the Tractarian period. The breadth of the concept is indicated by the appendix to the *Apologia* (Svaglic), pp. 254–62, where Newman lists eighteen characteristics of liberalism. At the outset of this, he gives a concise definition, 'the Anti-dogmatic Principle' – although this is to 'tell us very little about it', ibid., p. 255. In his *Biglietto Speech* (1879) he summarised his life's work as the battle against liberalism in religion

and defined it as 'the doctrine that there is no positive truth in religion, but that one creed is as good as another', quoted in Ward, II, p. 460.

147 *Arians*, p. 22.
148 *Ibid.*, pp. 366.
149 *Ibid.*, p. 270.
150 *Ibid.*, pp. 329–30.
151 *Ibid.*, p. 372.
152 *Ibid.*, pp. 308.
153 *Ibid.*, p. 391.
154 *Ibid.*, p. 308.
155 *Ibid.*, p. 307.
156 *Ibid.*, p. 304–5.
157 *Ibid.*, p. 304.
158 *Ibid.*, p. 305.
159 *Ibid.*, p. 307.
160 *Ibid.*, p. 8. Rowan Williams, *Arius, Heresy and Tradition* (London, 1987) p. 3, declares that Newman was original in locating the heresy's origin in Antiochene exegesis, rather than Neoplatonism.
161 *Arians*, p. 8.
162 *Ibid.*, p. 11.
163 *Ibid.*, p. 18.
164 *Ibid.*, p. 113.
165 See *Essay on Development*, pp. 305–6, his discussion of the origins of Nestorianism.
166 Williams, *Arius*, p. 4; by contrast with the Syrian Church, 'The Alexandrian Church is held up . . . as the very exemplar of traditional and revealed religion'.
167 Charles Frederick Harrold, 'John Henry Newman and the Alexandrian Platonists', *Modern Philology*, 37 (1940), p. 282.
168 *Ibid.*, 287.
169 For 'figuration', see Hans Frei, *The Eclipse of Biblical Narrative* (New Haven and London 1974) p. 2.
170 The edition referred to throughout will be: Joseph Milner, *The History of the Church of Christ Previous to the Reformation* [in 6 vols.], Vols. I and II (London: Religious Tract Society, undated). It was originally published in York, 1794–1809, being completed after his death by his brother Isaac.
171 See 'Milman's View of Christianity', *Essays Critical and Historical*, II, p. 186: 'Gibbon is almost our sole authority for as subjects near the heart of a Christian as any can well be.'
172 J.D. Walsh, 'Joseph Milner's Evangelical Church History', *Journal of Ecclesiastical History*, 10, (1959) p. 186. On the other hand, Harrold, 'Newman and the Alexandrian Platonists', pp. 284–5, n. 26, is more positive about the continuing influence of Milner upon Newman.

173 For republicated patterns, see Walsh, 'Milner's Evangelical Church History', pp. 179, 185. Newman did acknowledge the influence upon him, when composing his first *Essay on Miracles*, of Milner's theory of history: 'that upon the visible Church came down from above, at certain intervals, large and temporary *Effusions* of divine grace', *Apologia*, p. 22.
174 Yngve Brilioth, *The Anglican Revival*, p. 35.
175 Quoted in Walsh, 'Milner's Evangelical Church History', p. 177.
176 *Ibid.*, p. 176.
177 Joseph Milner, *History of Christianity*, I, p. 142.
178 *Ibid.*, p. 139.
179 *Ibid.*, I, pp. 207–10, 224 and 326–7, where Origen is blamed for originating Arianism.
180 *Ibid.*, I, p. 185. He is treating of the heretic Theodotus.
181 *Ibid.*, I, p. 201. See also pp. 383–4.
182 *Ibid.*, I, p. 201.
183 Compare Newman's account of Ammonius Saccas' accomodation of Christianity to his eclecticism or 'Neologism' (*Arians*, pp. 104–6), with Milner's description of this philosopher's corruption of the true doctrine of Justification by platonic philosophy. Joseph Milner, *History of Christianity*, I, pp. 188–9.
184 *Ibid.*, I, p. 384. Similarly Julian the Apostate is compared with Hume, see Walsh, 'Milner's Evangelical History', p. 179.
185 *Ibid.*, p. 179.
186 *Ibid.*, p. 183.
187 *Ibid.*, p. 138.
188 'If then this zeal for good works be the EFFECT of HIS redemption, how is it possible that a person who disbelieves the important doctrines essentially concerned in that redemption should have any zeal for good works.' Joseph Milner, *History of Christianity*, I, p. 379.
189 *Ibid.*, II, p. 59, 67.
190 *Ibid.*, II, p. 60, precisely as Newman does in *Arians*!
191 *Ibid.*, I, p. 380.
192 *Ibid.*, I, p. 379. Milner asserts that many passages testify to Origen's orthodoxy of belief. His 'ambiguities' may be explained by 'his well-known, curious and adventurous spirit of enquiry, in subjects on which he never meant to be positive'.

3. NEWMAN'S TRACTARIAN RHETORIC, 1833–1837:
THE ANALOGY CONTINUED

1 See Norman, *Church and Society*, p. 106.
2 For example, on Roman Catholic Emancipation, see Part I, ch.2, n. 17.
3 *Arians*, p. 406.

4 *Apologia*, p. 35.
5 *Verses on Various Occasions*, p. 181.
6 *Ibid.*, p. 145.
7 *Ibid.*, p. 102.
8 *Ibid.*, p. 89.
9 The *Letters* have a long and complex textual history behind them before their appearance in the *Collected Works, Historical Sketches*, I and II. They were extensively reworked for the first edn of *The Church of the Fathers*, in 1840, and also in 1857, for the new edn of this work, when some of the material was diverted to form *Primitive Christianity*. Numerous rephrasings, conflations, deletions and additions took place between 1833 and 1872/3, so that quotations in *Historical Sketches*, I and II are not a reliable guide for what Newman wrote in the original *Letters*. The original articles have been referred to at all times in the body of the text, but, for convenience, accompanying references to the collected works have been given, where applicable.
10 *Letter I, British Magazine*, IV, 1 October 1833, p. 421; *Historical Sketches*, I, p. 339.
11 *Ibid.*, p. 339.
12 *Ibid.*, p. 339.
13 *Letter I, British Magazine*, IV, p. 422; *Historical Sketches*, I, p. 341.
14 *Letter I, British Magazine*, IV, p. 424; *Historical Sketches*, I, p. 346.
15 *Letter I, British Magazine*, IV, p. 423; *Historical Sketches*, I, p. 342. (altered).
16 *Letter I, British Magazine*, IV, p. 425; *Historical Sketches*, I, p. 347.
17 *Letter I, British Magazine*, IV, p. 425; *Historical Sketches*, p. 347.
18 *Discussions and Arguments*, p. 41.
19 *Tract 15*, p. 11.
20 *Ibid.*, p. 11.
21 *Via Media*, II, p. 84.
22 *Ibid.*, pp. 89.
23 *Ibid.*, pp. 89–90.
24 *Ibid.*, p. 59.
25 For a full account of the young Newman's apocalypticism, and its political dimension, see Sheridan W. Gilley, 'Newman and Prophecy, Evangelical and Catholic', *Journal of the United Reformed Church History Society*, 3 (5), (March, 1985), pp. 160–88.
26 This connection has been observed by C.S. Dessain, *John Henry Newman* (London, 1966), p. IX; and more vividly by William Barry. *Newman*, p. 54: 'Savonarola condemned the Pagan Renaissance; Newman the French Revolution.'
27 *Discussions and Arguments*, p. 51.
28 *Ibid.*, p. 57.
29 Newman adds, 'a coincidence between actual events and prophecy sufficient to show us that the apparent contradiction in the latter

may be easily reconciled, though beforehand we may not see how', *Discussions and Arguments*, p. 68.

30 *Ibid.*, p. 58.
31 *Ibid.*, p. 59.
32 *Ibid.*, p. 59.
33 *Ibid.*, p. 59.
34 *Essays Critical and Historical*, I, p. 139.
35 *Ibid.*, p. 140.
36 *Ibid.*, pp. 157–8.
37 *Ibid.*, p. 158.
38 *Ibid.*, p. 160.

4. CONCLUSIONS: RHETORIC AND POLITICS

1 *Apologia*, p. 37.
2 *Ibid.*, p. 62.
3 J.C.D. Clarke, *English Society 1688–1832, Ideology, Social Structure and Political Practice during the Ancien Régime* (Cambridge, 1985) pp. 3–38 which surveys historiography.
4 *Ibid.*, p. 1.
5 *Ibid.*, p. 96.
6 *Ibid.*, pp. 272ff.
7 Even Edward Irving opposed the repeal of tests, *ibid.*, p. 350.
8 'The salient fact for the social historian of eighteenth century England is that Christian belief is initially almost universal, a belief calling attention to the history of a chosen nation conceived as a family', *ibid.*, p. 87.
9 *Ibid.*, p. 350.
10 *Tracts*, Vol. I, no. 2, p. 2.
11 Norman, *Church and Society*, pp. 73–5: it was possible, Norman argues, to make a distinction between non-party-political defence of the Establishment before 1832, and specific party involvement. Indeed, Toryism was not necessarily seen as party-political (p. 84). After Reform, this distinction was made more difficult to maintain (pp. 92–3).
12 *Letters and Diaries*, IV, p. 24.
13 *Ibid.*, p. 26.

5. NEW DIRECTIONS: THE MID-1830s

1 ed. J. Stevenson, *A New Eusebius*, (London, 1978) p. 340. According to Socrates' *History*, Arius accused his bishop, Alexander of Alexandria of 'introducing the doctrine of Sabellius the Libyan'.
2 In *Arians* Ch. I, Sect. v, 'Sabellianism', Newman offers some hesitant speculations about the possibility of a 'declension' from a 'more

orthodox' form of modalism (Christ *is* God), to something approaching Socinianism ('the Ebionite, or modern Socinian heresy', p. 123).

3 Newman's vocabulary is often backward-looking, to the Deist and Socinian challenges of the eighteenth century. Hence, the prominence of 'Socinian' and 'infidel' in his vocabulary. On the other hand, he can refer, looking forward, to the increasing secularisation of his own age, e.g. *Essays Critical and Historical*, II, 219. Here, be it noted, he uses the term 'infidelity' rather than 'atheism'.

4 For example, *passim* in *De Decretis Nic. Symb.*, esp., ch. 4 (PG XXV, 429B) ch. 5. (PG XXV, 431C), ch. 15 'ασεβουντες' (PG XXV, 419), PG XXV, 419), ch. 16, 'ασεβεια', (PG XXV, 419), ch. 30 (PG XXV, 471D), ch. 32 (PG XXV, 476). 781B, *Hist. Arianum*, ch. 75 PG XXV, 689A, *Epist. ad Serapion De Morte Arii*, ch. 4. In an 1871 note to *Arians*, Newman notes the connection between 'ασεβεια' and heresy, and 'ευσεβεια' ('piety' or 'godliness') and orthodoxy, *Arians* (1833). p. 286, n.5.

5 'the devil alone . . . is your father in this apostasy, who in the beginning sowed you with the seed of irreligion'. *Library of Nicene and Post-Nicene Fathers of the Christian Church*, 2nd Series, Vol. IV, *Select Works and Letters of St Athanasius*, trans., J.H. Newman (Michigan: Eerdmans, 1980) pp. 168–9. This translation dates from 1841–2. See Migne, *Patrologia Graeca*, 1857, Vol. xxv, col. 465D.

6. PATRISTIC RESEARCH: THE EDITION OF DIONYSIUS OF ALEXANDRIA

1 *Letters and Diaries*, IV, p. 202, To Henry Wilberforce, 10 March 1834.

2 J.F. Bethune-Baker, *Introduction to the Early History of Christian Doctrine* (London, 1951), pp. 113–18, ch. VIII, 'The Correspondence Between the Dionysii'; Kelly, *Early Christian Doctrines* (London, 1972), pp. 133–6; ed. Stevenson, *New Eusebius*, pp. 268–71, document nos. 235, 236.

3 In the Libyan Pentapolis, see Kelly, *Early Christian Doctrines*, p. 133. Dionysius, Bishop of *Rome*, in his contribution to the controversy, alludes to an exaggerated and erroneous reaction to 'Sabellius' opinions', ed. Stevenson, *New Eusebius*, p. 268.

4 Kelly, p. 133, indeed, sees Dionysius of Alexandria as the 'best-known exponent of Origen's subordinationist strain'.

5 See Kelly, *Early Christian Doctrines*, p. 134; Bethune-Baker, *Introduction*, pp. 116–17.

6 Although without directly accusing him. The Pope is courteously vague, 'I am told that some among you . . .,', ed. Stevenson, *New Eusebius*, p. 268.

7 For a translation, see Newman's own of the *De Sententia Dionysii*, most readily available in ed. Schaff, *Nicene and Post-Nicene Fathers*, Vol. IV, *St Athanasius: Select Works and Letters*, Oxford and New York,

1892, pp. 181–2. See also Stevenson, *New Eusebius*, pp. 269–70 for discussion of the nuances of the analogies by the two Dionysii.

8 Ward, *Life of Newman*, II, p. 576, To Canon Jenkins, 27 February 1877.

9 *Letters and Diaries*, IV, p. 320, to John William Bowden, 10 August, 1834.

10 *Ibid.*, p. 320. Newman therefore tells Bowden 'not to trouble himself' about Mohler's book on St Athanasius.

11 *Letters and Diaries*, III, p. 43.

12 *Ibid.*, p. 65.

13 *Ibid.*, pp. 104–5.

14 *Letters and Diaries*, IV, pp. 311, n.1.

15 Newman began work on 10th March, 1834, *Letters and Diaries*, IV, p. 202, and ended on 30 August 1835, *Letters and Diaries*, V. There are references to the work in progress throughout this period: *Letters and Diaries*, IV, pp. 253, 274, 280, 283, 291, 293, 311, 320, 360; V: 97, 104, 107, 118, 120, 122, 132.

16 *Letters and Diaries*, IV, pp. 283, 293; V, 97.

17 *Ibid.*, pp. 293, 310–11, in July 1834.

18 *Ibid.*, IV, p. 311.

19 *Ibid.*, p. 320.

20 *Ibid.*, p. 360.

21 *Letters and Diaries*, V, p. 104.

22 *Ibid.*, p. 118.

23 *Ibid.*, p. 122.

24 *Ibid.*, p. 132.

25 *Ibid.*, p. 132.

26 Birmingham Oratory Archive, B. 2.8.

27 i.e. Sextus.

28 Eusebius, *Ecclesiastical History*, Penguin edn, p. 289 (7.1.6.) 'The doctrine now being propagated at Ptolemsis in Pentapolis is an impious one, characterised by shocking blasphemy against Almighty God, Father of our Lord Jesus Christ; utter disbelief in His only-begotten Son, the word made man; and indifference to the Holy Ghost.'

29 Birmingham Oratory Archive, B. 2.8.

30 *Ibid.*, B. 2.8.

7. THE HAMPDEN CONTROVERSY

1 *Letters and Diaries*, IV, p. 323, 20 August 1834.

2 Trevor, *Pillar and the Cloud*, pp. 173–7, gives a vivid account of the atmosphere and personalities involved in this first stage of the controversy over Hampden, centring on matriculation for Dissenters.

3 *Letters and Diaries*, IV, p. 371, 28 November 1834.

4 *Letters and Diaries*, V, pp. 50–1, 23 March 1835.

5 *Ibid.*, p. 65, 3 May 1845.

6 See Trevor, *Pillar and the Cloud*, pp. 174, 176.

7 *Letters and Diaries*, V, pp. 73–4, 22 May 1835.

8 *Ibid.*, V, p. 74, letter of Hampden to Newman, 22 May 1835.

9 *Ibid.*, p. 83, Hampden to Newman, 23 June 1835. In the *Collection of Pamphlets* there was that of Wilberforce, *Foundations of the Faith Assailed* (1835).

10 *Letters and Diaries*, V, p 83, 23rd June 1835.

11 The sentence in Hampden's letter of 23 June 1835, was 'Would you have dared to act in such a way, had you not taken the advantage of the sacred profession?' *Letters and Diaries*, V, p. 83.

12 Newman wrote to J.W. Bowden, 7 July 1835, that Hampden 'affirms that I should have been afraid so to have acted except under shelter of my "sacred profession", which means, as Froude says, that he, to *prove himself a Christian*, would have fought a duel with me, but for my being in orders. This is ingenious'. See, *Letters and Diaries*, V, p. 93.

13 Hampden's imputations were 'altogether disallowed' and 'gravely' protested against, *Letters and Diaries*, V, pp. 83–4.

14 See Trevor, *Pillar and the Cloud*, pp. 183–190, 'The Persecution of Hampden'. Arnold's famous attack upon the Tractarians, as 'Oxford Malignants', appeared in April 1836, in the *Edinburgh Review*, and was part of the second phase of the controversy, about the Regius Professorship.

15 See ch. 7.

16 In view of his protest in late November 1834, to Hampden, who had sent him a copy of his pamphlet, *Observations on Religious Dissent*, see n.(3) above. However, Newman knew of Hampden's position from late August 1834. See his letter to Rose, n.(1) above.

17 Oxford: J.H. Parker and London: Rivingtons, 1833. This work was delivered as the *Bampton Lectures* in the previous year, 1832, and will be hereafter referred to as Hampden, *Bampton Lectures*.

18 Diary for 31 March 1835, *Letters and Diaries*, V, p. 53. The controversy had been proceeding since late 1834, see nn.(1) and (3) above.

19 *Elucidations of Dr Hampden's Theological Statements* consisted largely of quotations from Hampden's *Bampton Lectures* and *Observations on Religious Dissent*, in order to demonstrate Hampden's virtual Socinianism, under nine sections: doctrinal truths, Trinity, Incarnation, Atonement, Sacraments, original sin, the soul, morals, positive statements. When the prospect of Hampden's appointment to the Regius Professorship had got out, Newman was in a position to compile his *Elucidations* very quickly – he wrote the pamphlet

overnight, having had dinner in his rooms, *Diary* for Wednesday, 10 February 1836, *Letters and Diaries*, v, p. 231.

20 R.D. Hampden, *Observations on Religious Dissent* (Oxford, London, 1834) p. 14.

21 *Ibid.*, pp. 11–12,

22 *Ibid.*, pp. 11–12,

23 *Ibid.*, p. 12.

24 *Ibid.*, p. 12.

25 *Ibid.*, p. 13.

26 Hampden, *Bampton Lectures*, p. 92.

27 *Ibid.*, p. 13.

28 i.e. in the derogatory sense of indifference to religious truth. Hampden distinguishes a better sense of the word – one who is eager 'to conciliate dissentients, further than his allegiance to his own church is conceived to admit', Hampden, *Observations*, p. 29.

29 *Ibid.*, p. 36.

30 *Ibid.*, p. 33, 'The real unity of the Church is, after all, an invisible one.' The doctrines of particular denominations will therefore inevitably be relative rather than absolute.

31 *Ibid.*, p. 33.

32 *Ibid.*, pp. 22–3.

33 *Ibid.*, pp. 23–4.

34 *Ibid.*, p. 27.

35 *Elucidations*, pp. 5–6.

36 Hampden, *Bampton Lectures*, p. 278.

37 *Apologia*, p. 169.

38 Although Hampden is very careful to distinguish himself from the early Tractarians. This is probably the meaning of his deprecation of the 'party sense' of the word: he is glancing at something like Newman's use of 'rationalism' as a polemic on behalf of High Church opinions, 'This term, having been lately appropriated to a particular class of theological opinions, may require the explanation, that it is here used in the general sense corresponding with its etymology', *Bampton Lectures*, p. 37, n.(b).

39 *Ibid.*, p. 37.

40 *Ibid.*, p. 54.

41 *Ibid.*, pp. 376–7. Hampden's picture of the Church unwillingly being forced by heresy to use logic to defend itself is identical to Newman's in *Arians*, ch. ii, section 3, pp. 168–9. See also *Parochial and Plain Sermons*, ii, p. 28, Sermon iii, 'The Incarnation'. This is not necessarily to suggest mutual influence here: Newman shows no awareness of the *Bampton Lectures* when writing *Arians*, nor does Hampden allude to *Arians* in his *Bampton Lectures*. It may, perhaps, be suggested that they both belong to the same 'Romantic' antipathy to the logical and merely propositional.

42 Hampden, *Bampton Lectures*, v, pp. 60–1.
43 *Ibid.*, v, p. 77.
44 *Ibid.*, v, p. 77.
45 *Ibid.*, p. 88.
46 *Ibid.*, p. 88.
47 For this phrase of Hampden's, see *Bampton Lectures*, p. 278.
48 *Arians*, pp. 185–6.
49 Hampden, *Bampton Lectures*, p. 149.
50 *Ibid.*, p. 88.
51 *Ibid.*, p. 91.
52 *Ibid.*, p. 89.
53 *Ibid.*, pp. 112–13.
54 *Ibid.*, pp. 114–15.
55 *Ibid.*, pp. 117–18.
56 *Ibid.*, pp. 117–18.
57 *Ibid.*, p. 148.
58 *Ibid.*, p. 148.
59 *Ibid.*, p. 148.
60 *Ibid.*, p. 148.

8. BLANCO WHITE

1 Blanco White had left his position with Whately and gone to Liverpool, to become Unitarian in January, 1835, *Letters and Diaries*, v, p. 51, n.1. However, Newman only heard about it on 20th March, *Letters and Diaries*, v, p. 48, *Diary* for 20 March 1835. Blanco had no reason to tell Newman: they were no longer close friends.
2 Newman says that ties of friendship had been severed between them, after the publication of *Arians* in 1832, *Letters and Diaries*, v, p. 103, n.2, since the work expressed sentiments which would have been 'simple misery' to Blanco.
3 Whose *clientela* was an opposing camp to that of Newman's by the mid-1830s.
4 See Martin Murphy, 'Blanco White's Evidence', *Recusant History*, 17(3) (May, 1985), p. 263. 25 years later, Newman paid tribute to the now dead Blanco's personal qualities and testified his affection for him, *Present Position of Catholics in England*, Lecture IV, sect. 3, pp. 142–3.
5 *The British Critic, Quarterly Theological Review and Ecclesiastical Record*, xx (July 1836), Art. VIII, 'The Brothers Controversy, being a genuine correspondence between a clergyman of the Church of England and a layman of Unitarian opinions', p. 167. Newman's review of his book adverted to the Socinianism of Hampden and Blanco White.
6 A copy of this letter does not exist, although a note about it by Newman does, *Letters and Diaries*, IV, p. 103. Blanco White noted in

his diary for 23 March 1835, that he had received a letter from Newman which was 'nothing but a groan, a sigh from beginning to end', ed. John Hamilton Thom, *The Life of the Rev Joseph Blanco White*, 3 vols. (London, 1845) Vol. II, p. 117. Blanco's rather cynical comment here upon Newman's anguish contrasts with his dignified reply to his former friend's letter.

7 *Letters and Diaries*, V, p. 49, 23 March 1835.

8 *Ibid.*, p. 123. Writing to his sister, Jemima, on 9 August 1835, Newman describes Blanco White's by then irrevocable decision as 'like a madness', it 'seems like insanity'.

9 Murphy, 'Blanco White's Evidence', *Recusant History*, 17 (3), May, 1985, p. 269, *Letters and Diaries*, V, p. 50.

10 *Letters and Diaries*, V, p. 56, To Henry Wilberforce, 5 April 1835.

11 Blanco White was generally, but without evidence, held to be behind Hampden's *Bampton Lectures*, because of his knowledge of scholasticism: 'Blanco White's Evidence', p. 268, Liddon, *Life of Pusey*, I, p. 271.

12 *Letters and Diaries*, IV, p. 169. J.F. Christie, writing to Newman on 5 January 1834, comments upon the *Second Travels*: it is 'nominally at least by Blanco White, not the Archbishop. Of course it would contain the notions of the latter, though developed by another hand'. Whately was right to think that he would be blamed for Blanco White's defection, Murphy, pp. 267–8. Moreover, Newman associated Blanco and Whately as belonging to a 'certain school', *Letters and Diaries*, V, p. 51.

13 O'Faolin, *Newman's Way*, pp. 236–7, is, however, surely wrong to suggest that Newman himself belonged to this web, and that Blanco's view of the defectibility of language derives from Newman's *Arians*. In the latter Newman balances the defective language of the economy by the concept of mystery, in which the economy is rooted. All liberals, however, including Blanco, attacked 'mystery'.

14 Murphy, 'Blanco White's Evidence', pp. 269–70, even suggests that Newman's reading, in 1845, of Blanco White's posthumous journals pushed him over the edge to Rome, because in them he saw the terrible consequences of rationalism.

15 *Letters and Diaries*, V, To J.W. Bowden, 3 August 1835, 'I have just seen Bl. White's most miserable book – there are some instructive confessions in it.'

16 There are four almost verbally identical references to this idea in Newman's letters, between 3 August 1835, and 9 August 1835: *Letters and Diaries*, V, pp. 114, 115, 116, 120. Newman's expression is an almost exact quotation from Blanco White, *Observations on Heresy and Orthodoxy* (London, 1835) Preface, p. viii, 'Sabellianism is only Unitarianism disguised in words.'

17 *Letters and Diaries*, V, p. 116, To R.H. Froude, 9 August 1835.

18 Blanco White *Observations*, p. vi.
19 *Ibid.*, p. x.
20 *Ibid.*, p. vi.
21 e.g. *Parochial and Plain Sermons*, II, pp.167–8. 'Self Contemplation', written in January or February 1835, where latitudinarian indifferentism to dogmatic truth is identified with Bible-Protestantism. There are hints here that Newman sees the latter as 'Sabellian' also, because it leads one 'to consider that inspiration speaks merely of divine operations, not of Persons'. (p. 167).
22 Blanco White, *Observations*, p. vi.
23 *Ibid.*, p. viii.
24 *Tract 73*, in *Essays Critical and Historical*, I, pp. 78–9.
25 Blanco White, *Observations*, p.viii.
26 Both Froude and then Newman attacked this extreme nominalistic view of language in articles in the *British Critic*, in 1836: R.H. Froude, *The British Critic*, XIX (1836), pp. 211–19. Newman, *The British Critic*, XX (July, 1836), pointed out that Blanco White, a Socinian, was arguing like an Anglican latitudinarian, p. 174.
27 Blanco White, *Observations*, Letter 1, p. 5.
28 *Ibid.*, p. 5.
29 *Ibid.*, p. 5.
30 *Ibid.*, p. 5.
31 *Ibid.*, p. 11.
32 *Ibid.*, p. 11.
33 *Ibid.*, Letter 1, p. 16.
34 *Ibid.*, p. 27.
35 *Ibid.*, pp. 27–9.
36 *Letters and Diaries*, IV, p. 316, To Henry Wilberforce, 3 August 1834.
37 *Letters and Diaries*, V, pp. 120–1, To Elizabeth Newman, 9 August 1835.
38 *Ibid.*, p. 121.
39 *Parochial and Plain Sermons*, III, no. 12.
40 Newman's patristic studies may be assumed to be in the background, between October 1834 and August 1835, although he did not begin to study Apollinarianism in depth, until six months after this sermon was preached. This may explain why his doctrinal line in this sermon is not entirely clear, and why he speaks, somewhat vaguely, of 'Nicene theology' when making Christological points.
41 *Parochial and Plain Sermons*, III, p. 169.
42 *Ibid.*, p. 169.
43 *Ibid.*, p. 170.
44 *Ibid.*, p. 171.
45 *Letters and Diaries*, V, p. 51, 23 March 1835. For the bearing of Hinds' 'notions about Inspiration', i.e. his internal evidencing, and the link

in Newman's mind between this and Sabellianism, see ch. 10, 11 on Erskine.

46 Hinds was Whately's domestic chaplain. They were also friends from schooldays and as undergraduates, W. Tuckwell, *Pre-Tractarian Oxford. A Reminiscence of the Oriel 'Noetics'* (London, 1909) pp. 54, 129.

47 For a detailed consideration of this incident, see Part 1.

48 See E. Jane Whately, *Life and Correspondence of Richard Whately* (London, 1957), p. 60. The charge originated from a passage in the Appendix to his *Logic* (1826), dealing with 'Person', in which Whately declared that, in the case of the Trinity, Person meant not an individual but a 'character'. This would bring him very close to modalism, see *Life*, p. 61, Tuckwell, *Pre-Tractarian Oxford*, p. 72. Ironically, it was this very work, the *Logic*, with which the young Newman had assisted his one-time mentor.

49 *Letters and Diaries*, II, p. 367. The call never came. Newman later attributed this fact to their divergence, perceived by Whately, not by himself: 'He knew me better than I knew myself'.

50 *Ibid.*, pp. 360, 369, 372.

51 *Ibid.*, p. 363, in *Diary*, Thursday, 29 September 1831.

52 The divergence of Newman and Whately was more gradual than is stated in the *Apologia* where it is declared tht the 'formal break' came over Catholic Emancipation in 1829, *Apologia*, p. 14, the occasion of Whately's humorous revenge for Newman's anti-Emancipation stance, in which he invited him to dinner and placed him among a group of port-drinking 'two-bottle orthodox'. Newman dates his depature from Whately's *clientela* at this date, ibid., p. 14. However, even by 1831, they were friendly and Whately was happy to offer him promotion. But it was not until November, 1834, that Newman made clear his differences of principle over the Church–State issue. In the preceding month, a ripple of indignation on Whately's part reached Newman from Dublin, because of rumours that Newman had absented himself from Holy Communion when Whately visited Oriel. Newman denied this, but began to make clear his disagreement with Whately's public stance over the Irish Church, see *Letters and Diaries*, IV, pp. 356–9. By March, 1835, Newman could lump together Whately with Arnold, Hampden and Blanco White. They were all liberals and all Sabellian, *Letters and Diaries*, V, p. 51.

9. APOLLINARIANISM

1 References to his edn end on 12 November 1834, *Letters and Diaries*, IV, p. 360, and do not begin again until Thursday, 16 July 1835, *Letters and Diaries*, V, p. 97.

2 Newman worked on Dionysius throughout July and August, 1835, *Letters and Diaries*, V, pp. 97, 104, 107, 118, 120, 122, and came to a

halt on 30th, p. 132. He first read Blanco White's *Observations on Heresy and Orthodoxy* on 10 August 1835, *Letters and Diaries*, v, p. 123 and was still referring to it at the end of the month, *ibid.*, p. 134.

3 *Letters and Diaries*, v, To R.H. Froude, 9 August 1835.

4 *Ibid.*, p. 122, To Jemima Newman, 9 August 1835.

5 *Ibid.*, p. 132, To Frederick Rogers, 30 August 1835.

6 *Ibid.*, p. 114, To John William Bowden, 3 August 1835.

7 *Ibid.*, p. 115, To Hugh James Rose, 6 August 1835.

8 *Ibid.*, p. 118, To R.H. Froude, 9 August 1835.

9 *Ibid.*, p. 119.

10 *Ibid.*, p. 120.

11 *Ibid.*, p. 120.

12 *Ibid.*, p. 120.

13 Birmingham Oratory Archive, B.2.8 (C).

14 *Ibid.*, p. 1.

15 *Ibid.*, p. 1.

16 *Ibid.*, p. 1.

17 *Ibid.*, p. 1.

18 *Ibid.*, p. 1.

19 *Ibid.*, p. 2.

20 *Ibid.*, p. 2. A variant reads 'they' for 'he'.

21 *Ibid.*, p. 3. This moves Apollinarianism close towards the Patripassian form of Sabellianism.

22 *Ibid.*, p. 3.

23 *Ibid.*, p. 3.

24 In the Birmingham Oratory Archive, B.3.5.

25 *Apollinaris' history*, p. 1.

26 It is in the Birmingham Oratory Archive.

27 E.g. in the version which appears in *Tracts Theological and Ecclesiastical*, Newman introduces a new phrase which succinctly epitomises his 1835 view of the hidden relation between apparently divergent heresies – 'underground communications', see. p. 305. This phrase does not appear in the 1835 MSS.

28 *Apollinaris' history*, p. 1.

29 *Ibid.*, pp. 1–4.

30 *Ibid.*, p. 5.

31 *Ibid.*, p. 6.

32 *Ibid.*, p. 7.

33 *Ibid.*, p. 7.

34 *Ibid.*, pp. 8–12.

35 *Ibid.*, pp. 12–14.

36 *Ibid.*, pp. 16–19.

37 *Apollinaris' history* was partly used in the *British Magazine Letter* on the Church of the Fathers, July 1836, no. XVI. In 1840, Newman omitted some chapters of the 1st edn, including 'Apollinaris'. This shortened,

revised edn is the one appearing in *Historical Sketches*, II, (1873). Newman further edited the omitted chapters and brought them together in *Historical Sketches* I (1872), under a new title, 'Primitive Christianity'. The Apollinaris article appears in 'What Says the History of Apollinaris', chap. 3.

38 i.e. *Apollinaris' history*, pp. 16–19.
39 *Ibid.*, p. 16.
40 See Part I, *passim*.
41 *Apollinaris' history*, p. 16.
42 It was a common argument, for example, on the part of the Roman Catholicism of Louis XIV, the school of Bossuet. See O. Chadwick's account of Bossuet's *Variations of Protestantism* in *From Bossuet to Newman. The Idea of Doctrinal Development* (Cambridge, 1957) p. 9.
43 *Apollinaris' history*, p. 17.
44 *Ibid.*, p. 18.
45 *Ibid.*, p. 18.
46 *Ibid.*, p. 18.
47 *Ibid.*, p. 18. For 'detestable', Newman wrote, as a variant, above the line, 'extravagant'.
48 *Ibid.*, p. 19.
49 *Apollinarianism* is a privately printed paper, dated 22 August 1835, for which the MS does not exist. It bears a close relation to the draft, *The Defection of Apollinaris*, B.2.8(C), in its structure. Newman wrote the notes up and published them, with emendations in *Tracts Theological and Ecclesiastical*, pp. 301–27, 'The Heresy of Apollinaris'.
50 *Apollinarianism*, p. 2, see *Tracts Theological and Ecclesiastical*, pp. 303–5.
51 *Apollinarianism*, p. 2.
52 *Ibid.*, p. 1. Newman declares his independence of the textbooks, particularly those tinged with French Enlightenment rationalism: 'J. Basnage and Bayle's Dictionary are intolerable, and *most* unfair, selecting from Apollinaris' opinions just what they choose.' This implies that Newman was ploughing deliberately through the sources himself and comparing his findings with the textbooks.
53 *Apollinarianism*, n. to p. 2. This appears, in substance, in *Tracts Theological and Ecclesiastical*, n. on ch. 2. pp. 303–4.
54 *Apollinarianism*, p. 2.
55 *Ibid.*, p. 2. (This passage does not appear in *Tracts Theological and Ecclesiastical*.)
56 *Arians of the Fourth Century*, p. 304. Newman is referring to the Semi-Arians (see Part I).
57 *Apollinarianism*, p. 2.
58 *Ibid.*, p. 2.
59 *Ibid.*, p. 3.
60 *Ibid.*, p. 3.
61 *Ibid.*, p. 3.

62 *Apollinarianism*, pp. 6–7.
63 *Ibid.*, p. 7.
64 *Ibid.*, p. 7.
65 *Ibid.*, p. 7.
66 *Ibid.*, p. 7.
67 *Ibid.*, p. 7.
68 *Ibid.*, p. 7.
69 *Ibid.*, p. 8.
70 *Ibid.*, p. 8.
71 *Ibid.*, p. 9.
72 *Ibid.*, p. 9.
73 *Ibid.*, p. 11.
74 *Ibid.*, p. 11.
75 *Ibid.*, p. 11.
76 *Ibid.*, p. 11.
77 *Ibid.*, p. 12, no.2. Those belonging to this party were called 'synusiasts'.
78 i.e. according to *nous*.
79 *Ibid.*, pp. 5, see also p. 11.
80 *Ibid.*, p. 12.
81 *Ibid.*, p. 12.
82 *Ibid.*, p. 12.
83 *Ibid.*, p. 12.
84 *Ibid.*, p. 12.
85 *Ibid.*, p. 12.
86 *Ibid.*, p. 12.
87 Newman's phrase is 'others, nay Apollinaris himself', *Ibid.*, p. 12.
88 *Ibid.*, p. 12.
89 *Ibid.*, p. 13.
90 *Ibid.*, p. 13.
91 *Ibid.*, p. 12, n.
92 *Ibid.*, facing p. 12.
93 See Tertullian *Adversus Praxean*, ch. 27, Ante-Nicene Christian Library, ed. Roberts and Donaldson, Vol. xv, *The Writings of Tertullian*, Vol. ii, pp. 395–9.
94 *Adv. Praxean*, p. 397.
95 *Apollinarianism*, p. 13 (marginal note). By 'Paul', he means Paul of Samosata.
96 *Ibid.*, p. 13.

10. 'TRACT 73 ON THE INTRODUCTION OF RATIONALIST PRINCIPLES INTO REVEALED RELIGION'

1 See, for example, Claude Welch, *Protestant Thought in the Nineteenth Century*, i (London, 1972), p. 52.

2 This subject fully treated in Robin Selby, *The Principle of Reserve in the Writings of John Henry Newman*.

3 Hume cast doubt on the external evidence for the truth of Christianity in *Enquiries Concerning Human Understanding*, chs. 10–11, and in *The Natural History of Religion*.

4 Erskine's approch to evidencing is fully presented in Steve Gowler, 'No Second-hand Religion: Thomas Erskine's Critique of Religious Authorities', *Church History* (American Society of Church History), 54, (June, 1985), p. 207.

5 *Ibid.*, p. 207.

6 H.F. Henderson, *Erskine of Linlathen* (London and Edinburgh, 1899), p. 132: F.D. Maurice said the book was a major influence on him.

7 *Ibid.*, p. 31.

8 See especially *University Sermons*, No. II, 'Influence of Natural and Revealed Religion Respectively', (1830), p. 18. For a full discussion of Newman's approach to the proof, see A.J. Boekrad and H. Tristram. *The Argument from Conscience to the Existence of God* (Louvain, 1961).

9 For example, *University Sermons*, No. IV, 'Usurpations of Reason', p. 70.

10 Newman criticised, as early as *Arians*, 'the practice of stimulating the affections, such as gratitude or remorse, by means of the doctrine of the Atonement, in order to the conversion of the hearers,' pp. 47–8.

11 Unpublished: MS Birmingham Oratory Archive.

12 *Critical Remarks upon Dr Chalmers' Theology, Birmingham Oratory Archive*, A.9.1. (1834), p. 1.

13 *Ibid.*, p. 2.

14 *Ibid.*, p. 2.

15 *Ibid.*, p. 2.

16 *Ibid.*, p. 3.

17 '. . . in no case do I make the gospel doctrine *as such* the instrument of a change from disobedience to obedience', *Critical Remarks*, p. 4.

18 *Ibid.*, p. 6.

19 *Ibid.*, pp. 3–4.

20 *Ibid.*, pp. 3–4.

21 *Ibid.*, p. 3.

22 *Ibid.*, p. 4.

23 *Ibid.*, p. 11.

24 *Letters and Diaries*, V, p. 51.

25 Rev. Samuel Hinds, *An Enquiry into the Proofs, Nature and Extent of Inspiration and into the Authority of Scripture.* (London and Oxford, 1831)

26 See Part I: ch. 1.

27 Hinds, *Enquiry*, p. 39.

28 *Ibid.*, p. 9.

29 *Ibid.*, p. 28.

30 *Ibid.*, p. 28.

31 Hinds *Enquiry* p. 28.
32 *Ibid.*, p. 31.
33 *Ibid.*, p. 43.
34 *Ibid.*, p. 50.
35 *Ibid.*, p. 51.
36 *Ibid.*, p. 66.
37 *Ibid.*, p. 69.
38 *Ibid.*, p. 92.
39 *Ibid.*, p. 93.
40 *Ibid.*, p. 93.
41 *Ibid.*, pp. 175ff.
42 Lee H. Yearley, *The Ideas of Newman. Christianity and Human Reliogosity* (London and Pennsylvania, 1978), p. 6.
43 *Ibid.*, p. 110.
44 *Tract 73, Essays Critical and Historical*, I, pp. 43–4.
45 *Ibid.*, p. 40.
46 *Ibid.*, p. 41. It is the event of divine *disclosure* which produces mystery, 'What was hidden altogether before Christ came, could not be a mystery; it became a mystery, then for the first time, by being disclosed at His coming.'
47 *Ibid.*, pp. 41–2.
48 *Ibid.*, p. 41.
49 Newman was attacking a particular *kind* of system. One need not conclude that he would be hostile to all systematic theology, because in *some* sense revelation is itself systematic. As S.W. Sykes remarks, 'A door, one might say, is left slightly ajar for the further development of the idea of system, inherent indeed in revelation, but in part at least mysterious ('a vast system unrevealed'), *The Identity of Christianity* p. 105. It is a very narrow chink: the system of revelation is '*un*revealed'.
50 *Tract 73*, p. 42.
51 *Ibid.*, pp. 52–3.
52 *Ibid.*, p. 47.
53 *Ibid.*, pp. 33–4.
54 See below, sect. IV, on Schleiermacher.
55 *Tract 73*, p. 56.
56 *Ibid.*, p. 56.
57 *Ibid.*, p. 55.
58 Although it had been brought to public prominence by Blanco White's *Observations on Heresy and Orthodoxy*.
59 *Tract 73*, p. 56.
60 *Ibid.*, p. 57.
61 *Ibid.*, p. 57.
62 *Ibid.*, p. 57.
63 For example, the notorious accusation of 'malignancy' by Thomas

Arnold in 'The Oxford Malignants and Dr Hampden', *The Edinburgh Review or Critical Journal*, LXIII (1836), pp. 225–39.

64 Jacob Abbott, 1803–79, author of *Rollo at Work, Rollo at Play, Rollo in Europe*, studied at Andover Theological Seminary, taught natural science and mathematics at Amherst College, 1824–9, and founded Mount Vernon School for Young Ladies in Boston. A Congregationalist minister, his *Young Christian* was very popular. *The Corner Stone* was written as sequel to this. See *Encyclopaedia Britannica*, 11th edn (Cambridge, 1910), Vol. I, p. 26.

65 John Pye Smith, 1774–1851, Congregationalist minister and theological lecturer at Homerton College. He had published the *Scripture Testimony to the Messiah*, 2 vols. (London, 1818–21) (See DNB). Newman, *Tract 73*, p. 83, describes him as 'one of the most learned, orthodox and moderate of the Dissenters of the day', but reproves him for his preface to *The Corner Stone*, because 'expressly specifying the Unitarians, he requires us to adopt Mr Abbott's language in order to reconcile them to us'.

66 Jacob Abbott, *The Corner Stone, or a Familiar Illustration of the Principles of Christian Truth*, with a Preface by John Pye Smith, DD (London, 1834). This edition is the one used by Newman. Two other editions also appeared in England in 1834: (i) ed. Rev P. Phillip (London, 1834). (ii) abridged Henry Blunt (London, 1834).

67 Abbott, *Corner Stone*, 'Preface', p. vii, 'Not a page had I read of any other production of the author.'

68 *The British Critic, Quarterly Theological Review and Ecclesiastical Record*, XIX (1836).

69 Abbott, *Corner Stone*, pp. 16, 19.

70 *Ibid.*, pp. 2–3.

71 *Ibid.*, pp. 337–63.

72 *Tract 73*, p. 83.

73 *Ibid.*, p. 76.

74 *Ibid.*, p. 74.

75 *Ibid.*, p. 73.

76 'My father, who had been the pastor of one flock for more than sixty years, once said to me that that book had done more than any single book of his time to give character to the new phase of theology in New England, which began about 1820, and in which Dr N.W. Taylor, Dr L. Beecher, Dr Moses Stuart, and many others, were prominently concerned.' William Hanna, *Letters of Thomas Erskine of Linlathen*, 4th edn (Edinburgh, 1884) pp. 26–7. See also Henderson, *Erskine of Linlathen*, p. 31.

77 In 1821, 1822 and 1824, *Encyclopaedia Britannica*, p. 26.

78 See ch. 10. IV on Schleiermacher below: Newman had a poor understanding of the context and intentions of Schleiermacher's translator, Moses Stuart.

79 *Tract 73*, p. 72.
80 *Ibid.*, p. 74.
81 *Ibid.*, p. 74.
82 *Ibid.*, p. 85.
83 *Ibid.*, p. 74.
84 *Ibid.*, p. 74.
85 *Ibid.*, p. 76.
86 *Ibid.*, p. 76.
87 *Ibid.*, p. 76.
88 *Ibid.*, p. 72.
89 *Ibid.*, p. 76.
90 *Ibid.*, p. 79. See ch. 8 on Blanco White.
91 *Ibid.*, p. 79.
92 *Ibid.*, p. 78.
93 *Ibid.*, p. 81.
94 *Ibid.*, p. 81.
95 *Ibid.*, p. 81.
96 *Ibid.*, p. 75.
97 *Ibid.*, p. 87.
98 Y. Brilioth, *The Anglican Revival*, p. 223. See also *Letters and Diaries*, XI, p. 135, To Henry Wilberforce, 10 March 1846, where Newman declares that the idea that Jesus 'grew in virtue' as 'untrue and wrong', 'heresy', and 'very startling, except we say it in the sense of his manifesting and having the exercise of virtues'. More recently, Roderick Strange in his study, *Newman and the Gospel of Christ* (Oxford, 1983), adverts to his high Christology but declares, 'For Newman there could be no more total affirmation of the reality of Christ's manhood than to equate it with his Godhead', p. 56. He is concerned to defend Newman from all appearance of docetism. It is doubtful if his treatment of Abbott lays any such doubts to rest. If Newman was not docetic, he verges on the Apollinarian.
99 *Parochial and Plain Sermons*, III, no. 12 (8 March 1835), p. 164.
100 *Ibid.*, III, p. 166.
101 *Parochial and Plain Sermons*, VI, no. 5. (26 April 1836), p. 62.
102 *Ibid.*, p. 62.
103 Newman does not *explicitly* deny that Christ had a human *psyche*.
104 *Parochial and Plain Sermons*, III, p. 150. The passage is in fact full of ambiguities, e.g. the following lines suggest that Newman is uncomfortable with Christ's psychological suffering, even though he acknowledges its reality: 'Perhaps it was intended to set before us an example of a special trial to which human nature is subject, whatever was the real and inscrutable manner of it in Him, who was all along supported by an inherent divinity'. On the other hand, his strong sense of the *unity* of Christ forced him to accept the suffering of the Divine: 'When He spoke, it was literally God speaking; when he

suffered, it was God suffering', *Parochial and Plain Sermons*, VI, p. 72, 'The Incarnate Son a Sufferer and Sacrifice', no. 6. 1 April 1836. However, Newman also had problems with a fully human Jesus until much later, *Letters and Diaries*, XI, p. 135.

105 *Parochial and Plain Sermons*, III, p. 150.
106 *Tract 73*, p. 91.
107 *Ibid.*, p. 86.
108 Newman quotes this, *Tract 73*, p. 86. See Abbott, *Corner Stone*, pp. 50–1.
109 *Tract 73*, p. 88 quoting Abbott, pp. 53–4.
110 *Ibid.*, p. 89 quoting Abbott, p. 59–60.
111 *Ibid.*, p. 88 quoting Abbott, pp. 54–5.
112 *Ibid.*, p. 88.
113 *Ibid.*, p. 88.
114 *Ibid.*, p. 89.
115 *Ibid.*, p. 90.
116 *Ibid.*, p. 90.
117 *Ibid.*, p. 87.
118 *Ibid.*, pp. 86–7.
119 C.S. Dessain, 'Cardinal Newman and the Eastern Tradition', *Downside Review*, 94 (1976), pp. 83–98.
120 *Tract 73*, p. 87.
121 *Ibid.*, p. 87–8.
122 *Ibid.*, p. 88.
123 Strange, *Newman and the Gospel of Christ*, p. 75, refers to Newman's language denying a growth of virtue and knowledge in Christ, and, p. 88, to the absence in Him of human emotional frailty. Strange's attempt to defend Newman's Christology is, accordingly, hard to account for.
124 *Tract 73*, p. 100, 'Note to Essay II'.
125 *Ibid.*, p. 100.
126 A review of *The Corner Stone* in *The British Critic*, XIX (1836), attacked Abbott's work as the fruit of the 'republican school of politics' and pours contempt upon its popular form of expression, p. 190. The unidentified reviewer would have been a Tractarian sympathiser, for it was in 1836 that the magazine became a Tractarian organ, see Esther Rhoads Houghton, '*The British Critic* and the Oxford Movement', *Studies in Bibliography* (Papers of the Bibliographical Society of the University of Virginia), XVI (1963), p. 119. The reviewer detects in Abbott's presentation of Atonement the underlying assumptions of utilitarianism, that justice is a matter of expediency, *ibid*, p. 197. Newman's treatment is milder: he draws no such conclusions.
127 For example, in 'Primitive Christianity', *Historical Sketches*, I pp. 339–41.
128 This idea was very strongly expressed a few years after *Tract 73*, in

'The Patristical Idea of Antichrist', *Discussions and Arguments*,
pp. 56–70, where the increasing secularisation of society in political
liberalism is regarded as approaching apostasy.

129 Newman's essay on 'The Anglo-American Church', written in 1839,
shows alarm at the proliferation of bizarre heresies of the American
backwoods, where Baptists, Quakers and Shakers held sway, 'In
reading such accounts how are we thrown back into the times of
early Church History, and find ourselves among the Valentinians,
Marcionites, Cataphrygians, Ebionites, Manichees, and all other
prodigies to which the presence of the true Church gives rise, as the
sun breeds reptiles . . .' *Essays Critical and Historical*, I, p. 327.

130 *Tract 73*, p. 95.

131 *Ibid.*, p. 95. Bull's *Defence of the Nicene Faith*, Vol. II, Bk 3, ch. 1,
p. 409, refers to 'Socinians, Arians and all other maintainers of what
the same Caius calls the "God-denying apostasy"'. Bull is referring
to Eusebius, who uses the phrase to describe the adoptionist theology
of Theodotus the Cobbler, see *Ecclesiastical History*, trans. G.A.W.
Williamson (Penguin Books, 1965) Bk v, ch. 28, section 5, p. 236.
The Greek phrase is της αρνησιθεου αποστασιας.

132 Gowler, 'No Second-hand Religion', pp. 202–3.

133 *Essays Critical and Historical*, I, pp.96–9.

134 The following works contain Schleiermacher's characteristic theology
of 'feeling'. They were all untranslated into English at the time
Newman was writing:
On Religion, Addresses to its Cultured Despisers, 1799, revised edns, 1806,
1821, 1831.
Brief Outline of the Study of Theology, 1811, 2nd edn, 1830.
The Christian Faith, 1821–2, 2nd edn, 1830–1.

135 The *Addresses*, by showing that religion is a psychological phenomenon *sui generis*, bypass the problems involved in proving the propositional *truth* of doctrines; they argue from human experience, rather
than external authority, H.R. Mackintosh, *Types of Modern Theology*
(London and Glasgow, 1969) pp. 66–71.

136 Friedrich Schleiermacher, *The Christian Faith*, ET of 2nd German
edn, ed H.R. Mackintosh and J.S. Stewart (Edinburgh, 1976)
pp. 6–7. 'Feeling' is presented by Schleiermacher as an awareness
that one is thinking. Synonymous with 'feeling' is 'immediate self-
consciousness'. That feeling which characterises the religious
impulse, or 'piety', is an awareness of oneself as standing out of
existence, pp. 8–9, which in turn calls attention to the unavoidable
fact of our contingency, the backcloth of all self-consciousness. This
feeling is called 'God-consciousness' and is the basis of the doctrines
of salvation and of the natures of Christ.

137 Schleiermacher, *The Christian Faith*, section 63, pp. 262–4.

138 *Ibid.*, section 8, pp. 361–5. Redemption has to be a *new* element, a

break-through into history, which is communicated and experienced as human 'feeling'.

139 *Ibid.*, Ch. 2, 'The Method of Christian Dogmatics', Schleiermacher, *Christian Faith*, p. 98.

140 Schleiermacher dismisses traditional Christological categories of person and nature ('utter fruitlessness', p. 394, *The Christian Faith*), and prefers to re-present Christology in terms of 'God-consciousness'. The 'divinity' of Christ is, then, the perfection of His 'God-consciousness', p. 397. Jesus was a *human* person, with human ego and personality, but also with a fully receptive and continuous God-consciousness, an immense receptive power – and in this latter, as communicated to us in salvation, his 'divine nature' consists, p. 388.

141 Schleiermacher, *The Christian Faith*, p. 738.

142 *Ibid.*, p. 748.

143 *Ibid.*, sections 171–3, pp. 738–51.

144 Sykes, *Identity of Christianity*, pp. 86–7.

145 E.g., in a letter to J.W. Bowden, 13 July 1834. Newman was examining, with Bowden's help with the German, *Möhler's Life of Athanasius*. Newman says that he will learn German if Möhler, via Bowden, should prove fruitful, *Letters and Diaries*, IV, p. 303. See also p. 320, where Newman also considers learning German.

146 For Pusey's visits to Germany and his meetings with Schleiermacher, see Liddon, *Life of Pusey*, I, pp. 70–108. For the origins of the controversy with Rose, pp. 147–74.

147 Newman recorded the appearance of Pusey's 'little book' in his 1828 Diary. In a letter to his sister Harriet, 4 June 1828, he conveys little else but confusion, 'It is very difficult even for his friends and the clearest heads to enter into his originality, fullformed accuracy and unsystematic impartiality. I cannot express what I mean.' Writing to Samuel Rickards, 7 August 1828, Newman criticises the difficult style of Pusey's book, as the work of a man in haste. *Letters and Diaries*, II, pp. 74, 98.

148 Pusey, *Historical Enquiry*, p. 48, Pusey contrasts the renewal of feeling, piety and emotion ('earnest inward piety') with the dry 'orthodoxism' (a term borrowed from Neander) of seventeeth- and eighteenth-century Protestantism. Pusey met Schleiermacher in Berlin in 1825 and attended his lectures on N.T. and on Practical Theology, in 1825–6, Liddon, *Life of Pusey*, I, p. 95. Pusey recorded his admiration for Schleiermacher in a footnote of his *Historical Enquiry*, 'that great man, who, whatever be the errors of his system, has done more than any other (some very few perhaps excepted) for the restoration of religious belief in Germany' (Quoted in Liddon, *Life*, I, p. 95).

149 Yearley, *Ideas of Newman*, p. 149.

150 *Ibid.*, p. 149.

151 *Tract 73*, 'Postscript', p. 96.

152 *The Biblical Repository and Quarterly Observer*, 18 (April 1835) pp. 265–353, and 19 (July 1835), pp. 1–116.
153 *Ibid.*, 18, pp. 270–6.
154 Yearley, *Ideas of Newman*, p. 149; Sykes, *Identity of Christianity*, p. 301, n.9.
155 As the translator, Moses Stuart, makes clear, *Biblical Quarterly*, 18, p. 279.
156 *Ibid.*, pp. 270–6.
157 *Ibid.*, p. 329.
158 'If the Sabellian views had peaceably obtained admission, in the sequel they would doubtless have received more accurate and definite limitations. But they were overwhelmed in the stronger opposite current, before they had time to be fully unfolded'. *Biblical Repository*, 19, p. 39.
159 *Biblical Repository*, 19, pp. 61-2.
160 *Ibid.*, 18, p. 273.
161 *Ibid.*, 19, pp. 53–4, p. 61, 'development of personality within the Godhead'.
162 *Ibid.*, 18, p. 22.
163 i.e., in the $3\frac{1}{2}$ pages of his 1836 Postscript, *Tract 73*, pp. 96–9.
164 *Ibid.*, p. 97.
165 *Ibid.*, p. 97.
166 Schleiermacher, *The Christian Faith*, p. 749.
167 *Tract 73*, 'Postscript', pp. 97–8.
168 *Ibid.*, p. 99.
169 *Ibid.*, p. 99.
170 *Ibid.*, p. 97.
171 *Biblical Repository*, 18, pp. 309–10, p. 316.
172 *Ibid.*, 19, p. 82: Newman's sixth quotation in *Tract 73*, 'Postscript', p. 98.
173 *Ibid.*, 19, p. 82.
174 *Ibid.*, 19, p. 104.
175 Sidney E. Ahlstrom, *A Religious History of the American People* (Yale University Press, 1972) p. 392.
176 *Ibid.*, p. 394.
177 *Ibid.*, p. 396.
178 *Ibid.*, p. 402: 'Unitarianism was a halfway house on the road to infidelity'.
179 *Biblical Repository*, 19, p. 115.
180 Quoted by Newman, in a series of nine quotations, in the 'Postscript' to *Tract 73*, p. 99.
181 *Letters and Diaries*, III, p. 16, to J.W. Bowden, 15 February 1832. Newman was opposing the election of Horace Hayman Wilson, a layman, and distinguished orientalist, to the Oxford Chair of Sanskrit. Wilson had been a surgeon in India and was rumoured to have

lived with a woman there. Newman championed a sound clergyman, of known moral uprightness, though admittedly inferior scholarship, William Hodge Mill.

182 *Letters and Diaries*, II, Diary for 8 June 1829, and 31 July 1829, pp. 147, 155. See also Liddon, vol.I, pp. 164, 167. Rose accused Pusey of disbelieving in the inspiration of Scripture. Pusey's *Historical Enquiry*, Part II clarified his position, which was opposed to crude literalism, and used patristic material to substantiate his case. Newman assisted Pusey with this.

183 Liddon, *Life of Pusey*, I, pp. 147–8. Rose's book, *Discourses on the State of Protestantism in Germany* arose out of four lectures delivered in Cambridge in May 1825, and was published in Cambridge in the same year, in the context of general English ignorance of German theology, Liddon, I p. 147. Newman heard another voice surprisingly prepared to be positive about German theology: even R.H. Froude was, in 1832, reading Herbert Marsh's translation of Michaelis' *Introduction to the New Testament*, and was 'much interested by it'. Letter to Newman, 10 January 1832, *Letters and Diaries*, III, p. 5.

184 *Essays Critical and Historical*, II, p. 244. Schleiermacher is 'eloquent' about moral regeneration, but 'silent on the redemption from death'. Milman's note is uncertain if this is indeed the teaching of *The Christian Faith*; Milman consulted an expert friend, H.H. Milman, *History of Christianity*, 3 vols., (New edn, London, 1884) Vol. I, p. 341. It is true that Schleiermacher says that the bodily resurrection cannot be derived from the principles of his systematic theology, *The Christian Faith*, p. 420, 'we cannot conclude that because God was in Christ he must have risen from the dead and ascended into heaven'.

185 *Essays Critical and Historical*, II, p. 210.

186 *Letters and Diaries*, XI, in a letter to James Hope, 28 November 1845.

11. THE 'ELUCIDATIONS' ON HAMPDEN

1 *Letters and Diaries*, V, pp. 228–9.

2 *Ibid.*, p. 231.

3 *Elucidations*, p. 11.

4 *Letters and Diaries*, V, p. 210, To Thomas Bowden, 23 January 1836.

5 *Ibid.*, p. 251, To Simeon Lloyd Pope, 3 March 1836.

6 *Ibid.*, p. 251.

7 See ch. 10, on Schleiermacher.

8 This is a reference to Hampden's *A Course of Lectures Introductory to the State of Moral Philosophy* (1835). Rose wrote about it to Newman, *Letters and Diaries*, V, p. 189, 1 January 1836. See also Newman to Froude, *ibid.*, p. 191 for the phrase 'worse than the Bamptons'.

12. APOLLINARIANISM REVISITED

1 *Letter 1* appeared in the *British Magazine* on 1 October 1833, and the last, *Letter XX* on 1 May 1837.
2 *British Magazine*, 1 July 1836, Vol. x (London, 1836, pp. 35–41.) Referred to hereafter as *Letter XVI*.
3 See above, ch. 9.
4 The controversy over Hampden's appointment to the Regius Professorship was still fresh. Arnold's article on the 'Oxford Malignants' appearing in the Edinburgh Review in April. In May the University Convocation, swelled by indignant non-resident members who came up from the country, voted against Hampden, Trevor, *Pillar and the Cloud*, pp. 186, 188–9.
5 *Letter XVI*, p. 35.
6 *Ibid.*, p. 36.
7 For a discussion of these sentences, see above ch. 9.
8 This biographical material appears, with a few alterations, in *Primitive Christianity*, ch. 3, sections 1–2, *Historical Sketches*, i, pp. 392–7.
9 *Letter XVI*, p. 36. See *Primitive Christianity*, pp. 392–3.
10 Apollinaris 'wrote & dedicated to Julian [the apostate emperor] a refutation of paganism on grounds of reason', *Letter XVI*, p. 36, *Primitive Christianity*, p. 393.
11 *Letter XVI*, p. 38, *Primitive Christianity*, p. 396.
12 *Letter XVI*, p. 38, *Primitive Christianity*, p. 396.
13 *Apollinaris' history*, (1835) MS, pp. 11–12.
14 *Letter XVI*, p. 38, *Primitive Christianity*, p. 396.
15 *Letter XVI*, p. 38. (*Primitive Christianity*, omits the phrase).
16 i.e. *Letter XVI*, pp. 39–41. (It does not appear in *Primitive Christianity*.)
17 *Letter XVI*, p. 39.
18 *Ibid.*, p. 39. (The 'refusal' to draw out the lesson is an example of the rhetorical device of *occupatio*.)
19 *Ibid.*, pp. 39–40.
20 *Ibid.*, p. 41.
21 A liberalist is an advocate of liberalism, usually in the sense which became current in the early nineteenth century – i.e. an advocate of political liberalism, one in favour of reform in the direction of greater democracy. See OED.
22 *Letter XVI*, p. 40. For Butler and probability, see Part iii.
23 *Ibid.*, p. 40.
24 *Ibid.*, p. 40.
25 *Ibid.*, p. 40.
26 *Ibid.*, p. 40.
27 *Ibid.*, p. 40.
28 *Ibid.*, p. 40.
29 *Ibid.*, p. 40: 'the simple question before us is, whether, *in matter of*

fact, any doctrine *is* set forth by revelation as necessary to be believed *in order* to salvation'. (Newman's emphases), and a few lines further on, 'The question is simply about the matter of fact.'

30 *Letter XVI*, p. 40.
31 *Ibid.*, p. 40.
32 *Ibid.*, p. 40 – because the numbers of witnesses involved are considerably greater than in a law case.
33 As he becomes in the *Essay on Development*, pp. 74ff, when he repudiates the Vincentian Canon.
34 Newman did not really face up to this problem until the 1840s. See Part III.
35 *Letter XVI*, p. 39.
36 *Letters and Diaries*, V, p. 135.
37 The Theological Society was mooted in July 1835, see *Letters and Diaries*, V, p. 94, and commenced in November with a general paper by Pusey, *ibid.*, p. 164. At the second meeting, Newman read a paper on the rule of Faith – i.e. a justification of the 'Via Media' position, hammered out originally in controversy with the Abbé Jager, *ibid.*, p. 164. (See Part III). It was soon interpreted as a party cell: the Heads of Houses were by January 1836, 'much annoyed' at it, *ibid.*, p. 191. In a letter of 17 February 1836, to J.W. Bowden, Newman sees the role of the Theological Society as related to the struggle with Hampden and the 'neologians' (so his holograph, p. 236, n.3.) of his party: the Theological Society is intended to 'restrain the vagueries of such as he', *ibid.*, p. 237. Such a Society would be useful in the task of heresy hunting, 'pushing formal investigations' into Hampden's teaching, should he be promoted to a high position, *ibid.*, p. 237. Moreoever, the increasing conflict between Government and Church will, Newman predicts, increase the 'consequence' of the Society. Newman, then can hardly be seen as initiating a Society of impartial scholars.
38 See ch. 9.

13. SABELLIANISM REVISITED

1 *Letters and Diaries*, V, p. 153, 18 October 1835, i.e. one month after the writing of *Tract 73*, i.e. 16 September 1835, *ibid.*, p. 146.
2 *Letters and Diaries* VI, p. 133, 12 September 1837.
3 See *Dictionary of National Biography*, p. 133, and *Letters and Diaries*, VI, p. 385.
4 See *ibid.*, p. 389.
5 In *Tract 73*, Newman described Pye Smith as 'one of the most learned, orthodox and moderate of the Dissenters of the day', and reproves him for recommending 'Mr Abbott's language' as a means of reconciling Unitarians to Trinitarian Christians, *Essays Critical and Historical*, I, p. 93.

6 *Letters and Diaries*, VI, p. 133.

7 *Ibid.*, p. 133.

8 See the full title to the *Lectures on the Prophetical Office*: 'viewed relatively to Romanism and *Popular Protestantism*', (my emphasis).

9 This abuse would, as Newman constantly argued, lead eventually to infidelity. See Basil Willey, *Nineteenth Century Studies*, p. 77: 'it was Protestantism, which, by exalting Scripture and "private judgment" had opened the way to schism and sect, and finally to infidelity.'

10 See ch. 10, *Tract 73*, and (B) of this section, concerning Schleiermacher.

11 This was his case against Hampden. Newman saw latitudinarianism as synonymous with an acceptance of both heresy and infidelity for reasons of expediency. See *Prophetical Office*, p. 61, *Tract 85*, pp. 129–30, where such an attitude is seen as an evacuation of all truth.

12 *Prophetical Office*, p. 20, *Via Media*, I. See text, below. 'Latitudinarian' was a term from early Hanoverian divinity, describing the school of Tillotson, Cragg, p. 61.

13 See below, and *passim* in the *Lectures on the Prophetical Office*.

14 As Newman argues in *Tract 73* in his critique of liberalism as 'Sabellian' – see ch. 10.

15 See Part III ch. 15, (c).

16 *Prophetical Office*, Introduction, sect. 14, *Via Media*, I, p. 19.

17 *Via Media*, I, p. 20.

18 *Ibid.*, p. 20.

19 See Part I, ch. 2, for the influence of H.J. Rose's discussion of German rationalism and 'neology'.

20 *Prophetical Office*, *Via Media*, I, p. 20.

21 *Ibid.*, p. 44. This matter will be considered in detail in Part III.

22 *Ibid.*, p. 84.

23 *Ibid.*, p. 90.

24 *Ibid.*, p. 89.

25 *Essays Critical and Historical*, I, p. 42.

26 *Via Media*, I, pp. 89–90.

27 *Ibid.*, pp. 91–2.

28 *Ibid.*, p. 89.

29 *Ibid.*, p. 93.

30 *Ibid.*, I, p. 99.

31 *Ibid.*, p. 99.

32 *Ibid.*, p. 99.

33 *Ibid.*, p. 99.

34 As was Erskine, see ch. 10.

35 *Via Media*, I, p. 99.

36 *Ibid.*, p. 99.

37 *Via Media*, I, p. 100.
38 Delivered at St Mary's, Moorfields, Lent, 1836, and published in the same year, 2 vols. (London, 1836).
39 *Via Media*, I, p. 101.
40 *Ibid.*, p. 100.
41 Newman implies surprise and regret, *Ibid.*, I, p. 100, 'one might have hoped that the religion of Rome would have been clear of the fault into which the rival system has been betrayed'. By 'rival system' he means 'the popular Protestantism of the day'.
42 *Ibid.*, p. 102.
43 *Ibid.*, p. 101, Newman quotes Wiseman's view 'that there is something in Roman teaching "beautifully contrasted to the eye of the philosopher"' with the 'imperfections' of Protestantism.
44 *Ibid.*, p. 101.
45 *Ibid.*, p. 101.
46 Wiseman, *Lectures*, p. 39: internal evidencing is an 'error'. It is a circular argument – the moral excellence by which we vindicate revelation itself is revealed. It is not, in any case, the Bible which changes men for good – but doctrines derived from it preached by the Church. He sees it as associated with the Protestant right of private judgment, by which, he argues, it would be necessary for each believer to be 'internally convinced', of any belief that he holds, *ibid.*, p. 8.
47 *Ibid.*, p. 13.
48 *Ibid.*, p. 15.
49 *Ibid.*, p. 15.
50 *Ibid.*, p. 11. On the other hand, shifts of perspective upon error reveal its faults, *ibid.*, p. 12.
51 In fact, what sounds to Newman rationalistic is the appeal to the *beauty* of Roman Catholicism's formal coherence, Wiseman, *Lectures* pp. 28, 30–1.
52 Conviction is essentially practical. Acceptance of Roman Catholicism necessarily entails the 'Catholic' principle of obedience to the Church, *ibid.*, p. 16.
53 In other words, Wiseman comes close to Newman's later position, in the *Grammar of Assent* (1870)!
54 Newman's preferred method of analysis, in any case, works by discerning unintended 'tendencies'. This is the essence of his critique *à la* 'Sabellianism'.
55 Wiseman's sixth and seventh lectures consider the 'Practical Success' respectively of the Roman Catholic and Protestant rules of faith.
56 Wiseman, *Lectures*, p. 164.
57 *Ibid.*, pp. 22–3.
58 Newman does not refer to Wiseman's statistics in the *Prophetical Office*, but does refer to this aspect of Wiseman's apologetic in his

earlier review of Wiseman's *Lectures, British Critic,* xx (January 1835), p. 402.

59 Wiseman, *Lectures,* p. 8.

60 *Ibid.,* p. 8.

61 *British Critic,* xx, p. 374.

62 *Prophetical Office, Via Media,* i, pp. 104–5.

63 There is a contradiction here to Newman's earlier approach, in the final pages of *Letter XVI,* Apollinaris, when he *defends* 'technicality'. See ch. 12.

64 *Via Media,* i, p. 106.

65 *Ibid.,* p. 117.

66 *Ibid.,* p. 99.

67 See ch. 8.

68 Newman referred to 'such vile persons as O'Connell', *Letters and Diaries,* v, p. 124. He sees him as the popular demagogue, bullying the government to make concessions damaging to the Church of England, *Letters and Diaries,* ii, p. 132. He is 'disgusted' that anyone should defend him, *Letters and Diaries,* v, p. 119.

69 *Via Media,* i, p. 40.

70 *Ibid.,* p. 44.

71 'Milman's View of Christianity', *Essays Critical and Historical,* ii, pp. 186–248. Milman's earlier *History of the Jews* (1825) had treated the Old Testament as secular history and sought natural explanations for miracles, Storr, p. 113. *The History of the Jews* had already antagonised Newman, *Letters and Diaries,* ii, p. 299, to Simeon Lloyd Pope, 28 October, 1830, 'It seems to me that the great evil of Milman's work lies, not in the matter of the history, but in the prophane spirit in which it is written ... the irreverent, scoffing Gibbon-like tone.'

72 'Milman's View of Christianity', p. 186, 'It is notorious that the English Church is destitute of an Ecclesiastical History; Gibbon is almost our sole authority for subjects as near the heart of a Christian as any can well be.'

73 *Ibid.,* p. 187, 'he has not pleased us'.

74 See ch. 10 (iv) above.

75 'Milman's View of Christianity', pp. 187–90. Milman is quoted as disclaiming 'polemic views', and as striving for a 'calm, impartial, dispassionate tone', p. 190.

76 *Ibid.,* p. 200.

77 *Ibid.,* p. 188.

78 *Ibid.,* p. 198.

79 *Ibid.,* p. 229.

80 *Ibid.,* p. 229.

81 This distinction is pointed out by J. Derek Holmes, *Newman and the Use of History,* Unpublished Ph.D. Dissertation, Cambridge, 1969, p. 134.

82 'Milman's View of Christianity', p. 229.
83 Newman adds, 'We are sure that Mr Milman does not see the tendency of the line of thought of which both his present and his former work give such anxious evidence.' *ibid.*, p. 229.
84 *Ibid.*, pp. 226–7.
85 *Ibid.*, p. 202.
86 *Ibid.*, p. 203.
87 *Ibid.*, p. 302, 'The great doctrines which the Socinian denies are Our Lord's divinity and atonement.'
88 *Ibid.*, p. 203.
89 *Ibid.*, p. 203.
90 *Ibid.*, p. 203.
91 *Ibid.*, p. 203.
92 *Ibid.*, p. 203.
93 *Ibid.*, p. 203.
94 *Ibid.*, p. 242.
95 *Ibid.*, p. 213.
96 *Ibid.*, p. 213.
97 *Ibid.*, p. 213.
98 *Ibid.*, p. 213.
99 *Ibid.*, p. 213.
100 *Ibid.*, p. 188, quoting, in the *Catechism* the answer to the question, 'What meanest thou by this word sacrament?' see Alf Härdelin, *The Tractarian Understanding of the Eucharist*, (Uppsala, 1965), which deals with the Tractarian use of the sacramental *idea* against Evangelicals and liberals alike. In Newman the sacramental principle combined many trends and interests: (i) the balancing of economy and mystery, (ii) Butler's analogy, (iii) Platonism, (iv) the Alexandrian Fathers, pp. 65–70. See also John Coulson, 'Newman on the Church – his Final View, its Origins and Influence', in ed. Coulson and Allchin, *Rediscovery of Newman*, pp. 123–143, for Newman's view of Church as 'the objectified presence or "Body" of Christ in the world, who is encountered sacramentally'. p. 130.
101 Charles Frederick Harrold, 'John Henry Newman and the Alexandrian Platonists', p. 289. See also Louis Bouyer, 'Newman et le platonisme de l'âme anglaise', *Revue de Philosophie*, IV (1936), p. 289.
102 A.M. Allchin, 'The Theological Vision of the Oxford Movement', in ed. Coulson and Allchin, *Rediscovery of Newman*, p. 54.
103 *Milman's View of Christianity*, p. 213.
104 *Ibid.*, p. 203.
105 Henry Hart Milman, *The History of Christianity from the Birth of Christ to the Abolition of Paganism in the Roman Empire*, 3 vols., (London, 1884) Vol. I, pp. 356–7. This edition is virtually unchanged from that of 1840, see *Preface*, p. iii.
106 Duncan Forbes, *The Liberal Anglican Idea of History*. (Cambridge,

1952), p. 110. This led to the concept of 'progressive revelation': what was revealed at one state in human history will be inappropriate to another and be superceded by a more developed view.

107 Forbes, pp. 16, 20ff, 30, 56–7.
108 *Ibid.*, pp. 132–3.
109 *Ibid.*, pp. 65ff.
110 Milman, *History*, I, pp. 92–3.
111 *Ibid.*, I, p. 240.
112 *Ibid.*, II, p. 352.
113 *Ibid.*, II, pp. 410–11.
114 *Ibid.*, III p. 411, for both forms of heresy.
115 *Ibid.*, III p. 408.
116 *Ibid.*, III, pp. 314–18.
117 *Ibid.*, III, p. 314.
118 *Ibid.*, III. pp. 313–14.
119 *Ibid.*, III. pp. 318–19.
120 *Ibid.*, III, p. 319.
121 *Ibid.*, I, Appendix III, p. 109.
122 Milman gives the German in a footnote, 'Christi übernatürliche Geburt, seine Wunder, seine Auferstehung und Himmelfahrt bleiben ewige Wahrheiten, so sehr ihre Wirklichkeit als historische Facta angezweifelt werder mag.' 'so sehr ihre' etc. is more clearly translated, 'even if their reality as historical facts may be called in question'. Strauss is not flatly denying historical facts, but saying that they are less important than the 'eternal truths' which are independent of them.
123 Milman, *History*, I, p. 110.
124 *Ibid.*, I, pp. 110–12. Milman sides with the more conservative Neander, whose historical researches he declares to coincide with his own, pp. 114–15.
125 *Ibid.*, I, pp. 263–4.
126 *Ibid.*, I, pp. 284–5.
127 *Ibid.*, I, p. 300.
128 *Ibid.*, I, p. 308.
129 *Ibid.*, I, pp. 340–1. 'The resurrection of Jesus is the basis of Christianity; it is the groundwork of the *Christian* doctrine of the immortality of the soul', p. 340.
130 *Ibid.*, I, p. 341, note.
131 *Ibid.*, p. 208.
132 *Ibid.*, p. 236.
133 Forbes, *Liberal Anglican Idea of History*, pp. 5–6.
134 *Ibid.*, pp. 7–8. Liberal Anglicans disliked the view of rationalists such as James Mill, who saw the progress of civilisation as inevitable.
135 *Ibid.*, p. 101; 'this sense of crisis was common to the Liberal Anglicans and to the Oxford reformers'.

136 Forbes, p. 107. Liberal Anglicans thought that a degree of rationalism could be accommodated, but there came a point when it had to be resisted, – i.e., when it began to threaten belief in God and His Providence, and the 'essential truths of Christianity'.

137 This phrase is used by Edward Farley, *Ecclesial Reflection, An Anatomy of Theological Method*, (Philadelphia, 1982) cited by Gowler, 'No Second-hand Religion', p. 206.

138 'Milman's View of Christianity', p. 219.

14. HERESY, TYPOLOGY AND THE ENCODEMENT OF EXPERIENCE

1 The idea of a culture as a system whereby experience is encoded derives from Claude Lévi-Strauss, *Structuralist Anthropology*. It is applied to modern literature by Terence Hawkes, *Structuralism and Semiotics* (London, 1977) p. 56, where he refers to authors' 'construction of the world they appear only to describe'. This may be extended to Newman's use of Christian Antiquity.

2 The phrase is borrowed from the title of Northrop Frye's *The Great Code. The Bible and Literature* (London, 1981). He, in turn borrowed it from Blake's 'The Old and New Testaments are the Great Code of Art', p. xiv. Frye is interested in the way the Bible sets up an 'imaginative framework – a mythological universe', p. ix.

3 Hans Frei, *The Eclipse of Biblical Narrative*, pp. 26–7.

4 Boekrad, *Personal Conquest*, refers to Newman's 'Husserlian' phenomenalism; Walgrave, *Newman the Theologian*, to his 'psychologism'. See next note.

5 In a disagreement between two great Newman scholars, Boekrad and Walgrave, Newman's possible closeness to the positions he is criticising is revealed. In 1944, Walgrave saw Newman's 'practical psychologism' as a weakness, i.e. 'an attitude of thought on account of which one is convinced of having given the ultimate explanation of a thing when one has given a psychological explanation'. Boekrad defended Newman against the charge: Newman's doctrine of conscience presents man phenomenologically in order to reveal the transcendence of human nature, Boekrad, pp. 262–6. Walgrave later moderated his position: Newman's 'psychologism' was not reductionist but neither was it conclusive as an argument for reaching metaphysical truth, pp. 334–41.

6 *Essays Critical and Historical*, I, p. 55.

7 See Thomas M. Parker, 'The Rediscovery of the Fathers in the Seventeenth-Century Anglican Tradition', in ed. Allchin and Coulson, *Rediscovery of Newman*: the Church Fathers permeated only slowly into Anglicanism, because of the unavailability of printed editions, until the seventeenth century. See also S.L. Greenslade, *The English*

Reformers and the Fathers of the Church: an Inaugural Lecture (Oxford, 1966). Owen Chadwick, *From Bossuet to Newman*, p. 5, gives a different explanation: Anglican and Roman positions about the interpretation of Scripture were mutually exclusive – it was not a field of argument. Both, however, could agree that the early centuries were normative – so here they could argue; historical research became the food for polemic. Newman's interest in the Fathers of the Church preceded his acquaintance with seventeenth-century Anglican theologians, Parker, pp. 41, 49, 42, 38. He came to the seventeeth-century divines when compiling *Arians*, and discovered their theology more fully between 1834 and 1836, p. 47.

15. CONSTRUCTION

1 Thomas S. Kuhn, *The Structure of Scientific Revolutions*, (Chicago, 1970) p. 10. By 'paradigms' are meant 'models from which spring particular coherent traditions of scientific research'. To share a paradigm involves commitment to the same 'fundamentals', which lay down 'the same rules and standard for scientific practice', *ibid.*, p. 11. The paradigm is, then, normative for belief and practice in the scientific community which holds it.

2 *Apologia*, p. 117.

3 'Via Media' refers to the concept, *Via Media* to the work of that title.

4 *Apologia*, p. 147.

5 *Ibid.*, p. 156.

6 Chadwick, *From Bossuet to Newman*, p. 13.

7 *Ibid.*, p. 13.

8 Bossuet and the Gallicans applauded Bull's attack upon Petavius, because they saw it as a defence of their anti-papal, anti-Jesuit position, see F.L. Cross, *John Henry Newman* (Glasgow, 1932) p. 107; Jean Guitton, *La Philosophie de Newman* (Paris, 1933) p. 151.

9 Chadwick, *From Bossuet to Newman*, p. 17.

10 Church history had become the common ground for debate between Roman Catholics and Protestants, since they could not agree about rules to argue about Scripture. Thus all historical research fed polemic, *ibid.*, p. 17.

11 See the opening sentence of St Irenaeus, *Adversus Haereses*, in *The Treatise of Irenaeus of Lugdunum Against the Heresies*, 2 vols. (London, S.P.C.K., 1916.)

12 *Ibid.*, I, 22. 1. For a summary of passages from Irenaeus, showing his view of the doctrine as prior to heresy, devolving upon the bishops by tradition from the apostles, see Bettenson, *Early Christian Fathers*, pp. 89–92. See also Jean Daniélou, *Gospel Message and Hellenistic Culture* (London, 1980) pp. 139–57. The Church, according to Irenaeus, has a duty to preserve and guard the deposit handed down to

it, Daniélou, p. 147. The priority and apostolicity of the deposit can be proved – against the Gnostic claim to a secret tradition – by its unity, which the identity of tradition throughout the world witnesses, *ibid.*, p. 149.

13 *De Praescriptione Haereticorum*, chaps. vii–xiv, ed. Roberts and Donaldson, (A.–N.C.L.) *Tertullian*, pp. 8–19.

14 Walter Bauer, *Orthodoxy and Heresy in Earliest Christianity*, (Philadelphia, 1971), Introduction, pp. xxiii–xxiv, where Bauer summarises, and then distances himself from, the 'classical' view. George Strecker in the Foreword to the 2nd German edn summarises Bauer's 'thesis' as follows: 'In earliest Christianity, orthodoxy and heresy did not stand in relation to one another as primary to secondary, but in many regions heresy is the original manifestation of Christianity', p. xi.

15 H.E.W. Turner, *The Pattern of Christian Truth. A Study in the Relations between Orthodoxy and Heresy in the Early Church*, (London, 1954) p. 26.

16 *Ibid.*, p. 29.

17 Dionysius Petavius (Denys Pétau)'s *De Dogmatibus Theologicis* provoked a debate about pre-Nicene orthodoxy. See below.

18 See ch. 15 (c), below.

19 Turner, *Pattern of Christian Truth*, pp. 9–10. Such evidence of fluidity is 'sufficient to cast grave doubt upon any form which presupposed that heresy represented a series of deviations from a fixed and static doctrinal norm', p. 9.

20 This was translated in 1851 and formed part of the *Library of Anglo-Catholic Theology* (Oxford, 1851).

21 *Arians*, p. 170.

22 *Apologia*, p. 156, 'Bp. Bull's theology was the only theology on which the English Church could stand.' In *Difficulties of Anglicans*, Newman always mentions Bull as a pillar of the 'Via Media' position, *Difficulties*, i, pp. 2–3, 5–7, 8, 224, ii, p. 45.

23 *Letters and Diaries*, ii, p. 371, To Samuel Rickards, 30 October 1831. He calls the 'standard divines' – among them Bull – 'magnificent fellows but ... Antiquarians or Doctrinists, not Ecclesiastical Historians'.

24 See the discussion of Newman's purposes in composing *Arians*, in Part i.

25 *Apologia*, p. 26. Actually, Newman is hesitant – he 'takes it for granted' that it was from Bull.

26 *Ibid.*, p. 145.

27 Bull accused Petavius of denigrating the pre-Nicene Fathers to promote papalism, *Defence*, p. 11. The fullest account of the problem of Petavius' intentions is Paul Galtier, 'Pétau et La Préface de Son De Trinitate', *Recherches de Science Religieuse*, 1921, pp. 462–7: Petavius' historical analysis is concerned to lay bare the distorting

influence of Platonism upon Christianity in the pre-Nicene age, which led to a subordinationism anticipatory of Arianism (pp. 462–3), while in his *Preface* to the *De Dogmatibus Theologicis*, he maintains that orthodoxy is unchanging (p. 263). Galtier surveys the theories to account for this discrepancy: that he wrote the *Preface* under obedience (Turmel, O. Chadwick), that the Sorbonne required it before it would authorise printing (Bayle, Godet), or that he 'repented' of his denigration of the Fathers (Bossuet), but dismisses them all, p. 465. Galtier sees Pétau as pursuing two distinct but not irreconcilable purposes: in the body of the work, he operated as historian, in the *Preface* as dogmatic theologian, p. 471. In any case, the *Preface* was not an afterthought: it was written co-terminously with the rest of the work, pp. 466, 472–3.

28 Galtier, 'Pétau', p. 464.

29 Petavius, *De Dogmatibus Theologicis*, L.I., ch.V, no. 8: ed. Vives, t.II, p. 316A, quoted in Galtier, p. 463, (my translation of Latin). The ante-Nicenes all believed that, the *Word*, existed from all eternity and was connatural with the Father, but, with varying degrees of distinctness, they taught that, before the Creation, Christ was not fully a *son*; this is because the Word *became* Creator – and sonship, although taking place outside time, nevertheless had a direct relation to the act of creation. Augustine saw the view as heretical, De Haer. 50, see Jean Guitton, *La Philosophie de Newman*, Appendix A, 'Newman et Les Pères Antenicéens,' p. 149.

30 *passim*, Bull, *Defence of the Nicene Creed*, e.g. p. 47, explaining fluidity of terminology by reference to an orthodox *meaning* underlying it. The antithesis emerges very sharply in the following sentence, p. 84, 'And thus far of the word homoousion, "of one substance". Let us now deal with the thing itself.' He then commences an examination of the Fathers' teaching in chronological order, based upon this antithesis. See also, *ibid.*, p. 447, 'For what purpose is it to wrangle about words and modes of speaking, when we are agreed about the thing itself.'

31 *Ibid.*, p. 410.

32 *Ibid.*, p. 248.

33 *Ibid.*, p. 83. (Arianism is a later form of Gnosticism), also, p. 397.

34 Here Bull is reliant upon Tertullian, *Adversus Praxean*, ch. 8, which he quotes *ibid.*, p. 82.

35 *Ibid.*, pp. 661–2, where Bull answers the question 'If Arius was so completely heterodox, how could it, in so short a time after it arose, prevail to such an extent,' by reference to Arian fraudulence ('fraude'), which deceived 'many over-credulous bishops'.

36 See below, the following quotation.

37 Bull. p. 598.

38 *Ibid.*, p. 598.

39 Bull sees Petavius himself as an obedient Jesuit: he had to destroy the unanimity of the early centuries, in order to advocate papal Infallibility – the Fathers are made heretics to keep the Roman Church sound, *Defence*, pp. 11–12.

40 Christopher Sand (Sandius) was the appellation of two Socinian theologians, father and son, of the late seventeenth century. They were both Arians, that is, they attacked Trinitarian orthodoxy by reference to a revisionist interpretation of the pre-Nicene age, rather than, as the pure Socinians, relying on reason alone, see Robert Nelson, *Life of Dr George Bull*, (London, 1713) p. 280–1. It was the younger Sand who wrote The *Nucleus Historiae Ecclesiasticae*. Sand had, like his father, studied at Königsberg, but also at Oxford. He was based in Amsterdam. The *Nucleus* was his most important work: 'a history of Arianism, ancient and modern, by way of showing that primitive Christianity was Arianism, which can be traced in a continuous stream down to the present'. He also wrote *Bibliotheca Antitrinitariorum* (1684), a biographical survey of all antitrinitarian writers since the Reformation, with an account of their writings, Earl Morse Wilbur, *A History of Unitarianism, Socinianism and Its Antecedents*, (Harvard U.P., 1947) p. 512. Newman owned a copy of the *Nucleus*, which remains in the Birmingham Oratory, Edgbaston. Bull refers to Sandius in the Introduction to his *Defence* pp. vii-viii, and to the 'modern defenders of Arianism', p. x. Bull is arguing against the tenet of the Arian branch of Socinians who held that *before* Nicea only the *Father* was believed to be God, p. 5. According to Nelson, p. 282, Bull's *Defence* was only partially completed when Sandius' work was published and circulated in England. His friends urged him to complete the work, which was eventually published in 1685 under the patronage of the Bishop of Oxford, Nelson, *Life of Bull*, p. 284.

41 The spread of their influence resulted in a questioning of 'tests', initiating the agitation about 'subscription' to articles. See Leslie Stephen, *History of English Thought in the Eighteenth Century*, 2 vols., 2nd edn (London, 1881), Vol I, pp. 421–5: in the second half of the eighteenth century, 'Unitarianism became the prevailing creed of the most intelligent dissenters', p. 421. See also, Clarke, *English Society*, p. 320.

42 Gibbon sees the Trinitarian controversies in the early Church as a 'high and mysterious argument derived from the abuse of philosophy', *The History of the Decline and Fall of the Roman Empire*, Vol. II, ed. Bury (London, 1898) pp. 335–7, where, like Petavius with whom he sympathises (p. 100), he sees Platonism as the underlying error. Orthodoxy in trying futilely to reconcile Sabellianism and Tritheism was essentially circular, p. 346, an 'invisible and tremulous ball', p. 349.

43 *University Sermons*, VII, 'Contest Between Faith and Sight', 27 May 1831, p. 126, where Newman refers to Gibbon without naming him: 'the celebrated work of a historian of the last century, who, for his great abilities, and, on the other hand, his cold heart, impure mind and scoffing spirit, may justly be accounted as, in this country at least, one of the masters of a new school of error, which seems to have accomplished its destinies, and is framed more exactly after the received type of the author of evil, than the other chief anti-Christs who have, in these last times, occupied the scene of the world'. However, Newman read Gibbon in the Long Vacation of 1818 and was captivated by his style and undertook an analysis and imitation of it, see Ward, I, p. 34; ed. Tristram, *Autobiographical Writings*, p. 41; and the reminiscence in *Idea of a University*, pp. 322–3. Newman declared in the Introduction to his *Essay on Development*, 'Perhaps the only writer who has any claim to be considered an ecclesiastical historian is the unbeliever Gibbon', Ward, I, p. 34. He ruefully acknowledged in his review of Milman's *History of Christianity*, that Gibbon was 'almost our sole authority for subjects as near the heart of a Christian as any can well be', *Essays Critical and Historical*, II, p. 186. He regrets that Milman, 'who is not a Gibbon but a clergyman' has not provided a replacement of 'the infidel history', *ibid.*, p. 187. At the beginning of 'Part II, Historical', Newman lists his 'authorities' for the rest of the volume, amongst which is 'Gibbon's Roman History', *Arians*, p. 243, n.1.

44 *Arians*, pp. 189–99.

45 *Ibid.*, p. 189.

46 *Ibid.*, p. 191.

47 *Ibid.*, p. 194.

48 *Ibid.*, p. 197.

49 *Ibid.*, p. 197.

50 *Ibid.*, p. 198.

51 Of Newman's treatment in *Arians*, ch. 2, sect. IV, R.H. Broker declares, *The Influence of Bull and Petavius on Cardinal Newman's Theory of the Development of Doctrine*, (Rome, 1938) p. 28, 'Newman not only took his examples of patristic teaching from Bull, but also followed Bull in his attitude towards the treatment of these Fathers.' This is, in fact, truer of Newman in his 'Via Media' phase (1834 onwards) than of *Arians*.

52 *Arians*, p. 185.

53 *Ibid.*, p. 184–5.

54 *Ibid.*, p. 184–5.

55 *Ibid.*, p. 185.

56 M. Jamie Ferreira, *Doubt and Religious Commitment. The Role of the Will in Newman's Thought* (Oxford, 1980) p. 67, compares Newman's understanding of religious language with that of Wittgenstein: to

Newman, belief issues from 'a way of life'. Ferreira is discussing the *Grammar of Assent* (1870), but the same might be said of Newman's treatment of early Church life and belief in *Arians*. Similarly, P.J. Fitzpatrick, 'A Study in the Grammar of Assent', II (*Irish Theological Quarterly*) p. 219: for Newman and Wittgenstein, 'It is our *life* that shapes what is the setting that gives sense to our doubts and assertions.'

57 *Arians*, p. 185.
58 See ch. 17 for a detailed discussion of the development of doctrine.
59 *Arians*, p. 185.
60 *Ibid.*, p. 185.
61 *Ibid.*, p. 186.
62 See Selby, *Principle of Reserve*, pp. 1–43. The doctrine of *reserve*, the secrecy of the early Church, conveys their reverence which holds them back from publishing their dogmas (*Disciplina Arcani*). On the other hand, the early Fathers unfolded the meaning of mysteries in expressions which were economies, a symbolic mode of expression.
63 *Arians*, p. 91.
64 *Ibid.*, pp. 51, 54.
65 *Ibid.*, p. 57.
66 *Ibid.*, p. 168.
67 *Ibid.*, p. 168. See also, Wordsworth, *Preface* to *The Lyrical Ballads*, p. 741, *Poetical Works*, (ed. Hutchinson) (Oxford: OUP, 1969)
68 *Ibid.*, p. 148.
69 *Ibid.*, p. 149.
70 *Ibid.*, p. 149.
71 *Ibid.*, p. 150.
72 *Ibid.*, pp. 148–9.
73 *Ibid.*, pp. 150–1. This seems contradictory.
74 *Ibid.*, p. 149
75 *Ibid.*, p. 149.
76 *Ibid.*, p. 152.
77 *Ibid.*, p. 152.
78 See J.M. Cameron, 'Newman and the Empiricist Tradition' in Coulson and Allchin, *Rediscovery of Newman*, pp. 76–7, and J.M. Cameron, *The Night Battle* (London, 1962) pp. 203–10. See also ch. 17, below.
79 *Primitive Christianity*, *Historical Sketches*, I, p. 347. See Part I, ch.3.
80 Butler declares his method to be 'practical', being based upon the 'common pursuits of life', *Analogy of Religion*. (Select Christian Authors, no. 17 (undated)), p. 176. For Butler's account of probability, see his Introduction, *ibid.*, pp. 171–207.
81 See George Kennedy, *Classical Rhetoric and its Christian and Secular Tradition from Ancient to Modern Times* (London, 1980) p. 20: in the

courts, appeal to probability concerning the commission of a crime was regarded as more reliable than testimony.

82 *Records of the Faith* were translations of extracts from patristic texts appended to the *Tracts for the Times*, to support their arguments. The translations of the *Library of the Fathers* commenced in 1835, Newman and Pusey being the instigators, Ward, I, p. 57.

83 See *Via Media*, I, pp. 271–22. (*Prophetical Office*).

84 The article *Via Media* consists of Tracts 38 and 41 (25 July, and 24 August 1834), published in *The Via Media of the Anglican Church*, II, pp. 19–48, 28.

85 *Via Media*, II, p. 41.

86 *Ibid.*, pp. 23, 48.

87 *Ibid.*, II, p. 31.

88 *Ibid.*, p. 32. Newman means that the Tridentine articles do not differ in *kind* from the *39 Articles* as being secondary additions to meet particular heresies. They differ from the *39 Articles* in being simply 'untrue'. But Newman does not put himself so strongly: after all, it is difficult to imagine the Tractarian position being *fully* consistent with the *Articles* either. Hence Newman takes refuge in a weaker word – 'unsound'.

89 *Ibid.*, p. 32.

90 *Ibid.*, p. 32.

91 *Ibid.*, p. 32.

92 *Ibid.*, p. 40.

93 *Ibid.*, p. 40, 'Yes'.

94 *Ibid.*, p. 40, n.4.

95 *Ibid.*, p. 40, i.e. The *39 Articles*.

96 *Ibid.*, p. 41, 'Yes'.

97 *Ibid.*, pp. 40–1.

98 Anglican theology of the eighteenth century, notably that of Waterland, saw the distinction between fundamentals and non-fundamentals as a matter of clarity and obviousness, such that the unlearned could understand them. The fundamentals were contained in Scripture, Günter Biemer, *Newman on Tradition*, pp. 9–10.

99 Harrison had his first letter published in the *Universe*, on 18 September 1834, see Louis Allen, *John Henry Newman and the Abbé Jager*, (London, 1975) p. 21.

100 Sykes, *Identity of Christianity*, p. 102.

101 Vincent of Lerins, *The Commonitory*, *Library of Christian Classics*, IX 'Early Medieval Theology' (London, 1957) p. 37.

102 *Ibid.*, p. 38.

103 Allen, *Newman and the Abbé Jager*, p. 22.

104 *Ibid.*, p. 23.

105 *Ibid.*, pp. 23–4.

106 *Ibid.*, pp. 22, 26.

107 Allen, *Newman and the Abbé Jager*, p. 35.
108 *Ibid.*, p. 36.
109 *Ibid.*, p. 36.
110 *Ibid.*, p. 36.
111 *Ibid.*, p. 36.
112 *Ibid.*, p. 36.
113 *Ibid.*, p. 36.
114 *Ibid.*, p. 40.
115 *Ibid.*, p. 40.
116 *Ibid.*, p. 40.
117 *Ibid.*, p. 40.
118 *Ibid.*, p. 40.
119 *Ibid.*, p. 40.
120 e.g. *Via Media*, ii, p. 36.
121 Allen, *Newman and the Abbé Jager*, p. 66.
122 *Ibid.*, p. 76.
123 *Ibid.*, p. 81.
124 *Ibid.*, p. 81.
125 *Ibid.*, p. 81.
126 *Ibid.*, p. 81.
127 *Ibid.*, p. 87.
128 *Ibid.*, p. 98.
129 *Ibid.*, p. 86. See also p. 92, Newman quotes Athanasius *De Synodis*, ch. 41, 'but as far as those who receive its (Nicea's) whole Creed, except the word consubstantial (*Homoousion*), but doubt about it, *we must not regard them as enemies*, for our opposition to them is not as if we thought of them as Arians, and impugners of the Fathers, but we converse with them as *brothers with brothers*, who hold the same sense as we do, only hesitate about the word'.
130 *Ibid.*, p. 86.
131 *Ibid.*, pp. 94–5.
132 *Ibid.*, p. 95.
133 *Ibid.*, p. 95.
134 *Ibid.*, pp. 107, where Jager, replying to Newman's 2nd Letter points out that all previous controversy *equated* 'fundamental' with 'necessary for salvation' and that it was only Newman himself who had made a distinction between the expressions. In correspondence between Newman and Froude, the latter, too, criticised Newman's distinction, quoted by Allen, p. 179.
135 Nicholas Wiseman, *Lectures on the Principal Doctrines and Practices of the Catholic Church*, delivered at St Mary's Church, Moorfields, Lent, 1836, 2 vols. The effect of these lectures was described to Newman by J.E. Tyler, on 3 March 1836, see *Letters and Diaries*, v, p. 252.
136 These lectures were eventually published as the *Lectures on the Prophetical Office of the Church*.

137 *Letters and Diaries*, v, pp. 246–7.

138 *Ibid.*, p. 91.

139 The monthly *British Critic* had been founded in 1793. In February 1836, Newman became a contributor; by July 1838, he had become the editor, see Houghton, *British Critic and the Oxford Movement*, pp. 119–20.

140 *British Critic*, xx, July, 1836, published in *Essays Critical and Historical*, I, 3, pp. 102–37.

141 *Essays Critical and Historical*, pp. 373–403 – Wiseman's *Lectures on the Church*, published October 1836, written in September, see *Letters and Diaries*, v, p. 350.

142 Newman was writing up his *Lectures on the Prophetical Office*, from already existing material, in November, 1836, *Letters and Diaries*, v, p. 385.

143 See 'Note on Essay III,' *Essays Critical and Historical*, I, p. 137, in which Newman describes *Apostolical Tradition* as 'being a continuation of a series of protests' against Hampden's theology, in the build-up to the latter's appointment to the Regius chair.

144 *Apostolical Tradition, Essays Critical and Historical*, I, pp. 112, 113–4, 117.

145 *The British Critic*, xx, 1836, pp. 373–403, published in October, 1836. The article was actually written on 6 September 1836, while *Apostolical Tradition* appeared in the *British Critic* in July, see n. 93 above.

146 *British Critic*, xx, p. 377.

147 Benjamin Harrison, who had started the debate with Jager, criticised Newman's view that there was no development to the fundamental Creed and suggested that 'fundamentals' should mean 'simply the rock on which the Church is built', see Allen, p. 155. Newman popularised his terminology, bringing in 'essentials' to gloss 'fundamentals' but would not concede any developments in the Creed to have taken place. Newman described Harrison's criticisms as 'mad' and 'violent', p. 162, and appealed to Hugh James Rose for his judgment.

148 *British Critic*, xx, p. 378.

149 *Ibid.*, p. 378.

150 *Ibid.*, p. 379. Newman is quoting the 1571 Convocation.

151 *Ibid.*, p. 380.

152 *Ibid.*, p. 38off., where Newman quotes Laud, Stillingfleet, Hammond and Ussher on the distinction between fundamentals and essentials, and non-fundamentals and non-essentials.

153 *Ibid.*, p. 383.

154 *Ibid.*, p. 383.

155 *Ibid.*, p. 384.

156 *Ibid.*, p. 384.

157 See *Letters and Diaries*, v, p. 385.

158 *Via Media*, I, p. 212.

159 *Ibid.*, I, p. 40.

160 See *Ibid.*, p. 44: 'we find that the necessary difference between us and them is not one of essential principles, that is it is the difference of superstition, and not of unbelief, from religion'.

161 *Ibid.*, p. 61.

162 For example, in Lectures IX–X of *Lectures on the Prophetical Office*, 'On the essentials of the Gospel'. By 'essentials', Newman means the fundamentals, *ibid.*, p. 215.

163 *Ibid.*, p. 234, where Newman declares that the *39 Articles* are 'Articles of religion' not of "*faith*".'

164 The Creed, which contains the fundamentals or essentials, is 'the primitive condition of communion, or fundamental faith', *ibid.*, p. 217. Articles of religion, however, are not terms of communion: they may, though, be useful in securing the order and unity of the Church in a time of heresy, *ibid.*, p. 234.

165 *Ibid.*, p. 203, where 'Catholic agreement' is contrasted with 'local opinions'.

166 Newman frequently presents the Creeds as broad outlines of the essential faith, *ibid.*, p. 222, where he refers to the 'Symbol, or Rule, or Summary of Christian Doctrine', or *ibid.*, p. 249, 'outline of sound words'. See also pp. 212, 196–7. The *Homoousion* was introduced into the Nicene creed 'merely in explanation of a great article of faith, held from the first, but then needing, from circumstances, a more accurate wording', *Via Media*, I, p. 228.

167 i.e., the view that the first five centuries of Christianity are normative for doctrine. This idea of the first 500 – or sometimes 400 – years goes back to Elizabethan divinity: Newman quotes a parliamentary act of the first year of Queen Elizabeth, which names the first four Ecumenical Councils (AD 325–451). Anglicanism has tended, in fact, even in its theology courses up to this day, to consider AD 451, the date of the Council of Chalcedon, as the *terminus ad quem* for the normative Christian past. Newman, however, records the great diversity of view upon the extent of time to be included: Ken has 800 years, Bramhall 600, Hammond and Stillingfleet 680, while van Mildert was prepared to go as late as the great Schism (1054), see *Via Media*, I, pp. 205–6. Newman's honest record of this variety of opinion somewhat weakens his argument on behalf of Tradition. He imagines a weakening of the purity and authority of the Church, until a point arrives when Antiquity can no longer be regarded as 'normative' in view of the seriousness of the schisms that have taken place: 'The principle is clear, the fact obscure.' *ibid.*, p. 207. Newman agrees with his Anglican forebears that the VIIth Ecumenical Council of 787 (2nd Nicea) cannot be accepted. He considers it only

of local authority, p. 208 – but clearly draws back from it, as did other Reformation Fathers such as Bramhall, because it decreed 'worship of images' or icons. In practice, Newman is a quinquesecularist: all his defences of Christological orthodoxy take Chalcedon as the norm.

168 *Via Media*, I, p. 44.
169 *Ibid.*, p. 43.
170 *Ibid.*, p. 44.
171 *Ibid.*, p. 244.
172 *Ibid.*, p. 233.
173 See *ibid.*, pp. 254ff.
174 *Ibid.*, p. 254.
175 *Ibid.*, p. 258.
176 *Ibid.*, p. 259.
177 *Ibid.*, p. 224.
178 Newman sees the Church as always having known its own mind: dogmatic definitions are the clearing-up of verbal ambiguities – *ibid.*, p. 225.
179 *Ibid.*, p. 228.
180 *Ibid.*, p. 225.
181 *Ibid.*, I, p. 226.
182 Athanasius would not, however, let them hold any public *office* in the Church, *ibid.*, p. 231.
183 *Ibid.*, p. 231.
184 *Ibid.*, pp. 252–3.
185 *Ibid.*, p. 252.
186 *Ibid.*, p. 252.
187 *Ibid.*, p. 252.
188 *Ibid.*, p. 252.
189 *Ibid.*, p. 142.
190 *Ibid.*, p. 142.
191 *Ibid.*, p. 142.
192 *Ibid.*, I, p. 143.
193 *Ibid.*, I, p. 143.
194 *The Catechetical Lectures of St Cyril of Jerusalem*, trans., Richard W. Church, 1838, in *Library of the Fathers of the Holy Catholic Church*, No. 2. (Oxford, 1845); the *Preface* (pp. i–xxii) was also written in 1838.
195 For example, Fr. G.D. Dragas, in 'Newman's Greek Orthodox Sense of Catholicity', *Ecclesiasticus* (Darlington, 1984) p. 100.
196 i.e. 1839, see Part III.
197 see Liddon, *Life of Pusey*, I.
198 The *Catechetical Lectures* have no notes, but by 1842, Newman was surrounding his translations with compendious annotations – see his *Select Treatises of St Athanasius*.

199 *Catechetical Lectures*, p. xii.
200 *Ibid.*, p. ii.
201 *Ibid.*, p. iv. Cyril preferred Acacius' formula 'like in all things, to Athanasius' 'of the same substance'.
202 *Ibid.*, p. x.
203 i.e. when Newman was losing confidence in the 'Via Media', see ch. 16(b), below.
204 He means Eusebius of Caesarea and Meletius.
205 *Catechetical Lectures, Preface*, p. x.
206 *Ibid.*, p. xvii.
207 *Ibid.*, p. vii.
208 'Holy Scripture in Its Relation to the Catholic Creed', 1838, *Discussions and Arguments*, III, pp. 109–253.
209 *Ibid.*, p. 211.
210 *Ibid.*, p. 199.
211 *Ibid.*, p. 199.
212 *Ibid.*, p. 252.

16. COLLAPSE

1 *Apologia*, p. 114.
2 *Ibid.*, p. 115.
3 *Ibid*, p. 115.
4 i.e. *Difficulties of Anglicans*, lectures delivered in the Oratory Church in King William Street, Strand, London, starting 9 May 1850. Catholics and non-Catholics attended, Ward, I, pp. 231–2.
5 i.e. the *Apologia* (1864), on the occasion of Charles Kingsley's imputation of his intellectual integrity.
6 *Apologia*, p. 93.
7 See ch. 15 (c), above.
8 *Apologia*, p. 105.
9 *Ibid.*, p. 114.
10 Ward, II, *Life of Newman*, pp. 2ff.
11 *Apologia*, p. 114.
12 *Apologia Pro Vita Sua*, ed. with introdn. and notes, Martin T. Svaglic (Oxford, 1967), p. 540, n. on 108–24.
13 *Apologia* p. 115.
14 *Difficulties of Anglicans*, I, p. 373.
15 See ch. 17 below.
16 Birmingham Oratory, B.2.9. Referred to hereafter as *The Monophysite Heresy* (Longer MS).
17 Also entitled *The Monophysite Heresy*, it is prefaced by the following declaration, in Newman's hand: 'The following is an abstract of a MS of this date, with Notes and References.' It is pp. 17–31 of a printed

booklet also containing the printed paper on *Apollinarianism*. This will be hereafter referred to as *The Monophysite Heresy* (Printed Digest). Never published, it resides in the Birmingham Oratory.

18 Birmingham Oratory, B.2.8.C. This will be referred to as *Monophysitism* (Shorter MS).

19 *The Monophysite Heresy* (Longer MS), p. 2.

20 *Ibid.*, p. 2.

21 *Ibid.*, p. 3.

22 *Ibid.*, p. 3.

23 *Ibid.*, p. 51.

24 Newman quotes the authorities (e.g. Vasquez) against the viability of the distinction, but eventually decides that there was, indeed, a school of opinion that might be described as 'Semi-Arian,' *The Monophysite Heresy* (Longer MS), p. 51.

25 *Ibid.*, p. 51.

26 *Ibid.*, p. 53.

27 *Ibid.*, pp. 54–5.

28 *Ibid.*, p. 58. They could appeal via Cyril back to Athanasius.

29 *Ibid.*, pp. 68–9.

30 *Ibid.*, p. 68.

31 *Ibid.*, p. 1.

32 *Ibid.*, p. 4.

33 *Ibid.*, p. 4.

34 *Ibid.*, p. 23: Touching this objection, Newman admits, 'There is much truth in this.'

35 *Ibid.*, p. 23.

36 *Ibid.*, p. 24.

37 *Ibid.*, p. 24.

38 *Ibid.*, p. 9.

39 *Ibid.*, p. 9.

40 *Ibid.*, p. 7.

41 *Ibid.*, p. 8.

42 *Ibid.*, p. 9 – note on left-hand side of page.

43 *Ibid.*, p. 11.

44 *Ibid.*, p. 12.

45 *Ibid.*, p. 12.

46 *Ibid.*, p. 12.

47 *Ibid.*, p. 12.

48 For example, *passim* in *Tract 73*, see Part II.

49 *The Monophysite Heresy* (Longer MS), p. 28.

50 *Ibid.*, p. 28.

51 *Ibid.*, p. 40.

52 *Ibid.*, p. 40.

53 *Ibid.*, p. 40.

54 *Ibid.*, p. 42.

55 *The Monophysite Heresy* (Longer MS), p. 45.
56 *Ibid.*, p. 47.
57 *Ibid.*, p. 47.
58 *Ibid.*, p. 48.
59 *Ibid.*, p. 48.
60 *Ibid.*, p. 48.
61 *Ibid.*, p. 48.
62 *Ibid.*, p. 48.
63 *Ibid.*, p. 48.
64 At the very end is a summary of the proceedings leading up to the Council of Chalcedon.
65 *The Monophysite Heresy* (Longer MS), pp. 34ff.
66 *Ibid.*, p. 70.
67 *Ibid.*, p. 70.
68 *Ibid.*, p. 72.
69 'It was observed in the beginning of these remarks that it [the principle that *physis* = person] was held by the Monophysites in common with Nestorians, Arians and Sabellians, A participation in the principle involved a participation in its consequences. As applied to the doctrine of the Trinity, it led to the direct conclusion either that there is but one Person in the Godhead because there is but one Divine Nature; or that there are Three Persons; that is, it led to Sabellianism or Tritheism,' *ibid.*, p. 72.
70 *Ibid.*, p. 76.
71 *Ibid.*, p. 76.
72 *Ibid.*, p. 77.
73 For the idea of heresy's development towards infidelity, see Part II.
74 *The Monophysite Heresy* (Longer MS), p. 26.
75 *Ibid.*, p. 26.
76 *Ibid.*, p. 26.
77 *Ibid.*, p. 26.
78 *Ibid.*, p. 26.
79 *Ibid.*, p. 28.
80 i.e. *Monophysitism* (Shorter MS).
81 *Ibid.*, p. 2.
82 *Ibid.*, p. 2. 111
83 This was a stock typologisation of the patristic age, which Newman follows, *Monophysitism* (Shorter MS), p. 2.
84 *Ibid.*, p. 2.
85 *Ibid.*, p. 3.
86 *Ibid.*, p. 3.
87 *Ibid.*, p. 5.
88 *Ibid.*, p. 5.
89 *Ibid.*, p. 5.
90 *Ibid.*, p. 6.

91 i.e. pp. π, ϱ, σ.
92 *Monophysitism*, (Shorter MS), p. 9, 'There was no difference of opinion what the true doctrine concerning the Eternal Son was . . .'
93 *Ibid.*, p. 9.
94 See *Apologia*, p. 116.
95 *Ibid.*, p. 9.
96 Mozley, II, p. 286.
97 Nicholas Wiseman, 'The Anglican Claim of Apostolic Succession', *The Dublin Review*, VII (August, 1839), p. 144.
98 *Ibid.*, pp. 144–5.
99 *Ibid.*, p. 146.
100 *Ibid.*, p. 149, 150, 155.
101 Wiseman points to the argument of Cresconius who maintained that it was not necessary to be in active communion with the universal Church to be Catholic, *ibid.*, p. 160. Wiseman presents Ticonius as the leader of 'a High Church party', which was attempting to revive Catholicity as universality within the Donatist Church. Perhaps Ticonius represents Newman.
102 Wiseman, 'The Anglican Claim', p. 178.
103 Mozley, II, p. 286.
104 *Ibid.*, p. 287.
105 Published in *Essays Critical and Historical*, II, under development of the Cyprianic concept of the Church's unity, 'Epicopatus unus est, cuius a singulis in solidum pars tenetur' ('The episcopate is one and each bishop shares in its fulness'). Newman argues that consequently every Church is independent of every other, being in itself the whole universal Church, p. 31. He sees it as possible to be Catholic without being in communion with Rome.
106 Mozley, II, p. 249, 24 November 1843.
107 *Essays Critical and Historical*, II, p. 51.
108 *Ibid.*, p. 51.
109 *Ibid.*, p. 51.
110 *Ibid.*, p. 13.
111 *Ibid.*, p. 13.
112 *Ibid.*, pp. 13–14.
113 *Ibid.*, p. 13.
114 *Ibid.*, p. 14.
115 *Ibid.*, p. 14.
116 *Apologia*, p. 73.
117 *Ibid.*, p. 73.
118 *The Ecclesiastical History of M. L'Abbé Fleury from the Second Ecumenical Council to the End of the Fourth Century*, Translated, With Notes, and 'An Essay On the Miracles of the Period', (Oxford: J.H. Parker, and London: Rivingtons, 1842) p. vi. Newman's 'Advertisement' is dated 4 June 1842.

119 *Apologia*, p. 73. The word 'photograph' had, in fact, come into the language in 1839 – see OED.
120 *Fleury*, I, p. v.
121 *Ibid.*, p. vi.
122 Mozley, II, p. 283.
123 The 'Advertisement' refers to 'Herbert's translation' (London, 1728), *Fleury*, I, p. vii.
124 Mozley, II, pp. 284–5.
125 *Ibid.*, pp. 284–5.
126 *Ibid.*, p. 281.
127 *Ibid.*, p. 284.
128 *Ibid.*, p. 400. This first volume contains hardly anything about heresy.
129 *The Ecclesiastical History of M. L'Abbé Fleury From* AD *429 to* AD *456*. Translated with Notes (Oxford: J.H. Parker and London: Rivingtons, 1844). The 'Advertisement' is dated 8 November 1844, referred to hereafter as *Fleury*, III, pp. 15, 51, 136, 284.
130 Even here, there are only gentle hints, see ch. 17 (c), below.
131 *Apologia*, p. 120.
132 Mozley, II, to J.W. Bowden, 10 October 1841, p. 352.
133 *Ibid.*, p. 353.
134 *Tract 90*, 'Remarks on Certain Passages of the 39 Articles', *Via Media*, II, p. 259–356.
135 The furore commenced in March, 1841.
136 See *Apologia*: Newman's 'protest' against association with not only the Lutheran and Calvinist Churches, p. 145, but also the Jacobite, Nestorian and Monophysite ones, p. 143.
137 *Ibid.*, p. 147.
138 *Ibid.*, p. 139.
139 *Ibid.*, p. 139.
140 Mozley, II, p. 392.
141 *Apologia*, p. 139.
142 *Ibid.*, p. 139.
143 *Select Treatises of St Athanasius*, (Library of Fathers Translation, 1844) p. 49, n.(p).
144 *Ibid.*, p. 157, n.(i).
145 *Ibid.*, p. 103, n.(t).
146 *Ibid.*, p. 103.
147 *Ibid.*, p. 103.
148 *Apologia*, p. 103.
149 *Ibid.*, p. 139.
150 So, for example, *ibid.*, p. 343; Newman gives an account of Athanasius' exegetical method in terms of the Vincentian canon and the Tractarian Rule of Faith; 'he is explaining what is obscure or latent in Scripture by means of the Regula Fidei. "Since the canon of Scripture is perfect", says Vincentius, "and more than sufficient for

itself in all respects, what need of joining to it the ecclesiastical sense? because from the very depth of Holy Scripture all men will not take it in one & the same sense etc." '

17. RHETORIC REFASHIONED

1 *Apologia*, p. 234.
2 J.J. Byrne, 'The Notion of Doctrinal Development in the Anglican Writings of J.H. Newman', *Ephemerides Theologicae Lovanenses*, XIV (1937), p. 230, n.1.
3 Ward, *Life of Newman*, I, p. 94.
4 *Apologia*, p. 234.
5 *Essay on Development*, p. 90.
6 Ward, *Life of Newman*, I, p. 176.
7 *Ibid.*, p. 176.
8 *Ibid.*, p. 86.
9 *Ibid.*, p. 83. See Gilley, *Newman*, p. 229.
10 *Ibid.*, p. 83.
11 *Essay*, p. 72.
12 Ward, *Life of Newman*, I, p. 159ff.
13 J.J. Byrne, 'The Notion of Doctrinal Development in the Anglican Writings of J.H. Newman,' p. 265.
14 The letter is unpublished. I am grateful to Gerard Tracey of the Birmingham Oratory for this information.
15 See ch. 15, above.
16 See Part II, *passim*.
17 The *Copybook on Development* is in the Birmingham Oratory.
18 The letter is dated 10 November 1840, and is written from Oriel College: it resides, unpublished, in the Birmingham Oratory Archive.
19 Birmingham Oratory Archive, letter 10 November 1840.
20 Birmingham Oratory Archive, letter 10 November 1840.
21 Fleury, *Ecclesiastical History*, III, p. 272, n. (o).
22 Newman had two translations available to him, a French translation of *Unity in the Church* (pubd. 1839) and an English one of the *Symbolic Theology*, but there is little evidence that he studied either, see Chadwick, *From Bossuet to Newman*, pp. 111–12.
23 Fleury, *History*, III, p. 272, n. (o).
24 *Ibid.*, III, p. 359, n.(h).
25 *Ibid.*, III, p. 345, n. (c).
26 *University Sermons*, pp. 312–13.
27 Cameron, ed. Coulson and Allchin, *Rediscovery of Newman*, pp. 81–2: the immediate 'impression' upon the mind was seen by Hume as richer and more vivid than the combination of these into ideas. Newman applied this model to revelation: the object of faith is

unknown in itself: it makes a vivid impression on us, which is later systematised in dogmas.

28 *University Sermons*, p. 329.
29 *Ibid.*, p. 330.
30 *Ibid.*, p. 331.
31 *Ibid.*, p. 330.
32 *Ibid.*, p. 332.
33 *Ibid.*, p. 350.
34 *Ibid.*, p. 316.
35 'Wonderful, to see how heresy has but thrown that idea into fresh forms, and drawn out from it farther developments, with an exuberance which exceeded all questioning, and a harmony which baffled all criticism', *University Sermons*, p. 317.
36 *Ibid.*, p. 318.
37 *Ibid.*, p. 318.
38 *Ibid.*, p. 337.
39 *Ibid.*, p. 320.
40 *Ibid.*, p. 351.
41 *Apologia*, p. 198.
42 *Essay on Development*, p. 154.
43 Nicholas Lash, *Newman on Development* (London, 1975) p. 154.
44 'The Reformation of the 11th Century', *Essays Critical and Historical*, II, p. 250.
45 *Essay*, pp. 100–1.
46 Lash, *Newman on Development*, p. 97.
47 *Ibid.*, p. 106.
48 *Essay*, p. 316.
49 *Ibid.*, p. 318.
50 *Ibid.*, p. 318.
51 *Ibid.*, p. 322.
52 *Ibid.*, p. 29.
53 *Ibid.*, p. 328.
54 Newman still uses this idea in the *Essay*, p. 329.
55 *Ibid.*, p. 275.
56 With the words 'they were received back into the communion of the Catholic Church', *ibid.*, p. 332. Newman's peroration then begins with 'Dreary and waste was the condition of the Church'.
57 *Ibid.*, pp. 332–3.
58 *Ibid.*, p. 309.
59 *Ibid.*, p. 309.
60 *Ibid.*, p. 313.
61 *Ibid.*, p. 305.
62 *Ibid.*, p. 305.
63 *Ibid.*, p. 305.
64 *Ibid.*, pp. 308–9.

65 *Essay*, pp. 336–42.
66 *Ibid.*, pp. 93–100.
67 *Ibid.*, p. 95.
68 *Ibid.*, p. 99.
69 *Ibid.*, p. 100.
70 *Ibid.*, pp. 356–65.
71 *Ibid.*, pp. 401–2.
72 *Ibid.*, p. 403.
73 *Ibid.*, p. 404.
74 *Ibid.*, p. 409.
75 *Ibid.*, p. 411.
76 See *Ibid.*, pp. 124–6, on the 'continuity of Principles' as a test of a true development.
77 *Ibid.*, p. 360.
78 *Ibid.*, p. 360.
79 *Ibid.*, p. 360.
80 *Ibid.*, p. 360.
81 Broker, *Influence of Bull and Petavius on Newman*, pp. 6–7, accepts, unquestioningly, F.L. Cross' article in the *Church Quarterly Review*, January, 1933. Broker ignores the problem of Petavius' position on the status of post-Nicene dogma, see ch. 15 (b), n.51, above.
82 *Essay*, pp. 401–12.
83 *Ibid.*, p. 401.
84 *Ibid.*, p. 402.,
85 *Ibid.*, p. 402.
86 *Ibid.*, p. 202.
87 *Ibid.*, p. 202.
88 *Ibid.*, pp. 353–5.
89 *Ibid.*, p. 132.

CONCLUSION

1 For example, Oscar Cullmann announces a tension between the basic facts of biblical history, and the faith which constitutes them as revelatory, *Christ and Time* (London 1965), p. 23.
2 See S.W. Gilley, 'Newman and Prophecy', for Newman's apocalyptic re-description of the present: he shared the view of 'most conservative Evangelicals, in seeing the spirit of Antichrist in the infidelity of political liberalism', p. 180. Indeed, the ferment of apocalypticism generated by Edward Irving, the *enfant terrible* of Evangelicalism in the 1830s fed upon the prevailing anxiety at social and political changes, see Newsome, pp. 6–7. Newman was closer to Irving than Newsome admits: whereas Newsome sees him as directing his polemic against the Irvingites, Dr Gilley has shown that Newman's

own world-denying spirituality in the face of political events has much in common with Irving's apocalypticism, 'Newman and Prophecy', pp. 170–1.

3 Claude Welch, *Protestant Thought in the Nineteenth Century*, I, ch. 9. pp. 190–241.

4 Welch, pp. 193–4, regards this 'refusal' as characteristic of mid-nineteenth-century movements suffused by 'the pervasive mood of restoration (or preservation and defence) and of churchly self-consciousness'.

5 See Williams, *Arius*, p. 5: 'The Arians of the Fourth Century is, in large part, a tract in defence of what the early Oxford Movement thought of as spiritual religion and spiritual authority.'

6 Newman's list of 'authorities' at the beginning of his historical narrative of Arianism lists mainly archaic sources for his secondary material. The 'moderns' he mentions are Tillemont, Petavius, Maimbourg, and Gibbon! See *Arians*, p. 242. He does not cite what was then a recent work on Arianism – that of the contemporary German Church historian, Neander, but then, he could not read German.

7 See ed. Henri Frankfort, Mrs H. Frankfort, John Wilson, Thorkild Jacobson, *Before Philosophy* (Pelican, 1949) pp. 11, 15: 'The thought of the ancient Near East appears wrapped in imagination'; ancient authors *thought* mythically.

8 *Epistola ad Serapion de Morte Arii*, PG, col. 689, sect. 5. The phrase 'πρηνης γενομενος ελακησε μεσος' ('and falling headlong he burst open in the middle') is lifted directly from the account of Judas' death in the book of Acts, 'Now this man purchased a field with the wages of iniquity; and falling headlong, he burst open in the middle and all his entrails gushed out', Acts 1:18. Athanasius made a direct parallel between the deaths of Arius and Judas.

9 John Lawrence Mosheim, *An Ecclesiastical History Ancient and Modern from the Birth of Christ to the Beginning of the Eighteenth Century* (London: 1815) p. 112.

10 Milner, *History of the Church of Christ*, II, p. 54, 'When they came nigh unto the forum of Constantine, a sudden terror, with a disorder of the intestines, seized Arius. In his urgent necessity, he requested to be directed to a place of private retirement. Agreeably to the information he received, he hastened behind the forum; and there he poured forth his bowels with a vast effusion of blood. Such was the end of the notorious Arius.'

11 *Letters and Diaries*, III, p. 78, To H.J. Rose, 16 August 1832. Newman invoked Gibbon, 'Even Gibbon, I believe, thinks his temperate notice of Arius' death striking.'

12 *Arians*, p. 276.

13 *Ibid.*, p. 276.

14 *Ibid.*, p. 277. Newman is here discussing the legitimacy of applying

such an approach to events to occurrences in the contemporary situation.

15 Newman defended miracles as part of God's 'moral government' of the universe, *Two Essays on Biblical and Ecclesiastical Miracles*, p. 12. They form part of a whole system by which the human conscience is roused and sharpened by divine interposition, *ibid.*, pp. 12, 16–17, 20, 26, 33.

16 A.M. Fairbairn, *Catholicism Roman and Anglican* (London: Hodder and Stoughton, 1899) p. 103.

17 Williams, *Arius*, p. 6.

18 Gérard Verbeke, ed. J.D. Bastable, 'Aristotelian roots of Newman's illative sense', *Newman and Gladstone. Centennial Essays* (Dublin, 1978) pp. 177–96.

19 Susan Carole Funderburgh Jarratt, *A Victorian Sophistic: The Rhetoric of Knowledge in Darwin, Newman and Pater* (Ph.D. Dissertation, University of Texas at Austin, 1985).

20 *Ibid.*, p. 5.

21 *Ibid.*, p. 95.

22 Walter Jost, *Rhetorical Thought in John Henry Newman* (University of South Carolina, 1989).

23 *Arians*, p. 30–2 (Aristotle), pp. 28, 33 (Sophists). See Part I, ch. 2.

24 Newman's rhetorical denunciations of rhetoric, e.g. *Arians*, p. 31, belong to an ancient tradition going back to Plato's *Gorgias*.

25 *Arians*, p. 31, i.e. Part I, Section II, 1.

26 Marginal annotation on his own copy of *Arians*.

27 Marginal annotation to Newman's copy of *Arians*.

28 Martin Dibelius, *From Tradition to Gospel* (Cambridge and London, 1971) chap. 1.

29 Verbeke, 'Aristotelian roots of Newman's illative sense', p. 178: Newman helped to draft Whately's *Elements of Logic* in 1822. Whately's *Logic* has a close relation to his rhetoric, because he sees the latter as a subordinate branch of the former.

30 Rhetoric is generally regarded as becoming obsolescent by the late 1820s, see Jarratt, *Victorian Sophistic*, p. 1, Kennedy, *Classical Rhetoric*, p. 240.

31 Kennedy, *Classical Rhetoric*, p. 240: Whately's *Rhetoric* 'the last major treatment of the subject in the classical tradition'.

32 Richard Whately, *Elements of Rhetoric* (London, 1841).

33 *Ibid.*, p. 8.

34 Sykes, *Identity of Christianity*, p. 81, describes Newman and Schleiermacher as 'two *modern* theologians of unquestionable stature, "fathers" of, respectively, modern Protestant and modern Roman Catholic theology'.

35 For example, Lash, *Newman on Development*, Introduction, p. 4, where he argues that to take Newman 'seriously as a theologian' will

redeem English Catholicism, and especially the hierarchy from reactionary fear of the historical consciousness.

36 For example, Father George Dragas' account of 'Newman's Greek Orthodox Sense of Catholicity', see p. 427, n. 195.

Bibliography

A. PRIMARY SOURCES

I. EDITIONS OF PUBLISHED WORKS CITED

Apologia Pro Vita Sua cited as *Apologia*. London: Longmans, Green and Co., 1887. This edition will be referred to throughout, unless otherwise stated.

Apologia Pro Vita Sua cited as *Apologia* (Svaglic). ed. with introduction, and notes, by Martin T. Svaglic. Oxford: Clarendon Press, 1967.

The Arians of the Fourth Century cited as *Arians*. 3rd edn, London: Lumley, 1871.

Certain Difficulties Felt by Anglicans in Catholic Teaching Considered: I, In Twelve Lectures Addressed in 1850 to the Party of the Religious Movement of 1833 cited as *Difficulties of Anglicans*, I, London: Longmans, Green and Co., 1885.

Discussions and Arguments on Various Subjects cited as *Discussions and Arguments*. London: Longmans, Green and Co., 1885.

Elucidations of Dr Hampden's Theological Statements cited as *Elucidations*. Oxford: J. H. Parker and London: Rivingtons, 1836.

An Essay on the Development of Christian Doctrine, the Edition of 1845 cited as *Essay on Development* or *Essay* ed. with introduction, J.M. Cameron. Pelican Books, 1974.

Two Essays on Biblical and on Ecclesiastical Miracles cited as *Essay on Miracles* (I). 5th edn, London: Longmans, Green and Co., 1885.

Essays Critical and Historical, I, 7th edn, London: Longmans, Green and Co., 1887.

Essays Critical and Historical, II. 7th edn, London: Longmans, Green and Co., 1887.

An Essay in Aid of a Grammar of Assent cited as *Grammar of Assent*. 6th edn, London: Longmans, Green and Co., 1887.

Historical Sketches, I. 6th edn, London: Longmans, Green and Co., 1886.

Historical Sketches, II and III. London: Longmans, Green and Co., 1885.

Lectures on the Doctrine of Justification. 3rd edn, London, Oxford and Cambridge, 1874.

On Consulting the Faithful in Matters of Doctrine. ed. John Coulson. Glasgow: Collins Flame Classics, 1986.

Parochial and Plain Sermons, I. New edn, London: Rivingtons, 1837.

Parochial and Plain Sermons, II. New edn, London: Rivingtons, 1834.

Parochial and Plain Sermons, III. New edn, London: Rivingtons, 1834.

Parochial and Plain Sermons, IV. New edn, London: Rivingtons, 1837.

Parochial and Plain Sermons, V. New edn, London: Rivingtons, 1837.

Parochial and Plain Sermons, VI. New edn, London: Rivingtons, 1831.

Parochial and Plain Sermons, VII. New edn, London: Rivingtons, 1832.

Parochial and Plain Sermons, VIII. New edn, London: Rivingtons, 1832.

Preface to the Catechetical Lectures of St Cyril of Jerusalem. Library of the Fathers of the Holy Catholic Church, No. 2, trans. R.W. Church. Oxford: Rivingtons, 1845.

Lectures on the Prophetical Office of the Church Viewed Relatively to Romanism and Popular Protestantism, in the *Via Media of the Anglican Church,* Vol. I, cited as *Prophetical Office.* 2 vols. London: Longmans, Green and Co., 1885.

Sermons Bearing on Subjects of the Day. New edn, London, Oxford and Cambridge: Rivingtons, 1896.

Tracts for the Times by Members of the University of Oxford. 5 vols. London: Rivingtons, 1836.

Tracts Theological and Ecclesiastical. New impression, London, New York and Bombay: Longmans, Green and Co., 1902.

University Sermons: Fifteen Sermons Preached Before the University of Oxford, 1826–43. ed. D. Holmes. London: SPCK, 1970.

Verses on Various Occasions. New impression, London, New York and Bombay: Longmans, Green and Co., 1903.

The Via Media of the Anglican Church Illustrated in Lectures, Letters and Tracts Written Between 1830 and 1841, Volume II. cited as *Via Media* II.

2. ARTICLES AND REVIEWS BY NEWMAN (NOT IN PUBLISHED WORKS)

The British Critic, Quarterly Theological Review and Ecclesiastical Record, XIX, XX, London: Rivingtons, January, 1836:

pp. 373–403, Review of Wiseman's *Lectures on the Principal Doctrines and Practices of the Catholic Church.*

pp. 166–99, Review of 'The Brothers Controversy'.

British Magazine and Monthly Register of Religious and Ecclesiastical Information, Parochial History and Documents Respecting the State of the Poor, Progress of Education etc. cited as *British Magazine,* Vols. IV–XI, 1833–37. London: Rivingtons. 'Letters on the Church of the Fathers' appeared, in 20 instalments between October 1834, and May 1837.

3. TRANSLATIONS

The Ecclesiastical History of M. L'Abbé Fleury from the Second Ecumenical Council to the End of the Fourth Century, vol. I, 381–400. Translated with Notes, and *An Essay on the Miracles of the Period*. Oxford: J.H. Parker and London: Rivingtons, 1842.

The Ecclesiastical History of M. L'Abbé Fleury From 400 to 429, Translated with Notes. Oxford: J.H. Parker and London: Rivingtons, 1843.

The Ecclesiastical History of M. L'Abbé Fleury From AD 429 to AD 456, Translated with Notes. Oxford: J.H. Parker and London: Rivingtons, 1844.

Select Treatises of St Athanasius, Archbishop of Alexandria, In Controversy with the Arians, Translated, With Notes and Indices. 2 vols. Oxford: J.H. Parker and London: Rivingtons, 1844, for the Oxford Library of the Fathers.

4. LETTERS, DIARIES, JOURNALS AND AUTOBIOGRAPHICAL MEMOIRS

John Henry Newman. Autobiographical Writings. ed. and introdn. Henry Tristram. London: Sheed and Ward, 1956.

The Letters and Diaries of John Henry Newman, vol. I. ed. Ian Ker and Thomas Gornell, S.J., cited as *Letters and Diaries*, I. Oxford: Clarendon, 1978.

The Letters and Diaries of John Henry Newman, vol. II. ed. Ian Ker and Thomas Gornell, S.J., cited as *Letters and Diaries*, II. Oxford: Clarendon, 1979.

The Letters and Diaries of John Henry Newman, vol. III. ed. Ian Ker and Thomas Gornell, S.J., cited as *Letters and Diaries*, III. Oxford: Clarendon, 1979.

The Letters and Diaries of John Henry Newman, vol. IV. ed. Ian Ker and Thomas Gornell, S.J., cited as *Letters and Diaries*, IV. Oxford: Clarendon, 1980.

The Letters and Diaries of John Henry Newman, vol. V. ed. Ian Ker and Thomas Gornell, S.J., cited as *Letters and Diaries*, V. Oxford: Clarendon, 1981.

The Letters and Diaries of John Henry Newman, vol. VI. ed. Gerard Tracey, cited as *Letters and Diaries*, VI. Oxford: Clarendon, 1984.

Letters and Correspondence of John Henry Newman During His Life in the English Church, With a Brief Autobiography, ed. at Cardinal Newman's request, Anne Mozley, 2 vols., vol. II, cited as *Mozley*, II. London: Longmans, Green and Co., 1891.

5. UNPUBLISHED MATERIAL

(a) *Manuscript sources (Birmingham Oratory, Edgbaston)*

A12.11 Rough Notes Preparatory to *The Arians of the Fourth Century*.
Newman's marginal annotations to his personal copy of *The Arians of the Fourth Century*, copy inscribed, 'John H. Newman. Nov. 5, 1833'.
B3.5 Notes on Apollinarianism. One sheet, dated 12 August 1835.
B2.8c. Notes on Apollinarianism. One sheet on 'Apollinarian sects'.
B3.5. Notes on Eutychianism and Apollinarianism. One sheet, entitled Eutychianism, is dated 5 July 1839.
Apollinaris' history. Dated 19 August 1835 (pp. 19).
B.2.8. (c). *The Defection of Apollinaris*. 15 August 1835.
B.2.8. Copybook on Development. Dated 'March 7th, 1844. In festo. S. Th.'
B.2.8. Manuscript of projected edition of Dionysius of Alexandria, 1834–5.
B.2.8. Fragment on Incarnational Heresies (?1839).
B.2.8.c. Untitled MS on Monophysitism (pp. 11), 1839.
B.2.9. *The Monophysite Heresy*. Dated 23 August 1839 (pp. 83).
B.3.5. Note on the Homoousion, 19 September 1835.
D.18.1. Large indexed MS notebook on Theological Topics. Entries from 1826–68. Inscribed 'John H. Newman. Oriel College, 1826. quod in ecclesia salutem feliciter vortat.'
A.9.1. *Critical Remarks on Dr Chalmers' Theology* (1834).
Sermon, *On the Mediatorial Kingdom of Christ*, No. 160, preached on 15 April 1827.

(b) *Printed material (Birmingham Oratory, Edgbaston)*

Apollinarianism. Dated 'August 22, 1835'. This is a privately printed document, pp. 1–16.
The Monophysite Heresy. Dated 23 August 1839. Inscribed as follows: 'The following is an abstract of a MS of this date, with Notes and References.' Privately printed document, pp. 17-end.

SECONDARY SOURCES

Abbott, Jacob. *The Corner Stone, or a Familiar Illustration of the Principles of Christian Truth*, with a Preface by John Pye Smith, D.D. London: Seeley and Burnside, 1834.
Ahlstrom, Sydney E. *A Religious History of the American People*. New Haven and London: Yale University Press, 1972.
Allen, Louis. *John Henry Newman and the Abbé Jager. A Controversy on Scripture and Tradition (1834–1836)*. Edited from the original manuscripts and the French version. London: Oxford University Press, 1975. (University of Durham Publications).
Aquinas, Thomas. *Summa Theologica*. Rome: Leonine Edition, 1928.

Aristotle. *The 'Art' of Rhetoric*. Trans. and introd. John Henry Freese. Loeb Classical Library. London: Heinemann; Cambridge, Mass.: Harvard University Press, 1954.

Arnold, Thomas. 'The Oxford Malignants and Dr Hampden.' *The Edinburgh Review or Critical Journal*, 63, 1836, pp. 225–39.

Barry, William. *Cardinal Newman*. London: Hodder and Stoughton People's Library, 1927.

Bastable, James, D. (ed.). *Newman and Gladstone. Centennial Essays*. Dublin: Veritas Publications, 1978.

Battiscombe, Georgina. *John Keble. A Study in Limitations*. London: Constable, 1963.

Bauer, Walter (ed. Robert A. Craft and Gerhard Krodel). *Orthodoxy and Heresy in Earliest Christianity*. Trans. Philadelphia Seminar on Christian Origins. Philadelphia: Fortress Press, 1971.

Bethune-Baker, J.F. *An Introduction to the Early History of Christian Doctrine*. 9th edn London: Methuen and Co., 1951.

Bettenson, Henry (ed.). *The Early Christian Fathers*. Oxford: Oxford University Press, 1976.

Biemer, Gunter, *Newman on Tradition*. Trans. Kevin Smyth. London: Burns and Oates, 1966.

Boekrad, A.J. *The Personal Conquest of Truth According to J.H. Newman*. Louvain: Editions Nouwelaerts, 1955.
'Newman as Theologian. His Candour and Loyalty.' *Cardinal Newman Academic Symposium*. Rome, 1975.

Boekrad, A.J. and Tristram, H. *The Argument from Conscience to the Existence of God*. Louvain, 1961.

Bouyer, Louis. *Newman. His Life and Spirituality*, with a Preface by the V Rev Monsignor H. Francis Davis. Trans. J. Lewis May. London: Burns and Oates, 1958.

Bremond, Henri. *The Mystery of Newman*. Trans. H.C. Corrance, with an Introduction by Rev. George Tyrrell. London: Williams and Norgate, 1907.

Brendon, Piers. *Hurrell Froude and the Oxford Movement*. London: Paul Elek, 1974.

Brilioth, Yngve. *The Anglican Revival. Studies in the Oxford Movement*. London: Longmans, Green and Co., 1933.

Broker, Rev Ralph H. *The Influence of Bull and Petavius on Cardinal Newman's Theory of the Development of Christian Doctrine*. (Extract From a Thesis Presented to the Faculty of Theology in the Pontifical Gregorian University, Rome.) Rome: Gregorian University, 1938.

Bull, Bishop George. *A Defence of the Nicene Creed, out of the Extant Writings of the Catholic Doctors, who Flourished during the Three First Centuries of the Christian Church, in which also is incidentally vindicated The Creed of Constantinople Concerning the Holy Ghost*. Oxford: Library of Anglo-Catholic Theology (J.H. Parker, publisher), 1851.

Butler, Joseph. *The Analogy of Religion Natural and Revealed, To the Constitution and Course of Nature*, with an Introduction by Daniel Wilson, Bishop of Calcutta. London: William Collins, Select Christian Authors, no. 17, (undated).

Byrne, J.J. 'The Notion of Doctrinal Development in the Anglican Writings of J.H. Newman.' *Ephemerides Theologicae Lovanenses*, 16, 1937, pp. 230–86.

Cameron, J.M. *The Night Battle. Essays*. London: Burns and Oates, 1962.

Chadwick, Owen. *From Bossuet to Newman. The Idea of Doctrinal Development*. Cambridge University Press, 1957.

The Victorian Church. London, 1970.

Cicero. *De Oratore*, Books I and II. Trans. E.W. Sutton; introd. H. Rackham. London: Heinemann; Cambridge, Mass.: Harvard University Press, 1952.

Clarke, J.C.D. *English Society 1688–1832, Ideology, Social Structure and Political Practice during the Ancien Régime*. Cambridge: Cambridge University Press, 1985.

Coulson, J. and Allchin, A.M. (eds.). *Rediscovery of Newman: An Oxford Symposium*. London: SPCK Sheed and Ward, 1967.

Cragg, C.R. *From Puritanism to the Age of Reason. A Study of Changes in Religious Thought within the Church of England, 1660 to 1700*. Cambridge: Cambridge University Press, 1950.

Cross, F.L. *John Henry Newman*. Glasgow: Philip Allan, 1932.

Cullmann, Oscar. *Christ and Time*. English Translation, Floyd V. Filson. London: SCM, 1965.

Daniélou, Jean. *Gospel Message and Hellenistic Culture*. London: DLT, 1980.

de Man, Paul. *Allegories of Reading. Figural Language in Rousseau, Nietzsche, Rilke and Proust*. New Haven and London: Yale University Press, 1979.

Dessain, C.S. *John Henry Newman*. London: Nelson, 1966.

'Cardinal Newman and the Eastern Tradition.' *Downside Review*, 94, 1976, pp. 83–98.

Dibelius, Martin. *From Tradition to Gospel*. Trans. B.L. Woolf. Cambridge and London: James Clarke and Co., 1971.

Dragas, George D. *Ecclesiasticus: Orthodox Church Perspectives, Models and Eicons*. Darlington, 1984.

'Conscience and Tradition: Newman and Athanasius in the Orthodox Church.' *Newman Studien Elfte Folge*, 1980.

Eagleton, Terry. *Literary Theory. An Introduction*. Oxford: Basil Blackwell, 1983.

Egner, G. *Apologia Pro Charles Kingsley*. London: Sheed and Ward, 1969.

Ender, Erwin. 'The Economy of Salvation and Justification. On the Question of Salvation in Newman's Life and Thought.' *Cardinal Newman Academic Symposium*. Rome, April 1975.

Erskine, Thomas, of Linlathen. *Remarks on the Internal Evidence for the Truth of Revealed Religion.* 10th edn, Edinburgh: David Douglas, 1878.

Eusebius of Caesarea. *Ecclesiastical History.* Trans. G. A. Williamson. Penguin Books, 1965, (1981 Reprint).

Fairbairn, A.M. *Catholicism: Roman and Anglican.* London: Hodder and Stoughton, 1899.

Ferreira, M. Jamie. *Doubt and Religious Commitment. The Role of the Will in Newman's Thought.* Oxford: Clarendon Press, 1980.

Fitzpatrick, P.J. 'A Study in the Grammar of Assent, II.' *Irish Theological Quarterly* (n.d.).

Forbes, Duncan. *The Liberal Anglican Idea of History.* Cambridge: Cambridge University Press, 1952.

Frankfort, Henri *et al.,* (eds.) *Before Philosophy.* (Pelican, 1949).

Frei, Hans W. *The Eclipse of Biblical Narrative. A Study in Eighteenth and Nineteenth Century Hermeneutics.* New Haven and London: Yale University Press, 1974.

Froude, Richard Hurrell (ed. J.H. Newman). *Remains of the Late Richard Hurrell Froude, M.A. Fellow of Oriel College Oxford.* 2 vols. Vol. I London: J.G. and F. Rivington, 1838.

Review of Joseph Blanco White 'Observations on Heresy and Orthodoxy' and 'Second Travels of an Irish Gentleman'. *The British Critic, Quarterly Theological Review and Ecclesiastical Record,* Vol. xix, 1836, pp. 204–25.

Frye, Northrop. *The Great Code. The Bible and Literature.* London: Ark, 1981.

Gadamer, Hans-Georg. *Philosophical Hermeneutics.* Ed. and trans. David E. Linge. Berkeley, Los Angeles and London: University of California Press, 1977 (pbk.).

Galtier, P. 'Pétau et la Préface de son *De Trinitate.*' *Recherches De Science Religieuse,* 1921, pp. 462–76.

Gibbon, Edward. *The History of the Decline and Fall of the Roman Empire.* 7 vols. Vol. II. London: Methuen and Co., 1898.

Gilley, Sheridan. 'Newman and Prophecy, Evangelical and Catholic.' *Journal of United Reformed Church History Society,* 3(5), March, 1985. *Newman and His Age.* London: DLT, 1990.

Gowler, S. 'No Second Hand Religion: Thomas Erskine's Critique of Religious Authorities.' *Church History. American Society of Church History,* 54 (2), June 1985, pp. 202–14.

Greenslade, S.L. *The English Reformers and the Fathers of the Church: an Inaugural Lecture.* Oxford, 1966.

Guitton, Jean. *La Philosophie de Newman: Essai sur L'idée de Développement.* Paris: Boivin and Co., 1933.

Hampden, Renn Dickson. *Observations on Religious Dissent.* Oxford: J.H. Parker and London: J.G. and F. Rivington, 1834.

The Scholastic Philosophy Considered in Its Relation to Christian Theology.

(The Bampton Lectures, 1832.) Oxford: J.H. Parker, and London: J.G.F. Rivington, 1833.

Hanna, William (ed.). *Letters of Thomas Erskine of Linlathen.* 4th edn, Edinburgh: David Douglas, 1884.

Härdelin, Alf. *The Tractarian Understanding of the Eucharist. Acta Universitatis Upsaliensis. Studia Historico-Ecclesiastica Upsaliensa, 8.* Uppsala, 1965.

Harrold, Charles Frederick. 'John Henry Newman and the Alexandrian Platonists.' *Modern Philology,* 37, 1940, pp. 279–91.

Harvey, Van A. *The Historian and The Believer. The Morality of Historical Knowledge and Christian Belief.* London: SCM, 1967 (pbk.).

Hawkes, Terence. *Structuralism and Semiotics.* London: Methuen and Co., 1977.

Henderson, Henry F. *Erskine of Linlathen. Selections and Biography.* Edinburgh and London: Oliphant, Anderson and Ferrier, 1899.

Hinds, Rev. Samuel. *An Enquiry into the Proofs, Nature and Extent of Inspiration and into the Authority of Scripture.* London: B. Fellowes; Oxford: J. Parker, 1831.

Holmes, J. Derek. *More Roman than Rome.* London: Burns and Oates, 1978.

'Newman and the Use of History.' Unpublished Dissertation. Cambridge, 1969.

'Personal Influence and Religious Conviction. Newman and Controversy.' *Cardinal Newman Academic Symposium.* Rome, 1975.

Horner, Winifred Bryan (ed.). *The Present State of Scholarship in Historical and Contemporary Rhetoric.* Columbia and London: University of Missouri Press, 1983.

Houghton, Esther Rhoads. *The 'British Critic' and the Oxford Movement.* Reprint from Studies in Bibliography, Papers of the Bibliographical Society of the University of Virginia, XVI, 1963, pp. 120–37.

Irenaeus. *The Treatise of Irenaeus of Lugdunum Against the Heresies.* Trans. F.R. Montgomery Hitchcock. 2 vols. London: SPCK, 1916.

Jarratt, Susan Funderburgh. *A Victorian Sophistic: the Rhetoric of Knowledge in Darwin, Newman and Pater.* Ph.D. Dissertation, University of Texas at Austin, 1985.

Jost, Walter, *Rhetorical Thought in John Henry Newman.* University of South Carolina, 1989.

Kelly, J.N.D. *Early Christian Creeds.* Third edn, London: Longmans, 1972. *Early Christian Doctrines.* 5th Revised edn, London: Adam and Charles Black, 1977.

Kennedy, George. *Classical Rhetoric and Its Christian and Secular Tradition from Ancient to Modern Times.* London: Croom Helm, 1980.

Ker, Ian. *John Henry Newman.* A Biography. Oxford: Clarendon Press, 1988.

Kuhn, Thomas S. *The Structure of Scientific Revolutions.* 2nd edn, University of Chicago (International Encyclopaedia of Unified Science), 1970.

Lash, Nicholas. *Newman on Development.* London, 1975.

Lecler, Joseph, S.J. *Toleration and the Reformation* (Vol. 1). Trans. T.L. Westow. London: Longmans, 1960.

Liddon, Henry Parry. *Life of Edward Bouverie Pusey.* 4 vols. Vol 1 (1800–36). 4th edn, London: Longmans, Green and Co., 1894.

Lonergan, Bernard J.F. *Method in Theology.* 2nd edn, London: Darton, Longman and Todd, 1975.

Lynch, T. 'The Newman–Perrone Paper on Development.' *Gregorianum,* 16, 1935, pp. 402–47.

Machin, G.I.T. *Politics and the Churches in Great Britain, 1832 to 1868.* Oxford: Clarendon Press, 1977.

Mackintosh. H.R. *Types of Modern Theology. Schleiermacher to Barth.* London: Fontana Library, 1969.

Martin, Brian W. *John Keble, Priest, Professor and Poet.* London: Croom Helm, 1976.

McCloy, Shelby T. *Gibbon's Antagonism to Christianity.* New York: Burt and Franklin, 1933.

Middleton, R.D. *Newman at Oxford. His Religious Development.* Oxford, London, New York, Toronto: Oxford University Press and Geoffrey Cumberlege, 1950.

Migne (ed.). *Patrologia Graeca.* 1857.

Milman, H. H. *The History of Christianity From the Birth of Christ to the Abolition of Paganism in the Roman Empire.* 3 vols. New edn, London: John Murray, 1884.

Milner, Bishop. *The End of Religious Controversy.* London: Catholic Truth Society, 1912.

Milner, Joseph. *The History of the Church of Christ Previous to the Reformation.* 6 vols. Vols. I and II. London: Religious Tract Society, undated.

Mosheim, John Lawrence. *An Ecclesiastical History Ancient and Modern From the Birth of Christ to the Beginning of the Eighteenth Century.* Trans. with notes, Archibald Maclaine. London: Blackie and Son, 1851.

Moxon, Reginald Stewart. *Modernism and Orthodoxy. An attempt to Re-assess the Value of the Vincentian Canon in Regard to Modern Tendencies of Thought.* London: James Clarke and Co., 1924.

Mozley, Rev T. *Reminiscences Chiefly of Oriel College and the Oxford Movement.* 2 vols. Vol. I. 2nd edn, London: Longmans, Green and Co., 1882.

Murphy, Martin. 'Blanco White's Evidence.' *Recusant History,* 17(3), May 1985, pp. 254–73.

Nelson, Robert. *The Life of Dr George Bull, Late Lord Bishop of St David's, with the History of those Controversies in which he was engaged and an Abstract of those Fundamental Doctrines which he Maintained and Defended in the Latin Tongue.* London: Printed for Richard Smith, 1713.

Newsome, David. *The Parting of Friends.* London: John Murray, 1966.

    'Justification and Sanctification: Newman and the Evangelicals.' *Journal of Theological Studies,* 15 (New Series), April, 1964.

Norman, E.R. *Church and Society in England 1770–1970. A Historical Study* Oxford: Clarendon Press, 1976.
The English Catholic Church in the Nineteenth Century. Oxford: Clarendon Press, 1984.
Norris, Thomas J. *Newman and His Theological Method. A Guide for the Theologian Today.* Leiden: E.J. Brill, 1977.
O'Faolin, Sean. *Newman's Way.* London: Longmans, Green and Co., 1952.
Overton, J.H. *The English Church in the Nineteenth Century, 1800–1833,* London: Longmans, 1894.
Pailin, David A. *The Way to Faith. An Examination of Newman's 'Grammar of Assent' as a Response to the Search for Certainty in Faith.* London: Epworth Press, 1969.
Pannenberg, Wolfart. *Basic Questions in Theology.* Bristol: SCM, 1970.
Prestige, G.L. *Fathers and Heretics.* London: SPCK, 1958.
Pusey, E.B. *An Historical Enquiry into the Probable Causes of the Rationalist Character Lately Predominant in the Theology of Germany, to which is Prefixed A Letter from Professor Sack, upon the Rev H.J. Rose's 'Discourses on German Protestantism',* London: Rivingtons, 1828.
Ramsey, Michael, 'Hugh James Rose and the Oxford Movement.' Talk given to the Lightfoot Society, Durham University, 12 February 1985.
Raven, Charles. *Apollinarianism. An Essay on the Christology of the Early Church.* Cambridge: Cambridge University Press, 1923.
Reardon, Bernard M.G. *From Coleridge to Gore. A Century of Religious Thought in Britain.* London: Longmans, 1971.
Ricoeur, Paul. *The Rule of Metaphor. Multi-disciplinary Studies in the Creation of Meaning in Language.* Trans. Robert Czermy with Kathleen McLaughlin and John Costello, S.J. London: RKP, 1978.
Robbins, William. *The Newman Brothers. An Essay in Comparative Intellectual Biography.* London: Heinemann, 1966.
Rose, Rev. Hugh James. *The State of the Protestant Religion in Germany, In a Series of Discourses Preached Before the University of Cambridge.* Cambridge: J. Deighton and Sons, and London: C. and J. Rivington and G.B. Whittaker, 1825.
Rowell, Geoffrey (ed.). *Tradition Renewed. The Oxford Movement Conference Papers.* London: DLT, 1986.
Sacramentum Mundi. New York and London: Burns and Oates, 1968.
Schaff (ed.). *Nicene and Post-Nicene Fathers,* vol. IV *St Athanasius: Select Works and Letters.* Oxford and New York: Eerdmans, 1892.
Schleiermacher, F. *The Christian Faith.* Trans. H.R. Mackintosh and J.S. Stewart. Edinburgh, 1976.
'On the Discrepancy Between the Sabellian and Athanasian Method of Representing the Doctrine of the Trinity.' Trans. M. Stuart. *The Biblical Repository and Quarterly Observer.* 18, April 1835; 19, July, 1835.
Schmidt. *Newman and Postmodernism: A Study of Newman's Prose Non-Fiction*

and its Relation to Poststructuralist Literary Theory. University of Minnesota, Ph.D. Thesis, 1985.

Scott, Thomas, *The Force of Truth. An Authentick Narrative*, 8th edn, London: L.B. Seeley, 1808.

Selby, Robin C. *The Principle of Reserve in the Writings of John Henry Cardinal Newman.* Oxford: Oxford University Press, 1975.

Seynaeve, Jaak. *Cardinal Newman's Doctrine on Holy Scripture.* Louvain: Publications Universitaires de Louvain, and Oxford: Basil Blackwell, 1953.

Sheridan, Thomas L. *Newman on Justification.* New York: Alba House, Society of St Paul, 1967.

Stead, G. Christopher. 'Rhetorical Method in Athanasius.' *Vigiliae Christianae*, 30 (March 1976), pp. 121–37.

Stephen, Leslie. *History of English Thought in the Eighteenth Century.* 2 vols. 2nd edn, London: Smith, Elder and Co., 1881.

Stevenson, J. (ed.). *A New Eusebius.* London: SPCK, 1978.

Storr, Vernon F. *The Development of English Theology in the Nineteenth Century 1800–1860.* London: Longmans, 1913.

Sykes, Stephen. *The Identity of Christianity.* London: SPCK, 1984.

Taylor, Mark C. *Deconstructing Theology.* New York: Crossroads Publishing Co., and Chicago: Scholars Press, 1982.

Tertullian (ed. Roberts and Donaldson). *The Writings of Tertullian* vol. II. *Ante-Nicene Christian Library*, vol. xv.

Thom, John Hamilton (ed.). *The Life of Joseph Blanco White Written by Himself with Portions of his Correspondence.* 3 vols. London: John Chapman, 1845.

Trevor, Meriol. *Newman: the Pillar and the Cloud.* London: Macmillan and Co., 1962.

Tristram, Rev. Henry (ed.). 'John H. Newman on the Acta of Faith.' *Gregorianum*, 18, 1937.

Tuckwell, Rev. W. *Pre-Tractarian Oxford. A Reminiscence of the Oriel 'Noetics'.* London: Smith, Elder and Co., 1909.

Tulloch, John. *Rational Theology and Christian Philosophy in England in the Seventeenth Century.* 2 vols. London and Edinburgh: William Blackwood and Sons, 1872.

Turner, H.E.W. *The Pattern of Christian Truth. A Study in the Relations between Orthodoxy and Heresy in the Early Church.* London: Mowbray, 1954.

Velocci, Giovanni. 'The Perception and Theology of Providence in Newman.' Trans. Fr. P. Boyne, O.C.D. *Cardinal Newman Academic Symposium.* Rome, 1975.

Vickers, B. (ed.). *Rhetoric Revalued. Papers from the International Society for the History of Rhetoric.* New York: Medieval and Renaissance Texts and Studies, 1982.

Vincent of Lerins (attrib.). *The Commonitory. The Library of Christian Classics.* Vol. IX, Early Medieval Theology. London: SCM, 1957.

Walgrave, J.H., O.P. *Newman the Theologian.* Trans. A.V. Littledale. London: Geoffrey Chapman, 1960.

'Faith and Dogma in the Theology of Cardinal Newman.' *Cardinal Newman Academic Symposium.* Rome, 1975.

Walsh, J.D. 'Joseph Milner's Evangelical Church History.' *Journal of Ecclesiastical History,* 10, 1959, pp. 174–87.

Ward, Wilfrid. *The Life of John Henry Cardinal Newman.* 2 vols. London: Longmans, 1913.

Welch, Claude. *Protestant Thought in the Nineteenth Century,* 1, 1799–1870. New Haven and London: Yale University Press, 1972.

Whately, E. Jane. *Life and Correspondence of Richard Whately.* London, SCM, 1957.

Whately, Richard. *Elements of Logic.* 9th edn, London: Longmans, 1866.

Elements of Rhetoric, comprising an Analysis of the Laws of Moral Evidence and of Persuasion, With Rules for Argumentative Composition and Elocution. 6th edn, revised. London: B. Fellowes, 1841.

White, Rev. Joseph Blanco. *Observations on Heresy and Orthodoxy.* London: J. Mardon, 1835.

Wilbur, Earl Morse. *A History of Unitarianism. Socinianism and Its Antecedents.* Cambridge, Mass.: Harvard Univesity Press, 1947.

Willey, Basil. *Nineteenth Century Studies. Coleridge to Matthew Arnold.* 6th Impression. London: Chatto and Windus, 1968.

Williams, Rowan. *Arius. Heresy and Tradition.* London: DLT, 1987.

Wiseman, Nicholas. *Lectures on the Principal Doctrines and Practices of the Catholic Church, delivered at St Mary's, Moorfields, Lent, 1836.* 2 vols. London: Joseph Booker, 1836.

'The Anglican Claim of Apostolic Succession.' *The Dublin Review,* 7 (August and November 1839). London: Dolman, 1839, pp. 138–80.

Yearley, Lee H. *The Ideas of Newman. Christianity and Human Religiosity.* University Park and London: Pennsylvania State University Press, 1978.

Index